GENEALOGICAL HISTORY

OF THE

TOWN OF READING, MASS.

INCLUDING THE PRESENT TOWNS OF

Wakefield, Reading, and North Reading,

WITH

CHRONOLOGICAL AND HISTORICAL SKETCHES,

FROM 1639 TO 1874.

BY HON. LILLEY EATON.

"The hills are dearest, which our childish feet
Have climbed the earliest; and the streams most sweet
Are ever those at which our young lips drank, —
Stooped to their waters o'er the grassy bank."
— WHITTIER.

Copyright 1994
Heritage Books, Inc.

-Notice-

The foxing, or discoloration with age, characteristic of old books, sometimes shows through to some extent in reprints such as this, especially when the foxing is very severe in the original book. We feel that the contents of this book warrant its reissue despite these blemishes, and hope you will agree and read it with pleasure.

Entered according to Act of Congress, in the year 1874,
BY JOHN S. EATON,
In the Office of the Librarian of Congress, at Washington.

Facsimile Reprint
Published 1994 by
HERITAGE BOOKS, INC.
1540-E Pointer Ridge Place, Bowie, Maryland 20716
(301) 390-7709

ISBN 1-55613-989-6

A Complete Catalog Listing Hundreds of Titles on
Genealogy, History, and Americana
Available Free on Request

CHAPTER XII

MISCELLANEOUS.

TOPOGRAPHY, MANUFACTURES, PUBLIC BUILDINGS, LIBRARIES, POPULATION, VALUATION, ETC.

IT was said by the ancient Woburn historian, Johnson, in writing of Reading in 1651, that "Reading hath her habitation in the very centre of the country," meaning, we presume, that its location was in the centre of that portion of New England which was then settled. And now after the lapse of more than two centuries, the territory of old Reading, including the present towns of Wakefield, Reading, and North Reading, is still the centre of a periphery not less considerable and important; for within a radius of fifteen miles of its central point, are no less than eight flourishing cities, viz. Boston, Salem Lynn, Chelsea, Charlestown, Cambridge, Lowell, and Lawrence, containing a population of more than 350,000; with many large towns within the same circle.

This territory of the Readings contains about thirty square miles, or about 18,000 acres; of which Wakefield contains 4,568 acres, and its central village is in latitude 42° 30' 26" N., and in longitude 71° 4' 42 W., and is ten miles from Boston.

Reading contains 5,941 acres, and its central village is in latitude 42° 32' N., and in longitude 71° 6' W., and is twelve miles from Boston.

North Reading contains 7,649 acres, and its central village is in latitude 42° 34' 31" N., and in longitude 71° 5' W., and is fifteen miles from Boston. The whole territory is bounded *northerly* by Andover, *easterly* by Middleton, Lynnfield, and Saugus, *southerly* by Saugus, Melrose, and Stoneham, and *westerly* by Stoneham, Woburn, and Wilmington. The central village of Wakefield is two and one half miles southeast from that of Reading; the central village of North Reading is three miles northeast from that of Reading, and five miles north of that of Wakefield. The entire territory is agreeably diversified with hill and plain, woodland and meadow, lake and river. There are no lofty eminences. Its soil is generally fertile and productive. There is a fair share of water scenery. Ipswich River, taking its rise in the meadows of Wilmington and in Haggett's Pond, in the northwesterly part of North Reading, forms the boundary line between the westerly portions of Reading and North Reading, and then runs through the central part of North Reading, and passing through the town of Middleton empties into Ipswich Bay. Quannapowitt Lake, in Wakefield, contains four hundred acres, and Crystal Lake, also in Wakefield, contains one hundred acres. Saugus River, composed of two streams that flow from the two lakes in Wakefield, and which unite near the eastern boundary of Wakefield, runs through the town of Saugus and empties its waters into Lynn Harbor. These rivers, lakes, and ponds afford considerable water for mills and factories, furnish much romantic scenery and many fine building sites.

WAKEFIELD.

The town of Wakefield is *mainly* a place of manufactures and trade, but includes many pleasant fields, gardens, and orchards. Its principal manufactures are those of boots and shoes, rattan goods, iron castings, medicines, razor straps, shoe tools, etc. The boot and shoe business, mainly ladies' shoes, has long been an important branch of industry in the place. As long ago as 1677, the town assigned to Jonas Eaton "the privilege of wood and herbage on a tract of land, on condition that he remained in town, and followed the trade of a *shoemaker*." He remained, and many of his descendants and successors, from that year to this, have exercised that honorable handicraft. The manner of carrying on this branch of industry has greatly changed within the last few years. Formerly nearly every shoemaker was his own "Boss"; that is, "he worked his own stock"; he cut, his wife and daughters bound, and his sons and apprentices, with sometimes a few journeymen, finished up the work. His principal market was Boston, to which place, sometimes in saddle-bags and on horseback, and sometimes in a shoe cart, he transported and peddled from store to store his goods.

The introduction into this manufacture of labor-saving machinery, a full supply of which is too expensive for small operations, together with the greatly increased demand from a widely extended market, for boots and shoes, has thrown their manufacture into large establishments, so that while the amount of goods manufactured has increased, the number of those who carry on the business, has diminished.

The value of boots and shoes now (1868) annually manufactured town exceeds $400,000. The number of shoe factories averages abou twelve. Until within some forty or fifty years the journeymen shoemakers received their pay for their labor largely by way of barter, — in groceries and other articles at their employers' own prices. Much credit is due to Hon. Thomas Emerson, Col. James Hartshorn, Col. Lemuel Sweetser, and others, who, some fifty years ago, introduced a system of entire cash payments for labor, much to the advantage of the employees, — a system which still continues.

About the year 1822, Dr. Nathan Richardson removed from Reading, where he had long been a successful practitioner, and settled in Wakefield. Dr. R. had been accustomed to prepare sundry articles of medicine, especially sherry wine bitters, which had become justly celebrated for their excellent medical and health-giving properties. After his removal to Wakefield, in connection with his son, Dr. Solon O. Richardson, and subsequently by the son alone, the preparation of these medicines was improved, systematized, and their sale widely extended, and the fame thereof spread the country over; the business in 1868 amounting, it is said, to $100,000 annually.

RAZOR STRAPS. — The manufacture of the celebrated "Emerson Razor Straps" was commenced in Wakefield more than fifty years ago. Charles Emerson, the original inventor and manufacturer, was a native of Wakefield, and a resident here, when the first *strap* was made. He subsequently removed to Charlestown, where he and his successors continued the business; but razor straps, similar to Emerson's and not inferior to them in excellence and beauty, are still made in Wakefield by the Messrs. Atwell, to the amount of $25,000 annually.

SHOE TOOLS, especially *awls*, of an improved kind, were manufactured in Wakefield, by Thomas Woodward, Senior, as early as 1810, perhaps earlier. It is believed that he was the first *American* manufacturer of such articles, and his tools, particularly his *awls*, being far better and more finely finished than those imported from England, soon came into general use. His grandson, James F. Woodward, still continues the business in Wakefield, and on a much larger scale than his ancestor, and now manufactures some $25,000 worth annually.

RATTAN WORKS.

The rattan works of the late lamented Cyrus Wakefield, Esq., in their present magnitude and completeness, are a marvel of patient energy and perseverance. From the smallest beginning, under the greatest difficulties, they have grown to the most entire and perfect success. They are located on Water Street, and occupy the mill privilege and homestead known in the early history of the town as "Green's Mill."

At the time of the purchase by Mr. Wakefield of this property, in 1855,

RATTAN WORKS.

it consisted of two mill ponds, one on each side of the road, and a few small buildings, which had been used for various manufacturing purposes, together with the old "Green" dwelling-house. The premises

RATTAN WORKS.

were first occupied by Mr. Wakefield for the manufacture of rattan into skirt-reeds and baskets. When its use for skirts was superseded by steel, his attention was given to the production of cane for chair-seating by hand labor. The experiment of this process was not brilliant, and Mr. Wakefield soon saw that the whole enterprise would end in failure, unless some arrangement could be made to use machinery. This, with his accustomed energy, he set himself about, and finally succeeded. From this time his course was onward, and soon the cane manufactured at these works was in demand all over the United States.

The different processes of manufacture may be briefly described as follows: The raw material, as it is imported, is of all sizes, and must be first assorted; it is then straightened, washed in huge revolving boxes, and scraped, by which it is brought nearly to a uniform size in its whole length. The next step is peculiar: each separate stick of rattan being passed through a machine which divides the outside surface into five, six, seven, or eight strands, as the case may be, and leaving a smooth, round centre, the length of the original stick. This is called the pith, and is used for baskets, etc. etc. The strands are then shaved smoothly and tied in bunches containing one thousand running feet, bleached, put up in bundles of one hundred bunches, and the finished chair cane is ready for the market. The shavings, which have been referred to, are utilized by being spun into a coarse yarn, then woven into carpeting and mats, braided for open mats, etc. etc. In 1863, the number of hands employed was about two hundred. This number gradually increased, until in 1873 it exceeded one thousand. The present works consist of one brick machine shop, 158 x 60, of four stories, eight large workshops and store-houses, and a number of smaller buildings, and occupy ground to the extent of about four acres. The power required to run the immense machinery contained in the buildings is furnished chiefly by two magnificent steam-engines of two hundred and fifty horse-power each. This sketch would not be complete without mention of the names of Mr. Amos W. Chapman, the present superintendent; Mr. Chas. W. Trow, master mechanic, and inventor of much improved machinery; and Mr. William Houston, foreman of the mat and carpet department, whose ingenuity and untiring perseverance has brought this branch of the business to its present state of perfectness. Many others are also worthy of honorable mention, but the length which this sketch has already reached, forbids further extension.

SCHEDULE OF GOODS MANUFACTURED. — Seating cane for chairs;

matting, many varieties; mats of all kinds; baskets of all kinds; chairs for ladies, gentlemen, and children; cradles, cribs, tete-a-tetes, sofas, baby carriages, window shades, brooms, brushes, table mats, wall screens, fire screens, wall pockets, slipper holders, clothes beaters, etc. etc.; rattan used in the manufacture of whips, umbrellas, corsets, saddles, etc. etc.

THE BOSTON AND MAINE FOUNDRY.

Near the centre of our town, and close beside the track of the Boston and Maine Railroad, stand several brown and dingy buildings, of various shapes and sizes, surrounded by dust and smoke, and to which, in the morning, numbers of stalwart men may be seen wending their way. The stranger passing in the cars is told that this is the Boston and Maine Foundry, but of the extent of the business carried on here, the classes of goods manufactured, and the various new and improved processes employed, even most of our own residents are ignorant.

Like many other important enterprises, this foundry had its commencement in a comparatively small business, but its growth has been rapid and continuous. Previous to the year 1854, stoves and other articles of iron for household use were made of imperfect and ancient patterns, and needlessly large and heavy. During the early part of that year, Mr. A. J. Blanchard, residing at South Reading, having dissolved his connection with Messrs. Hartshorn & Ames, iron founders at Nashua, N. H., conceived the plan of erecting an iron foundry on the line of the Boston and Maine Railroad, in what was then a part of Stoneham, and producing iron goods of improved patterns and construction. He selected a piece of land belonging to Mr. Cyrus Wakefield, and which, although thickly covered with oak, he considered well suited to his purpose. Consulting with Messrs. Charles Tarbell, William Stewart, and J. F. Dane, with whom Mr. Blanchard soon after became associated in partnership, it was determined to purchase this site, if possible, and proceed to the erection of buildings suitable for the business. On conferring with Mr. Wakefield, who was then, as well as since, well known and respected for his liberality and public spirit, the project immediately met his hearty co-operation.

Work was commenced in clearing the land, building material was collected, and early in the fall of 1854, the corner-stone of the original buildings was laid by Mr. Blanchard, and the work vigorously pushed forward by Messrs. Blanchard, Tarbell, Stewart, and Dane, under the firm name of Blanchard, Tarbell & Co., with a capital of $20,000.

The buildings originally erected were, — 1st, a moulding room 150 feet in length, 60 feet wide, and one story high, with arched roof, large windows, and well ventilated, and which is still standing; 2d, a build-

FOUNDRY BUILDINGS.

ing 65 feet long, 56 feet wide, and two stories high, connected with the former, and which was used for a store-house and mounting room. This has since been rebuilt and greatly enlarged.

Within the space of four months, the first productions of the new firm were placed on the market, and they gave employment to about fifty men. The amount of the first year's business was such that larger capital was required to make those additions and improvements that would enable them to supply the demand for their goods. Overtures having been received from parties to invest in the enterprise, it was finally determined to form a stock company, which was organized Feb. 4, 1856, under the present style of the "Boston & Maine Foundry Co." This company consisted of the members of the old firm of Blanchard, Tarbell & Co., with the addition of Messrs. Sewall G. Mack, Cyrus Wakefield, and others. Sewall G. Mack was elected president; T. C. Whittemore, secretary; and A. J. Blanchard, agent and business manager. The capital stock was increased to $30,000, and the real estate, stock, and good-will of the firm of Blanchard, Tarbell & Co. were purchased by the company.

The tract of land which was deeded to the company by Mr. Wakefield March 15, 1855, comprised about 65,000 square feet.

The business of the company steadily increased each year under the skilful management of Mr. Blanchard, aided in "hard times" by the calm and far-seeing advice of Mr. Wakefield, and the clear and able judgment of Mr. Mack, until June 29, 1866, when a serious fire checked the business, and involved the company in heavy loss. The most untiring and vigorous efforts of the employees, firemen, and citizens only sufficed to save the moulding room, the rest of the buildings being totally destroyed. This loss was the more disastrous because occurring at a time when the company had on hand a large stock of manufactured goods and raw material. Five hundred tons of castings were melted or broken by the fall of the building, and a large quantity of wood patterns was destroyed. The loss by the fire was $80,000, with $50,000 insurance.

The company immediately commenced clearing away the ruins, and in a short time the present building, 125 feet long, 56 feet wide, and 4 1-2 stories high, occupied the site of the one destroyed. Many alterations and improvements were adopted in the new building, and new and improved machinery introduced, as suggested by the long experience of Mr. Blanchard, so that at the commencement of 1867 the foundry and its connections were the most complete and convenient of any in New England.

The loss having amounted to the sum total of the original capital, it became necessary either to increase the capital stock or to meet the cost of these improvements from the profits of the business. The former being considered the safest and most convenient plan, $60,000 was added, making the capital stock $90,000, and with these improved facilities the business was correspondingly increased.

It has ever been the endeavor of the company to secure the best of raw material, and skilful and experienced employees to work it, thereby manufacturing first-class goods, and to sell them at the lowest prices. Through the able management of their foreman, the late lamented Mr. T. B. Walker, a thoroughly practical moulder, experienced in the charge of men, and who was greatly beloved by them, the company has gained the credit of manufacturing some of the finest castings in the market.

They now manufacture every description of cast-iron goods for domestic and plumbers' use, besides much jobbing from outside parties. Here also are manufactured the well-known car-seat fixtures, the invention of Mr. George Buntin, which may be found far and wide over the country in the cars of nearly all our railroads.

Two furnaces are employed, one constantly, and the other as a relief in case of accident, and a powerful blower furnishes the blast. From twelve to fifteen tons of pig and scrap iron are daily melted in these furnaces, for which there are required about three tons of coal. The iron and coal, as well as the moulders' sand and other raw material, are landed directly from the cars, upon a large platform which is at a suitable level for immediate delivery to the furnaces. A storehouse 135 ft. x 35 ft. has been built beside the track, for the reception of sand, and capable of holding 300 tons of sand and 300 tons of small coal.

In 1862 and 1864 there were added to the original moulding room two others, called the west and south shops, each of the same dimensions as the first. There are employed in these rooms about 75 moulders, under the care of Mr. J. G. Savage, who are busily engaged during the early part of the day in the preparation of the moulds for the reception of the iron. The furnace is "charged up" about twelve o'clock, and about three o'clock the iron is in a suitable state for "pouring off," as it is called, when each of these moulders, with a long-handled ladle, takes his turn at the spout of the furnace, and soon the dingy room is lighted up by the glare of the molten iron, which is hurriedly carried to all parts of the building and carefully poured into the moulds. In a few minutes the articles are cooled and hardened, and the "flasks," as wooden boxes used for moulding are technically called, are emptied of the sand, and various shapes of iron with which they are filled.

The sand is scraped into a corner and repeatedly used, while the moulded articles, which are rough and covered with sand, are removed to another room, scarcely equalled for its dust, where the loose particles of sand are brushed off from the larger articles with a wire brush, and the smaller articles are packed into a revolving cylinder which speedily accomplishes the same thing.

In the morning the slag from the previous day's charge is removed from the furnace, and being placed in a cylinder with iron balls and made to revolve, the slag is broken up and sifted out, while the pieces of iron with which it was mixed remain in the cylinder in suitable form to be again used.

After the sand has been brushed from the goods, they are taken, should they be parts of a stove, to the mounting room, where thirty men, under the charge of Mr. Edwin E. Gates, are employed in fitting the various parts to each other. Each piece is tried carefully, and ground upon emery wheels until a perfect joint is secured, which is then filled with a cement which makes it practically air tight. These castings are now packed away in the store-room, ready for shipping to the dealers in hardware, or they are set up complete for use, the company being prepared to fill orders for all descriptions of cooking and parlor stoves in either form.

Many of the articles of hollow ware, such as pots, kettles, saucepans, urns for parlor stoves, etc., are in these days lined with enamel, which makes them smoother and easier to clean, and prevents them from rusting. The Boston & Maine Foundry Company were formerly obliged, in order to supply the wants of their customers in this line, to ship the goods to New York, where the enamelling was done, and then they were sent back. The cost of this enamelling was thus found to be a heavy outlay, as well owing to the freight both ways, as to the cost of the enamelling; and about a year since, Mr. Blanchard, with his usual enterprise, determined to erect enamelling works, and thus do his own work on his own premises, as well as to be prepared to do enamelling for other parties in New England who were also then obliged to send to New York. A building 45 x 55 feet, two stories high, was therefore erected, and two furnaces for enamelling constructed, as well as a smaller furnace for the manufacture of the enamel, which is a species of glass. Into this smaller furnace, which is capable of containing several hundred pounds, the mixed materials are placed, and melted together When properly mixed, the mass is allowed to run into a tank of cold water before the furnace, which makes it brittle, and breaks it into small pieces. It now resembles saltpetre, some pieces being clear and transparent, while others are more opaque. It is afterwards dried and finally ground. The articles to be enamelled are carefully turned and cleaned of all roughness, and the enamel is then applied. The ware is afterwards placed in the oven and heated to a cherry red, and on removal is found to be coated with the fine white enamel so well known as "porcelain lining."

This company was the first in this country to produce enamelled bath tubs. When Mr. Blanchard first stated his intention of making them, he was assured by those experienced in such matters, that he would find it an impossibility. He was determined, however, to make the attempt, and in eight weeks from making the pattern, a perfect bath-tub of cast-iron, lined with enamel, was completed. This department is under the charge of Mr. L. Lefferts, an experienced enameller, who is assisted by ten men.

Previous to 1871, all the wooden patterns used by the company in the moulding of their various goods, were made by Mr. Edward Mingay, of 164 Portland Street, Boston; but the business of the company increased to such an extent that it was necessary to do this part of the work here, and last year a two-story building was erected, 90 x 55 feet, the upper story of which is used for making wood-patterns, and the lower story for brass-founding and polishing. The pattern room, which is thought to be the finest in New England, is under the charge of Mr. L. M. Bates, and there are facilities for the employment of from twelve to fifteen men. As each part must be an exact fac-simile of the finished article, some idea may be gained by examining the parts of a stove, for instance, of the ingenuity and skill necessary to form these out of simple wood.

The patterns used in the moulding room are subjected to such constant use, that wooden patterns would soon wear out; consequently the wood patterns are usually employed only for the production of iron ones, which last for a long time. These iron patterns are cast in the usual manner in the moulding room, from whence they are taken to the pattern finishing room, where they are carefully finished and fitted. This department employs four men, under the charge of Mr. Joseph Chadwick. A large room is filled with these iron patterns, containing a copy of every design ever produced by the company.

In the brass foundry there are facilities for the melting of a ton of brass daily, and for the employment of ten men, and it is under the charge of Mr. Geo. Savage. Here the company manufacture all their brass rivets, and a great amount of car supplies.

In the polishing room portions of some of the goods are ground bright on emery wheels, and especially the arms of the Buntin car seats, and other articles, which are to be nickel-plated.

A carpenter's shop is attached to the works, which employs four men, under Mr. Curtis Clifford, in making the flasks and other needed carpenter's work.

The company employ two tin and sheet iron workers in manufacturing parlor stoves, and tin-ware for the cook stoves ready for the market, although most of their goods go into the hands of dealers who prefer to furnish these. This department is under the charge of Mr. Josiah R. Goddard.

A fine steam-engine of forty-five horse power, under the charge of Mr. John Rayner, furnishes power for the machinery of the various departments of the works.

The whole number of men employed by the company is about one hundred and seventy-five, and a finer class of men can be found in no manufacturing establishment in the country. In 1854, Mr. Blanchard, having in mind the comfort of his men, built a bath-house, the first of its kind in New England, with a tank in the centre, supplied with hot and cold water, and containing also a shower bath. The floor is of cement, so graded that perfect drainage is secured. Each man changes all his garments on entering the works in the morning, and resumes them after a bath at night; and here may be seen, or might if we were privileged to be present, such a display of physical development as would cheer an admirer of muscular Christianity. An old steam boiler, raised to the top of the south moulding room, and supplied by a force pump in the engine room, furnishes a tank from which the bath-room and all parts of the works requiring water are supplied.

It is necessary that all the moulders' sand should first be dried and finely ground and sifted. Formerly this was accomplished by hand; but in 1865, Mr. Joseph G. Savage invented a machine for grinding and sifting by power, and now the sand, after being dried in a room heated by steam, is put into the machine in this room, which performs in a few hours daily what formerly required the constant labor of three men.

Between the moulding rooms and the main store-house a brick wall with iron doors greatly reduces the danger of fire. In the store-house, running from basement to attic, a fine elevator is placed, furnished with Fairbanks platform scales to weigh all goods shipped. This is a feature introduced by Mr. Blanchard. The building is four and a half stories high, with capacity for the storage of one thousand tons of castings, which are manufactured largely in advance of orders, so that the company are able to fill any reasonable demand at any time.

By means of the elevator, the goods are delivered on the floor directly on a level with the cars, which stand on a side track at the door of the works; and so perfect are the arrangements for shipping goods that in all kinds of weather they may be sent without danger of exposure or injury by wet. Many goods are shipped north and south, and thence east and west without change of cars; but so extensive is the business of the company that they employ a shipping clerk in Boston to attend to the transfer of goods, which must be re-shipped there. The shipping of goods is under the care of Mr. Joseph Scully, the efficient clerk, who, by his courteous and gentlemanly bearing, has made himself a favorite of the employees, as well as all who have dealings with him.

Nearly all the buildings are so connected by covered passage-ways that all the business can proceed without the slightest interruption from the weather, and it may be safely said that in its facilities for the reception of raw material, the delivery of goods, and the general conduct of business, this establishment is not surpassed, if equalled, by any of its kind in the country.

The monthly pay-roll of the company is $10,000 or $12,000, the disbursement of which, and its consequent distribution in the community, adds not a little to the material prosperity of the town. Its employees are thinking men, and form an important portion of the producing class, on which the prosperity of a community depends; and on the whole, it is difficult to compute the value and influence of this establishment in our midst, — an influence yet in its infancy, and destined to be greatly enlarged by the inevitable increase and extension of the business.

The company have a fine office and sales-room in Boston, at 46 Canal Street, fronting also on Market and Friend Streets. This store is 145 x 22, and seven stories high, and here they have on exhibition samples of all the goods manufactured by them.

The Citizens' Gas Light Company, of Reading, Wakefield, and Stoneham, was organized in 1860, with a capital of about $93,000. Its gas house and works are located in Wakefield, but its pipes extend to Reading and Stoneham. It manufactures annually, at present (1868), about 4,000,000 cubic feet of illuminating gas, which sells for about $20,000.

Edward Mansfield, Esq., is its *president;* Thomas Winship, *secretary* and *treasurer;* B. B. Burbank, Esq., *superintendent; directors*, Stephen Foster, of Reading; Luther Hill, of Stoneham; William Hurd, of Stoneham; E. Mansfield, of Wakefield; J. F. Emerson, of Wakefield; Thomas Emerson, of Wakefield; C. Wakefield, of Wakefield (deceased).

Various other branches of manufacturing industry might be enumerated and described, if space permitted. Suffice it to say, that the total value of goods annually manufactured in Wakefield (including the value of ice, of which $100,000 worth are annually gathered) exceeds, it is estimated, $1,500,000.

The number of employees necessary to carry on this amount of manufactures, gives occasion for a lively and extensive mercantile business, and so we find that there were in Wakefield (in 1868) stores as follows: —

For groceries, grain, etc., 8; dry and fancy goods, 4; clothing, 3; shoes and boots, 3; apothecaries, 3; provisions, 3; fruit and confectionery, 2; furniture, 2; wood, coal, and lumber, 2; wood and ice, 1; jewelry, 2; bread, 1; shoe findings, 1; hard and tin ware, 1; periodicals, 1.

The annual sales, by these stores, was supposed to amount to $500,000, in 1868.[1]

NEWSPAPERS.

In 1854, the publisher of "The Middlesex Journal," a weekly, printed at Woburn, offered to establish a South Reading Department in his paper, if the people of South Reading would furnish the matter. Whereupon several persons, "a combination of gentlemen" they were called, undertook the duty. The introductory article was written by Professor Tweed, in behalf of the South Reading editors, and was published April 15, 1854.

They say in that article that they "propose to help make it the medium of communication among our townsmen; hoping also to cultivate a better acquaintance with our friends in the circle of towns in which our homes are set. As a free circulation of pure air is necessary to the full development and play of our bodily organs, so is a free circulation of thought and feeling requisite to a healthy social system; and we hope by means of this *register* to admit and let off streams

---

[1] Since the preparation of these statistics, the business of Wakefield has very *largely* increased; but we are unable to furnish the exact figures for 1873.

from the current of daily life around us, which may tend in some measure to the promotion of virtue, intelligence, and good neighborhood."

This "combination of gentlemen" included B. F. Tweed, Edward Mansfield, P. H. Sweetser, L. Eaton, J. S. Eaton, Jonas Evans, and others. Soon, however, it was found that Edward Mansfield, Esq., possessed the peculiar talent and the willing disposition to indite and collect the necessary items to make the weekly contributions, and by degrees the whole labor of so doing was devolved upon him, and for a whole decade he performed this service with great ability and punctuality, and without remuneration, making the South Reading Department of the "Middlesex Journal" a most useful and desirable visitor. Mr. Mansfield's valedictory was published Dec. 24, 1864, and thus ended our connection with the Woburn journal.

In 1858, W. H. Hutchinson, Esq., from Boston, established the "South Reading Gazette," which was published by him and his successor for about three years, and was a very useful and entertaining weekly.

In 1868, A. A. Foster, Esq., of Wakefield, commenced the publication of the "Wakefield Banner," a weekly sheet of respectable size, which was merged in the "Citizen," a paper which continues to be issued by the "Citizen Association," and which receives liberal support.

The "Wakefield Banner," a weekly, edited by W. H. Twombly, Esq., is also now published.[1]

LIBRARIES OF WAKEFIELD.

At the beginning of this century there was a library in this place, called the "Social Library." The writer has not been able to trace it to its origin, but it is supposed to date back some fifty years in the last century. And one evidence for this belief is the very antique appearance of some of the books, and especially of the book-case, as remembered in their earliest years by some of our oldest present citizens. It consisted chiefly of books on theological subjects, by Baxter, Aliene, Doddridge, and such standard authors, and on ecclesiastical history. It was usually kept at the residence of the pastor of the Congregational church. About the year 1812, Mr. Lilley Eaton (father of the late Hon. Lilley Eaton) was elected librarian. The library was increased by the addition of some volumes of history and other works, and removed from the residence of Rev. Reuben Emerson to the store of Mr.

---

[1] The two papers have recently been united, and one weekly paper is now issued under the title of "The Wakefield Citizen and Banner."

Eaton in the large building still standing at the corner of Main and Salem Streets.

At one time prior to this date, conflicting opinions in regard to the character of the books to be added by purchase, or some other cause, created unpleasant differences, destroyed harmony, and led to a decided change in the list of subscribers and the government of the library. Some members withdrew their names and their support, having previously, however, drawn out as many books as would be equal in value to their shares in the library, and never took the trouble to return them.

This library continued in a vigorous state for many years, until supplanted by one of more modern date. Its last act was in the beginning of the year 1836, when its treasurer passed over the balance of funds in his hands to the treasurer of the Franklin Lyceum, for the benefit of its library, though its active existence closed more than a year before.

In the early part of the year 1831, the young men of the town, including those connected with the "South Reading Academy," formed an association called the "South Reading Franklin Lyceum," and later in the same year established a library in connection with it, known as the "Franklin Library." This consisted more of works of art and science, civil history, travels, geography, medicine, etc.

In 1834, negotiations were entered into between the "Social" and the "Franklin" libraries, with a view to uniting them in one. Committees were appointed by the two bodies to favor the object, and at a meeting of the proprietors of the Social Library, held Dec. 3, 1834, it was agreed to make over all the books belonging to the Social Library to the Franklin Library, on condition that each member of the former should of right be a member of the latter library. This condition was accepted by the proprietors of the Franklin Library at a meeting held on the 26th of the same month, and a committee was chosen to receive the books and book-case, in behalf of the Franklin Library. This library was accessible six days in the week, and occupied a very important place in the community for many years. It was liberally patronized by old and young, especially in the earlier days of its history.

Though established in 1831, a librarian does not appear to have been appointed until the fall of 1832, and the first record found of the delivery of books is under date of October, 1833. The names of those who drew the first books from this library are, Abner Breeden, Asaph Evans, and Samuel Kingman; and the last books drawn therefrom, on Dec. 5, 1849, were taken by Rev. Reuben Emerson, Moses Boardman, William Chamberlain, Henry W. Brown, and Rev. Mr. Clayes.

Its first librarian was Hon. Lilley Eaton; its last was Abel F. Hutchinson, Esq.

In the year 1838, great interest was felt by many of the young men in the subject of phrenology, that was attracting general attention about that time. L. N. Fowler, Esq., of New York, an extensive phrenological lecturer, visited this town, and spoke enthusiastically of the new "science," as it was called. Some of his lectures were delivered before the Franklin Lyceum, followed by lectures from other gentlemen upon the same subject. The members of the Lyceum also discussed the correctness of its principles in set debates, and waxed warm in the presentation of their arguments, *pro* and *con;* and during the month of September, 1840, the secretary of the Lyceum, Franklin Poole, Esq., delivered a course of nine lectures before that body upon that favorite topic. In connection with this phrenological excitement, some twenty-five or thirty of the young men formed themselves into a club, in order more thoroughly to prosecute their investigations, and to become more intimately acquainted with a subject so attractive, and seemingly so important. Among other books, they procured the entire works of Spurzheim, which they read with avidity, and examined craniums, until they thought they could tell a man's character by the bumps on his head. This collection of books was styled the "Phrenological Library," and many of its founders are still with us, men of marked intelligence, prominent and deserving citizens.

In March, 1842, the Legislature passed a resolve appropriating fifteen dollars for each school district in the State that would raise an equal sum to establish in each district a common school library. Soon after this generous encouragement from the State, such libraries were established in most, if not in all, the districts in town.

These books were selected and prepared by the Board of Education with great care, free from politics and sectarian bias. They were taken home, like books from other libraries, and read by the scholars and their parents. In some households, probably, these were the principal new books to which they had access, and consequently were very highly prized. These libraries met an important want in the education of the young, especially, who had not then such facilities for securing the use of profitable books as now. Though these libraries performed a valuable office for a time, they had not the elements of permanency; for, as the teachers were constantly changing, upon whom depended much of their efficiency, the books were neglected, and allowed to be carried away without proper care for their return, and finally, as libraries, were disused. It is not known that any of the books found their way into a subsequent library. Such as have not been appropriated to individual use, or destroyed, may doubtless be found boxed up, or on the shelves, or in the old closets of the school-houses of the several districts.

Some years subsequent to the last mentioned date (1842), another library was organized, known as the "Prescott Library," of which very little can be said, inasmuch as the prime movers in it have deceased, and no record of its beginning, continuance, or ending is known to exist. It was named, as is supposed, after Prescott the historian, as it contained his works as its prominent feature. It was kept in a little room at one corner of the hall in the old town house. Its subscribers (probably about fifty in number) were among the most intelligent and energetic of our citizens, many of whom still remember the interest they felt in perusing the books, without any particular impression as to the date of its origin, or to incidents in its life.

In 1856 was formed the Public Library of South Reading, now known as the Beebe Town Library of Wakefield, its name having been changed, in 1868, in honor of Lucius Beebe, Esq., a generous contributor to its funds. A place was fitted up for it in one of the lower rooms of the old town house, where it remained until 1871, when it was transferred to an apartment in the new town house especially provided for its use. At the commencement there was a public reading-room connected with it, where might be found the most important newspapers and other periodicals, gratuitously furnished by the liberality of some of the citizens.

The act of the Legislature, authorizing towns to raise money to establish and support public libraries, was passed during the session of 1851, and the town of South Reading, having already shown its liberality in making appropriations for the support of free schools, was among the first of the country towns of this Commonwealth to avail itself of the provisions of the statute, and establish a free town library.

At the annual town-meeting this year (1856), held March 3d, it was voted that it was expedient to establish a public library for the use of the inhabitants, and the sum of $500 was raised and appropriated for that purpose, with the expectation that the books from the former libraries of the town, owned by individual subscribers, would be donated to this library, as also contributions were anticipated from associations and individuals. At that meeting seven persons were elected as trustees.

At this stage of the history of libraries, we see nearly all those previously mentioned now converging to a point.

As a large river is fed by many little streams, so nearly all the libraries that previously existed in town became tributaries to our present free library.

These tributaries were not large, but proportionate to the body that received them.

As nearly as can be ascertained, the present library in its start received donations as follows: volumes from the "Social," "Franklin," "Phrenological," and "Prescott" library associations, 259; from Mechanics' Association, 130; from pupils of the high school, from exhibitions, 121; other individuals, 217; total, 727; being about the same number of volumes that were furnished by the town the first year. During the second year, the scholars of the high school, and citizens in various capacities, contributed upwards of $200 in addition to the town appropriation.

This library has met with constant favor from the people since its commencement. The town has made some appropriations for it every year, and individuals have borne testimony to their interest in its welfare. In 1867, Lucius Beebe, Esq., presented it with five hundred dollars, to be spent in the purchase of books, to which generous gift he has since added several hundred volumes, selected expressly for this library. In 1872, another liberal-minded, public-spirited individual, Mrs. Harriet N. Flint, donated to the town the sum of one thousand dollars, the income of which is to appropriated to the purposes of the Beebe Town Library.

Trustees in 1873. — Edward Mansfield, chairman; Lucius Beebe; M. J. Hill, secretary; Chester W. Eaton, treasurer; D. H. Darling, J. O. Burdett, Cyrus Wakefield (died in October).

In 1860, Mr. John Reynolds, from Concord, Mass., establisher of agricultural libraries, procured twenty-one subscribers in this town to an association called the South Reading Agricultural Library. Certificates were issued at five dollars each, and were dated Jan. 31, 1860. Although this organization was designed to advance the interests of agriculture, it must not be supposed that only farmers were members of the club. The various interests of the town were represented, being composed of five merchants, four farmers, three carpenters, two manufacturers, two physicians, and one each of five other occupations.

In 1861, the members of this association transferred their several shares in said library to the South Reading Horticultural Society, on condition that said Horticultural Society should raise fifty dollars in aid of the library, and consider the members of the Library Association as members of the Horticultural Society, entitled to all its privileges, which included an equal right to the use of the library.

This collection consisted of some 150 or more valuable books, which for several years were sought after and read with a great deal of profit by the various classes in the community, as the improved state of our gardens, fields, etc., will bear unmistakable testimony. This library is still in existence, in good condition, and open to its members. Though the books are not so much drawn out for reading as formerly, they are consulted as works of reference.

POPULATION AND VALUATION.

READING.			SOUTH READING.			NORTH READING.	
A. D.		No.	A. D.		No.	A. D.	No.
1765,		1530					
1776,		1984					
1790,		1802					
1800,		2025					
1810,		2228	1812,	Incorporated.			
1820,		*2797	1820 (Estimate),		1000		
1830,		1806	1830,		1311		
1840,		2193	1840,		1517		
1850,		3108	1850,		2407	1853,	Incorporated.
1855,		2522	1855,		2758	1855,	1050
1860,		2662	1860,		3207	1860,	1193
1865,	{ Ma. 1158 / Fe. 1278 }	2436	1865,	{ Ma. 1494 / Fe. 1750 }	3244	1865,	{ Ma. 488 / Fe. 499 } 987

A. D.	POLLS.	VALU.	A. D.	POLLS.	VALU.	A. D.	POLLS.	VALU.
		£ s. d.						
1791,	462	3,225 17 1						
1802,	496	$17,468 00						
1812,	596	19,772 00						
1821,	425	14,747 43	1821,	293	$9,263 51			
1831,	511	385,501 00	1831,	412	247,084 00			
1840,	691	463,024 61	1840,	449	279,409 00			
1850,	906	1,071,042 00	1850,	630	755,019 00			
1860,	732	1,269,570 00	1860,	868	1,861,319 00	1860,	325	$527,890 00
1863,		1,299,648 00	1863		1,803,903 00	1863,		552,565 00

WAKEFIELD.

TOWN VALUATION, 1873.

Real Estate	$3,146,235
Personal	898,227
Total	$4,044,462

* This number includes the population of South Reading, which was not taken separately.

AMOUNT OF ANNUAL APPROPRIATIONS.

For town charges	$71,275 00
" State tax	5,152 50
" County tax	2,935 26
Total	$79,362 76

RATE OF TAXATION, $18.50 ON $1,000.

Number of polls	1,960
" " dwelling-houses	941
Acres of land taxed	3,913

ASSETS AND LIABILITIES OF THE TOWN, MAY 1, 1873.

School-houses	$91,000
Other public buildings	113,200
Public grounds and parks	40,000
Other real estate	3,000
Cemetery	1,000
Public library	4,200
Fire apparatus	7,000
Trust fund	1,100
Other assets	4,200
Total assets	$264,700
Town debt	$139,467 63

NUMBER OF INHABITANTS, 6,041.

Males	2,922
Females	3,119
Under five years of age	678
Over five and under fifteen years	1,061
Fifteen and upwards	4,302

THE OLD BUILDINGS OF WAKEFIELD.

The march of improvement, very rapid and noticeable recently, is fast removing the ancient landmarks from our midst; and a few years hence the visitor will search in vain for the traces even of their former existence.

To give space for the erection of the new High School Building, the

"Old Prentiss House" was removed from the site it had so long occupied; and in view of its removal, the following lines seem eminently appropriate, and worthy of preservation: —

> "Farewell to the house where my father was born,
>   I shall never behold it again;
> Its roof and its walls will soon fall to the ground,
>   Thro' the interposition of men.
>
> "'T would be foolish to weep o'er this wreck of a home,
>   Which was once of South Reading the pride;
> The 'parsonage house' of an earlier day,
>   Where a past generation have died.
>
> "These walls once resounded with innocent mirth,
>   When children ran over the floor;
> Wit, culture, and beauty were found by its hearth,
>   And piety guarded its door.
>
> "Death came to its chambers and took in his prime,
>   The pastor, the father, the guide;
> And the grave-yard adjacent will tell how his sons
>   And daughters lay down by his side.
>
> "The children remaining were scattered abroad,
>   From Kentucky to picturesque Maine;
> And around the warm hearth, once so cheerful and bright,
>   They never collected again.
>
> "These walls now so desolate, aged, and lone,
>   My affection and interest claim;
> For thro' every mutation and stage of decay,
>   They have borne the family name.
>
> "Farewell to the house where my father was born;
>   May its timbers and boards help to make
> Some beautiful place, which descendants may love,
>   As do I, for the ancestor's sake!"

THE "OLD HART HOUSE"

Was removed from its ancient site in 1857, and at that time, the author of this history wrote, with reference to it, as follows: —

"The history and traditions connected with this venerable old mansion, long owned and occupied by the late Hon. John Hart, M. D., so far as we have been able to obtain them from a hasty inquiry, are as follows: —

"It was erected about one hundred and fifty years ago, by the Smith family. It appears that among the early settlers of Reading was a

John Smith, with his sons John and Francis, who purchased of the Indians, for a jack-knife, and some other articles of cutlery, a considerable tract of land in the southeasterly part of what is now South Reading, extending from the northerly shore of 'Smith's Pond,' long so called (now 'Crystal Lake'), into that part of the town called 'Little World.' The first house erected by this family stood very near the spot now occupied by the station of the South Reading Branch Railroad.

"Francis Smith succeeded his father at the old homestead; married Ruth, daughter of Elias Maverick, of Charlestown; had six sons and three daughters; was selectman, innholder, and authorized by the General Court 'to draw wine for travellers'; was a deacon, and died in 1744, aged 85 years.

"He gave to each of his six sons a farm out of his own. Their names were John, Isaac, Abraham, James, Benjamin, and Elias. One lived on the place now the town farm; one on the place now owned by Mr. Lowell Emerson; one on the place now owned by Dea. Ezekiel Oliver; one on the 'Walton farm,' near Dea. Oliver's; one, probably Isaac, occupied the house which is the subject of this article; and one, Benjamin, succeeded his father on the homestead. We say that Isaac *probably* lived in the house now being removed, because of the fact we are not certain, and because we find from an old map of South Reading, made about one hundred years ago, that this house was then occupied by Isaac Hart; and as we learn that the Smith and Hart families were related, we infer that this Isaac Hart may have been the successor, perhaps the namesake and relative, of said Isaac Smith. Dr. Hart purchased the place about the year 1783, and occupied it until his decease in 1836. After the death of his widow in 1838, the house and a portion of the farm were sold to strangers; since then it has been rented to various and changing tenants, and now at last it has rolled away. Venerable old edifice! that has long been a landmark in geography, as the old maps of the county will testify; that was esteemed almost as fixed and permanent as old Cedar Mountain, at whose base it stood; that was once among the most spacious and respectable dwelling-houses of the town; that stood among the highest in the assessors' valuation; distinguished as the abode of wealth, gentility, and professional power; the home of wisdom, refinement, and hospitality, and the nursing-place of beauty and literature,— O! how lost and fallen from its ancient standing and renown! *Change* has now come over it; the auctioneer has seized it, the shambles have encompassed it; and after having been for a while a medium of barter and exchange, it has at last become *currency*, and has been *passed off.* It has gone — the place that so long knew it will know it no more. 'Thus passeth the glory of the world away.' How suited is this event to

RESIDENCE OF THE LATE CYRUS WAKEFIELD.

remind us all that the 'houses we live in' will soon fall, and to suggest the importance of securing a title to that house 'not made with hands, eternal in the heavens.'"

If it were within our power and province to reproduce from the dusty archives of the vanished years the traditionary records connected with ALL these ancient dwellings (now so rapidly disappearing from their former sites), such records would furnish, we presume, very many entertaining reminiscences; but the limits assigned us forbid such an attempt, and we proceed to a brief inspection of

THE NEW BUILDINGS OF WAKEFIELD.

Descriptions of the Town Hall, and of the High School Building, appear elsewhere in these pages; and among other new and imposing public and private structures, we select a description of the new Baptist Church edifice, of which a correct illustration has been furnished.

THE NEW BAPTIST CHURCH.

Our citizens have watched with general pride and interest the gradual but steady growth of the beautiful house of worship which the Baptist Society have been rearing in a most commanding and eligible location at the corner of Main and Lafayette Streets.

In the spring of 1871, the capacity of their former edifice having become inadequate, the society determined upon the erection of a new one, and secured for that purpose the large area now occupied by them as above mentioned. Having secured this territory, building operations were speedily commenced, and work upon the foundation was in progress, when on the night of the 21st of June, 1871, their old edifice nearly opposite, at the corner of Main and Crescent Streets, was destroyed by fire. Since the fire, the erection of the present completed structure has been pushed with zeal, but not with that haste that would necessitate lack of care or workmanship. The beautiful building, as it stands in its completeness, prominent among the adorning features of our main avenue, is as nearly perfect in all its details as it is well possible for the work of man to be, and compels more than denominational pride and gratification. Ground was broken for the new edifice early in June of 1871, and the building had received the principal external finish before winter closed in. The final internal touches have been completed, and a general survey of this elegant ornament and honor to our town will not be without interest to our readers.

BAPTIST CHURCH, WAKEFIELD.

The building is of wood, and of the Romanesque order, which has the past few years become quite the favorite with church-builders; and the style in this structure has been nearly maintained in its purity, combining the sharply pitched roof, the bastioned tower, the minaret and pinnacles, and the lofty spire incident to this order of architecture.

The building is of the stone tint, popularly known as French gray, and the prevailing tone forms a pleasing contrast with the green of its surroundings, and the brighter colors of its illuminated windows. The dimensions of the building are 105 feet on the north side, from the front of the tower, which projects two feet on either angle from the main structure to the rear end; 103 feet on the south side, 71 feet across the front end to the point of the tower, and 69 feet to the rear end. The distance to the eaves is 41 feet, and to the ridge of the roof 75 feet. The height of the tower and spire to the point of the vane is 180 feet, making it the loftiest spire in this region. The height of the minaret is 100 feet, and to the tip of the pinnacle is 75 feet. The front of the building and the tower are finished in narrow sheathing, furred out from the building and thoroughly laid, forming a plain but elegant finish, admirably calculated to give the full effect of the capitals, corbels, dentels, etc., with which it is richly relieved. The front façade, which faces east, is additionally relieved by heavy pilasters; by an exceedingly tasteful portico (strongly brought out by the unusually fine character of its ornamentation, the dentel work of its pediment, the carvings of its pinnacles, and the capitals of its columns being both unique and beautiful); by a grouped arrangement of the windows, and by the salient angles of the tower (which is by far the finest we remember to have seen); by mosaic belts, which are brought in with fine effect both on it and on the spire and upon the minaret, and by the heavy mullioned windows of the tower, which are unusually fine. The sides and rear end of the building are finished with clapboards having an ogee edge, and both side elevations are relieved by sheathed buttresses, nine on each side, capped with metal and tastefully headed. The southern façade is further relieved by a convenient portico in harmony with the general order of the building, and of similar ornament, opening upon the wide concrete driveway leading to the carriage sheds in the rear of the church. A doorway at the rear angle also relieves this façade, making three entrances to the building. The architraves of the windows, their circular heads, and the coving finish, are all especially fine.

Ascending the easy slope from the broad sidewalk by a wide path of concrete, we pass through the main entrance. On either hand, as we enter, are doors leading to the cellar, the stairways thereto being amply lighted. Directly in front are two pairs of doors, giving entrance to the main vestry, and at the extreme of the main hall at each end a flight of stairs ascends to the hall of the main audience room. The floor of the hall is of hard pine, the large door-mats being let into the same. The wall finish is a delightful combination of ash and black walnut. The stairways have hard pine treads and risers, with ash and black walnut stringers, and highly wrought black-walnut balustrades of unique patterns. The wall is of smooth finish, the ceiling being tinted a French gray, with lines of blue, red, and Bismarck brown, the walls being of a light tint shading upon buff. Three gas-burners, of three lights each, light the lower hall, which also receives light from the semicircular ornamental window over the doors and the stairways, and lighted by the windows on either side set with stained glass, the windows of the lower story being filled with flecked glass. Ascending the stairway, we reach the upper hall, which is similar in most respects to the lower, but having a heavy black-walnut balustrade about the large aperture which opens in the floor, giving light, air, and roomy appearance to the lower hall. From this hall four pairs of doors opening *outward* give entrance to the main auditorium. A stairway at either end gives access to the balcony, the finish-trimmings of the walls and woodwork being the same as below stairs, as are also the gas-fixtures.

The doors throughout the interior of the building are of ash, with black-walnut mouldings, except the inside of the doors of the main audience room, which are solid black walnut.

Entering the principal chamber of worship, than which few can be more beautiful, one is charmed with the simple elegance of the entire whole. The lofty ceiling divided into two planes by the longitudinal ribs, and by a difference of a few feet of elevation, and subdivided by transverse beams, presents a fine harmony of colors, the panels of the upper plane being tinted cerulean-blue, picked with gold and shaded by pannellings of delicate brown; the lower plane furnishing a combination of flesh tint, blue, buff, and bistre, the flesh tint prevailing, and serving as a ground for the blue fret-work openings for ventilation.

Across the front of the church a wide, low balcony extends, its front finished in the arcade pattern, and supporting two imposts with Roman chaptrels, from which springs an arch having in its reveal the illumined group of windows of the centre of the church front, the centre one bearing the representation of the cross and the crown. Over this arch appears the inscription in illuminated text, "My house shall be called a house of prayer." The pulpit platform, the front of which is finished richly in arcade of black walnut, as is also the desk itself, supports also two imposts, with Roman chaptrels supporting an arch some 26 feet in diameter, beneath which is the pulpit alcove, divided by a heavy walnut balustrade into areas for the choir and for the preacher. Beneath that occupied by the preacher, the large baptistery is located, capable of holding some eighteen hundred gallons, and supplied with heating facilities, and the most complete arrangements for use. On the north side of the alcove is located the organ-box, and on the south two doors, one affording entrance and exit to the choir, and the other passage to and from the rear vestry entrance, the lower rear hall, the pastor's study, etc. The wall faces at either hand of the alcove are heavily mullioned, that on the north embracing the richly figured organ pipes, and that on the south containing in its three divisions under the captions, Worship, Salvation, and Service, selections of Scripture in illumination, while over the pulpit arch there appears, in old English, the text, "To you is the word of His Salvation sent."

The fresco upon the rear wall of the pulpit alcove presents corresponding columns of Roman design to those supporting the arch, and in the centre panel an open Bible, the whole being well executed, while the Rose window is the finest in the building.

There is a notable absence of stucco about the interior; the mouldings, dentels, drops, brackets, corbels, consoles, all being of carved wood, and of the most enduring class, and highest style of art. The walls are of a general neutral tint, finely relieved by their pickings of color and the Persian belt that sweeps the heads of the windows, and encircles the house.

The whole building is provided with extraordinary facilities for lighting, and the pendants from the ceiling of the main auditorum are specially tasteful in their color (blue) and their design. The lighting arrangements are such that the whole house can be lighted and fed from a small overflow pipe, until such time as it may be desirable to turn on the main. The most ample and sensible arrangements for ventilation both from the floor and ceiling are perfect, there being twelve ceiling and four floor ventilators, with extra opportunities of cold air supply to furnaces from within and without.

The auditorium is 67 feet by 78 feet long, exclusive of the pulpit and gallery alcoves, and is intended to seat, with the gallery, one thousand persons. The pews are of a new pattern, are of black walnut, highly ornamented and finished, and are more pleasing in their general effect than any we know of. The carpets are a pleasant combination of red and black, in two-ply, and are uniform throughout the house.

The elegant marble Howard clock upon the face of the balcony was the gift of the children of the late Lilley Eaton, Esq., father of the late Hon. Lilley Eaton. Descending to the lower front hall, we open one of the double doors, descend a few steps, and are in the main vestry, finished like the rest of the building in ash and black walnut, and divided by a sash and wood partition (capable of being raised and so uniting all) from the adjoining subordinate rooms.

Too much praise cannot be bestowed upon the wonderfully substantial, skilful, and elegant character of the construction of this edifice. Few buildings in any section of the country can boast of more conscientious and efficient care in their arrangements for stability, strength, and convenience, and the result is alike creditable, in a high degree, to the architect and builders.

RAILROADS.

The railroad facilities now enjoyed by the inhabitants of Wakefield are so ample and important as to merit a brief description.

The extension of the Boston and Maine Railroad (opened in 1845) from Wilmington to Boston, thus placing this town on its main line, furnished easy and frequent communication with Boston, as also with the northern sections of the State and of New England, and contributed largely to the growth of the town.

The later construction of the Danvers Railroad (nine miles to Danvers) and of the Newburyport Railroad (from Danvers, twenty-one miles to Newburyport), both of which are leased and operated by the Boston and Maine Railroad, opened avenues to another portion of the State; while the South Reading Branch Railroad (eight miles to Peabody), operated by the Eastern Railroad, placed the means of reaching Salem by rail within reach of our inhabitants.

Thus, by successive developments, the present town of Wakefield has become an important railroad centre; being very nearly equidistant from the cities of Boston, Cambridge, Somerville, Chelsea, Lynn, Salem, Lawrence, and Lowell, with the immediate prospect of a closer connection with the latter city by means of the Andover and Lowell Railroad (now being constructed), and enjoying means of easy communication with other flourishing cities and towns, not distant from those above named.

As might be expected, possessing so desirable a location and offering so many attractive situations, the recent growth of our town in population and resources has been alike noticeable and rapid.

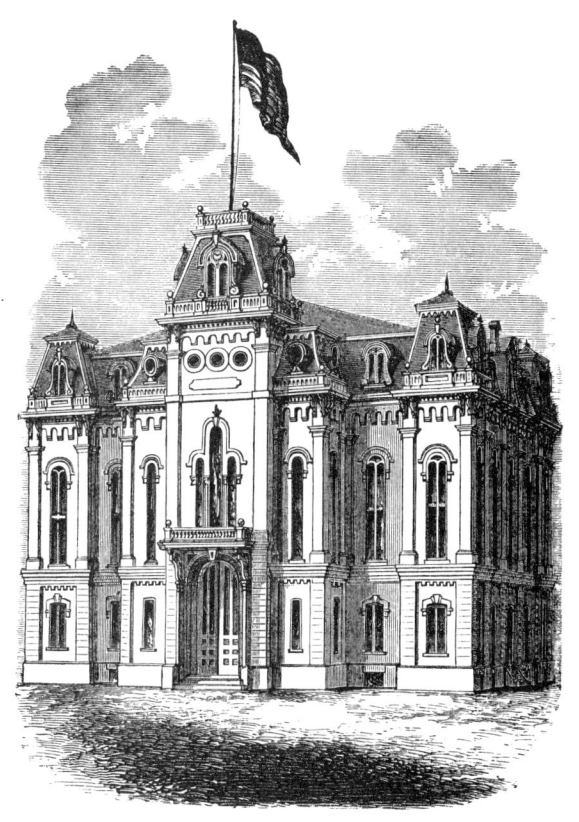

WAKEFIELD HALL.

In this sketch we have space for but few statistics, and we insert the following figures, that the curious in such matters may clearly note the changes of the recent years.

On the completion of this portion of the Boston and Maine Railroad, in 1845, it was predicted that the present town of Wakefield would furnish that road with *thirty* daily passengers.

We have no record for that year; but in 1848, the whole number of passengers during the year, for all points, was 45,574, or an average of 146 daily passengers.

In 1873, the number of *Boston* passengers alone was 320,172, or an average of 1,025 daily passengers.

In 1848, the whole amount of passenger and freight receipts at South Reading was $12,532.00.

In 1873, the *Boston* passengers to and from Wakefield furnished the sum of $53,186.00.

THE PRESENT TOWN OF READING.[1]

THE POST-OFFICE.

The Post-office was first established in this town in 1811, in a building that stood where the bank now stands. Col. Nathan Parker was postmaster. He was succeeded in 1815 by John Weston, Esq., who held the office until his death, in 1849. It was kept for a time in the Weston house at "Hill End," and then for a short period in Johnson's store, that stood where Thomas Pratt's garden now is. It is said that Mr. Ambrose Kingman had charge of it for a time, and kept it in his house. It was then removed, and kept in a house nearly opposite Lyceum Hall, just south of W. R. Perkins's house, since removed. John P. Sherman, druggist, was the next postmaster, appointed probably in 1849 or '50, and the office was kept in the north side of the building occupied by Beard's watch store. He resigned on account of ill-health. Capt. Thomas Richardson became his successor, and was followed when the administration changed, or some time subsequently, by Horatio M. Cate, who was appointed by President Pierce. He removed the office to the market building. In the course of two or three years, C. D. Brown was appointed to the place, and held it till the appointment of Mr. Gleason, the present postmaster, by President Lincoln, in May, 1861. Mr. Gleason removed the post-office from

---

[1] The following pages in this chapter have been prepared and contributed by Hiram Barrus, Esq., of Reading.

the market building near Stephen Foster's, to Lyceum Hall building. It is a noteworthy fact that not one of Mr. Gleason's predecessors is living.

For many years the Concord stage brought one mail a day from Boston, over the "turnpike," now Main Street. When the stage came to the top of the hill, in the south part of the town, in sight of the village, the driver blew a powerful blast with an immense tin horn, which was the signal for getting another set of horses ready on his arrival, that he might change his team without delay.

After several years, Mr. Samuel W. Carter, who had been doing a general express and freight business since about 1821-2, put another stage on the route between here and Boston, carrying the Stoneham mail and passengers. He drove four horses, said to have been one of the best teams that went into Boston.

After politics began to affect the post-offices, another party was appointed to carry the mail to Stoneham, *via* Malden. Many were disaffected at the change, and a meeting of the citizens of Reading resulted in sending Mr. H. G. Richardson to Washington to lay the matter before the Postmaster-General. This was in 1843. On Mr. Richardson's arrival at the Capitol, he obtained an introduction to the Postmaster-General through a former postmaster of Washington city, with whom Mr. Richardson had had business transactions for many years. The Postmaster-General, Mr. Wickliffe, received Mr. R. very cordially, and introduced him to Mr. Hobbie, the First Assistant Postmaster General, who listened attentively to Mr. Richardson's statements, and directed him to call the next morning at 10 o'clock. With characteristic promptness Mr. R. was on hand at the moment, and was assured that his requests would be granted, and the papers promptly forwarded.

An interesting incident occurred while Mr. Richardson was sitting in the Postmaster-General's office. An old man who had been for some time quietly sitting there, said to Mr. R., "Young man, where do you belong?"—"In Boston, Massachusetts."—"Your name?" "Richardson."—"Well, my name is Richard M. Johnson. I am glad to see you. I am always glad to see a citizen of Massachusetts."—"I am glad to see you, sir, responded Mr. Richardson, who also referred to the ex-Vice President's fight with Tecumseh. Col. Johnson continued, "Yes, I have reason to remember it. You see I still carry the marks of those days." He then exhibited his arm, which was deeply engraved with frightful scars. Reference was made to his age. "Young man," said he, firing up with what must have been something of his youthful vigor, "young man, if my services were again needed, I would mount my horse soon as ever." Mr. Richardson returned, and the desired arrangements were soon established. Mr. Carter continued to carry the mail till after the opening of the Boston and Maine Railroad, which commenced running its trains through this town July 1, 1845.

LIBRARIES.

The first library in the West Parish, now Reading, was established Sept. 27, 1791, and was known by the name of "The Federal Library." It was owned and managed by an association which held its first meeting at the date above given. Rev. Peter Sanborn, Dea. Timothy Pratt, John Emerson, John Temple, and John Weston, were a committee "to take care of the affairs of the society." Mr. Sanborn was the first librarian, and seems to have served till 1814. It had a membership of about sixty persons. Rights of membership were sold at first, at a dollar each, which was afterwards increased to two dollars, and an annual tax of twenty-five cents.

In 1817 the association assumed the form and powers of a corporation. Abijah Weston was chosen clerk; John Weston, librarian; David Emerson, treasurer. The number of members increased to seventy-five, and the librarian was paid five dollars per annum for his services. The records close in 1830. The books were sold at public auction Jan. 24, 1831. Jonathan Frost and Charles Parker, the committee making the sale, reported the number of books sold 273. Net proceeds $97.12, to be divided among fifty-seven proprietors. This closed the existence of the "Federal Library" at the age of forty years.

The next was known as the "Franklin Library." The application of the proprietors for a meeting to organize was dated Dec. 25, 1841. It was signed by Stephen Foster, Dr. Kendall Davis, H. G. Richardson, and others. The organization was completed Jan. 1, 1842. John Batchelder, 3d, was elected president; Geo. Bancroft, vice do.; Oliver Peabody, clerk, treasurer, and librarian; Kendall Davis, Thomas Sweetser, Stephen Foster, Nathan P. Sherman, Haven P. Cook, Chas. Newman, Loea Parker, curators. The constitution and by-laws were signed by one hundred and three persons, who probably included nearly all that ever belonged to the association. The terms of admission were two dollars for each member, with an annual tax of fifty cents. Dr. H. P. Wakefield succeeded Mr. Batchelder as president in 1855; Milo Parker followed in 1858; J. H. Bancroft, 1860; Stephen

Foster, 1862. In 1869, by vote of the members, the library — four hundred and sixty-two volumes — was transferred to the trustees of the Reading Public Library. The last meeting of the members was held Jan. 7, 1871, practically dissolving the association after an existence of thirty years.

The Agricultural Library Association was formed in March, 1860. N. P. Pratt, Esq., was its first president; Thos. E. Prescott, vice-president; J. W. Manning, secretary; Thos. Richardson, librarian. The members paid each five dollars as admission fee. Mr. Richardson continued to serve as librarian till his decease in April, 1864. Miss Emily Ruggles was his successor. The books, numbering one hundred and sixty-six volumes, were transferred to the town library in January, 1869. Mr. Manning was the only person who served as secretary of the association.

The present public library was established by votes of the town passed March 2, 1868, and Nov. 3, 1868. The trustees chosen were: Ephraim Hunt, Edward Appleton, Chauncey P. Judd, Francis H. Knight, Hiram Barrus, and William Proctor; the amount of money appropriated, five hundred dollars. The trustees organized by the choice of E. Hunt, president, and F. H. Knight, secretary and treasurer. The whole number of volumes procured during the first year was 823. Of these, 199 volumes were presented by school districts Nos. 5, 8, and 9; 186 by the Appleton family; 18 by F. H. Knight; 210 by purchase; and the remainder by donations from various sources. The library, located in the high school building, was opened for circulation of books Feb. 17, 1869, Miss Mattie H. Appleton, librarian. During the following year the library received a donation of five hundred dollars from Dr. Horace P. Wakefield, which amount was offered in 1867, on condition that the town should appropriate an equal sum for the founding of a public library. In 1871, a donation of one hundred dollars was received from the estate of T. Ward Hartshorn; Loton Parker presented 228 volumes; Edward Appleton and sister, 38; Rev. Dr. Barrows, 15; John B. Lewis, Jr., 100; and, with other liberal donations from friends of the institution, added to the purchases by the town, the number of volumes in the library, reported March, 1871, was 2,475. F. O. Dewey, Esq., the largest donor since that date, presented in 1873, a complete set, numbering 115 nicely bound volumes, of "Littell's Living Age."

Dr. Hunt resigned his position as trustee of the library in April, 1871. F. O. Dewey was chosen his successor, and Edward Appleton, president. Stephen Foster, Esq., succeeded C. P. Judd, Esq., in 1872.

The remaining trustees belonging to the original board are still in service. Miss Appleton resigned her position as librarian in the summer of 1873, and Miss Alice Temple was appointed. The library was removed the same season to the Perkins building, corner of Woburn and Lowell Streets. The whole number of books then reported as catalogued was 3,237 volumes. The whole number of volumes taken out for circulation during the year was 14,671.

THE READING CHRONICLE.

The publication of the "Reading Chronicle" was commenced in 1870 by H. C. Gray, Esq. The first number was issued Saturday, May 28th. The first local item relating to Reading announces that a veteran association has been formed, and Col. C. D. Wright has been chosen commander. Another item refers to the death of Mrs. C. Augusta Soule, Aug. 20th, at Newark, N. J., sister of Dr. E. Hunt, of this town, and formerly a teacher in the Reading High School. Reference is also made to the Reading Brass Band, which flourished for several years; and to the services of Wm. H. Temple as auctioneer, who still continues to act in that vocation. S. Temple & Co. advertise millinery goods, now succeeded by Miss Charlotte Buck; R. M. Boyce offers coal for sale; Charles Schweizer supplies bread, cake, and pastry from his bakery, now carried on by J. & T. Carley; J. W. Manning, nurseryman, offers fruit trees, in large variety, and fifty kinds of grapes, which business he still pursues with undiminished energy.

THE READING FEMALE ANTISLAVERY SOCIETY.

The preamble of this society explains its purposes and objects in the following language: —

"Whereas we believe that slavery is contrary to the precepts of Christianity, dangerous to the liberties of the country, and ought immediately to be abolished; and whereas we believe that the citizens of New England not only have the right to protest against it, but are under the highest obligations to seek its removal by moral influence; and whereas we believe that the free people of color are unrighteously oppressed, and stand in need of our sympathy and benevolent co-operation; therefore, recognizing the inspired declaration, that God hath made of one blood all nations of men for to dwell on all the face of the earth, and in obedience to our Saviour's golden rule, 'All things whatsoever ye would that men should do unto you, do ye even so to them,' we agree to form ourselves into a society to be governed by the following constitution."

The object of the society is declared to be, to endeavor, by all means sanctioned by law, humanity, and religion, to effect the abolition of slavery in the United States; to improve the character and condition of the free people of color; to inform and correct public opinion in relation to their situation and rights, and obtain for them equal civil and political rights and privileges with the whites.

The payment of three dollars constituted a membership for life, or the payment of twenty cents, membership for a year, with power to vote in all meetings. The society met in Union Hall, and organized March 22, 1833, choosing the following officers: Mrs. Sarah Reid, president; Mrs. Sarah Parker, vice-president; Mrs. Hepzibah S. Temple, secretary; Mrs. Esther Kingman, treasurer; Mrs. Julia P. Eaton, Mrs. Susan S. Perkins, Mrs. Sophronia Kingman, Mrs. Susan W. Peabody, Miss Lucy Parker, counsellors.

The first name on the list of members was that of Mrs. Polly Chute, wife of Daniel Chute, Esq., a lady then about seventy years of age.

The first vote of the society, after adopting their constitution, was for appropriating money to Mr. Garrison's mission. The records being defective at this point, a letter of inquiry to Mr. Garrison elicited the following interesting reply: —

ROXBURY, March 4, 1874.

DEAR SIR: In answer to your letter of inquiry, I would state that I have carefully examined the early copies of the "Liberator," and I find that the historical honor belongs to Reading of giving birth to the first Female Antislavery Society ever formed in this country. . . .

In the month of May of that year, 1833, I went on my first antislavery mission to Great Britain; and among the credentials I carried to commend me to the respect and confidence of British abolitionists was an approving testimony from the Reading Female Antislavery Society, which, in the dearth of such testimonies at that time, was of real service to me, and elicited so kind a response from the antislavery ladies of England as to cause the following action: —

"At a meeting of the Reading Female Antislavery Society, on the 29th of October, 1833, called for the purpose of hearing the letters sent to us from the ladies in England, and also to dispose of their presents, the following resolution was adopted: —

"*Resolved*, That to the ladies of England we extend the hand of affection, reciprocate their good feelings, and cherish their presents as mementoes of those, our fellow-beings, who are groping in worse than Egyptian darkness, and whom they, in common with us, are striving to put in possession of all those rights which nature and nature's God ever intended they should enjoy."

This society continued for several years to be an efficient antislavery instrumentality, and helped to give a strong impetus to the whole movement. You very justly say, — "The time has come when such efforts are remembered with respect," — and

I am glad to know that you are "desirous that the ladies of Reading should have all the honor they deserve"; and that I conceive to be very great.

But Reading has not only the honor of having formed the first female antislavery society, but also the first male society auxiliary to the New England Antislavery Society. The latter was formed on the 13th of March, 1833, a few days prior to the former. Its officers were: president, Rev. Jared Reid; vice-president, Capt. Jonas Parker; secretary, Horace P. Wakefield; treasurer, Ambrose Kingman; counsellors, Enoch Peabody, Jesse Frost, Hiram D. Sweetser, Henry Kingman, Caleb McIntire.

This society was also very active and efficient. For some time Reading continued to be "the banner town" in the antislavery conflict.

Respectfully yours,
WM. LLOYD GARRISON.

HIRAM BARRUS, ESQ.

It is unfortunate that the letters from the ladies of England cannot be found. They were probably destroyed in the fire that consumed the house of Mr. Ambrose Kingman, in 1865. The presents referred to consisted of a china tea-set, each piece ornamented with a picture representing a kneeling slave, with manacled hands raised in the attitude of prayer. These were distributed among the members, and are still preserved with religious care.

The records of the society show that it was actively engaged in carrying out its professions. Frequent contributions of money were made to the antislavery societies in Boston and New York, and to special objects. Appropriations were made in behalf of Miss Prudence Crandall, of Canterbury, Conn., who was "suffering under the wicked law of that State for endeavoring by her personal instructions to elevate the intellectual and moral character, and thus improve the condition, of a portion of the free people of color." Aid was sent to Rev. S. J. May, agent of the American Antislavery Society; to Rev. H. Wilson and Father Hanson, for the support of colored schools in Canada; to the African captives taken in 1840 on board the brig "Amistad"; to Rev. Charles T. Torrey, the antislavery martyr; to the New York and Boston vigilance committees in charge, probably, of the famous underground railroad. Antislavery documents were circulated among the people, and lectures by distinguished advocates were given in behalf of the cause. Names were obtained and petitions sent to Congress against the admission of slave States, and among those presented by John Quincy Adams, for the abolition of slavery in the District of Columbia, was one forwarded from this society.

The records of the society close in 1850. Mrs. Sarah G. Temple was then chosen president; Mrs. Rebecca Parker, vice-president; Mrs. Nancy A. Gleason, secretary; Miss Elizabeth Gardner, treasurer. The counsellors were Mistresses Clarissa E. Weston, Selina Cheney, Sarah Wakefield, Elizabeth Porter, Roxana G. Weston.

RAILROADS AND EXPRESSES.

The Boston and Maine Railroad, when first built, did not run through this town. Its trains from Wilmington to Boston passed over the track of the Lowell Road.

In January, 1843, Mr. W. R. Perkins, learning that an effort was making for extending the railroad from Wilmington through Woburn to Boston, immediately set to work to divert it from that, to its present route. Messrs. Stephen Foster and Sylvester Harnden, with Mr. Perkins, visited Haverhill to see the president of the road, Mr. West, who met them on the following day, with Mr. Hayward, the engineer, at Wilmington, and went over the proposed route. A hasty survey resulted, and in ten days from the start, the petition for the road was brought before the Legislature, with plans and estimates.

Substantial aid was rendered by Messrs. Thaddeus B. Pratt, Joshua Prescott, Thomas Sweetser, H. G. Richardson, Daniel Pratt, Abiel Holden, Warren Perkins, and others of Reading; and Hon. Lilley Eaton, Dr. Thaddeus Spaulding, Benj. B. Wiley, and others of South Reading, now Wakefield.

A charter was procured after a short but memorable struggle, and the road was located over the present route. The speech of Dr. Wakefield, then a member of the House from Oakham, during the contest, is still remembered and referred to, as one of his best and most successful efforts. It presented the claims of this route in a strong light, and greatly aided in securing the passage of the act of incorporation.

The first train over the road was from Portland, in the afternoon of July 1, 1845. Mr. Calvin Temple was station agent here then, and continued in the service till Jan. 1, 1866. The fare to Boston was at first thirty cents, but it was soon reduced to twenty-five, and packages of fifty tickets were sold as family tickets at twelve and one half cents each.

The old depot, used for more than a quarter of a century by the people of this town, was the largest structure of the kind, and originally designed to be the best and most convenient, on the Boston and Maine Railroad, out of the city. It sheltered both tracks, and was more than one hundred feet in length. It was erected in 1845, and came near destruction at the time of the burning of the wood-sheds and freight house, April 18, 1868. The present depot, on the side of the track, has been in use about two years. Another new depot has been erected near Mr. O. Foote's, a half mile north of the present station.

Of the original conductors, Messrs. Tucker and Smith are still employed. Aborn, conductor, was then station agent at South Reading, and Smart was conductor of a freight train. Mr. Wm. Carter has been conductor since 1855. Mr. Clark, the present station agent, succeeded Mr. Temple.

Mr. Ebenezer Emerson did a general express and freight business between Reading and Boston for many years previous to 1820. He drove a team of two yoke of oxen and a horse. He usually started for Boston in the afternoon, stopping at Charlestown for the night, went into the city the next morning, gathered up his load and returned to Reading before he slept, unless he slept by the way, for he often did not reach home till midnight. He sometimes spent a day extra on the way doing a job of plowing or other team work for persons who desired his help. Evidently the steam whistle had not worked people up to the appreciation of telegraph lines and lightning trains as mediums for doing business at that time. About the year 1821 or '22, Mr. Carter, as before stated, commenced the express and freight business, using horses, going to the city twice a week and returning the same day. There were three stores here that did considerable business at that time, — Thomas Pratt's, Thomas Parker's, and Daniel Pratt's.

Mr. Carter sold his express and freight business soon after putting on his stage, to Capt. Thomas Richardson. Mr. Stowell succeeded him, and at his death the business fell into the hands of Mr. Cummings, the present efficient proprietor of the original line.

Mr. C. H. Lang has, since his return from service in the late war, been also doing a successful business in that department.

Our modern facilities for rapid conveyance and intercourse with all parts of the country and the world, do not enable us to appreciate the difficulties that surrounded our forefathers. Long journeys were made chiefly on horseback or on foot. Forty-five years ago, Erie canal packet boats were a popular means of conveyance for travellers from Albany to Buffalo.

Heavy freights were transported by ox teams. "Going West" for a long period did not imply going beyond the bounds of Massachusetts. Early in the present century, "The West" was understood to be in central, and then in western New York; or in the "Western Reserve," Ohio, and so onward till it finally had as little of definiteness in its meaning as had "The North" in England, when Pope wrote: —

> "Ask where's the North, — at York, 't is on the Tweed ;
> In Scotland, at the Oreades ; and there,
> At Greenland, Zembla, or the Lord knows where."

The early roads were little more than bridle paths from one neighborhood to another, —

> " Winding as old roads will,
> Here to a school-house, and there to a mill."

Those who had horses used the pannier, a sort of basket, or the wallet, a bag that, like the pannier, hung on each side of the horse, over his back, in which parcels were carried.

Squire Sweetser, now in his eightieth year, relates that when a small boy, he went in company with two of his brothers to Poole's mill to catch alewives, taking a horse with them to aid in bringing home the fish. One boy rode astride the horse, and one in the wallet on each side. They had unexpectedly good luck, and caught several bushels of fish, which they carried home upon the horse. Instead of the expected commendation for their successful expedition, they were mildly rebuked by their father for the unmerciful burden they had inflicted upon the horse.

Squire James Bancroft had a chaise as early as 1790.

Wagons began to be used a little previous to 1807. Rev. Mr. Sanborn had one of the first. Mr. Ephraim Weston at that time had a chaise, and probably there were others. Col. Nathan Parker had, about the same time, a farm wagon which had an iron axle, the first in use here.

During the winter months, hand-sleds were much used for the transportation of the lighter articles of commerce. Shoes, produce, etc., were carried to the cities, and supplies obtained for the family. Salem was more popular as a place for trade, till a comparatively recent date, than was Boston. Parties of several men, each with a loaded hand-sled, frequently went to Salem in company, going and returning the same day.

Newhall's tavern, near the present Lynnfield hotel, was the usual halting place for rest, refreshment, and the indispensable "mug of flip." One of these parties in a happy mood, before starting off homeward in the evening from this tavern, added a heavy stone to the load of one, who had rather boasted over the others of his superior strength and agility. The stone had a free ride to Reading, and the weariness it brought to the one that drew it was greatly enjoyed by those who perpetrated the practical joke. Mr. Phineas Sweetser, uncle of Thomas,

Esq., when once drawing his sled load of shoes to Boston, found the rivers so open that he was obliged to go around the city and come in over Roxbury Neck. After doing his business, he took on another load, and retracing his steps came home the same night, nearly exhausted.

MERCANTILE AFFAIRS.

The first intimation of there being a store in this part of the town is found among the writings of James Bancroft, Esq., in a paper dated May 15, 1761. It commences with the preamble, "Whereas I, James Bancroft, of Reading, have lately been at considerable expense to furnish myself with sundry sorts of West India goods (and other goods), as molasses, sugar, rice, tea, coffee, etc., and earthenware, in order to accommodate my neighbors, determining to sell the same as reasonably as they are sold at Medford, Charlestown, and Boston. . . . I think it might be an advantage to me by increasing my custom, and to others by accommodating them, if I might be approbated and have license to sell spirituous liquors." The paper asks for signatures signifying a willingness that he should be a retailer of spirits; but as no names are subscribed, and as there is no other evidence to suggest that he engaged in the sale of spirits, it is doubtful whether the paper was ever presented for signatures. How long he continued to sell the other kinds of goods named is unknown.

The first store of any importance in the village was that of William Johnson, which was built in the fall of 1801. It stood in the garden, just below the present store of Mr. Thomas Pratt. Johnson built a house in connection with it the next year, which was the second house built on the common, Rev. Mr. Sanborn's being the first. The Johnson house was removed in 1855 or '6, and is the house now owned by the heirs of Thomas Day. The house of Mr. Silas Smith was probably the next. The house of Mr. James Davis, then owned and occupied by Col. Nathan Parker, was built earlier, and was occupied for a long series of years as a tavern.

The store of Mr. Thomas Parker, on the lot near where the house of the late Sylvester Harnden stands, was probably opened about 1810, or soon after. Mr. Parker built a house adjoining it in 1828, which was removed to make room for Mr. Harnden's house, now owned by Col. Carroll D. Wright. Mr. Parker continued his store till his decease, Oct. 3, 1832.

Mr. Ephraim Weston had a store in the western part of the town as early as 1807, in connection with the shoe business. The store was continued by his sons till Mr. Holden took it for a year or two, and it was then resumed by Mr. Weston, who kept it till 1833. In that year his grandson, J. Brooks Leathe, purchased the goods, and continued the business till 1864, when he relinquished it to enter upon the duties of U. S. assistant assessor in the Internal Revenue Department. This office he held till the office of assessor was abolished in 1873.

Daniel Pratt, Esq., continued a dry goods and grocery store for many years in connection with his shoe business. Thomas Pratt, his brother, as intimated in another connection, was probably longer in the business than any other person that has lived here. For many years Reading was the centre of trade for Wilmington, Tewksbury, Middleton, and several other neighboring towns, and the stores here had a flourishing business. Medford rum was formerly a very popular article of traffic, and one of the stores is said to have sold it at the rate of a hogshead of one hundred and twenty gallons per week, while another was thought to have sold twice that amount.

Mr. Thomas Pratt has transferred his business to his son Thomas B., who continues to carry it on at the old stand, where it has been pursued for more than half a century.

Mr. William Parker commenced in the grocery and West India goods trade in 1830, in a store that stood near where W. R. Perkins's house is located. He afterwards occupied the store of D. Pratt, Esq., for a time, and then the Thomas Parker store. In 1841, he removed to the store he now occupies. This building was first erected for a store, in Wakefield. It was removed to Mr. Etson Damon's, and used for a time as a cabinet shop.

Mr. F. Fletcher opened a dry goods store here about 1855. He had previously been in the trade about ten years. He was first to occupy the late post-office room in Lyceum Hall building, which he left to be the first to occupy one of the stores in the Bank building, where he remained till he built his present store. He deals in ready-made clothing, and employs tailors for custom work.

Mr. Amos Temple was several years a dry goods dealer here in the store now occupied by Reed & Buck.

Mr. James Reid, who was formerly associated with Mr. Fletcher, commenced dealing in dry goods in 1866. He still pursues the business in company with Mr. George F. Buck.

Mr. Jonathan Frost began to trade in 1828, in the Spokesfield house, and in 1831 removed to his present residence. He still continues the business.

Miss Sukey Parker, daughter of Benjamin, had the first dry goods and millinery establishment here. It was kept in the store that stood where Mr. Foster's house is, previous to 1823, and afterwards in Market building till about 1850. The boys of her time remember an ancient looking picture, which she preserved with pious care, and impressed them with the belief that it was a likeness of the Saviour painted from the original. The present milliners are Mrs. Abbie Nichols, Miss Charlotte Buck, and Mrs. H. B. Remick.

Mr. Silas Smith kept a limited stock of dry goods for several years in the house built by him and still occupied by his widow, 90 years of age, the oldest person in town, save one. She was the daughter of Aaron Parker, and sister of Dea. Jabez D. Parker. Mr. Smith was the principal dealer in cotton sheetings, being manufacturer's agent for the sale in this vicinity. His son Cyrus was for a time engaged in the business, and kept a store in the same house.

Copeland and Bowser have been in business, in Gowing's Block, since its erection in 1871, commencing April 1st. They keep a general assortment of dry goods and gents' furnishing goods. Mr. Copeland had been for several years in the employ of F. Fletcher.

The store near the depot at the foot of Haven Street was built and occupied about 1851 by Mr. Franklin Putnam, who continued the grocery business for ten years. He was succeeded by Pierce Bros., Colman, and others, for short periods. Mr. T. T. Greenwood purchased the store and had charge of it for several years. He was succeeded by James H. Davis. Lucius Turner was in trade there from 1867 to April, 1873. S. N. Stone succeeds him.

Mr. Salma A. Gould built a store near the Woburn Street Schoolhouse two years since, in which he continues to trade.

John Adden kept a store in connection with his shoe business, at the corner of Main and Summer Streets, about thirty-five years since.

MEAT AND PROVISION TRADE.

In addition to the supplies furnished by the several stores, the town is served by three markets, kept by Messrs. Harnden and Tweed, T. C. Trow, and B. F. Adams. Mr. Charles Tweed was the pioneer in the business. Timothy Temple, Wm. H. Temple, L. G. Richardson, J. R. Morton, and others have formerly been employed in it. J. R. Brown has a fruit and provision store in the Appleton building near the depot.

SHOE STORES.

Those now doing business here in the retail shoe trade, are N. D. Stoodley, Ira Atkinson, J. A. Bancroft, D. F. Weston, S. Doucette.

Miscellaneous Stores.

F. J. Bancroft opened a store in 1873 for the sale of music and musical instruments.

Lewis E. Gleason has papers, periodicals, and a variety of other articles in the store connected with the post-office.

Mr. Francis Bartley succeeds James T. Norris in the sale of men's clothing and furnishing goods. M. Hanley deals in furniture. J. & T. Carley carry on the bakery which has been in operation several years. Robert J. Bell has a drug store near the depot.

Lyceum Hall.

The association that built Lyceum Hall was organized in the month of May, 1854, under an act of incorporation approved April 24th of the same year. Edward Safford, Samuel T. Ruggles, Ignatius Sargent, their associates and successors, were made a corporation, by the name of the Reading Lyceum Hall Association. The first meeting for the choice of officers was held May 29th. Horace P. Wakefield was chosen president; Sylvester Harnden, vice-president; Stephen Foster, secretary; Ignatius Sargent, treasurer; Alfred A. Prescott, Edward Safford, Reuben Weston, directors; C. P. Judd, John Damon, Thomas Richardson, standing committee. A building lot was purchased of Lilley Eaton for $927. Edward Safford contracted for the erection of the building at $4,800.

The frame of the original building was raised in November, 1854. When the work was completed, the cost of the building, furniture, and land amounted to about $8,000. A portion of this had been raised by subscription, ten dollars entitling a person to one share and the privilege of membership. Each member had a right to as many votes as he owned shares, provided no member had more than ten votes. The balance of the money not secured by the sale of shares was borrowed to pay the expenses. This was repaid from the yearly receipts before making any dividend among the stockholders. The first dividend was in 1859, of fourteen per cent, the second in 1860 of fifteen per cent. During the war the rents were reduced, and the profits also. The store now occupied by G. W. Atkinson was first rented by a union store association, and kept by J. S. Campbell. W. J. Wightman succeeded in 1857, and remained till 1865, when Mr. Atkinson took it. Capt. Thomas Richardson kept the drug store till 1862, selling out to John Dole, who sold to Dr. W. H. Willis, the present occupant, in 1865. Miss Emily Ruggles has occupied the same store she now does, from her commencement in business soon after the completion of the building. Miss Ruggles is also real estate broker. Mr. Gleason, the present postmaster, in May, 1861, removed the post-office from the market building near Stephen Foster's to Lyceum Hall building, where it still remains, though it was removed from the room now occupied by Mrs. Remick for millinery purposes to the present, in December, 1873. Ira Gray & Son had their clothing store in the story above till the erection of the bank building in 1860–61, to which place he removed. Since that time the rooms have been variously occupied. Clarkson Parker has for nearly five years used the room he now does for a barber shop.

The first movement for the building of Lyceum Hall was prompted by the felt need of the people for a hall suitable for public gatherings, and the wants of a small organization that has since merged into the Christian Union Society, for a place to hold their meetings. The efforts for obtaining funds by subscription for building the hall were nearly a failure. There was at that time little surplus wealth in town that could well be spared for such an investment. Mr. Stephen Foster and S. Harnden, impressed with the need of such a work, and foreseeing that the public would be ready to sustain it, engaged in the enterprise with others, and helped carry it forward to completion. In November, 1870, an additional piece of land was bought, that formerly belonged to the old estate of Dr. Daniel Gould, to which the first purchase from Mr. Eaton had originally belonged, and proceeded after some delay to the building of the extension just now being completed.

The present officers of the association are: E. Safford, president; Samuel Pierce, vice-president; Stephen Foster, secretary and treasurer; Reuben Weston, G. W. Atkinson, H. E. Cox, directors; C. W. Perkins, N. P. Pratt, standing committee. Mr. Foster has been secretary from the organization, and Mr. Weston one of the directors. Dr. H. P. Wakefield was continued as president till 1868, when his services for the State required his removal from town.

THE WATCH AND CLOCK BUSINESS IN READING.

Mr. Benj. E. Beard was probably the first in town who made the watch and jewelry trade a distinct business. He opened his store in 1847 in Harnden's building, and continued there till his death in 1868. His son, W. E. Beard, succeeded him, and in December, 1873, removed the business to Lyceum Hall building. He is assisted by Mr. D. A.

Emery. Dea. Amos Evans had been earlier engaged in watch repairing, which he long continued after Mr. Beard commenced the business. A Mr. Wheeler had also had a room in a small building on the east side of the street, below the Common, where he dealt in watches and repaired them. Mr. Daniel Putnam acquired many years ago a good reputation as a repairer of watches, and his friends claim he is still able to do better work than the average watch repairer. We don't know how well founded the claim is, but we are told that he is the possessor of a watch over a hundred years old that he maintains in good running order, though we think he did not make it.

The manufacture of clock cases was commenced in this town in the spring of 1832 by Mr. Jonathan Frost. He first began to buy clocks of Burr & Chittenden, of Lexington, who bought the movements or running part in Bristol, Conn., and made the cases themselves. Mr. Frost sent them out with other goods by his pedlers for a year or so. When he began the business for himself the movements cost him a trifle over eight dollars apiece, which price was finally reduced to seven and a half. Within the year 1832, Mr. [Frost formed a partnership with Daniel Pratt, Esq., for the manufacture, which continued for three years. After the close of the partnership, Mr. Frost suspended operations in that line for nearly two years, when he resumed and continued it till about 1850. Mr. Pratt had continued the business uninterruptedly during all this time. In 1838–39, he employed about twenty hands. Among his employees was Mr. B. E. Beard, to whom we have already referred. Another employee was Mr. Gilbert Green, now of Clinton, Mass., who deals in watches and jewelry, and has become wealthy. Several others in this town and in North Reading were also employed by Mr. Pratt in carrying on his business. Mr. Pratt supplied and sent out pedlers to dispose of his clocks till about 1846, when he opened a store in Boston, at 49 Union Street, in which business has been continued to the present time. For a year or two previous he had sent a considerable number of clocks to Calcutta, where a very good market was found. A clock with a fancy case, known as the "double Gothic," costing about five dollars here, sold there for about fifteen dollars in gold. They were frequently exchanged for the goods of the countries to which they were sent, which were imported and sold here. Since the decease of Mr. Pratt, in March, 1871, as well as for some years previously, the business has been carried on by Messrs. D. F. Pratt and B. M. Boyce, who now constitute the firm, under the name of "Daniel Pratt's Sons." F. W. B. Pratt, son of D. F., is employed with them. They have for about three years imported clocks from abroad. They are doing a rapidly increasing business in this line, which might well be expected, as they sell nice French clocks much cheaper than any other house in the city. The manufacture of clocks was discontinued here by Mr. Pratt about 1858 or 1859. The house on Linden Street, owned by Mr. Pease, and the shoe store on Haven Street, occupied by Major Stoodley, were, before removal to their present sites, occupied by Mr. Pratt in the prosecution of his business. The pedlers sold the clocks at prices ranging from twelve to sixteen dollars each. The brass movements were introduced about 1835 or 1836. The clock dealers, in speaking of clocks and time-pieces, make a distinction that is perhaps peculiar to themselves. If it strikes the hour it is called a clock; if it does not strike the hour, it is called a time-piece.

Cabinet-Makers.

Ambrose Kingman is said to have been the first to engage in this business here. He sold out to his brother Henry, who greatly enlarged it, and subsequently removed to New York, where it is still successfully prosecuted by his son William.

Luther Elliot, Hammond Flint, Amos Sweetser, Charles Carter, Henry F. Parker, J. W. Beers, S. T. Ruggles, John Cheney, Gardner French, D. B. Lovejoy, D. G. Richardson, James Davis, and others, were more or less engaged in this business.

Alden Batchelder has been in the manufacture of furniture about ten years, employing twenty to thirty hands. He sells his goods throughout the Union and Canada.

Dinsmore and Grouard have been more than twenty years manufacturing furniture. They were the first to make parlor desks, which had a large sale. They also make book-cases and chamber furniture, and employ about thirty hands. Their mill was built by William Badger about twenty-five years since. It passed into other hands, and was purchased about ten years since by Dinsmore & Grouard, and fitted up with a new engine and machinery.

Mr. Charles Manning and Mr. Frederick Miller are both engaged in making parlor desks.

Mr. Sylvester Harnden came here from Stoddard, N. H., about 1823, and worked at the furniture business with Luther Elliot, and afterwards, in company with Amos Sweetser, in a building that stood just south of W. R. Perkins's present residence. In 1827 or 1828, Mr. Harnden erected and used for a shop the building occupied for many years by B. E. Beard in the watch business. In 1831 he built the house now owned by his son, F. Harnden, and another shop a little in the rear. His business rapidly increased, and he employed for many years about seventy-five or eighty workmen.

In 1856 he engaged in the manufacture of refrigerators, under the patent of John C. Schooley, which, in connection with the furniture business, is still continued by his son, F. Harnden.

Mr. Harnden was a prominent man in town matters, always ready to aid in public improvements, and to do his share in sustaining the burdens and performing the duties required of a true citizen. He was a native of Wilmington; born 1804; died May 19, 1873.

COOPERS.

David Emerson, Joseph Young, Edward Young, John Nichols, David Ball, Samuel W. Brooks, Capt. Abijah Weston, Jabez Weston.

CURRIERS.

Oliver Colburn and George Flagg were curriers, and carried on business in the red house near the railroad crossing on Main Street, known as the "Dublin House."

WHEELWRIGHTS AND CARRIAGE-MAKERS.

Mr. Ambrose Kingman is remembered as the principal one here in the wheelwright business. Mr. Samuel Brown, on Haven Street, is a carriage-builder. In the same building, P. McCall makes harnesses.

MILLS.

Messrs. Dinsmore & Grouard, F. Harnden, Solon Parker, and H. Bachelder have steam mills for sawing lumber. Mr. John Burrill has a saw-mill operated by water power, formerly owned by Cleaveland Beard. This mill is probably referred to in a deed by Abraham Foster to Raham Bancroft, dated in 1730. There is also a saw and a grist mill at "Lob's Pound," where there was a saw-mill in 1694.

The first mill in this part of the town for sawing boards was probably the one often referred to in the early town records as the "saw-pit mill," which was near where Summer Street crosses Main. The little bridge just east of the corners retained the name "Soppit Bridge," till quite recently. Thomas Sweetser, Esq., recollects seeing the pit in which the under man stood while drawing his end of the saw. It is referred to as "Parker's mill" in the town records, but the oldest inhabitant now living does not know to which of the Parkers it belonged. There was once a saw-mill at the foot of the hill, about thirty rods west of the house of Capt. George Bancroft. It belonged to Thomas Bancroft, and a Merrow. It is believed to have been there in 1764. There was a tannery about twenty rods west of the mill, the relics of which have not entirely disappeared.

The reference to "Lob's Pound" suggests an inquiry as to the origin of the name. Dea. Wakefield says that some one told him, there was formerly a pound there for keeping colts in over night, and that the name "Lob" was a corruption of "nobby" or "nob," a child's pet name for a colt.

BLACKSMITHS.

Zadoc Richardson appears to have been in the business here from 1762 to 1772, and may have been for a much longer time. Eli Mead had a shop at the corner of Woburn and Washington Streets, date unknown. Samuel Pratt, who died in 1734, and who lived where Herrick Batchelder now lives, was a blacksmith. His son Samuel succeeded to his estate, and followed the same occupation. This Samuel left no children. His nephew, Benjamin, son of Lieut. Ephraim, of North Reading, was his successor. He died in 1842 at the age of 84. He was a soldier of the Revolution ; a town officer for more than twenty years ; deacon in the Old South Church more than forty ; and the father of thirteen children. His son Benjamin was the father of Benjamin, Joseph L., and Stillman M. Pratt, of the present time, and several daughters.

Mr. Joseph Spokesfield, whose shop stood where Edward F. Parker's house now is, was in the business sixty years ago. The early blacksmiths supplied the people with "wrought" nails, which were sold by count, not by weight, and made most of the tools used by the farmers and mechanics.

The more recent blacksmiths have been Cephas Parker, D. M. Damon, E. B. Eames, R. C. Totten, John Blunt, Theo. F. Gould. The last named four are still in business.

TIN-WARE AND STOVES.

T. Littlefield came from Wakefield to Reading in 1843, and opened a shop on Ash Street. He removed to the village in 1853, and to his present shop in 1860. He was the first to engage in the business in this town, and for a time had no competitor here, or in Wakefield, or in Stoneham. Several others have set up the business here for brief periods. Mr. Eugene De Jean has been engaged in it for about two years.

House Builders.

Amos Parker, father of Dana Parker, was one of the principal carpenters of eighty years ago. Dea. Caleb Wakefield served his apprenticeship with him, commencing March 29, 1801. Seventy years afterwards, within an hour of the time of the day at which he went to the house of Mr. Parker to begin his service, Dea. Wakefield called at the same house, now occupied by the son above named, and reminded the family of the fact, an incident of rare occurrence. The first house built by Dea. Wakefield was the tavern for Col. Nathan Parker, which stood where the bank building now stands. This was in 1806. It was three stories high, the first of that height built here. The old "try-rule" system of framing had been followed up to that time, which required every tenon and mortise to be fitted together and marked so that it could be known where every piece belonged. Dea. Wakefield followed that system called also "scribe" rule, and the critics decided he could not erect the building in that way. An interested party declared that the builder should pay a dollar for every false mortise made. But the frame was completed and raised without a mistake. The modern system called "square rule" was soon after generally introduced. In 1801, Dea. Wakefield purchased the first screw auger he had seen. Previous to that, mechanics had used what they called the "pod" auger. Up to 1806 the farmers used wooden shovels, which were sometimes plated, or "shod," upon the cutting edge with iron.

The following list embraces most of the principal carpenters and builders for half a century, coming down to the present time: —

Eben Eaton, John Nichols, Timothy Temple, Samuel R. Allen, Joseph Spokesfield, Daniel Creesy, Wendell Bancroft, David C. Temple, Wm. M. Phillips, Edward Safford, Nath'l W. Broad, Wm. Bryant, Edward C. Nichols, Ephraim Wight.

Masons.

Bridge Wakefield, William Wakefield, Stewart P. Wakefield, Capt. Joseph Gleason, N. H. Turner, S. M. Hall, Edward Parker.

Painters.

Abner Bancroft, Wm. H. Bancroft, Nathan Bancroft, Moses Nichols, J. C. Cook, Amos McIntire. M. H. Garfield, carriage and sign painter.

Manufacture of Shoes.

The first recorded evidence of the manufacture of shoes in this part of ancient Reading appears to be in the account book of Lieut.

Joseph Bancroft, commencing in the year 1758. He seems to have supplied the home market for about thirty years afterwards. In the summer of 1794 he charges John Temple, Jr., for making about four hundred pairs of shoes.

The manufacture of shoes as an article of trade seems to have fairly been commenced before this time. During the Revolution tradition connects the names of several persons with the business who were accustomed to carry their work to the city for a market. Among these was Ephraim Parker, who also kept the tavern in Squire Sweetser's old house on Washington Street. He employed several workmen in the business. Phineas Sweetser, uncle of the Squire, did a smaller business; and Mr. Daniel Damon, grandfather of Edgar, D. Myron, and Albert P. Damon, carried on the business as early as 1794, employing several hands. He learned the trade in Westford, where he seems to have been when the war of the Revolution commenced. After his return to Reading he lived in a house that stood where Mr. Francis Kingman now resides, and owned the land in that vicinity, including the grove now owned by Solon Parker. His first wife, Anna, died of small-pox in 1793, aged 28 years. She married at the age of 18, and in the short period of her married life, became the mother of seven sons and one daughter. The seventh son, Warren Damon, over eighty years of age, is now living in Amherst, N. H.

The first to engage extensively in the manufacture of boots and shoes here was probably Daniel Chute, Esq., about 1792. He prosecuted the business with great energy for about twenty years, but we have few details concerning the kind or amount of goods made by him. It appears that he not only employed many workmen here, but also at the same time in Byfield, his native town.

Mr. Jonathan Temple did business in making shoes, commencing as early as 1794, but to what extent is not known. He was for some time connected with Mr. David Pratt. Mr. John Temple carried on the business in the same neighborhood.

David Pratt, who came to Reading from Saugus about 1796, and lived where Edward Appleton, Esq., now resides, was early employed in the business. The first shoes he made he carried to Boston and Charlestown for a market. He employed at first three or four workmen, and carried the shoes in saddle-bags, over his own shoulders. He soon procured a horse and a two-wheeled vehicle, known then as a "milk cart," which he used for transporting his goods. People considered this a piece of extravagance, and predicted his failure. But his business increased till he eventually employed about a hundred workmen. His goods continued to be delivered in Boston, whence they were sent to the Southern States. They were packed in barrels, his boys Daniel and Thomas treading them down as they were put in, in order to get as many as possible into each barrel. In 1806 or '7, he bought the land where Thomas Pratt's store now is, and also the store that stood in the garden just below, which was formerly owned by William Johnson. In 1817 he built the house and store which his son Thomas has since continued to occupy. He intended it for a shoe factory and store; but he died in 1818, before completing his designs, and left them to be carried out by his two sons, Daniel and Thomas. They continued the business together for a few years, when they divided, Thomas continuing the store, and Daniel the shoe business. In 1826, Daniel removed to his late residence, which he continued to occupy up to the time of his death. He gave up the shoe trade and engaged in the clock business in 1832, as related elsewhere.

Silas Smith did considerable business in the shoe manufacture for several years, contemporary with Mr. Pratt.

Mr. Ephraim Weston was among the first who employed any considerable number of hands. As early as 1804, he made from five hundred to seven hundred pairs of shoes per month. He seems to have supplied quite a number of families with work, paying from seventeen to twenty cents a pair for making children's and misses' shoes, and twenty-five to twenty-nine cents for other kinds. Some kinds of children's shoes sold at that time in market, at forty-six cents a pair; women's shoes, from seventy-four to ninety-one cents. Red morocco skins cost twenty-five dollars per dozen. His goods for some years were sent to the West Indies, but were afterwards sent to Baltimore, to his son Asahel, who was engaged there in trade. The business was continued by his sons Aaron and Luther, and is now carried on by Clifford P. Weston, his grandson.

Mr. Warren Perkins, father of Charles W., came here from Middleton, and about 1807 began the manufacture of shoes, which he continued for about forty years. He employed from fifty to seventy-five hands in this and adjoining towns, whom he supplied with work. He built the house that stood where the Union church stands, which he long occupied, and which was subsequently the residence of Mr. William Parker.

Isaac Upton, Lilley Eaton, Lorenzo Parker, and —— Beers were also among the early manufacturers.

H. G. Richardson and W. R. Perkins were in company for seven years manufacturing shoes, commencing in 1835. Mr. Perkins continued it till 1846. In 1857, Mr. Richardson turned his attention to the hide and leather business, which he continued till his store was destroyed in the great fire in Boston in 1872.

John Adden commenced the manufacture of shoes about 1830. In 1845 he opened a general jobbing and wholesale store in New Orleans, which has been continued without interruption, save for a few years during the late war. In 1861, Mr. Adden formed a partnership with his son, J. H. Adden, and the business has since been conducted under the name of J. H. Adden & Co. They formerly employed nearly two hundred hands in the manufacture of their goods; but the introduction of labor-saving machinery has diminished the necessity for employing so many.

Mr. Abiel Holden, who came to this town from Stoneham, commenced the manufacture of morocco shoes, probably in the year 1822. He did business as the agent of Mr. Isaac Mead, of Charlestown, who furnished the morocco. Nearly every family in town at that time was employed in binding and stitching shoes for the different persons engaged in their manufacture. Mr. Stephen Foster came here from Wakefield in 1823, and was employed by Mr. Holden for many years in giving out and receiving the work, keeping books, etc. The business was carried on for a year or two, at Weston's corner, in the store of Ephraim Weston, and was then transferred to a house and store in the village that stood where Mr. Foster's house now stands. About 1830, Mr. Holden gave up the business into the hands of Mr. Foster, who continued the agency till the fall of 1834, when, upon the death of Mr. Mead, he bought the stock and continued the business on his own account. The leading business at that time was making what was known through the country as " Reading pumps," or men's dancing shoes. Mr. Foster continued manufacturing here till 1852, when he opened a store in Boston. He resumed manufacturing here in 1859, and in 1864 was joined by Mr. Charles W. Perkins. The company still continue the business.

Mr. Holden, who had been for several years employed as deputy sheriff, resumed the manufacture of shoes in 1840, which he continued till July, 1850, when he took in his sons with him. In August, 1862, the business fell into the hands of his sons, Arkaid, Clinton B., and William J., and is now continued under the name of Holden Brothers. Before the introduction of machinery they employed about fifty hands. For about fifteen years they have made, exclusively, children's and misses' shoes for the Southern market.

Mr. D. F. Weston began in 1835; has sometimes employed fifty hands;

manufactures children's and misses' shoes; had a store in Boston for several years for their sale.

Mr. Stillman E. Parker manufactures men's and women's shoes for the Southern market, employing about twenty-five hands in his manufactory, and furnishing work to about as many others outside. He commenced the business in 1845.

Mr. J. H. Bancroft has been engaged in the business for about twenty years, making children's and youths' sizes.

Mr. James A. Bancroft commenced in 1858 the manufacture of children's shoes, which he still continues. He employs from eight to twelve hands.

Among those who have, till a comparatively recent period, been engaged in the manufacture of shoes, are Joseph L. Pratt, the late Dea. Thomas H. Sweetser, Gilman C. Coggin, Roswell N. Temple.

Reading is known among the shoe trade as a town where infant shoes are a specialty.

The business for many years was small in the aggregate, and was conducted by women, who cut and made their goods, and then sold them at the country stores, or exchanged them with the travelling pedlers for the wares which they carried from door to door. Early in the present century, one or two men commenced the business on a more extensive scale, cutting out the shoes themselves, and employing women to make them up at a fixed price per pair. The soles were of thin sheepskin, tanned a russet color; but calico and velvet, as well as leather, were sometimes used for the uppers. The shoes were cut out and made by hand, and the whole process was a slow and tedious one, yielding to the manufacturers a profit less than the present wages of a good mechanic, while the women who made the shoes earned from two shillings to a dollar a week in addition to performing their household duties.

The introduction of the sewing-machine and other mechanical inventions has greatly developed the business, and there is as much taste displayed in the style and finish of infants' shoes as in any other branch of shoe manufacture. But little of the work is now done without the aid of machinery. The uppers are almost exclusively cut out with dies, the ornamental figures are put on by the aid of a stamp, while all the stitches, with the exception of sewing on the rosettes, are taken by a sewing-machine.

A woman, devoting her whole time to the work, now earns from six to twelve dollars per week, and some earn nine dollars besides doing their house-work.

It would hardly be supposed that so small an article as an infant's shoe afforded much room for variety. But there is quite as much change demanded in the style of shoes for the little folks as for the people of larger growth, and a wonderful skill and taste is displayed by our manufacturers in the production of these goods, while fond mothers are so eager for novelties that the manufacturer who produces a new style that pleases the fancy of the public is sure of a large demand and a good profit as long as he can keep it a secret from his brother manufacturers.

Some of the manufacturers secure themselves against competition by obtaining a patent for their favorite styles.

Although infants' shoes are made in small quantities in various other places, Reading is the centre of the business, and in styles and general character of its goods is the leading market of the country. The production is about 400,000 pairs annually, furnishing constant employment to nearly a hundred women. The principal manufacturers are G. A. Richardson, Clifford B. Weston, George E. Leathe, E. Bassett, John Burrill, J. W. Richardson & Co. There are also several ladies who manufacture dolls' shoes in great variety.

Geo. A. Richardson & Co., two years since, secured a patent for a sewing-machine for bottoming shoes, which makes a saving of nine or ten cents per pair in making children's shoes. They make yearly about 200,000 pairs, representing about eighty different styles, of which three are patented. They have eight or ten different patents on machines and shoes.

For the past fifteen years the business has been steadily increasing, and the products of our Reading manufacturers are found in every store in the Union, as well as in the British Provinces.

Manufacture of Hats, etc.

Nathan Weston, prompted by the high price of hats during the war of 1812, turned his attention for several years to their manufacture. The bodies were made by him of pasteboard, coated with a preparation of shellac and gum copal, to render them waterproof. For the outer covering, he used cotton plush. The cloth was prepared for this purpose by Adam Hawkes who had a fulling mill and clothiers' works in the eastern part of South Reading (Wakefield), near Lynnfield. Weston employed but little help, and did not prosecute his business with the energy that the merits of his work might well have prompted. He sold principally to customers in this vicinity.

It seems to be well authenticated that Weston was the first manufacturer, as well as inventor, of the silk hat. The cotton plush he used soon faded, and he was ultimately led, it is claimed, to the use of silk in order to remedy the defect. After the close of the war the price of hats became much reduced, and in 1819 he discontinued their manufacture. Having a patent under which he had made them, he allowed others the benefit of it, for which they paid him a royalty of twenty-five cents for each hat made by them. Mr. Thomas Sweetser (now Esq.) took up the business and carried it on here for one season, and then, in 1818, removed it to Charlestown. Mr. Warren Perkins was for a time employed in the business.

W. J. Wightman, Esq., commenced the manufacture of coach lace here in 1840, employing eighteen hands. He continued the business with encouraging success for seventeen years.

NECKTIE MANUFACTURE.

Damon, Temple & Co. (D. Myron Damon, A. P. Damon, and Joseph S. Temple) began the business in January, 1866, in the bank building, with about a dozen employees. The business increased till the number of hands in 1869 was about one hundred and twenty-five. During this latter year their factory on Woburn Street was erected. They were pioneers in making this line of goods a specialty. They opened a store in Boston at the time they began to manufacture here, and another at Chicago in 1867, to accommodate their Western customers. The Chicago store, with its contents, was burnt in the great fire of October, 1871, and the Boston store and goods in the great fire of November, 1872. In May, 1873, they were compelled to remove their goods to escape impending destruction from another extensive fire in Boston. Notwithstanding these serious drawbacks, their business has continued to flourish, and by adopting improved methods, they are now able, with one hundred hands, to turn out as much work as formerly with many more employees. They now import their silk and other materials direct from the foreign market. Twenty-five persons are employed in the distribution of their goods at their store in the city and elsewhere. The quality of their work is of such established reputation as to be demanded by the trade throughout the Union. They sell considerable quantities to "Zion's Co-operative Association" among the Mormons in Utah.

Organ Manufacture.

The first to engage in this business was Thomas Appleton. He was a native of Boston, where he began the manufacture in 1809, working in company with his brother-in-law, in Chambers Street, Boston, who built the first organ in this country. In 1810 he became a member of the firm of Hoyts, Babcock & Appleton, who put up a building for the manufacture of pianos and organs, on the site of Franklin's birthplace in Milk Street. After a few years he commenced business alone. In September, 1851, he came to Reading, and has occupied since that time the factory near the depot. He built thirty-five organs for churches in Boston: the first being for the church in Summer Street, recently removed; the second for the Handel and Haydn Society, which was long used in Music Hall. He also built organs for nearly every principal city of the United States, in all nearly thrice as many as for Boston. He built his last organ in 1868, when more than sixty years of age, for the Baldwin Baptist Church in Canton Street, Boston. This was one of his largest, and he designed it to be his best. Thirty years previously he had built one for the same church, then in Baldwin Place, which during all that time never cost the society a dollar for repairs. His organs, like himself, were honest clear through. He never counted the cost, but made every instrument as thoroughly as possible. He said he should be ashamed to pass a church that had in it an organ of his that was imperfectly built. He designed his work to last one hundred and fifty years as the best monument he could leave to perpetuate his memory. His instruments were noted for sweetness and purity of tone, as well as for perfection of machinery. His ear was remarkably accurate, and his musical judgment unerring. Dr. Shattuck, of Boston, employed him to select a piano for his daughter, and was so well pleased with the selection that he made him a present of two hundred dollars. Yet as a musical performer he set up for himself no claim. Indeed, he was accustomed to say he neither could "sing, whistle, nor play a jewsharp." He possessed a remarkable memory; could remember events that he witnessed more than eighty years before. He retained a vivid idea of the burning of the ropewalk on Atkinson Street, Boston, when he was seven years old, and the hanging of three pirates on the same day. A cage, with a post in the middle, was hauled on trucks from the jail-yard, where the Court-house now stands, to the Common. The pirates were hung to arms extending out from this post. This was also used for a whipping-post and pillory, and usually stood near the head of State Street.

He was a man of rare generosity, often giving or lending considerable amounts of money where needed, when he had no reason to expect the return of a dollar. He was a stranger to all feelings of malice or ill-will. One who knew him most thoroughly, says, "He was the best-tempered man I ever knew." An organ building firm were accustomed, in their efforts to compete with him, to speak in severe though unjust terms of him. When he heard of it he said, "They would feel better if they only had work enough"; and ever ready to return good for evil, he soon after procured for them a good contract. It is needless to add that they became his firm friends. He was temperate in his habits. Only a few days before his death he remarked to a friend, "I never smoked nor chewed tobacco, and was never intoxicated."

Mr. Appleton was a man of quiet and unobtrusive manners, tall and erect, with a genial face that bore a striking resemblance to that of General Washington. He was a cousin to the Messrs. Appleton, the well-known New York publishers, and a descendant of Thomas Appleton, one of the first settlers of Ipswich.

He died July 11, 1872, in the 87th year of his age.

Samuel Pierce began the manufacture of metallic organ pipes in 1847. It was the first attempt at making the business a specialty. It rapidly increased, and necessitated the building of his manufactory in 1852, which has subsequently been enlarged, to furnish room for the employment of about thirty workmen. Mr. Pierce finds a market for his pipes throughout the United States and Canada, among first-class organ-builders.

FIRE ENGINES.

The engine known as "Union No. 1," was purchased between the years 1813-15, by private contributions, chiefly from those who desired to become exempt from doing military duty. This exemption was by law allowed to those who belonged to a fire engine company, but the number belonging to a company was limited to about thirty-five. Those holding positions in this company, and becoming exempt for other reasons from doing military duty, were accustomed to sell out their rights, at fancy prices, to others who desired exemption.

Engine No. 2, the "Water Witch," was procured in 1825, for similar reasons, for a company formed in the neighborhood of Barnard's Hotel, then a part of this town. It was last used when the hotel was burnt, April 18, 1867. Its first captain who served was Nathaniel Batchelder, Jr.; its last, Hiram Batchelder, chosen in 1853.

Engine "Washington No. 3," was purchased of Charlestown, in

1836. The well near the common, so long used for the comfort of man and beast, was constructed by private contributions of money and labor for the purpose of obtaining a sufficient reservoir of water to supply this engine in case of fire.

In March, 1852, the shop of C. H. Goodwin on Salem Street, and in the same year, a barn belonging to Henry Kingman, were destroyed by fire. In May, 1853, Harnden's shop, where R. C. Totten's shop now is, was burnt, with lumber and other property valued at nearly $7,000. There was no fire department during these years, but the engines were worked by citizens. The frequent recurrence of fires alarmed the people, and a town-meeting was called which voted to procure another engine, a quantity of hose, and to build an engine house. On the sixth of June, a company was organized to take charge of the new engine, which was christened "Eagle No. 4." Nathaniel Vaughan, formerly member of the Boston fire department, was chosen its first foreman. The engine was built by Howard and Davis, of Boston. It was brought to Reading October 29th, and its arrival was celebrated by a large gathering of people. A large procession marched through the principal streets, a dinner was served in Harnden's shop just rebuilt, and a levee was held in the same place in the evening, in which the ladies participated. The successive commanders of this company have been Charles H. Lang, Ira W. Ruggles, N. Vaughan, Geo. A. Niles, W. L. Crowe, J. W. Coburn, James M. Day, David E. Crowell, and Wm. L. Crowe, who is now in office.

The Hancock, which formerly belonged to the city of Charlestown, and was there known as "Hancock No. 1," was purchased in 1869, for the use of the west part of the town, to take the place of Union No. 1, which was put out of commission. It had been stationed in that neighborhood since about 1865. The new house is to be completed for the occupancy of the Hancock on the first of April, 1874. It is located near the school-house on Woburn Street. This engine has a company of forty men, under command of Capt. S. T. Sweetser.

The town appropriated, in 1873, for building engine house and cisterns, $7,000; for purchase of hose for use of engine companies, $1,800.

For many years previous to 1854, the different organizations when engaged at fires were under command of fire-wards chosen by the town with other town officers; but in April of that year, a fire department was established under an act of the Legislature. Its chief engineers have been Benj. M. Boyce, from 1854 to 1861, inclusive; Nathan Carter, 1862 and '63; John Clifford, 1864; Dan'l Creesey, 1865; C. D.

Brown, 1866-67 (died in office); James McKay, 1868 to 1871; William H. Temple, 1872; Chas. H. Lang, 1873-4.

BANKING INSTITUTIONS.

An act to incorporate the Reading Agricultural and Mechanical Association was approved Feb. 10, 1831. Edmund Parker, Joshua Prescott, Warren Perkins, Abiel Holden, and Jonas Parker, with their associates, are named as corporators, with power to hold real estate not exceeding five thousand dollars in value; and the annual income of its personal estate not to exceed two thousand dollars. It had about fifty members. The shares, at first, were ten dollars each. The institution did business as a bank of discount and deposit, and its earnings for many years were applied to increase the amount of its capital. The par value of its shares was raised in 1838 to fifty, and ultimately to one hundred dollars each. In 1846, and subsequently to 1852, the dividends were five dollars per share; in 1853-7, six dollars; 1858-60, twelve dollars. Its customers were largely engaged in trade with the Southern States, which the war brought to an abrupt termination with disaster to many of their fortunes. The bank suspended operations and eventually closed up its affairs, without loss to its creditors.

The first board of officers was: Edmund Parker, president; Warren Perkins, vice-president; Jonathan Frost, secretary; Cyrus Smith, treasurer; Thomas Smith, Abiel Holden, Caleb Wakefield, and Eliab Parker, Jr., directors.

Hon. Edmund Parker was continued as president till his death in June, 1843, when Daniel Pratt, Esq., was chosen. Stephen Foster succeeded Cyrus Smith as treasurer in 1837. The present officers are Thomas Sweetser, president; S. Foster, vice-president; S. E. Parker, secretary; Jonathan Frost, treasurer.

The corporation has never forfeited its powers and privileges, and has the right to resume business whenever it sees fit.

The Reading Savings Bank was incorporated June 12, 1869, upon petition of Ephraim Hunt, William Proctor, and others.

The corporation organized July 14, 1869, by the choice of Ephraim Hunt, president; Thomas Sweetser, vice-president; N. P. Pratt, clerk and treasurer; H. G. Richardson, Stephen Foster, F. O. Dewey, Alfred Perkins, N. P. Pratt, Thomas Sweetser, William Proctor, F. H. Knight, Hiram Barrus, C. P. Judd, E. Hunt, all of Reading; Samuel P. Breed, of North Reading; and Lemuel Eames, of Wilmington, trustees; E. Hunt, N. P. Pratt, and Stephen Foster, board of investment. This list of officers remains nearly unchanged. Mr. Sweetser resigned as vice-president, and Mr. Dewey was elected his successor ; N. P. Pratt resigned his position on the board of investment, to which H. Barrus was chosen.

The annual report of the treasurer, dated Nov. 1, 1873, gives the sum of $181,224.76 as the total assets of the institution; and the amount due depositors, $179,454.63; leaving a surplus of $1,770.13. The band pays its depositors a semi-annual dividend of three per cent. It has won the reputation of being a safe institution for investments, which the financial panic of 1873 in no wise disturbed.

THE CEMETERY.

The first person buried in the cemetery was Ensign Nathaniel Parker, who died in Dec. 1737. There is a tradition that he was the donor of the land to the town, to be used for burial purposes. If the tradition is true, it is singular that nothing appears upon the records of the town or county corroborating it. The records of the town imply that it never alienated its title to the common, or to the old cemetery adjoining. Four years after the death of Ensign Parker, it conveyed five acres lying north of the old burying-ground, and bounded on it, to John Merrow. The few acres which lay between the common and the land granted to Merrow could not have belonged to the Boutwell farm on the east, or to the Bancroft farm on the west, without following most absurd boundary lines. Nor does it seem probable that Ensign Parker would have secured a title to the same, by purchase or otherwise, from the town, merely for the sake of returning it as a donation. If he did so under the promptings of a desire to leave a memorial of himself, it seems he made a mistake in not having his act perpetuated by some record, or at least a reference to it in his will.

A committee chosen by the old South Parish, in 1846, report at length upon the subject, March 16, 1848, taking the position that the town had always retained its ownership of the burial-ground till it was conveyed to the parish. The report of the committee indicates a most thorough examination of the whole matter, and their conclusions seem to be well founded.

In 1846, the parish chose Dr. Horace P. Wakefield, Sylvester Harnden, and Stephen Foster a committee to purchase land of Dana Parker, lying north of the old burying-ground, to lay out the same in lots and avenues, and make sale of lots for payment of expenses. The committee purchased thirteen acres of land, and employed Amasa Farrier, an engineer from Stoneham, to superintend the work of laying out the lots and avenues, and prepare a lithograph plan of the new cemetery. The cemetery was consecrated with appropriate services Nov. 25, 1846. Rev. Daniel Temple, the returned missionary, made the invocatory prayer. Rev. Aaron Pickett delivered the address. The consecrating prayer was by Rev. E. W. Allen. Several original hymns were sung. The pleasure of the occasion was seriously marred by the occurrence of a furious snow-storm.

In 1853, the parish relinquished its interest in the cemetery to the town, which thereupon resumed control of it.

March 7, 1870, the town chose a board of trustees, to have charge of the cemetery and of all moneys appropriated by the town, or contributed by individuals, for the improvement of the cemetery. The first board of trustees were Solon Bancroft, F. H. Knight, for three years; F. O. Dewey, Gilman C. Gleason, for two years; William Proctor and Thomas B. Pratt, for one year. The same persons have been continued by re-election to the present time. Three and a half acres of land have been purchased of Mr. Dana Parker, which extends the cemetery at the northwest corner to "Love Lane." The wall on Main Street has been nearly completed, and the trustees have brought the cemetery into a condition that is alike creditable to themselves and the town. There are few cemeteries that possess such diversity of surface in so small compass, or that are capable of being made so attractive. Mr. Gilman C. Gleason, the present efficient sexton, has had charge of the cemetery for many years.

SLAVES.

It is said that previous to the Revolutionary war nearly every large landholder here had also a slave. In 1754 there were twenty colored persons in town; in 1765, thirty-four; in 1783, twelve. It is probable that nearly all of these were, or had been, slaves. In 1744, Sandy, servant of Dea. Raham Bancroft, married Pegg, servant of Thomas Nichols. In 1771, Chester, servant of Dea. Samuel Bancroft, died. In 1723, Benjamin Pool advertises a negro man who had run away from him. In 1754, Raham Bancroft in his will orders his negroes sold. In 1774, Samuel Bancroft is charged by Joseph Bancroft for shoes for "Prince" and "Cato" and "Fillis." In 1764, Joseph Damon is charged for shoes for "Sesar." Cesar was probably a native of Africa. His face was scarred with tattoo marks. He is described as "a clever old man, and a favorite with the children," but inclined to get intoxicated. When in this condition, he said he "did n't know what the matter was, but things would go round and round just like a cart-wheel." It was said he could read his own Bible, but no other.

"Prince Merrow" was the name of another slave who seems to have gone into the army as a substitute.

"Keemer," formerly a slave in Woburn, removed to this town and married "Dinah," a slave belonging to the Pool family. He served in the army of the Revolution, and received a pension.

Sharper Freeman was formerly a slave to Mr. Breed, of Lynn. He was brought from Africa when about sixteen years old, and was believed to be the son of a king. He remembered the crying of his mother when he was brought away. He gained his freedom, as did several others in this town, by enlisting in the army, when he received the name of "Freeman." By the aid of Gov. Brooks and Dea. Wakefield, he obtained a pension. He died Jan. 4, 1833, aged about 90, and was buried in our cemetery.

Amos Potamia, son of Titus and Pegg Potamia, was born a slave in Wilmington, and baptized Nov. 24, 1765. He removed to this town and accumulated some property. He invested two thousand dollars in the Andover and Medford turnpike, which shared the fate of similar investments by his white neighbors, and was lost. He owned the house now belonging to Mr. John Bowditch. He was greatly esteemed as a man and was an active Christian. He never married.

TORNADOES.

This section of the State suffered considerable damage in the Great Gale of Sept. 23, 1815. Dea. Caleb Wakefield relates that a storm of rain with wind in the N. E. commenced on the previous evening and continued through the night. In the course of the next day the wind changed to S. E. and increased till about two o'clock, P. M. There was a case on trial before John Weston, Esq., that day, in which Dea. Wakefield was a witness. It became necessary to produce the commission he held as a captain of the military company to which he belonged. He went home for it, and the wind blew so strongly that on the way his horse was thrown down. On his arriving in the village the chimney of Mr. Silas Smith's house was blown down, giving his horse a sudden fright. On his way he noticed several sea gulls that had been driven hither by the wind, trying to make their descent into the Quannapowitt. They were repeatedly driven upward by the force of the tempest and finally disappeared. The wind did not appear to move with a power that the results proved it to possess. The trees were borne down and uprooted by it, as a sapling would be borne down by a strong man. An immense amount of timber was prostrated; and so great was the apparent destruction that Dea. Wakefield at first estimated his loss at a thousand dollars. The fallen timber on his premises produced 80,000 feet of boards, besides other lumber and wood not taken into the account. The sales turned the seeming loss into actual gain, and gave a net profit of five hundred dollars. The wood on the ministerial lands was extensively damaged, and in order to save the timber, the Old South Society was led to build their present house of worship, which was dedicated early in the year 1818. The granite for the underpinning and steps of the church came from Tyngsboro', whence it was brought over the Mitldlesex Canal to Wilmington, and delivered there, near the present railroad depot. These facts, like others connected with other subjects referred to in these historical sketches, seem too valuable to be lost, and are thrown in for safe keeping, though in a disjointed manner. The wind destroyed the sheds on the common near the old church (now Union Hall). It is asserted that the falling rain was so charged with the salt spray blown hither from the ocean, that its presence could be detected by the taste.

The tornado of 1857 occurred Thursday, August 13. It was accompanied by a thunder shower, and came about 7 or 8 o'clock in the evening. It commenced on the premises of E. Appleton, Esq., and thence took a southward course, prostrating a few apple-trees and fences on land of Thomas Sweetser. It seemed to expend its force principally in the south part of the town. The orchard of Dea. Thos. H. Sweetser was almost entirely prostrated, and the building occupied by him as a shoe factory completely wrecked. The school-house upon the hill, just above, was turned upon its foundations about six feet. The house of A. F. Converse was similarly displaced. The barn of John Parker was razed to the ground. A horse in it was carried over two walls and the street, but was found uninjured and quietly feeding. The house formerly belonging to John Weston, Esq., was partially destroyed, and Mrs. Austin who resided there was completely shut in by the ruins. D. F. Weston's buildings were considerably injured, as were others in the vicinity. The barn of Aaron Weston, at Weston's Corner, was partly unroofed. It also prostrated many trees on the Prescott farm. Considerable damage was done to the house of George C. Coney by the falling branches from the elms in front, and otherwise.

PERSONAL REMINISCENCES.

Thomas Sweetser, Esq., among the interesting reminiscences we have freely used, relates others that show some of the peculiar features of former times. His father, Thomas, Sen., at the age of forty years, married Miss Sarah Pratt, of Saugus, sister of David, the early shoe manufacturer of this town. His wedding suit, which was long preserved, consisted of the olden style coat of peach-blow color; a white vest, made of Marseilles quilt, with glass buttons; pants of nankeen color, reaching only to the knees, where they were met by white stockings, to which they were united with silver knee buckles. A beaver "cocked hat," costing sixteen dollars, and silver shoe-buckles, costing nine dollars, helped make up the outfit. The wife of Mr. Sweetser, at the age of eighteen, went out spinning for a shilling a week. She received for her first week's labor a silver piece known as the "Pine Tree Shilling," dated 1652, which she preserved during her life. It is now in possession of her son Thomas. It is somewhat worn, but could not be purchased for a week's work of the smartest woman of the present time, though wages have greatly advanced.

Mr. Sweetser, Sen., removed here in 1807, and bought the house of Ephraim Parker on Washington Street, which still remains, and is considered one of the oldest houses, if not the oldest, in town. It was kept as a tavern before and during the Revolution. It is said that several British officers boarded here while their army held Boston, and some interesting traditions are preserved relating to them. It is also said that some of the prisoners belonging to Burgoyne's army were quartered here, and it is related by others that they were accustomed to march around the pond for exercise. A brass spoon of quaint fashion was found in this house, with a minute impression of a stamp in the inside representing the British lion and other emblems. It is possible that the stamp may have been used to designate the furniture and utensils belonging to the royal troops.

After Mr. Sweetser came he removed a cedar gate-post which he was told had stood in its place forty years. It was again set in the fence fronting Mr. Sweetser's present residence, where it seems good for another century. There is a boundary post in Cedar Swamp, in this town, marked "R. B." (Raham Bancroft), that is supposed to be one hundred and forty years old.

Daniel Chute, Esq., after coming to this town, lived for about ten years in the parsonage of the Old South Society, now the residence of Mr. Grouard. Rev. Mr. Sanborn, who had been instrumental in inducing him to come here, for a time boarded with him, and subsequently married the niece of Mrs. Chute. The parsonage farm extended from the common, westward, to the Jaquith farm, the boundary line between the two passing just eastward of Mr. William Wakefield's garden. The Jaquith farm extended westerly and southerly to Washington Street, and northerly to the Bancroft farm. Mr. Chute bought the Jaquith place, and in 1802 built the house now owned and occupied by Mr. William Carter, the conductor, which was then the only house between the parsonage of Mr. Sanborn and the old Jaquith house. That part of Woburn Street which connects these houses, was laid out in 1798. In 1809, Mr. Chute erected, a little eastward of his house, a building which was for some years used for an academy. The school kept here was under the instruction of Misses Elizabeth Eaton and Susan Eaton, sisters of the editress of the "Friend of Virtue." One room in the building was used as the office of Dr. Abner Phelps, who came here about 1812. He was the father of Hon. Charles A. Phelps, formerly president of the Massachusetts Senate.

Mr. Chute prosecuted his business with an energy that for many years knew no rest, and was considered for those days quite wealthy. He was a man of strict integrity, excellent judgment, devoted piety, and universally respected. During the last thirty years of his life he was compelled, by ill health, to give up active business. He died March 21, 1843, in the eighty-third year of his age. He adopted the daughter of Rev. Mr. Sanborn, who married Samuel W. Carter, father of William Carter.

Mr. Chute was born in 1760, and married Polly Stimpson, of Reading. He was the tenth child of Daniel, born 1722; who was a son of James, who commenced a settlement in Byfield in 1681; who was son of James Chewte, register in Salem, Mass.; who was son of Lionel, who came from England to America in 1634 or '5. He was son of Lionel, son of Anthony, son of Charles, son of Robert, son of Edward, of Sussex, who sold the manor of Taunton to Lord Dunhare in 1502. Edward was son of Charles, born 1438, son of Robert, Esq., of Taunton, son of Henry, son of Edmond, son of Ambrose, son of George, son of Philip, Esq., son of Cuthbard, son of John, son of Alexander, born 1268. The Chute or *Chewte* family had a coat of arms, described as "Three swords barways *argent*, hilt and pummeled," *or*, which in plain English appears to be three swords placed horizontally across the face of a shield. Henry VIII added to this a lion of England, and a crest representing a hand, couped at the wrist, holding a broken sword. This was given to Philip Chewte, captain of Cumber Castle, and standard-bearer of the arms at the siege of "Bollonge" (Boulogne).

The genealogy from which this account is taken is written on an ancient parchment, now in possession of Rev. Ariel P. Chute, of Boston, a nephew of Daniel, Esq. It shows the coats of arms of the Chute family, and of other families with whom they intermarried. The Chute families still exist in England, some of the name retaining high official and social positions. Challoner Chute, who was a descendant of the senior branch of the family, was speaker of the House of Commons in Cromwell's Parliament. His estate was at the Vine in Hampshire, which is still in possession of his descendants.

John Damon, whose name appears upon the town records in 1652, came, it is said, with his son Samuel, from Reading, County of Northumberland, England. He may have been here some years earlier. In the list of those "who desire to be made freemen," in May, 1645, the name John *Damng* is given. The spelling of the name is unusual; but as none of that name appears afterwards, there is a fair presumption that John *Damon* is meant, especially as in the same list, Humphreys is spelled "Umphryes."

John Damon at first located near Bear Hill, where he built a house over the cellar which is still visible. The year of his death is uncertain. His son Samuel was born in 1656, which seems conclusive evidence that *he* was not born in England. On his way to or from church he was thrown from his horse and killed; and his wife, who was riding on the pillion behind him, was so injured as to be unable to walk for the remainder of her life. It is unknown when the family removed to what is since known as the John Damon farm. The present house was built in 1751 by his grandson Samuel, who used in its construction some of the material from the house preceding this. Some of these old boards used in the roof of the present house, are said to have been sawed by hand in what was called a saw-pit mill.

Samuel, Jr., born in 1756, lived with his father many years, expecting to succeed to the ownership of the farm. At length, however, he gave up his expectations to his younger brother John, and removed from town. The father soon after died, and Samuel desired a portion of the property to remunerate him for his long service to the aged parent, though he had no legal claim for it. John magnanimously paid his demand, and thus preserved the brotherly ties, where many, under similar circumstances, have sundered them. His subsequent prosperity soon replaced more than he had sacrificed for peace. His son John, born in 1795, sold the homestead a few years since, and now lives near, — his house occupying one of the lots belonging to the original farm.

In 1840, Dea. Wakefield, who administered upon the Damon estate, laid out that portion of it near the village, in streets and building lots. The streets were Union, Pleasant, Parker, and John. The last was so named out of respect to its then late owner, and may be considered as a compliment to each of those who bore the name, and owned the land, on which it was located. The ground occupied by Union Hall was donated for its use by Mr. Damon. After the laying out and sale of the lots by Dea. Wakefield, the Hon. Edmund Parker remarked to him, "Well, you have laid out your lots and sold them well, but you will never live to see half of them built upon." Whether the Squire misjudged as to the length of the good deacon's life, or as to the future prosperity and progress of Reading, need not be decided; but Dea. Wakefield, now nearly eighty-nine years of age, still in the enjoyment of life, health, and his faculties, lives to recall the prophecy, and remark that he has seen every lot built upon One of the lots which then sold for thirty-six dollars was divided, and one of the halves was recently sold for four hundred and fifty dollars.

Dea. Wakefield retains a vivid recollection of the memorial services held here after the death of Washington. The people from both the other parishes met here on that occasion. A procession was formed at the tavern of Col. Nathan Parker, under his superintendence, which marched to the church, the present Union Hall, which then stood on the south part of the common. A sermon was preached by Rev. Mr. Stone, of the North Parish. By vote of the town it was printed, and every family in town supplied with a copy. The title-page reads: "A discourse delivered at Reading, Feb. 22, 1800: the day recommended by Congress to the people of the United States, by their assembling, in such manner as might be convenient, and publicly testifying their grief for the death, and their respect for the memory of General GEORGE WASHINGTON. By Eliab Stone, A. M., minister of the second church in Reading. Boston: Manning and Loring, printers, near the Old South meeting-house."

Rev. Aaron Bancroft, D. D., born in Reading, Nov. 10, 1755, died in Worcester, Aug. 19, 1839, was said to have been one of the most accomplished scholars of the country. He was a volunteer in the battles of Lexington and Bunker Hill; was three years a missionary in Nova Scotia, graduated at Harvard, and was settled in Worcester in 1785. He published a life of Washington, and a volume of his own sermons. He was a son of Samuel, Esq., son of Capt. Samuel, son of Dea. Thomas, son of Lieut. Thomas, son of John, who died in Lynn in 1637. George Bancroft, the historian, is a son of Rev. Aaron.

James Bancroft, Esq., and captain in the army of the Revolution, was son of Dea. Raham, who was a brother of Capt. Samuel, the grandfather of Rev. Aaron. The only son of James, Esq., died unmarried. The ancestors of Lieut. Joseph Bancroft, — who was a cousin of Rev. Aaron, — for four generations, reaching back to John of Lynn, were each named Thomas. In the sixth generation, to which Lieut. Joseph belonged, there were fifty-three of the Bancroft name, but it is a singular fact that all the Bancrofts now belonging in Reading are the descendants of Lieut. Joseph, b. 1735, who m. Elizabeth Temple, and had five sons: Joseph, b. 1762, Timothy, b. 1764, Thomas, b. 1766, Nehemiah, b. 1768, and Jonathan, b. 1774. Capt. Joseph, Jr., had Joseph, father of John M., and Lewis H.; and Emery, father of Solon, Esq., Emery, and Frederic. Timothy had Timothy, father of Newton, Charles, James, Nathan, Wendell, and Moses; Capt. George, father of Thomas E., killed in the war of the Rebellion; Parker, father of Parker E. and Francis J.; Abner, father of Wm. Hazen; Bradley; John Hart. Nehemiah had James H., father of James A., the land surveyor and present town treasurer. Jonathan was father of Harrison.

Col. Nathan Parker was a leading man in this part of Reading. He kept the hotel where Mr. James Davis has resided for many years, near the head of Ash Street. It is not known when he commenced, but he is credited in 1781 with "a pale of toddy," and again with "1 quart *wetin* and 3 pints rum," which implied that he was then keeping tavern there, and it is probable that he continued to keep it until his removal to the new tavern in 1806, where the bank now stands. He was the first postmaster here, and held the office till the appointment of John Weston, Esq. The law passed by Congress imposing what was called "the direct tax," to raise money for paying the expenses of the war of 1812, was an unpopular enactment, and a meeting was called here which passed resolutions disapproving it. Col. Parker presided over the meeting, which gave offence to the President, and was the cause of his removal from the office of postmaster.

When John Weston, Esq., was appointed his successor, with due formality he waited upon the Colonel, and commenced a speech, saying, "It becomes my painful duty, sir, to inform you that the post-office is transferred " — " No pain to me, Squire," replied the Colonel, interrupting the speech, "I am glad to get rid of it."

The first wife of Col. Parker was Phebe, daughter of Ephraim Pratt. Hon. Edmund, and Rev. Dr. Nathan, afterwards of Portsmouth, N. H., were her sons. Col. Parker's second wife was widow Abigail Eaton, whose daughter m. Joshua Prescott, Esq., father of

A. A. Prescott, Esq. The children of the second wife were Thomas Parker, the storekeeper, and Susan, who m Thaddeus B. Pratt, Esq., father of N. P. Pratt, Esq. The third wife of Col. Parker was Lydia Stearns, of Bedford. Her daughter Phebe m. Thomas Pratt. Her son, Nathaniel, kept the hotel for a few years; Gould, Sarah, and Eunice m. and removed from town.

Hon. Edmund Parker, son of Col. Nathan, is remembered as a man of excellent judgment, sensible and practical, well known and popular throughout the county. He was a "Federal" and afterwards "Whig" in political sentiment, and repeatedly served as the representative of his town in the Legislature. He was councillor in 1840, and senator in 1841. He was a justice of the peace, and was often called upon to act as referee in cases decided by arbitration. Caroline, daughter of Hon. Edmund, m. James Davis, father of William Wallace.

The Parker families in this town all descend from Thomas, who embarked at London March 11, 1635, and came to Lynn. He was made freeman in 1637, m. Amy ——, d. 1683, aged 74 years; was probably a resident of Reading for upwards of twenty years. His son, Sergt. John, b. 1640, m. Hannah Kendall, 1667, had John, b. 1668, who had John, b. 1701, who had Jonas, 1728, who had Jonas, Aaron, William, and Amos. Jonas had Capt. Jonas, and Ephraim, father of Jerome and Clarkson. Aaron, b. 1756, m. Jerusha Damon, and had Aaron, b. 1788, who m. Rebekah, daughter of Capt. Joseph Bancroft, and had Dea. Stillman E., Henry F., and Rebekah, who m. John Adden, parents of John Henry. The other sons of Aaron, born 1756, were Jabez D., father of Samuel and Wyman; John; William, father of Warren, Edward, and William C.; and Rev. B. Wyman, the missionary. Polly, the daughter of Aaron, m. Silas Smith, parents of Sydney, who was asst. engineer on the "Kearsarge." William, son of Jonas, b. 1728, had Luther, father of William Strong; Sarah, who m. William Wakefield, parents of Frederick and Rev. William; Sophronia, who m. Henry Kingman, parents of William P. and Gilman D.; and Lavinia, who m. Daniel Nichols, parents of Howard P., Hartwell, and Wyman.

Amos, son of Jonas, b. 1728, m. Polly Taylor, and had Amos, who m. Nancy Batchelder, parents of Solon A.; and Dana, who m. Elizabeth Steele, parents of Milton D., who m. Melvina Bancroft, and Galen A., who m. Edna S., daughter of Hiram Barrus; Betsey, first wife of Amos Temple; Philomela, who m. Walter Damon, parents of Washington P.; and Harriet, who m., 1st, Samuel Dinsmoor; 2d, Jacob Smith.

Benjamin Parker, b. 1703, brother of John, b. 1701; had William, b. 1735, and Asa, b. 1740, and others. William had Richard, father of

William, Cephas, Theron, and Loton. Asa had Loea, b. 1782, m. Anna Bancroft ; parents of Loea, b. 1809, Asa and Harrison Loea, Jr., was father of Gilman L. and Elmore.

Thomas, the pilgrim, had Ensign Nathaniel, who was the first person buried in the Reading cemetery, b. 1651, d. 1737, who was the father of Lieut. Nathaniel, b. 1679, d. 1761, who had Capt. Nathan, b. 1719, who was father of Col. Nathan, b. 1748, d. 1815, and Dr. Nathaniel, who died in Salem at the age of 36, and Edmund, who died in the Revolutionary war. Ensign Nathaniel, who d. 1737, had Jonathan, b. about 1682, who m. Barbara Ilsley in 1706, and had Daniel, b. 1725, who m. Sarah, daughter of Benjamin Parker. Daniel, Jr., b. 1752, m. Sarah Richardson, 1780, and had Jonathan, b. 1783, who m. Susanna, daughter of Capt. Joseph Bancroft. They were the parents of Dea. Milo Parker.

Thaddeus B. Pratt, Esq., b. 1777, was father of Nathan P. Pratt, Esq., b. 1811, who m. Louisa Wakefield ; Abigail, b. 1809, m. Hon. H. P. Wakefield, M. D. ; and Louisa, b. 1814, m. Stephen Foster, Esq.

Mr. Pratt was an active business man, and a prominent citizen of the town ; had excellent judgment, was thoroughly honest, fearless in the expression of his opinions, and interested and active in everything that promoted the well-being of the town, and was often called to serve his fellow-citizens in official positions. He was son of Isaac, b. 1740, son of Timothy, b. 1702, son of John, who came to Reading about 1692, and who was the ancestor of most of the families of that name now in Reading. He was son of John, of Medfield, who died in 1707. His will is recorded in the Suffolk Probate Office, vol. 16, page 328. He was son of John, of Dorchester, who came from England, and was made freeman in 1634.

George Minot, lawyer, born in Haverhill, Jan. 5, 1817, graduated at Harvard, studied law with Rufus Choate, was admitted to the bar 1839, was for ten years editor of the U. S. Statutes at Large, published an edition of nine volumes of English Admiralty Reports, and was the editor of the well-known " Minot's Digest," of the Decisions of the Supreme Court of Massachusetts. He removed to Reading about 1847, and was the attorney of the Boston and Maine Railroad corporation, up to the time of his decease, April 16, 1858.

William F. Harnden, son of Amariah and Sally Harnden, a cousin of the late Sylvester Harnden ; was born in Reading, Aug. 23, 1812, and lived here till about fourteen years of age. He originated the express business, March 4, 1839, when, agreeably to previous announcement through the newspapers, he made a trip as a public messenger, from Boston to New York, *via* Boston and Providence Railroad, and a Long Island Sound steamboat. He had in charge a few booksellers' bundles and orders, and some brokers' parcels of bank-notes to deliver or exchange, for which he charged an adequate compensation. He also made arrangements for the rapid transit of freight, and the delivery of the latest intelligence to the press in advance of the mails. The business was rapidly extended, not only in this country, but to foreign countries. Mr. Harnden employed his brother, Adolphus H., as his agent over the route to New York. The latter lost his life, with young Weston of this town, in the ill-fated steamer "Lexington," which was burnt on Long Island Sound, Jan. 13, 1840. Mr. Harnden himself died in 1848. The business had increased to such an extent that ten years ago it was estimated that the aggregate capital employed in carrying it on was from ten to fifteen millions of dollars, yielding a return to the stockholders of nearly fifteen per cent.

Mr. Alfred Perkins, born in Dunbarton, N. H., Nov. 26, 1808, came to Boston about 1826 or '27, and engaged in the wood and coal business. He furnished fuel to the Boston and Maine Railroad corporation from the commencement of its business till he was appointed fuel agent by them, which position he held for seventeen years. He first came to Reading in 1844, but soon returned to the city. He repurchased in 1861 the residence here which, during the summer season, he continued to occupy till his decease, which occurred in Boston, Feb. 8, 1874. He was a genial man, extensively known, and greatly esteemed for his many virtues. The officers of the Savings Bank in Reading, of which he was a trustee, passed a vote of respect to his memory.

PERSONS RESIDING IN READING DOING BUSINESS PRINCIPALLY IN BOSTON.

Edward Appleton, Esq., was born in Boston. He received the Franklin medal in the Latin School in 1830, graduated at Harvard College 1835, and taught in the Latin School one year, and in Beverly Academy in 1842–3. He commenced studying civil engineering with James Hayward in 1838, and assisted him in the construction of the Boston and Maine Railroad. In 1842, he married Miss Frances Anne Atkinson, a relative of Theodore Atkinson, who died in 1769, the first husband of Lady Frances Deering Wentworth, one of the maids of honor to the Queen. The portrait of Lady Wentworth, who was a woman of great beauty, was painted by Copley the artist, and was recently sold in New York for two thousand dollars. The towns of Atkinson and Wentworth, N. H., received their names from her families. Mr. Appleton came to Reading in 1844, and continued his work upon the extension of the railroad through this town to Boston. He was subsequently employed upon the Ogdensburg Railroad, N. Y. State; and for several years upon railroads in Maine; then upon the South Reading Branch, and also in building the Saugus Branch railroads. In 1855 he spent nearly a year in the oil regions of Pennsylvania in railroad business, where he frequently saw the oil flowing off on the surface of the water in the creeks, but the discovery of the marvellous supply contained in the earth had not then been made. He was employed in engineering upon the Cambridge Horse Railroad — the first of the kind in this vicinity; then for six years in making surveys and constructing railroads in the State of Wisconsin. From 1862 to 1867, he was in the employ of the Boston, Hartford and Erie Railroad corporation. He served as one of the first Board of Railroad Commissioners in this State from 1868 to 1870. His son Thomas, civil engineer, is actively employed in the same profession.

Charles W. Abbott, born in Lowell, was for fourteen years in the employ of the Salmon Falls Manufacturing Co. as clerk and pay-master; came to Reading in 1869; is engaged in the wool commission business. "Has no political aspirations."

Milo L. Allen, born in Manchester, Massachusetts, 1838, removed to Lawrence, 1848, thence to Reading in 1873. Is clerk in the U. S. Treasury in Boston, having been appointed in 1870.

The Rev. Dr. Barrows, now about nineteen years a resident in Reading, marks a type of family slowly disappearing from New England. His early home was a family of twelve, Yankee on both sides of the house from Pilgrim days; a farm of sixty acres, and obstinate for boys' culture; parental common-sense; a spindle; a loom; annual barrels of home beef and pork; indefinite bushels of grain and vegetables; a few books well chosen and thumbed; a district school, well attended without regard to weather; and the Sabbath uniformly divided between home and the Lord's house, three miles away. The old-fashioned virtues, ideas, and knowledge ruled the home, more than a dinner, new jacket, or two-story house. The Bible and Catechism and New England Primer furnished moral lessons; Proverbs and Franklin's Aphorisms, the industrial and economical teachings. The Old Testament stories were never threadbare. Elijah's ravens, Elisha's bears, Daniel's lions, and Noah's menagerie always came out with a new feather, claw, or antic. Books were in the highest honor, and all printed matter was sacred. No winter snows were too lively or deep for the ox-sled and a load of neighborhood children on the way to school, where the firewood was four feet long, and many of the boys six. Naturally from such a home three of the sons entered college, yet with great pecuniary struggle. There were dark valleys and rough cliffs and miserable sloughs all the way. It was sawing and hoeing and mowing to pay bills in classics and mathematics, science and literature. Garden roots were cultivated by day and Greek ones by night, by the subject of this sketch, while in Andover; and in New York, Hebrew and private teaching by the hour, theological polemics in the Seminary, classes in Brooklyn and five-minute lunches on Fulton ferry, were all sandwiched together. So every bill was paid to its full face, and every borrowed dollar returned. This is wellnigh one of the lost arts in getting a liberal education, and therefore mentioned here. This struggle made labor a habit and fair success a rule with Dr. Barrows. Rare good health has allowed unbroken toil, — in a ministry of twenty-five years only two Sabbaths having been lost from the pulpit by sickness. Perhaps his habits of recreation should be named in this connection. His resting hours have been taken in kindling camp-fires all the way from New Brunswick to Colorado, as his Twelve Nights in the Hunter's Camp has sketched. If he has a weakness it is for a good fish-hook and fowling-piece away from home, and a spade at home in leisure hours.

In the spring of 1873 Dr. Barrows was appointed, by a unanimous and to himself totally unexpected vote, to the secretaryship of the Massachusetts Home Missionary Society, which office he now holds.

Mrs. Elizabeth Adams (Cate) Barrows, wife of the Rev. W. Barrows, D. D., was born in Pembroke, N. H. Her parents were Meshach Cate and Lucy (Adams) Cate. She was the second daughter, and the youngest of three children. Her early school days were spent in Boston. She afterwards took the full course at Bradford Academy, where she was graduated in 1842. Leaving as a graduate, she soon returned as a teacher, and so remained for about four years. Thence she went as an instructor to the Beacon Hill Seminary, Boston, an institution belonging to the Rev. Hubbard Winslow, D. D. From this school of young ladies Mrs. Barrows was called to be the principal of Wheaton Female Seminary, where she had the charge for about three years immediately prior to her marriage, which took place in 1849.

In addition to the instruction of many private pupils resident in the family, Mrs. Barrows has used her pen more or less for the public in Christian and literary periodicals, and in the production of several

Sabbath-school books. At the request of the Trustees of her alma mater, she prepared the Memorial of Bradford Academy, an octavo and illustrated volume, a well-merited tribute to that superior school, and an interesting contribution to the history of the Christian education of woman. The work gives large space to an outline memoir of that noble woman and pioneer in female education, Abigail Carleton Hasseltine.

Hiram Barrus, born in Goshen, Mass., July 5, 1822; brought up on a farm; fitted for college, but changing his plans, pursued his studies as opportunities presented.

He was employed in teaching portions of nearly every year from 1840 to 1852, and for a few terms subsequently. Was engaged from 1853 for several years in closing up the affairs of a manufacturing corporation, and managing suits at law connected with its affairs. Several questions growing out of these suits were carried to the Supreme Court, in which new and important principles were for the first time established. He was frequently engaged in his own and adjoining towns in settlement of estates in Probate Court, making out legal papers, and doing the usual routine business pertaining to the office of justice of the peace, to which he was appointed nearly twenty years since. In 1861, he received from his personal friend, Collector Goodrich, an appointment in the Boston Custom House, serving in several positions to which he had been promoted, without request on his part; he was appointed in 1864 to his present position, Assistant Cashier. In the spring of 1869, by order of the Treasury Department, he was detailed with Deputy Collector J. M. Fiske, to assist, in Washington, in revising and making uniform the system of blank forms used in keeping the customs accounts in the various ports through the country. He was subsequently recalled by the department to supervise the proofs of the revised system, as they passed through the governmental printing office. He came to Reading, May 19, 1863. He has occasionally contributed to the newspapers, and in 1865, published a serial history of his native town. Though not claiming to be an author, some of his writings have found their way into books published by others.

T. T. Briggs was born in Turner, Me., June 15, 1832; came to Reading Sept. 1867. He was engaged in the grocery trade from 1855 to 1862. Since March, 1870, he has been connected with Gilman L. Parker in the coffee and spice business, under the name of Briggs & Parker.

Mr. William Butler was a native of Oxford, Mass.; came to Boston in 1825, and removed to Reading in 1849 or '50. He was long engaged in the hardware business near Dock Square in Boston. In 1832 he also engaged in the manufacture of combs, which for many years he made an article of export. For several years he owned a number of vessels, and was engaged in commercial pursuits. The depression produced in that department of business, by the war of the rebellion, led him to go to England and France, where he disposed of his vessels, and then relinquished the business. His son, William, Jr., is in the employ of the Saxonville Manufacturing Corporation, of which his uncle, J. W. Blake, is treasurer.

Joshua Clark, born in Dennis, Mass., 1829, received his education at the academies of Dennis, Brewster, and Andover; came to Boston in 1848, and entered as clerk in the Shoe and Leather Dealers Bank. He has served in his present position as paying teller sixteen years. He removed to Reading in 1866, having previously resided in Medford six years, and in East Boston eleven.

Maj. A. M. Cook, born in New Durham, N. H., 1823, came to Boston, 1845; engaged in trucking and express business from 1854 to 1870.

He was commander of Cook's Battery in Boston, and was ordered to parade on the common, April 19, 1861, when Gov. Andrew informed them they might be ordered into service at any moment. A telegram was received that night of the assault upon our soldiers in Baltimore, and a request from Gen. Butler that more troops be forwarded immediately. Saturday, the 20th, was spent in hurried preparations, and at nine o'clock in the evening, the batteries, with horses and ammunition, were upon the cars, ready to move. They were delayed till sunrise in waiting for the Fifth Regiment, but then started and reached New York in the evening. There they embarked on the steamer "De Soto" for Annapolis. They were in Baltimore, with their field-pieces stationed in Monument Square, and at the Custom House and Post-office, when the Rebel Legislature was arrested. They returned home at the end of their three months' service. In 1862, Major Cook recruited the Eighth Massachusetts Battery, which enlisted for six months, and was in the battles of the second Bull Run, Chantilly, South Mountain, and Antietam. Major Cook was appointed superintendent of warehouses in the Boston Custom House, in Aug. 1861, which position he still holds. During his absence in the army the place was supplied by another. He came to Reading, July, 1871, and built his present residence in the following year.

Charles R. Corkins, born and lived at Whitingham, Vt., till the age of fourteen years. Removed to Charlestown in 1861, and to Reading in 1870. Has been for seven years engaged in the insurance business.

Francis O. Dewey, born in Berlin, near Montpelier, Vt., June 20, 1823; came to South Reading, now Wakefield, 1841, remaining five years in the employ of Mr. Burrage Yale; then commenced his present business in Boston, removing his residence to Brighton. He came to Reading, May 12, 1863, and still resides on the place formerly occupied by Frank Palmer, superintendent of the Merchants Exchange, in Boston.

Mr. Dewey is one of the largest dealers in New England in his branch of the glassware trade. His business extends throughout New England, Canada, and the British Provinces. His sons Edgar and Frank H. are engaged with him.

W. F. Durgin, a native of Peabody, lived in Bradford till he attained his majority; was educated at Atkinson and Middleboro' academies; taught school and lived several years at Martha's Vineyard, where he was employed as agent of a manufacturing company. In 1865, came to Boston and was engaged, first, in the office of the "Watchman and Reflector," and subsequently, in his present position, as the commercial editor of the "Advertiser." "Never held a political office." Removed to Reading in 1867, and to his present residence in 1873, which was built by him.

Wm. W. Elliott; foundry business; native of Mason, N. H.; came to Boston, and opened business in 1854; came to Reading, May, 1873.

Oscar Foote, born in Fairfield, Vt., May 5, 1826; came to Boston in 1850, and has since been principally employed in business connected with the market, and has done a large business in the Western pork trade.

He lived in Charlestown eight years, and came to Reading in September, 1864. Since living here he has built several valuable houses upon his homestead, which formerly belonged to the Temple family, and which continued in their name for a hundred and thirty-four years. Mr. Foote has laid much of it out in building lots, with suitable streets.

Jacob Graves, born in Vienna, Me., Dec. 5, 1829; entered on business in Faneuil Hall Market, 1847; came to Reading 1852, bought here 1864; does an extensive business in fancy fowls, and is the patentee of "Graves' Incubator and Artificial Mother," which entirely dispenses with the services of the hen (after the egg is laid) in hatching and raising chickens.

S. E. Gould, bridge contractor and builder, born in Warwick, Mass., 1810; soon removed to Newfane, Vt.; came to Boston, 1836, removed to

Reading, 1872. In 1856 was an alderman in Boston, and also served three years as assessor. He is proprietor of the store near his residence on Woburn Street.

Ira C. Gray, a native of Mendon, Mass., came to Reading in 1871. He has been in business in Boston, as dealer in gentlemen's furnishing goods, about twenty-five years.

Luther Hutchins came to Reading from Boston, 1862, where he had been employed for many years as constable in the criminal courts. He still holds a position connected with the Boston courts. He was a native of Kennebunkport, Me.

A. F. Hollis, of the firm of Hollis and Gunn, job printers, Boston, came from Berkshire County in 1840 or 1841, and to Reading in 1868. Previously resided at Jamaica Plain thirteen years.

William Hawes and Sons, Newell B., Jabez S., and William G., came from Holliston in 1868, and purchased the residence of "Father Kemp." The "St. Joachim" store, of which the brothers are the proprietors, was started by them, and was the first "dollar store" in Boston, and second in the country.

E. B. Harrrington, b. in Roxbury, was seven years in California, and has been in the leather trade in Boston twelve years. Removed to Reading in 1869.

A. G. R. Hale, Esq., born in Stowe, Mass., 1834, came to Reading from Cambridge in 1873, and resides on West Street. He was a graduate of Bridgewater State Normal School, spent several years teaching in Delaware, being called there by Gov. Cannon as tutor, served nine months in the Union army in the war of the rebellion, was subsequently admitted as a member of the Suffolk Bar by the Supreme Court. The degree of LL.B. was conferred upon him by Harvard University. Law office in Boston.

Andrew Howes, born in Chatham Aug. 26, 1826, went by sailing vessel to London in 1843, resided ten years in Essex in business as ship-joiner, came to Reading 1857, was with E H. Ryder & Co., ship-chandlers, for ten years, and has since been in the employ of H. & G. W. Lord, net and twine manufacturers. Mr. Howes represents the Middlesex District, No. 6, in the Legislature for the current year, 1874.

Ephraim Hunt, LL. D., b. Readfield, Me., Oct. 20, 1829; graduate of Waterville College; received his first honorary degree before attaining the age of twenty-one years; taught in the South 1853-4; became principal of the Boston English High School, 1854, and held the position fourteen years. He was then appointed principal of the Girls' High and Normal Schools, where he remained until the schools were divided in 1872. Dr. Hunt is the author of an "English Literature," a work of decided merit, published in Boston in 1871. He was one of the originators of the Reading Savings Bank, suggested by him, of which he is president.

C. P. Judd, Esq., born in Westhampton, Mass., Jan. 25, 1815, graduated at Yale College, 1840, read law with Judge Huntington; was a teacher in South Carolina two years and a half, admitted to the bar in Northampton, 1844, came to Reading, 1846, and kept an office here, over Mr. Reed's store, till 1860. He succeeded Geo. Minot, and still acts as attorney of the Boston & Maine Railroad. Mr. Minot and Mr. Judd married sisters, Misses Elizabeth and Sarah A. Dawes, of Cambridge. They were daughters of William Dawes, merchant, of Boston, son of Judge Thomas Dawes, son of Major Thomas Dawes, who drew the plan for Brattle Street Church in Boston, which was accepted, instead of one drawn by J. S. Copley, the artist. Major Dawes was one of the leading patriots of the Revolution. His house was occupied by the British when they were in possession of Boston. When they evacuated the city, they left an army blanket in the house, marked "G. R.," which is now in possession of Mrs. Minot, who, among other interesting relics, has a locket containing a braid of Gen. Washington's and John Adams's hair.

Robert Kemp, better known as "Father Kemp," was born in Wellfleet, Mass., June 6, 1821.

He came to Reading in 1853, and bought a farm, tried "fancy farming," and in one year sold two hundred and twenty five barrels of apples, at a profit of exactly eight cents a barrel; then took the "hen fever," which culminated one fine morning when he counted up his hundred chickens, and "turned" as suddenly, when, after the storm of the following night, he found his hundred chicks reduced to five.

The inspiration received from the songs of a few neighbors at his home one winter evening, suggested an "Old Folks' Concert." "Dress rehearsals" followed, and the evening of Dec. 6, 1856, saw the first performance of the kind. It was given in Lyceum Hall, Reading, which was packed with hearers. Other concerts followed, till it was decided to try *one* in Boston. It took. Tremont Temple was crowded, and ten concerts more were given there without any apparent diminution of the public enthusiasm. A singing tour to New York and Washington was planned, and the troupe was made up of forty-seven singers.

All the prominent places on the route gave them a cordial welcome and crowded houses. In the New York Academy of Music six thousand people listened to their singing. The largest hall in Philadelphia was crowded to hear them. In Washington they sung patriotic airs to President Buchanan, and appropriate music to his cabinet and the Congressmen.

They visited Mount Vernon and sang, "Why do we mourn," around the tomb of Washington. On their return homeward they continued their concerts in the principal cities with unvarying success. An Albany paper, among other things in their favor, said, "Seldom have our people had an opportunity of hearing church music rendered with such an inspiring effect and elevating influence."

The next year, 1858, a seven months' tour was made in the West, with similar results; and subsequently they continued their work in other States. While in Connecticut they met Abraham Lincoln on a political lecturing tour, who playfully suggested that he would like to swap audiences with them. After the rebel war-cloud began to darken the Southern horizon, they sang the "Star Spangled Banner" in Baltimore to a crowd of unionists and incipient rebels mid applauses and hisses.

In 1861 they visited England, and had rousing concerts in Liverpool, where they remained eight days, and cleared about five hundred dollars. One of the papers, in reference to their singing, said, "The vocalization was magnificent. Never have we heard voices more beautifully or equally blended. The effect produced was truly charming." In London and other places they secured good audiences, but their receipts were only about enough to pay expenses, which hastened their return home the same year.

Some of the original members of the company were Mrs. Sarah (Mark M.) Temple, R. N. Temple, Mr. and Mrs. Stillman M. Pratt, Mr. and Mrs. David Brown, Mr. and Mrs. E. P. Bancroft, Mr. and Mrs. F. J. Bancroft, Messrs. Brown and Needham Nichols, Henry Brown, Train Sweetser, Henry Temple, Daniel Foss (the "Grandfather with the big fiddle"), Edward Safford, doorkeeper; Mr. and Mrs. Rufus Pierce, of Stoneham; John Wiley, of Wakefield; Miss Abby Owen, of Lowell. Mrs. Emma J. Nichols, the popular solo singer, was long connected with the company. Mr. R. N. Temple played the flute in the orchestra till their return from Europe. He afterwards acted as agent for the troupe in their subsequent tours in this country. Father Kemp occasionally gives an Old Folks' Concert at the present time, and Music Hall is not capacious enough to receive all who rush to hear him and his antique choir.

F. H. Knight, a native of Lexington, was educated at Hancock Academy, N. H.; was five years with Jewett & Prescott, Boston; has been in his present business since 1851, first with Bates & Goldthwait, and since 1861, one of the firm of Goldthwait, Snow & Knight, carpet dealers. He came to Reading in 1862.

Henry Manley, born in Bridgewater, Aug. 31, 1841, graduated at the Normal School in that town, July, 1860. Taught in South Scituate and Easton. Was corporal in Co. K, 3d Mass. Vols., at Newbern, N. C., and vicinity, nine months in 1862-3. In 1864 he went, *via* Rio Janeiro, to the Cape of Good Hope, where he carried on the business of photography for nearly two years. Since February, 1869, he has been employed as assistant engineer of the city of Boston, and now has charge of the construction and repairs of the bridges within the city limits.

Wm. H. Nash, born in Wakefield, Dec. 17, 1827, soon removed to Salem, and received his education in the city schools. Came to Reading, 1843. Has done business in Boston several years.

Jas. D. Norris was in the gents' furnishing trade here from 1870 to 1873, first on Main, and then on Haven Street, Simes's Block. He sold his business here to Francis Bartley in 1873, and is now engaged with Lucius Turner and Milton D. Kingman, in Boston, as jobbers and manufacturers in the same business.

S. D. Niles, born in Orford, N. H., Oct. 22, 1829, was employed in Atlanta, Ga., seven years in teaching, and subsequently several years in the wholesale produce business. On the breaking out of the rebellion, misjudging as to the extent to which the rebels would carry their extreme measures, he was shut in, like many others of Northern sentiment and sympathies, to take his chances under rebel rule. In order to escape service in their army, he purchased a mill and became a miller to take advantage of the exemption that that afforded from military service. When that, by change of law, would no longer protect him, he purchased a newspaper office, and became an editor, which for a time secured him from being drafted. When Gen. Sherman took Atlanta, he established his head-quarters upon Mr. Niles's premises. Mr. Niles had changed his property as far as he was able into gold, which was secretly buried in his garden. It so happened that the tent of Gen. Sherman was erected directly over it. During the continuance of the firing Mrs. Niles sometimes abandoned their house and sought protection from the flying balls among the large trees near by. Mr. Niles became well acquainted with Gen. Sherman and his staff, among whom was Gen. O. O. Howard. The firing of cannon was heard one night in the far distance, and about two o'clock in the morning Gen. Sherman sent a messenger requesting the attendance of

Mr. Niles   He referred to the firing, and inquired of Mr. Niles his opinion as to where it was. The answer was satisfactory, and the General replied that it relieved him of a burden of anxiety.

Before Gen. Sherman left Atlanta on his march to the sea, he gave Mr. Niles and family a pass that enabled them to escape from their captivity; and after passing through many perils, they reached their friends in this vicinity. Mr. Niles purchased his present residence in March, 1865, and has since been variously employed in Boston.

Charles H. Nowell, pay-master of the Boston and Maine Railroad corporation, removed to Reading, March, 1872. He was born in Lowell, October, 1843, and graduated at the high school in that city.

S. G. B. Pearson, native of Wilmington, was a dealer in produce and provisions in Lawrence for eight years. Has been in Boston since 1866, dealing in hides. Came to Reading in 1869.

William S. Pease, born in Shrewsbury, Mass., 1830; graduate of Leicester Academy, 1845; has been variously employed as agent in New York and Boston. Removed to Reading, 1866.

William Proctor, born Oct. 5, 1826, in Deptford, Kent County, England, — the place where Peter the Great learned ship-building. Mr. Proctor served his apprenticeship in London at boot and shoe making, was in Nova Scotia three years, came to Boston, 1845, to Reading, 1851. Before coming to this country he served as non-commissioned officer in the rifle brigade, belonging to a regiment which went through the Crimean war, and had just returned to England from the Ashantee was. He was naturalized in 1849, and during our war of the rebellion was on every town committee here having in charge the supplying of men for service. He was representative from this district in the Legislature of 1866. He has been prominently engaged in promoting public improvements and the building of dwelling-houses in this town. He was one of the originators of the Reading Savings Bank, of which he has always been a trustee; and also of the public library, of which he is likewise a trustee.

Dr. A. C. Smith, a native of Unity, N. H., graduate of Baltimore Med. College, attended medical lectures at Dartmouth, 1838-9, and was in practice in Haverhill four years. Losing faith in drugs, he gave up his profession and became a teacher in Salem. Receiving an invitation from Rev. Dr. Stearns and others in 1845, he accepted the appointment of master of the Webster School in Cambridge, which he retained nearly thirty years. He had under his superintendence from six hundred to seven hundred pupils, and twelve assistant teachers. He removed to Reading in 1873, having formerly resided here a few years. He is still employed as teacher of penmanship in the Cambridge schools.

Charles D. Thomas, born in Williamstown, Mass., Nov. 16, 1831; received education at Mills' High School, and at Williston Seminary, Easthampton, Mass.; was engaged in 1857 in making a preliminary survey of Pacific Railroad, and in 1858, with Mr. Haupt, on the Troy and Boston Railroad; was assistant storekeeper in the Boston Custom House from 1861 to 1870, when, upon the decease of E. M. Brown, storekeeper, he was promoted to the vacancy, which position he still holds. He came to Reading in 1861 with Mr. Brown, who was a resident here for nearly ten years. Mr. Brown was a graduate of Williams College in 1843, and among other important positions held by him, was assistant sergeant-at-arms in the State House in 1859-60-61, and was clerk of the State Valuation during a portion of the time. He was for several years a member of the Republican State Committee. He was appointed storekeeper in the Custom House 1861. He was a man widely known and much respected.

G. M. Wethern, dealer in millinery goods, has a store in Boston; came to Reading 1872, and now occupies the house built by himself on Prospect Street.

Col. Carroll D. Wright, born in Dunbarton, N. H., July 25, 1840; removed to Reading in 1856; received his education in Reading High School and in academies at Washington, and Alstead, N. H., and Chester, Vt., and engaged in teaching; read law with Hon. W. P. Wheeler, of Keene, and afterwards in Boston with T. Willey, Esq. In August, 1861, he enlisted in 14th Regiment N. H. Volunteers, and was commissioned lieutenant by Gov. Berry; was commissary of brigade at Poolesville, Md.; officer in charge of central prison, and adjutant to provost-marshal, Washington, D. C.; aid-de-camp to Gen. Martindale, military governor of department of Washington, and there had charge of all guards at bridges, ferries, etc., in and around Washington. In October, 1863, was appointed adjutant of his regiment, and was employed as assistant adjutant general in district of Carrollton, La., and of the 1st brigade, 2d division of the 19th corps, in Louisiana, and during Sherman's campaign in the Shenandoah in the autumn of 1864, when he was commissioned colonel. He was admitted to the bar in Keene, N. H., October, 1865; and in August, 1867, to practise in the courts of Massachusetts, and of the United States. He was elected to the State Senate from the Middlesex Sixth District in 1871, and again in 1872. As chairman of the Senate Committee on Military Affairs, he remodelled the militia system of the State, which was adopted by the Legislature.

In 1873, Col. Wright was appointed by Gov. Washburn chief of the Bureau of Statistics of Labor. His first official report to the Legislature of 1874 is a work that gives evidence of extensive research, and a full comprehension of the duties involved in the position he holds.

Col. Wright has attained a deserved reputation as a lecturer. He has thoughts, and has the happy faculty of presenting them in an attractive manner.

George E. Abbott, architect, has an office in Pemberton Square.

E. S. Batchelder, salesman, with Rogers & Co., came from Exeter, N. H.; has resided in Reading several years.

Osgood Eaton, tuner, has been for several years with Mason & Hamlin, organ manufacturers.

Luther Elliott, broker, has resided here several years.

John C. Gleason, bookkeeper with F. Harnden.

Dudley F. Hunt, of the firm of F. W. Hunt & Co., came to Reading in 1873.

Edmund A. Hyde, firm of Cutter, Hyde & Co., fancy goods and toys, was a native of Bangor, Me.; has been in Boston about eighteen years; came to Reading 1870.

Wm. M. Horne, iron dealer, came to Reading in 1873.

Charles H. Lang, Jr., clerk, with the Wakefield Rattan Co.

J. Mitchell, Jr., bookkeeper, with Rogers & Co., born in Wellfleet; came to Boston about fifteen years since, and to Reading in 1871.

Walter H. Perkins, clerk, with H. C. Thacher & Co.

Harley Prentiss is employed as chief clerk in the freight department of the Fitchburg Railroad Co.

Geo. A. Parker is bookkeeper, Clark & Co., on India Street.

Galen A. Parker, bookkeeper with Kelham, Fitz & Co,

O. A. Ruggles, salesman, with Calder & Otis.

Henry Robinson, firm of E. Thompson & Co.

Wm. S. Richardson, clerk, with Geo. P. Banchor.

Frank M. Smith, clerk, with Frye, Phipps & Co., born in Lowell; has been eight years in Boston; came to Reading in 1869.

Daniel Stockwell, general insurance business, came to Reading in 1870.

Wm. M. Weston, broker, dealer in watches, jewelry, etc., has long resided in Reading.

PHYSICIANS.

Dr. F. F. Brown was born in Sudbury in 1834; graduate of Amherst College, 1855; teacher three years; studied medicine at Harvard and at Berkshire Medical Institution; was assistant surgeon in the 48th Massachusetts Regiment in 1862-3; came to Reading in April, 1864.

Dr. E. G. Barton, surgeon dentist, a native of Moriah Centre, N. Y., graduate of the Boston College of Dental Surgery; came to Reading in 1870.

Dr. Sarah A. Colby, born in Sanbornton, N. H.; graduate of Philadelphia Medical College, 1861; was for several years in general practice in Manchester, N. H.; removed to Reading Sept. 30, 1869; and opened an office in Boston, to which her present practice is confined.

Dr. J. H. Hanaford was born in New Hampton, N. H., in 1819. He pursued his preparatory studies at the institute in that town, and in Pembroke, N. H.; graduated in New York city; practised medicine at Nantucket six years; at Beverly, seven; at Reading, ten. He has been employed as editor and correspondent of several newspapers and literary publications; and is the author of "Ocean Melodies," and "Lights and Shadows of Sailor Life," published in Boston. Has taught in schools of all classes. His wife, Rev. Phebe A. Hanaford, a relative of Dr. Franklin, was born at Nantucket in 1829, and was married at the age of 17. She has been editress of " Ladies Repository," and " Myrtle," published in Boston; and employed also as teacher. She is more extensively known as a preacher. She was settled first, at Hingham; then at Waltham; afterwards at New Haven; now at Jersey City. Her published works are, "The Captive Boy," "The Young Captain," "Our Martyred President," "Life of Abraham Lincoln," "Frank Nelson," " Field, Gunboat, Hospital, and Prison," "The Soldier's Daughter," "The Life of George Peabody," "From Shore to Shore," "The Life and Writings of Charles Dickens."

Howard A. Hanaford, son of Dr. J. H. and Rev. P. A., graduate of Tufts College, preaches at Wellfleet, Mass.

Dr. Samuel H. Elliott, surgeon dentist, born in Haverhill, Mass.; resided in Lowell fifteen years; followed his profession in Lawrence eleven years; in Haverhill, twelve; removed to Reading in November, 1869. Retired from practice.

Dr. F. B. Kimball, born in Bridgeton, Me., March 27, 1829; graduated at Harvard Medical College 1858; practised in Kennebunk three years; was three years with 3d N. H. Reg. Vols., and as surgeon had charge of hospital six months at Beaufort, S. C., and subsequently of Marine Hospital at Wilmington, N. C. He was at the taking of Morris Island; at the bombarding of Fort Sumter, and the attacks on Battery Wagner, and at the taking of Fort Fisher, where the carnage compelled twenty-four hours unremitting labor at the operating table. After the war he practised in Manchester, N. H.

In September, 1869, he came to Reading, where he still resides; and, in addition to the usual duties of his profession, occupies the chair of Instructor of Histology in the Medical Department of Boston University.

Young America in Business.

Barrows & Foote (Morton, son of Rev. Dr. Barrows, and Perley, son of O. Foote, Esq., minors) have a printing-press in Reading, and furnish bill-heads, business cards, etc., doing their work in a very neat manner.

[The Barrows and Barrus families in this country are nearly all descended from John Barrow, of Plymouth, in 1665–92. He had Robert, who remained in Plymouth, and Benajah, Joshua, and Ebenezer, who went to Attleboro'; and Deborah, who m. 1687, Archippus Fuller, of Plympton, and Mary, who m. 1698, John Wormall, of Duxbury.

Robert had John, a portion of whose descendants lived in Rochester; Capt. George, b. 1670, ancestor of the Plympton families; Dea. Samuel, of the Middleboro' branch; Elisha, of Rochester; Robert and Thomas, of the Mansfield, Conn., line.

Capt. George had Samuel, b. 1700, who had Noah, b. 1727, and Samuel, b. 1733.

Noah had William, father of Rev. Dr. Barrows, of Reading; Samuel had Lazarus, who had Levi, father of Hiram Barrus, of Reading.]

CHAPTER XIII.

BURIAL-GROUNDS.

For many years after the first settlement of the town, the "Common," so called, in the First Parish, extended northerly from its present limits to the "Great Pond," and included all that territory that lies west of Main Street, and between what is now Church Street and said pond, as far west as the homestead of the late Col. James Hartshorn. That portion of this territory which was recently occupied by the town house and engine house, and including the town-house lot, and perhaps a part of the adjoining blacksmith's shop lot, was the earliest burying-place of old Reading. Here, for about fifty years, was the only place of interment for the fathers and mothers of the first generation of settlers, with the children who early died.

Many of these first graves, it is presumed, were without monuments, and as the ground was for a long time unfenced, many of the gravestones, earliest erected, were broken down and destroyed. The land around the graves was subsequently sold, the purchaser being bounded by the graves. In process of time, therefore, the portion of land allowed as grave-yard was reduced to very contracted dimensions, and much of the land occupied by the dust of our ancestors was disturbed by the plough of the agriculturist, and yielded a crop that made literal the figurative language of Scripture, that "all flesh is grass."

Upon the erection of the town-house, in 1834, the town of South Reading purchased what was the town-house lot, or so much thereof as had not been sold, took up the old gravestones, many of which were broken and defaced, and placed them in a continuous row on the easterly side of the lot; and, if the particular *dust* which they memorialized did not *lye beneath* them, it is certainly true that the *stones* did *lie above* them.

The following are some of the more noticeable inscriptions upon these old gravestones: —

"Memento te esse mortalem."
"Fugit Hora. Vive memor læthi. Fugit hora.
"C. ye 2d.

"Here lyes the body of Capt. Jonathan Poole, who deceased in the 44th year of his age, 1678.

> "Friends sure would prove too far unkind,
> If, out of sight, they leave him out of mind;
> And now he lyes, transform'd to native dust,
> In earth's cold womb, as other mortals must.
> It's strange his matchless worth intomb'd should lye,
> Or that his fame should in oblivion dye."

NOTE. — This stone contains the oldest date and the most artistic and elaborate work of any of the old monuments in this yard, representing, in relief, swords, hour-glass, coffin, spade, pickaxe, cross-bones, etc.

> "Memento te esse mortalem.
> "Fugit hora. Vive memor læthi. Fugit hora.

"Here lyes the body of John Person, Senor, aged 64 years. Deceased April 17, 1679."

> "Memento mori. Fugit hora.

"Here lyeth within this arched place the body of Deacon Thomas Parker, who was *won* of the foundation of the church, who dyed the 12th of August, 1683, aged about 74."

In 1688–9, the town erected its second church, and located it a few rods northwest of the present Orthodox church in Wakefield; and around this church, soon after its erection, in accordance with ancient custom, that has made *church*-yards and *grave*-yards synonymous terms, our fathers began to inter their dead, and thus and here commenced their *second* burial-ground. This ground has been enlarged from time to time considerably beyond its early limits. For more than one hundred and fifty years, it has been the chief place of sepulture for what is now the town of Wakefield. Here rest the ashes of the greater portion of its former inhabitants. Consequently it possesses a most lively interest, as the place where many a noble, many a beautiful, and many a loved form has been enshrined.

We shall, therefore, be excused for inserting a considerable number of its inscriptions. The earliest date upon any stone in this yard, is in memory of Lieut. Thomas Bancroft, aged 69, who deceased Aug. 19, 1691.

The first three ministers of the first parish were, it is believed, buried away from Reading; the first at Watertown, the other two at Boston, among their relatives.

"The Rev. Mr. Jonathan Pierpont, late pastor of the church of Christ, in Redding, for the space of twenty years, Aged 44 years; who departed this life June 2, 1709.

> "A fruitful Christian and pastor, who
> Did good to all, and lov'd all good to do;

>A tender husband and a parent kind,
>A faithful friend, which who, Oh who can find!
>A preacher that a bright example gave
>Of rules he preach'd, the souls of men to save;—
>A Pierpont, all of this, here leaves his dust,
>And waits the resurrection of the just."

" Here lyes interr'd ye body of ye Rev. Richard Brown, ordained Pastor of ye 1st church in *Reding*, June 25, 1712. His character bespeaks him faithful in his preaching, impartial in his discipline, and exemplary in his conversation; a man greatly beloved in his life, and much lamented at his death, which was Oct. 20, 1732, Aged 57 years."

" In this Sepulchre is reposited the mortal part of the Rev. Mr. William Hobby, A.M., late Pastor (the sixth in the order of succession) of the first church in the town of Reading,—learned, vigilant, and faithful; he was a preacher of the word of God, deservedly commended for his pure evangelical doctrine, replenished with erudition and piety, together with solid judgment and eloquence, being at length worn out with studies and labors, and most acute pains of long continuance, calmly resigning to the will of his Almighty Father, and earnestly aspiring after the Heavenly Habitation and Rest, he breathed out his soul into the hands of his Savior, June 18, Anno Christi 1765, Ætat. 58 years. He left, to profit his bereaved flock, a written monument of sage advice, in which, though dead, he speaks, in solemn strains."

" Sacred to the memory of Rev. Caleb Prentiss, late Pastor of the first church in this town, who passed into the world of spirits, Feb. 7, 1803, in the 57th year of his age, and 34th of his ministry. Faith, piety, and benevolence, with a kindred assemblage of Christian graces and moral virtues, adorned his public and private character, endeared his memory to a bereaved family, a mourning flock, his brethren in office, and all acquainted with his merits.

>" He tried each ar , reprov'd each dull delay,
>Allur'd to brighter worlds and led the way;
>Though gone, he is not dead,—no good man dies,—
>But like the day-star, only sets to rise."

" Here lyes ye body of Major Jeremiah Sweyen, Esq., who departed this life Aug. 13, 1710, in ye 69th year of his age.

>"'The memory of the just is blessed.'"

" Here lyes interred ye remains of Doct. Thomas Sweyn, who departed this life Apl. 22, 1759, aged 53 years.

" An useful, beloved physician,—an extensive blessing in life, and much lamented in death."

" In memory of Doct. Thomas Swain, who departed this life Oct. 26, 1780, Aged 30 years.

",Blessed with a penetrating genius, improved by application, he was a skilful and successful Physician, highly esteemed and beloved.

"Death, fearing the loss of his empire over the children of men, pointed a fatal dart, cut down this rising Genius, secured his own dominions and disappointed the hopes of many."

"Here rests what was mortal of Lieut. John Pool, who deceased Nov. 22, 1721, Aged 56.

"An humble christian, useful and sincere,
Much given to hospitality. lies here.

"Rich in alms to the poor, and in distress the widow's friend, father of the fatherless, a loving husband and a parent kind; a neighbor good and a most useful friend.

"All this was he, and more, but now at rest,
The memory of the righteous man is blest."

"Here lyes ye body of Mrs. Abigail Bancroft, wife of Mr. Raham Bancroft, who died Mar. 26, 1728, Aged 40.

"A prudent, pleasant wife was she,
An helpmate like the laboring bee,
Kind parent; — virtue's graces tell,
That she in those did most excel;
Full ripe for heaven, assur'd of bliss,
Long'd to depart to happiness.
If men forget to speak her worth,
This stone to ages sets it forth."

"Here lyes buried ye body of Mrs. Mary Smith, wife to Mr. Samuel Smith, who died Feb. 3, 1760, in ye 26th year of her age.

"Nipt in the beauteous bloom of life she lies,
A faded flower, bedew'd by numerous eyes;
Oh! could our tears revive so fair a flower,
Sure every eye would spring the quick'ning shower."

"Here lies buried the body of David Green, Esq., who, as a christian, was an ornament to his profession. He was improved in his day; faithful to his trust; and by his prudence and assiduity acquired the approbation and esteem of his acquaintance, and in a composed frame resigned his spirit on the 17th July, 1781, in his 67th year."

"Mrs. Rebekah Evans, widow of Thomas Evans, born Aug. 27, 1758; married Jan. 4, 1776; died of Palsy Apl. 22, 1835; Aged 77 years.

"I know that my Redeemer lives,
All that I need his goodness gives;
I'm calm and happy, blessed Lord!
My faith unshaken in thy word;
In praise I spend my parting breath,
And hail this joyful hour of death;
I've waited long to hear thy call,
My Father, Friend, my God of all!
I go to rest and bliss above,
To sing my great Redeemer's love."

"In memory of Joseph Walton, son of Lieut. Timothy Walton, who was drowned in Lynn, Sept. 17, 1792, in his 23d year.

> "Death, thou hast conquer'd me,
> I, by thy dart, am slain,
> But Christ has conquer'd thee,
> I shall rise again."

"In memory of Mr. Edmund Eaton, who lost his life by the fall of the Swing Bridge in Charlestown, Jany 1, 1800, Aged 33.
"Death often strikes unseen and unexpected. Frail is man. Scarce were the wishes of the New Year's morn exchanged, when fell the tender husband, brother, son. And *great*, as sudden, was the mourners' grief."

"In memory of Deacon Ebenezer Hopkins, who died Feb. 21, 1796, Aged 75 years.
"He was strong in the doctrine of free unmerited grace, and exhibited to the world that he had been with Jesus; and died with a firm hope of a glorious immortality.

> "The greatest purity
> Attain'd on earth, I would deny,
> Nor good confess in name or thing, —
> But Christ my Lord, my life, my King."

"In memory of Sophia Prentiss, daughter of the late Rev. Caleb & Mrs. Pamela Prentiss, who died Oct. 12, Aet. 25.

> "Taste, Fancy, Virtue, Piety, combined,
> Enlarg'd, improv'd her heaven born mind.
> To pale disease she gave her early breath,
> But *courted* more than *fear'd* the approach of death."

In 1846, the town burial-ground having become so fully occupied that the selection of eligible spots for single burials was difficult, and the securing of sufficient room therein for family lots wholly impracticable; and as there were no suitable adjacent lands obtainable with which to enlarge it, sundry individuals, perceiving the necessity for a new place of sepulture, and appreciating the desirableness and value of family burial lots, took measures for the formation of a private cemetery company, and became organized and incorporated under the General Laws by the name of the "Proprietors of the Lake Side Cemetery." This organization was effected in 1846. A tract of fourteen acres of land on the westerly side of the lake and bordering thereon, had been previously secured, at a cost of $1,400. The westerly part of this tract, reserving a street over the same, was soon after sold by the company for $1,200, and the balance, about seven acres, was enclosed and laid out into avenues, paths, lots, and bowers, from a design furnished by Chas. H. Hill, Esq, now of Wakefield.

The lots, about four hundred in number, were appraised at an average price of five dollars each, and on Oct. 15, 1846, the choice of these lots was sold at public auction, and about one hundred of them were taken.

On the same day of the sale the grounds were consecrated as a cemetery, by public exercises, in a bower of grape-vines, on the premises, consisting of a very able and pertinent address by Rev. Caleb Stetson, then of Medford, the singing of the following original hymns and other appropriate services by the resident clergy.

> "Together we have gathered now,
>   Upon the fair Lake Side, —
> Old men and gray, with wrinkled brow,
>   And youthful forms of pride, —
> We 've come with pleasing thoughts tho' grave,
>   This spot to consecrate,
> To bid the flowers their perfumes wave
>   Above death's iron gate!
>
> "And here we 'll build for those we love,
>   A tomb beneath the trees;
> That nature's song may swell above,
>   In sweetest melodies; —
> For friends and for *ourselves* a tomb,
>   When we are earth's no more,
> When are exchang'd its joys and gloom,
>   For brighter — fadeless shore.
>
> "And here, as oft in coming years,
>   Our children's children tread,
> Glad thoughts will rise to quell their fears,
>   Among the silent dead.
> Oh! hallowed spot! A cherished grave
>   Beneath the flowery sod!
> The *form* shall rest by sparkling wave,
>   The *spirit* with its God!"

> "When all life's cares with us are gone,
>   And we have reach'd our journey's bourne,
> With woes distress'd, with age oppress'd,
>   And longing for a place of rest;
> How sweet 't will be to find a home,
>   Where we can lay the weary frame,
> Mid fragrant flowers and vine-wrought bowers,
>   On this dear Lake Side seat of ours.

> "And know that we've secured a bed
> In this fair garden of the dead,
> Where friends will love to come and rove,
> And weep and hope and look above;
> Where roses will embalm the air,
> And warbling birds their requiems bear,
> And shady trees, with sighing breeze,
> And rippling waves our dirges raise.
>
> "Oh! sacred spot! may angels tread
> These mansions of the coming dead;
> Or, hov'ring o'er this field and shore,
> Illume these pathways evermore;
> Be ever ready, on their wings,
> Rising above all earthly things,
> To bear aloft to heavenly day
> The souls, who here have dropp'd their clay."

Additional territory has been purchased and reclaimed, from time to time, for enlarging the limits of the grounds, on which some one hundred additional lots have been laid out, making the present number of lots five hundred, of which nearly four hundred have been sold.

A plan of the cemetery lands, drawn by C. W. Eaton, Esq., assisted by Mr. B. F. Abbott, the efficient superintendent of the cemetery, who has always taken a lively and intelligent interest in its improvement, has been lithographed.

A still further addition of adjacent land has been secured for future enlargement of the cemetery. The present price of lots to residents is twenty-five dollars each. Any person, owning a lot, may become a member of the corporation by signing the by-laws.

This cemetery has been planted with trees, shrubbery, and flowers; many of its lots have been enclosed with iron fences, and adorned with marble and granite monuments, mausoleums, etc., and with its imposing water scenery, is already a most beautiful, romantic, and interesting spot.

The officers of the corporation at present, are:— President, Edward Mansfield; secretary, B. F. Abbott, and trustees, *ex officio*; treasurer, Edward Mansfield; trustees, Samuel Kingman, Hiram Eaton, E. S. Upham, Oliver Walton, 2d; superintendent, B. F. Abbott; sextons, Jotham Walton, and Oliver Walton, 2d.

CHAPTER XIV.

REBELLION HISTORY AND RECORD.

WHEN the clouds of the War of the Rebellion began to overshadow our beloved land, and the mutterings of their thunder began to be heard in the distance, the inhabitants of the three Readings, true to that spirit of liberty and patriotism which animated their fathers and predecessors in the war of the Revolution, were found to be almost unanimously loyal to the old flag, alive to the wickedness of the treasonable insurrection, and ready to go in for the defence and preservation of the Union at all hazards and at any cost. And when the reverberations of actual conflict filled the air, the people of these towns, in common with those of most other towns in the free States, uprose with alacrity and determined resolution boldly to meet the crisis.

There was at this time but one military organization, the "Richardson Light Guard," in the three towns. This company, with its armory and head-quarters at South Reading, was composed, mainly, of citizens of South Reading, but contained members from other portions of old Reading. It was a well-disciplined and flourishing corps.

By the wise foresight and sagacious action of Gov. Andrew, who seemed endued with prophetic ken, this company had been notified, some days before the attack upon Fort Sumter, to be in readiness at a minute's warning to rally and march to the defence of the Government.

To the honor of the company be it recorded, that they not only signified their willingness to be thus called upon, but also expressed a strong desire to do and dare in defence of the Union, and longed for an opportunity; and especially after the attack upon Fort Sumter, were earnest and even clamorous for orders to go.

It was then understood that orders to proceed to Washington would probably come soon; that the town bell would be rung upon their reception, when the Guards would be expected to rally at their place of parade.

On the ever memorable 19th of April, 1861, the desired orders came, and at 12 o'clock, noon, of that day, the old town bell struck its loudest peals, and all understood the stirring signal. The Guards hurried to the armory, and before 5 o'clock of the same day, Capt. Locke, with his company in full ranks, and all its members inspired with patriotic ardor and heroic zeal to fight in defence of their country's flag, was at the railroad station to take the train. And amid a crowd of earnest citizens, who had thronged about the railroad station to witness their departure, some of whom addressed to these departing heroes pathetic and glowing words of encouragement and hope, with exhortations to bravery and gallantry, and promises of support, of gratitude, and future fame; and amid the prayers, the tears, the tender leave-takings and farewells of relatives and friends, all electrified by the exciting news, just received, of the bloody tragedy which had that day occurred in the city of Baltimore, — amid all these stirring incidents and circumstances, and after an impressive invocation of Heaven's blessing upon the expedition by Rev. Mr. Phillips, these gallant soldiers went forth to glorious war.

LIEUT. J. H. WOODFIN.

The company were enlisted for three months; were stationed in Alexandria, in Virginia, where they performed valuable service in guarding and protecting the National Capital; fought bravely in the first battle of ull Run, in which some of their number were wounded, and three were taken prisoners.

At the expiration of their term of enlistment, the company (except the three soldiers who had been taken prisoners) returned to South Reading, where a public reception awaited them.

On their arrival at the railroad station, in South Reading, they were saluted by shouts of welcome from a great multitude of the inhabitants of South Reading, Reading, and other neighboring towns, and were addressed by Edward Mansfield, Esq., chairman of the board of selectmen in South Reading, in these appropriate words: —

Mr. Commander and Soldiers:

I can hardly realize that we are in the midst of a civil war, — that a portion of the States of this once united and happy Republic are in open and wicked rebellion against the constitutional government established and cemented by the blood of our fathers, — under which they and we have lived and prospered, and to which, in a great measure, we are indebted for our social and religious blessings.

I can hardly realize that the cry "to arms" has been echoed and re-echoed over hill and vale and mountain-top, to our New England homes, and that now the tramp of the war-horse and the glitter of arms present a spectacle awfully sublime on our American soil.

I can hardly realize that at the call, and in behalf of my fellow-citizens, I now stand before a portion of an American army, recently organized for the defence of our dearest rights, — for the better establishment and perpetuation of all that is sacred in government. Yet truth, which is sometimes stranger than fiction, declares this state of things to exist.

I recognize before me a part of our own community, from whom, for a time, we have been separated, who, when a dark and portentous cloud hung over the capital and the nation, and the administration inquired who would go to avert the impending danger, promptly responded, "Here are we, send us."

Yes, I recognize you, though the vertical sun of summer has bronzed your cheeks and in part disguised your manly brows; though the effacing fingers of care and toil have traced their lines upon your persons and your habiliments, — still I recognize you.

I recognize the forms that left us on the 19th of April last, just as the news reached the village that our neighbors had been struck down in Baltimore, and had been marred and slain by traitors. That was a thrilling moment, and all our hearts beat quickly with feverish emotions, as we bid you adieu for the present, feeling that we were looking upon some of your faces perhaps for the last time in life.

But our hearts still lingering with you, and with the cause you had espoused, we followed you in thought to Boston, to Annapolis, thence in part through an enemy's country, by railroad and on foot, until, way-worn and weary, you arrived at Washington to guard one of our most important public buildings from threatened destruction by an inveterate foe.

The scenes of hardships, of toils and sacrifices, of physical sufferings since endured, I need not, I *cannot* describe; they are already a part of your experience by too full a realization.

Real war is not the image which we have seen painted before us on occasions of parade and review. It has a sterner reality, reaching deep down into the soul, and moving to sighs and tears, and groans and blood.

With profound gratitude would we acknowledge an overruling hand in the care and protection over you in all your pathway of dangers and sufferings.

Though the peril to our country is not yet averted, though the victory is not yet achieved, you have thus far fulfilled the mission assigned to you; you have performed well your part in the great drama which is now being enacted, — and when the din of arms shall cease, when the smoke of battle shall be cleared away, and the history of this second war for our independence shall be written, then will Company B, of South Reading, claim an honorable mention on one of its brightest pages.

Worn out with marchings and with fatigues in actual service on the field of battle, we welcome you back to our quiet village to recover your exhausted natures. We welcome you to the kind congratulations of neighbors and citizens, who have met in these numbers with warm and sympathetic hearts to receive you. We welcome you to the sacred endearments of home, made doubly dear by a painful absence. We welcome you to the embraces of friendship, by companions, by children and parents, by brothers, sisters, and loved ones. We welcome you to the pure and invigorating air of freedom, which circulates nowhere so freely as in these more northern climes.

But our rejoicing to-day is tempered with sorrow. Of the seventy and nine who departed from us, where are the *three?* They are not here to receive our greetings; their friends in silence mourn; but their names and their valor shall be held in lasting remembrance. And may the glad sound which fell upon the ear of the patriarch of old,

"Joseph is yet alive," vibrate through our saddened spirits, and we yet be permitted to make merry with our friends, because these our brothers are alive again, though lost they now are found.

Soldiers and friends, in behalf of your fellow townsmen and citizens, I have extended to you this welcome, but they, through the president (Hon. Lilley Eaton) and other gentlemen, at another place, will give you a more hearty greeting in stronger and more eloquent words, to which mine were intended but as a prelude.

May the rights of the people to govern soon be established beyond the possibility of a contingency; and may the members of the Richardson Light Guard long live to uphold and enjoy the blessings of union and liberty, for which they have bared their bosoms so nobly.

At the conclusion of Mr. Mansfield's remarks, the company were escorted, amid the ringing of bells, the roaring of cannon, the display

MAJOR HORACE M. WARREN.

of banners, and the rejoicings of the people, to the common in South Reading, where, in a spacious tent, with greetings of rejoicing, in strains pathetic, with flowing verse and martial music, these bronzed heroes were welcomed to the festal boards, and to the homes and hearts of the people.

In the same year, soon after the departure of the Richardson Light Guard for the seat of war, Major John Wiley, 2d, of South Reading, who had been an accomplished officer in the volunteer militia, was anthorized to recruit a company of "three years' men," in South Reading and vicinity, which he succeeded in doing, and of which he was chosen and commissioned captain. The members of this company belonged principally to South Reading, but included some from Reading and other neighboring towns. They were attached to the Sixteenth Massachusetts Regiment, and went into camp at Cambridge in July, 1861, and left for the seat of war Aug. 17, 1861 (see roll of this company in this chapter).

This company served in Virginia in the grand army of the Potomac, and during its three years' term performed much severe duty, endured many hardships and fatigues, engaged in many hard-fought battles, and many of its members were either killed in battle, or died of wounds and disease, or of starvation in rebel prison pens; but it ever sustained the reputation of a brave, faithful, efficient, and gallant corps, and is entitled to the everlasting gratitude and highest honors of all loyal people.

LIEUT. B. F. BARNARD.

During the summer of 1861, the spirit of patriotism of the citizens in the three Readings was lively and overflowing. Contributions of those inestimable sinews of successful war, brave men, were proffered to the Government in profusion.

Drill clubs were formed in the several towns, composed of numerous members, young and old, who earnestly trained themselves in the tactics of war.

The Star Spangled Banner was unfurled from liberty pole and church tower, and from dwelling, school-house, and hill-top, all around us.

New flag-staffs were erected, and the heavens were gay with the bright symbols of liberty, union, and determined victory.

In South Reading and Reading, lofty masts were raised upon the respective commons, still standing, from which were unrolled, with imposing ceremonies, large and beautiful ensigns.

An account of the services at a flag-raising in South Reading, on July 4, 1861, may serve as [a specimen of many other similar occasions: —

A procession was formed near the town house, under the direction of N. S. Dearborn, Esq., chief marshal, consisting of the Yale engine company, Capt. Dunn, with engine following, drawn by horses; company of Massachusetts volunteers, Capt. Wiley (just recruited); South Reading drill club, Capt. Carpenter; the thirteen schools and a numerous retinue of citizens. The engine and horses were handsomely decorated, and the pupils made a fine appearance with wreaths, flowers, and appropriate banners.

The procession, preceded by the Malden Band, after marching through some of the principal streets, formed in front of the speaker's stand and awning, erected for the purpose, near the flag-staff, on the common, where the following exercises occurred.

The president of the day, Lilley Eaton, said: —

"*Ladies and Gentlemen*, — My duty on the present occasion is an honorable, a pleasant, and an easy one; for while it is not expected of me that I shall pour forth those streams of eloquent sentiment that the occasion demands and is calculated to inspire, still I have the honor to be intrusted with those magic keys, that at a touch will unlock and uplift the vocal gates, and let come a gushing flood of invocation and patriotism and harmonious enthusiasm that shall animate, refresh, and gladden all our hearts."

Whereupon the Rev. Mr. Phillips, of the Baptist Church, at the president's request, offered a most fervent and appropriate invocation.

The president then continued: —

"We are assembled on the anniversary of that declaration, which has made this day the consecrated birthday of our beloved country's independence; and we are met together under very unusual, peculiar, and exciting circumstances. Our government, the freest, wisest, and most prosperous that has ever existed; our grand palladium of liberty, law, union, and safety; that was secured by the toil, sufferings, and valor, established by the wisdom and sanctified by the blood of our heroic and sainted forefathers; a government beloved by the immortal Washington, and his illustrious compeers, is assailed by a most gigantic and wicked rebellion. Armed traitors, led by ambitious, unprincipled, and talented men, are seeking its overthrow; and are now, like the Goths and Vandals of old, hovering around the nation's capital, furious for its possession, and swearing that that starry banner, that symbolizes freedom, law, and union, that has waved triumphantly over many a battle-field, and commands respect in every clime and on every sea, shall be struck down and trampled in the dust.

But we rejoice to know, thanks to those brave Massachusetts soldiers who hastened early to Washington, that the Stars and Stripes still wave from the great dome of the Capitol; that our Government still lives and moves and has a being; that our chosen and honored civil and military chiefs still stand, tall and strong, wise and brave, fearless and hopeful amid the storm; that the genius of freedom from slumber is waking; that the sons of liberty, in valiant hosts, have rallied and rushed, and are still rallying and rushing, to the rescue. Joyfully and gratefully do we call to mind at this time, that at the first tocsin of alarm our own Guards, our sons, brothers, and husbands, were seen rallying, and at the earliest possible moment were observed hastening to the post of danger; that they are *to-day* standing in the front ranks of that bright array of loyal heroes, who are staying and forcing back that fearful tide of treason that threatens to overwhelm the land. We rejoice, too, to think and know that another company of our gallant sons is organized, and its members ready and earnest to join their brethren in the field. Their presence with us to-day adds interest to our exercises; but they are soon to depart to fight for freedom, for union, and for their country's flag; may they go resolute and cheerful; our best wishes and most fervent aspirations will go with them; may they return covered with laurels, — or, reposing upon them!

We forget not the reserved corps before us, no less patriotic and brave, who are educating themselves in military science, and preparing themselves to follow when necessary.

The firemen, too, are here, and we greet their presence, believing that, whenever their country calls them, they are ready, like Ellsworth's Fire Zouaves, to go forth to the contest, whether it be to *fight fire*, or fire and fight; and either or both will be well done (Dunn).

The schools are here, the coming hope of the country; we joyfully hail their smiling presence; may they catch the inspirations of the occasion, study its symbols, understand its memorials and stirring incidents, and make improvement in that knowledge and wisdom that will the better enable them to grow up into the stature of perfect and intelligent *free*-men.

Ladies and Gentlemen, — Amid all these eventful movements, exciting associations, and glorious memories, we meet to-day to unfurl anew the American ensign; to swing it from our new liberty pole; to swear fresh allegiance to our Star Spangled Banner, and to all the glorious principles of freedom, equal rights, law and union, which this bright flag symbolizes.

This is no party or sectarian color; it is the national flag, procured by the united contributions of all. It is, therefore, the "Union American Flag," and represents not only the Federal union of these States, but also that glorious, democratic union of the people, which recent treason and rebellion have served to produce and cement in the free States of this Republic.

I would fain wish that there still lingered among us one, at least, of those brave old Revolutioners, whose heroic deeds first gave meaning and beauty to this banner, that I might ask his aid in again unfurling it to the breeze; but, alas! the besom of time has swept them all away, — not one remains. With your permission, therefore, I will call upon our venerable and esteemed friend, Capt. and Hon. Thomas Emerson, who inherits some of the best blood of the Revolution, whose birth was nearly coeval with that of the Republic, and who loves the Government and Union which this flag represents. I will call upon him to unfurl, shake out, and lift up our new — our old — the starry banner of freedom, of union, of victory."

(Here the flag unrolled and rose majestically upward.)

The president continuing: —

"Let it rise to its mast-top — its topmost height! In the glowing words of our eloquent as well as excellent Governor, —

"Let it float on every wind, — to every sea and every shore, — from every hill-top and house-top let it wave; down every river let it run. Respected it shall be, not in Massachusetts only, but in South Carolina also, — on the Mississippi as on the Penobscot, — in New Orleans as in Cincinnati, — in the Gulf of Mexico as on Lake Superior, — and by France and England, now and forever. Catch it, ye breezes, as it swings aloft. Fan it every wind that blows ; clasp it in your arms, and let it float forever as the ensign of the Republic!"

The multitude were then addressed in eloquent and patriotic phrase, by Hon. Thomas Emerson, Hon. P. H. Sweetser, Rev. E. A. Eaton, and Prof. Elam Porter.

Poetic recitations by Mrs. E. C. Poland and Miss Sarah J. W. McKay followed.

The following original poem was then pronounced by John Sullivan Eaton, Esq.: —

> Beneath the flag our fathers wrought,
> We stand, to-day, most proudly ;
> Beneath that flag the fathers fought,
> Where cannon rattled loudly.
>
> That flag they bore on many a field,
> Rent with war's wild commotion —
> To victory, bore its star-gemmed shield,
> On bloody plain and ocean.
>
> Where fiery shells the hottest flew,
> Those gallant heroes bore it,
> Where Indian arrows pierc'd it through,
> And British lances tore it.
>
> It floated from the bending mast, —
> O'er the blue billows dashing ;
> While from the port-holes, red and fast,
> The fierce broadsides were flashing.
>
> While crashing ball and bursting shell
> Sent the firm timbers flying, —
> Clear, 'bove the smoke, it floated still,
> And sailors clasp'd it, dying.

> That flag has flutter'd in the air
> That sweeps the polar seas, —
> Its red and blue have glitter'd fair,
> Amidst the orange trees.
>
> Where winter stern, with icy bars,
> River and lake had fetter'd,
> The gallant Kane unfurl'd the Stars,
> With Union, golden-letter'd : —

Upon the ice-hill's topmost crest, —
  Beyond the sunlight lying, —
That noble leader, fearless, prest,
  And set our flag a-flying.

From Rocky Mountains' lofty crag, —
  No human footprint bearing, —
Was fair unfurl'd our nation's flag,
  By John Fremont, the daring.

On every sea, behold our sails,
  And ev'ry river flecking;
Behold that flag, on balmy gales,
  Each lofty peak bedecking!

On all the free pure airs of heaven,
  Its colors flash — undying —
By heroes, to their children given —
  They'll keep those colors flying!

Shall Treason, 'neath that starry flag,
  Its snaky head upraising, —
To depth infernal, seek to drag
  The Union, all are praising?

It may — it *has!* — E'en now, they march
  Along our Southern border, —
Led by a traitor, keen and arch —
  Those minions of disorder.

Are words of him who calmly sleeps
  Upon the earth's cold pillow,
In Marshfield's sod — while round him sweeps
  The broad Atlantic billow;

Are all the clear and warning words,
  By the great Statesman spoken —
In rush of trade, — in lapse of years, —
  Unheeded, and forgotten?

Not yet! The heroes' worthy sons
  Hold to the Union, steady;
With purpose firm, they man their guns;
  Are for the conflict ready.

When the war summons, startling, rang
    Along our Northern border —
How then, our sturdy yeomen sprang,
    In answer to that order.

From the white sands that belt the Cape,
    Wet with the spray of ocean,
To where the trees of Berkshire bend
    With fair and gentle motion ; —

From Essex' smooth and fruitful farms,
    Where flows the Merrimack ;
From Concord's glorious, hallow'd plains,
    Bright with the martyr's track ; —

From Bunker's swelling mount of green,
    Where stands the granite tow'ring,
Where Prescott fought and Warren fell,
    'Midst British bullets show'ring !

Our " Spindle City " sends its youth —
    First sacrifice to Freedom !
It sends, as well, its lawyers forth,
    When dangerous " cases " need 'em !

Our own dear town, with ready hand,
    Its treasures quick un-*Lock*-ing —
When rang the call, sent forth its " Guard,"
    'Round Freedom's banner flocking !

God guard them in their distant camp,
    By the Potomac's waters ;
And bring them safe to peaceful homes,
    To mothers, wives, and daughters !

From many a wild and rocky gorge,
    With mountain-spring outgushing —
New Hampshire's earnest, rugged sons,
    To guard their soil, came rushing.

From the far bounds of rocky Maine,
    Where rush Penobscot's waters —
Sprang forth the hardy lumber-men,
    Cheer'd by her blooming daughters.

From where the Hudson rolls in pride,
    By cro'nest, and the Highlands, —
Bearing, at length, his silver tide,
    Along Manhattan's islands ; —

On fair Ohio's waving grounds,
    In many a sunny valley,
The trumpet for the battle sounds —
    The sons of freemen rally!

O'er prairies green the columns wind,
    In firm and shining order;
And Western traitors wake, to find
    A "*Lyon*" on their border!

O'er all the acres, free and broad,
    With food for millions teeming,
Banners uplift and gay plumes nod,
    And bayonets are gleaming.

Our Eagle has his wings outspread,
    And floats on mighty pinion;
Our armies march with fearless tread,
    And shake the "Old Dominion"!

With Leaders true our columns press,
    To silence batteries, rebel;
The war-cry ringing as they charge —
    "*Ellsworth — Winthrop — Greble.*"

He who on bloody Mexic plains,
    Made sure and dread advances,
Now guides our military trains,
    And calculates the chances.

Brave Winfield Scott — enjoying fame,
    More worth than youthful Morphy's,
Moves new the pieces in this game,
    Where *Empires are the trophies!*

Calmly he sits, and views the field,
    As on a chess-board gazing;
While his firm squares which will not yield,
    Entrenchments strong are raising.

"Old Abraham," — the faithful one, —
    Alone has supervision;
And all the hero's moves are done
    With infinite precision.

The men he moves, as by a spring,
    Are, 'round his "Castle," closing,
And soon will "check" the "Cotton-King" —
    The foe he's now opposing!

Ne'er fear the end, nor chide delay;
   Hath *Heaven* no finger in it?
Treason, be sure, will *lose* the day,
   And Truth and Right will *win it!*

Be sure, a brighter day shall come,
   A calm and peaceful morrow;
No battle-shout, no roll of drum,
   No wailing cry of sorrow; —

Peace, with her olive-wreath, shall bind
   Our States, again United,
And plant with flowers the sunny fields
   War's cruel breath has blighted!

Flag of the free hearts' hope, float on!
   No single star dissever!
No stripe erased, no glory gone;
   Thus let it float, forever!

The exercises were interspersed with patriotic and inspiring songs by the choir, and stirring music by the band.

LIEUT. R. S. BECKWITH.

The 14th day of June, 1862, was signalized and made historic by the return to town of members of the Richardson Light Guard, who were taken captive by the rebels in the first battle of Bull Run, in July, 1861; and by the impressive ceremonies of a public reception, performed in South Reading in honor of those returned heroes, and in joy at their safe arrival.

Two of the returning soldiers, Sergeant Geo. W. Aborn and James H. Greggs, had arrived in Boston some days before, and the third, Frank L. Tibbetts, had reached New York, and was expected to reach Boston in season to accompany his comrades to South Reading on the day appointed to receive them. For some cause, to the universal regret, Mr. Tibbetts was not present.

Yale's mammoth tent was pitched upon the common. The tables therein for the festive repast were spread and loaded by the ladies of the town.

Edward Mansfield, Esq., was appointed president of the day; N. S. Dearborn, Esq., chief marshal; and L. Eaton, Esq., orator.

At one o'clock, P. M., the people of the towns of South Reading, of Reading, and of the surrounding towns generally, begun to assemble in crowds upon the common, and soon after a procession was formed, under direction of the marshal, consisting of the Richardson Light Guard, under command of Capt. H. D. Degen, who had succeeded to the captaincy, accompanied by the Boston Brigade Band; military and civic guests; reception committee in carriages; president, orator, and poet, in carriages; clergymen, town officers, public schools, citizens, etc.

The procession moved through some of the principal streets to the Junction railroad station, there to await the arrival of the three o'clock train from Boston, which was to bring the returning heroes.

Upon the arrival of the train it was found that Messrs. Aborn and Greggs, two of the rescued prisoners, were on board in charge of Capt. John W. Locke (recently the commander of the Guards, and subsequently appointed Lieut.-Colonel of the 50th Mass. Reg't), who immediately conducted them to the committee appointed to receive them, who were in waiting at the station.

Dr. S. O. Richardson, the chairman of this committee, and the godfather, namesake, and long tried friend of the Guards, took them by the hand, and thus addressed them: —

"*Gentlemen,*— This is indeed a happy moment to me, and one I shall never forget. I take pleasure in informing you that Messrs. Beebe, Wheeler, and myself have been delegated, in behalf of the citizens of South Reading, to greet you on this happy occasion, and bid you a thrice joyful welcome. We hope to show you by the ovation this afternoon, that although you have been from us a long time, as prisoners of war, our love for you has not diminished. You have shown us that on the battle-field you were full of pluck and fight, and nobly risked your lives to restore the Stars and Stripes to our glorious Union. Permit me to say you have done honor to yourselves, to this town, and as members of the Richardson Light Guard have conferred great honor on him for whom the corps is named. After leaving here, we hope to introduce you from the "Rebels' Field" of the South, to a "Man's-field" of the North, where you will receive a welcome by the "Lily" of the *field*, surrounded by a host of friends, with warm hearts and open arms, ready to receive and show you that you are not forgotten *even* at home."

The returned soldiers were conducted to a carriage and joined the procession, which took up a line of motion in return to the common; and passing through many of the principal streets, amid the ringing of bells, the booming of cannon, and the congratulations of the people, reached and entered the spacious pavilion.

After a sumptuous repast, prepared by the ladies of the town, and after a voluntary by the band, a hollow square was formed by the Richardson Light Guard in front of the speakers' stand, where the returned soldiers appeared and were introduced by the committee, through P. C. Wheeler, Esq., to the president of the day, Edward Mansfield, Esq., who descended from the platform to receive them and escorted them to seats provided for them. Then followed the singing of the "Star Spangled Banner" by the children, and a fervent invocation by Rev. C. R. Bliss, of the Congregational church.

The president then said : —

Fellow-citizens, Ladies and Gentlemen, — It was one of the most unwelcome duties that I was ever called to perform, to extend the parting hand, and utter farewell words, as more than one year ago the Richardson Light Guard left their friends and pleasant firesides, to protect the nation's capital, and to engage in scenes of strife and blood.

But life has its changes. Sorrow and joy follow each other sometimes in quick succession. The company went forth and wrote their names on the scroll of fame. Most of them in a few months returned from the dreadful conflict with the smell of fire upon them, and some with scars and wounds, and were joyfully welcomed by their numerous friends. But a stricken few remained, and a terrible suspense hung over us. The festive hour that witnessed our rejoicings over the many, was also an hour of lamentation and mourning. It was like "Rachel weeping for her children, refusing to be comforted because they were not." But later events proclaimed the welcome truth, "the missing ones are yet alive." Waning hope revives, the lost are found, the scalding tears may yet be wiped away. What has since transpired and been experienced will often be related in the social circle and at the fireside of home.

After long months of imprisonment by a cruel, a merciless and relentless foe, — in loathsome warehouses and gloomy Southern jails, — cut off from the comforts of home, from the sympathy of friends, and, I had almost said, from all communication with intelligent humanity,— these our friends are with us again to receive our congratulations, and to enjoy repose in the quiet of home.

And it is with a pleasure commensurate with a former sadness, that I now perform the part assigned me, and present them to one who has been appointed to receive them in behalf of the citizens, and who well knows how to speak fitting words of welcome on this joyous occasion

Friends, I refer to the Hon. Lilley Eaton, to whom I introduce and commit you; not now as prisoners in a Southern clime to a barbarous people, but as *free men*, breathing the free air of New England, and under the protection of the Stars and Stripes of our glorious old republic.

Mr. Eaton then delivered the following address: —

Mr. President, — I desire to thank you, sir, and through you the committee of arrangements, for this kind invitation; above all, I desire to thank heaven that I am permitted, on this rare and stirring occasion, amid this brilliant, crowded, and earnest assembly, with the symbols of loyalty, of union, of liberty, and of beauty, spread gayly around me, hearing and witnessing these exultant demonstrations, with the animating notes of victory coming in on the wings of every wind, — that I am permitted, under such glorious circumstances, to rise and declare my hearty concurrence and sympathy, and the sincere and united sympathy of all this concourse, with all these expressions of congratulation, of warm welcome, of joy and rejoicing, and of thanksgiving and gratitude to the great disposer of events, in view of the return at last of those heroic young men who, more than a year since, at the earliest call of their country, when in sudden and fearful peril, buckled on their armor, and hastened to the post of danger, to defend the sacred ark of their country's capital, to protect the government of the union, and to fight anew the battles of liberty; and who now, after exposure to bloody perils, having suffered severe hardships, privations, and imprisonment, and made to bear insults and reproach at the hands of malicious enemies, for ten long and weary months, have at length, thanks be to the God of battles for the great and glorious victories that have secured their release, been returned to us in life, health, and gladness.

Mr. President, and ladies and gentlemen, — Amid the memories of the exciting and startling events of the last year, as they come thronging upon the mind, as suggested by the present occasion, and the emotions of joy and pleasure awakened by recent victories, and in view of the presence here in our midst of these heroes, rescued from captivity and death, and of these other gallant youth, not less heroic and true and worthy, who have spilled their blood for their country and for us in the same great cause, and who, with the utmost propriety, are included in the list of those whom we this day delight to honor, — we say, amid these recollections of the past, the felicities of the present, and the hopes of the future, we know not what to say or how to speak ; we are overcome and confused by the magnitude of our privilege.

We read that the ancient saints, "when the Lord turned again their captivity, were like those that dreamed ; that their mouths were filled with laughter and their tongues with singing, and they were led to exclaim: 'The Lord has done great things for us, whereof we are glad.'"

Thus do we find ourselves: the past seems like a dream, the present full of joy, congratulation, thanksgiving, and hope.

But there are certain events and scenes recalled and revived by the facts of the present occasion, that seem to stand out in bolder relief than others. The first are those which occurred on the 19th of April of last year. The 19th of April! most memorable day in the calendar of liberty!

Who of us who heard it, will ever forget the rousing clangor of the old town bell, when at midday of that notable 19th, it pealed forth its startling tones of alarm and summons ? "To arms ! to arms ! The Greek ! The Greek!" We all understood its fearful import. Especially did our heroic band of volunteers understand it ; for at once, without delay, at "double quick," they came from all quarters, and were seen rushing forward and rallying at their rendezvous, and preparing for their departure ; and ere the sun went down in the west, we find them, all armed and furnished, and in full ranks, at the railroad station waiting for the train. Who of us who were present will ever forget that farewell at the station ! It will be recollected that at that time the political heavens were dark and threatening ; the federal city, with all its invaluable archives and treasures and prestiges, was in fearful peril ; its connection with the North was cut off ; we had just heard of the bloody massacre in the city of Baltimore, where our loyal troops who were hastening to the protection of the city of Washington, had been shot down by the "plug uglies" of secession while peaceably passing along the streets of the Monumental City; all was solicitude and apprehension. But we forget not the courage, zeal, and cheerfulness of that intrepid band, of whom our returned captives and their wounded companions were not least, with which, with tearful eyes to be sure, but with determined hearts, they bid farewell to their friends and fellow-citizens who were crowding around them, and that, amid the cheers and prayers and tears of all, then went fearlessly and boldly forth to fight, and if need required, to die in defence of the Union.

We are also reminded of the eventful battle of Bull Run. And although we are ready to admit that some of the circumstances connected with the progress and result of that fight were sad, regretful, and disastrous; yet it is our consolation to believe and know there were at least two great facts, brought out and wrought out by that battle, in which we can rejoice and glory, namely: —

1st. That the Massachusetts troops *generally*, and the 5th Massachusetts Regiment (to which our own friends belonged) *particularly* and *eminently*, did their whole duty bravely and arduously on that fearful occasion; that the Richardson Light Guards were in the thickest of that engagement; that they faced the cannon's mouth and flying missiles of the foe valiantly and fearlessly; that they spilled their blood on that field, as more than one of their number can witness; and that they did not retreat until they were ordered to do so; and that, even then, they fell back reluctantly, believing at that time, as many of them supposed, that they were just about to conquer the enemy.

Another glorious result, which, as we believe, that battle secured, was the salvation of the city of Washington; for although it is true that the enemy were not dislodged from their strongholds, yet it is also true that they were so damaged, crippled, and disabled that they were prevented ever afterward from making any offensive operations against us from that quarter, and the capital, until then in imminent danger, was thereby and thereafter rendered secure. And this was done in a great measure by Massachusetts soldiers, our own company included, both before and at that contest.

We had the privilege of visiting the army of the Potomac, a few days before the battle of Bull Run; and as we were returning from the encampments, passing through Alexandria, we stopped, with several others with whom we were riding in the same carriage, to visit a noted slave-pen in Alexandria, of which some of you have heard. We found the gateway guarded by a Union sentinel, — a Pennsylvanian, of German descent, — who demanded our *pass*. We told him we were Massachusetts men, who had called to take a look at the slave-pen, but that we had got a pass; and while we were producing it, he replied : " Massachusetts men ! God bless the Massachusetts boys ; for it was they who, by their promptness and heroism, saved yonder capital from pillage and destruction ; they are our truest and best soldiers. Just show me," said he, weeping, " that you hail from Massachusetts, and I want no other pass ; you can go where you please."

We mention this little incident to show the estimation in which our own soldiers are held at the seat of war. We greet these young men, therefore, as heroes true and honorable, and as so many saviors of their country's capital.

But we must just refer briefly to the state of feeling that was excited in our midst when the news of the Bull Run battle came home to our people.

At first we heard that the Fifth Massachusetts Regiment was in the front of the fight, was badly cut up, and that many of its men were killed and wounded, — how many and whom we heard not.

Then came the report that two of the Richardson Light Guard were certainly killed, two more badly wounded, and many were missing, but still no names.

Next came the story that Sergt. Aborn was killed by a cannon ball, Eustis and Greggs wounded, and Greggs and Tibbetts missing, and probably dead.

Oh who can depict the eager anxiety, the agonizing suspense, the deep sorrow, that pervaded all our minds at this eventful time !

Those were days of sadness and nights of sleeplessness with all of us.

" Many a voice was heard in Ramah, lamentation and bitter weeping ; " many a Rachel weeping for her children or dear friends, and refusing to be comforted, because they were not.

Not many days after the battle the Richardson Light Guard, their time of service having expired, returned to their homes ; three of their number, Aborn, Greggs, and Tibbetts, still missing, and their fate unknown ; none could then tell whether they were sainted heroes, gone up to their reward, or were languishing in the dungeons of the enemy. And although that returned company was received with joy and gladness, was honored with a public reception and festival, and was welcomed by a greater assembly than had ever before convened upon our common, who manifested the liveliest enthusiasm, as they looked upon the embrowned countenances and labor-marked frames of these gallant men; still a cloud of sadness and sorrow overshadowed all the proceedings on account of the missing ones.

Soon, however, the voice of heavenly mercy was heard, saying: "Refrain thy voice from weeping, and thine eyes from tears, for thy work shall be rewarded, and there is hope that thy children shall come again from the land of the enemy, to their own border"; and we then heard, that the absent ones still lived, although in imprisonment and affliction.

But *to-day* we have the unspeakable joy of knowing that such has been the success which has recently attended the armies of freedom so great is the number of conquered rebels, that the balance of trade in prisoners of war is greatly in our favor; that indeed these imprisoned traitors are becoming a drug upon our hands, and Yankee prisoners are commanding a premium; that instead of one rebel being equal in value to five Union men, as our enemies boastingly proclaimed at the onset, it now appears that the converse of that proposition is true, for our Government can now offer five of these revolting sinners for one true man.

We rejoice, therefore, that in consequence of this signal success, we are able to-day to greet the return of these young men to their long-lost homes.

We proffer them our heartiest welcome; we crown them with the laurels which they have so bravely, so nobly, so dearly won.

To them, to these other young heroes by their side, who have fought and bled for their country, to all our brave Guardsmen, whether present here to-day, or again absent at the post of danger and duty, and to all our patriotic and brave sons, who are fighting for the Stars and Stripes, we award the tribute of our gratitude and respect; we admit their title to a high niche among the benefactors and heroes of their country, and to a bright place upon the roll of fame.

In view, then, of the patriotism and prowess of all our young men who have so cheerfully enlisted for the defence of the Government; in view of the sufferings, wounds, and imprisonment of these our honored guests; in view of the present bright and hopeful prospects of our cause; and especially in view of our present joy and thanksgiving to the Father of mercies, for this return, it is meet and just that we should break forth into singing, with music and dancing, that we should kill the fatted calf and make merry with our friends, — "for these our sons were dead and are alive again, were lost, and now are found."

> "These brave men's perils now are o'er,
> Their glad return we sing,
> And loud and clear, with cheer on cheer,
> Our joyous welcomes ring.

> "Hurra! Hurra! — it shakes the wave,
>   It thunders on the shore,
> ' One flag, one land, one heart, one hand,
>   One nation evermore.' "

After "Home Again" was played by the band, Sergeant Aborn being called upon, gave a graphic history of his capture, of his imprisonment at Richmond, New Orleans, and Salisbury, and related many interesting incidents, which occurred during his ten months' incarceration.

Then followed singing by the children; and by the assembled multitude, to the tune of "America," the following hymn, written for the occasion by Hon. P. H. Sweetser: —

RECEPTION HYMN.

Land that our fathers trod,
The favored land of God,
  Light of the age!
Foul treason doth defame,
And with its tongue of shame
Becloud thy glorious name,
  Thy history's page!

Let selfish lips be dumb,
Let patriot spirits come,
  The true and brave,
And ask the mighty God, —
Who, by his chastening rod,
D splays his power abroad, —
  Our land to save!

May heaven our efforts bless,
And crown them with success,
  Hence, evermore.
O let our watchwords be
Unio and Liberty,
And Death or Victory,
  Till time is o'er!

Joy for the patriot dead,
Who rest in glory's bed —
  Their peaceful home!
How bright their virtues shine
With lustre all divine;
What sacred memories twine
  Around their tomb!

How well the heroes sleep!
Ye, who in sadness weep,
  Trust in his might
Who notes the sparrow's fall,
Whose love encircles all,
Whose power the dead shall call
  To life and light!

Through God's preserving care,
His bounties still we share,
  And hither come
To greet our sons who gave
Bold fight our land to save!
Welcome, ye tried and brave,
  Thrice welcome home!

Then followed a poem, composed and delivered by John Sullivan Eaton, Esq., full of glowing patriotism and sweetly flowing rhythm.

CAPT. T. McKAY.

A short and stirring speech from Capt. Brastow, of Somerville, music by the band, and singing by the children, concluded the public exercises of the day.

In the autumn of 1862, the Richardson Light Guard again came forward and offered to enlist for the nine months' service, were accepted and went into camp at Boxford. Samuel F. Littlefield succeeded to the command, in place of H. D. Degen, who had been chosen captain in place of Capt. Locke, but who was subsequently appointed quartermaster of the 50th Mass. Reg't, of which regiment Capt. Locke had been chosen lieutenant-colonel. This company at this time consisted mainly of residents of South Reading, but included members from Lynnfield, Melrose, and some other neighboring towns.

A new company was at this time recruited in Reading for the same nine months' service, the members of which belonged principally in Reading, but included recruits from North Reading, Wilmington, and some other places. This company was commanded by Josiah W. Coburn, of Reading, and also went into camp at Boxford.

Both companies were attached to the 50th Mass. Reg't, and left camp for the seat of war in November, 1862. They were sent to Louisiana and were joined to the expedition under Gen. Banks.

They were stationed for some time at Baton Rouge, were sent to guard exposed positions between Baton Rouge and Port Hudson, and engaged in various expeditions in the vicinity until May, when they were sent to Port Hudson to support the batteries in their assault upon that fortress, and were present at its capture. They returned home in August, 1863.

(See rolls of these companies in this chapter.)

In 1864 the Richardson Light Guard came forward for the third time in support of the government, and enlisted for one hundred days, and were stationed at Baltimore to protect that city from the threatened raids of the enemy.

During the continuance of the war the requisitions, made from time to time by government for additional recruits, were promptly complied with by the three towns, — the numbers furnished often exceeding the requisition.

Efficient military or war committees were appointed in the several towns, with authority, at whatever cost to keep the required quotas of men constantly full. Money for the purpose was appropriated freely and in full measure.

South Reading War Committee: D. B. Wheelock, Horatio Dolliver, John S. Eaton, Edward Mansfield, P. Folsom.

Reading War Committee: H. P. Wakefield, Sylvester Harnden, E. M. Horton, Gardner French, B. M. Boyce, S. E. Parker, and Wm. Proctor.

The families of the absent soldiers were liberally cared for. Soldiers' relief and sanitary associations, male and female, were formed in the several towns, which collected large sums of money and many necessaries, which were sent to the hospitals in various parts of the land. It is proper to mention, in this connection, that Mr. O. S. Moulton and John Sullivan Eaton, Esqs., of South Reading, who were performing service in the War Department at Washington, more or less of the time during the war, were very useful in searching out and aiding our sick and wounded soldiers in the various hospitals at and around Washington, in dispensing the charities which our sanitary society had raised, and in communicating the condition and wishes of the sick and dying heroes to their friends at home. Rev. Michael Burdette, formerly of South Reading, an army and hospital chaplain, performed similar service at New Orleans.

Mr. Eaton, aforesaid, being at Washington, at the return of our army to the capital, *en route* for home, after the surrender of the enemy, enjoyed the high privilege of witnessing the triumphal review of the victorious troops, which he describes as follows: —

MARCHING HOME.

Soft breezes sweep the broad Potomac channel,
    Whose waters seek the bay;
And full, on gilded dome and marble panel,
    Streams the clear sun of May.

Freshly, along the fair Virginian border,
    Swing forest flower and leaf;
Sadly, the ensigns droop in mournful order,
    For loss of nation's chief.

O'er sunlit crest, and o'er each fortress, guarded,
    The starry banner floats;
O'er cannon, ranged along the ramparts, swarded,
    With silent, brazen throats;

No death-notes from those polished portals pealing, —
    Their deadly duty done;
The riven clouds, a peaceful light revealing, —
    And Freedom's battle won.

Through crowded avenue, and laurelled arches, —
 'Neath the imperial dome, —
With steady step, each sun-browned soldier marches,
 A conquering hero, home.

With glad, triumphal strains, and pennons streaming,
 Move on the lines of steel ;
With glittering lances, and with sabres gleaming,
 The serried columns wheel.

On far, historic fields, all battle shrouded,
 Where awful carnage rolled,
Bore they, unawed, to victory unclouded,
 The flag with stainless fold !

On, unshrinking, through plowed and gory trenches
 Swept by the iron hail,
With a courage that falters not, nor blenches,
 Where bravest forms might quail, —

Right onward there, the slippery rampart scaling ;
 Across its bloody bars, —
Their breasts, their shields 'gainst deadly foes assailing,
 They bore the nation's stars !

'T is meet, within the city of the nation,
 Their standards they should plant ;
To soldiers worn and scarred, — a proud ovation, —
 And to their leader, Grant.

Proudly they ride — the heroes of the valley,
 Where crimson torrents ran, —
Who 'neath a peerless banner ride and rally —
 The braves of Sheridan !

Proudly they come, — the men who sang hosannas,
 As swept their columns wide,
With Sherman, marching over green savannas,
 To meet the ocean-tide !

Proudly they march, — the firm Potomac legions,
 With purpose fixed as fates, —
Fresh from Virginia's ransomed regions ;
 From Richmond's open gates.

Grandly they march, to sweet melodious measures,
 Proclaiming war's release ;
These guardians of a nation's priceless treasures,
 These conquerors of peace !

> As on the columns press, with notes victorious,
>   A *shadow* falls on me;
> The gallant heroes dead, *now crowned and glorious,*
>   Above these lines I see!
>
> Above, in air, where streams the sunlight clearest,
>   Those shadowy ranks appear;
> And with them, too, *our latest-lost and dearest,*
>   Bends from the shining sphere!
>
> Weave for the men so deathless deeds achieving,
>   Bright chaplets, ne'er can dim!
> Such laurels now the nation's love is weaving
>   For *these,* for *them,* for *him!*

SOUTH READING.

ALPHABETICAL LIST OF PERSONS WHO WERE IN THE MILITARY OR NAVAL SERVICE, DURING THE WAR OF THE REBELLION, FROM SOUTH READING.

Abbott, John, of South Reading, a widower, enlisted Feb. 14, 1865, in 2d Cavalry.

Abbott, Oramel G., of Reading, enlisted April 19, 1861, in Co. E, 5th Reg., for three months, as a private; re-enlisted May 1, 1861, in Co. D, 50th Reg., as 2d Lieut.

Aborn, George W., of South Reading, son of John and Elizabeth, enlisted April 19, 1861, as Sergt., for three months, in Co. E, 50th Reg.; was born May 24, 1834; married; taken prisoner at the battle of Bull Run, July 21, 1861, and confined at Richmond, Va., New Orleans, La., and Salisbury, N. C.

Aborn, Henry, of South Reading, a grocer, brother of the foregoing, was born in South Reading in 1831; enlisted Sept. 1862, in Co. E, of 50th Reg., for three months, as private; was discharged from the service by reason of disability.

Aborn, Sylvester P., of South Reading, son of Jotham and Rebecca; born April 5, 1840; was a private; enlisted Aug. 12, 1862, in the 2d Cavalry; was killed at the battle of Resaca, Ga.

Aborn, Warren, of South Reading, brother of the above; born Sept. 27, 1841; was a private and corporal; enlisted July 12, 1861, for three years, in the 16th Reg.; died in service, at South Reading, May 25, 1865.

Adams, Charles W., of South Reading, enlisted Aug. 20, 1864, in Co. K, of 4th Heavy Artillery.

OF THE TOWN OF READING.

Adams, Oliver S., of Reading, enlisted April 19, 1861, in the 5th Reg., as private, for three months.

Adams, Samuel H., a moulder, born 1818, at Cape Elizabeth, Me.; enlisted as a private, July 7, in Co. E, 16th Reg., for three years; was married; discharged for inability, Aug. 28, 1861.

Allen, John F., son of John and Eunice; born in Wilmington; was a cordwainer, of South Reading; enlisted July 8, 1861, for three years, in Co. E, 16th Reg.; was private and Corporal; was taken prisoner.

Alpaugh, Wm. E., enlisted in Co. A, of 1st Batt. of Heavy Artillery.

Alexander, John F., of South Reading, son of John and Sarah; born in Boston, March 3, 1835; was a blacksmith; married; enlisted Sept. 2, 1861, for three years, in Co. H, 26th Reg.; a private.

Anderson, Charles E., of South Reading, son of James and Elizabeth F.; born in Boston, Nov. 16, 1838; a cordwainer; served with the Richardson Light Guard in the three months' campaign; taken prisoner May 13, 1863; parolled after seven days; wounded Dec. 13, 1863, near Fredericksburg, in arm and side; discharged Nov. 1865; re-enlisted as Sergeant in Vet. Res. Corps, Co. G, 6th Reg.

Anderson, J. Henry, brother of the preceding; born in Lynnfield, Sept. 24, 1840; enlisted for three months in Co. E, 5th Reg.; a cordwainer; re-enlisted, July 18, 1862, in Co. K, 24th Reg.; was wounded in left hand on Seabrook Island, May 3, 1863.

Andrews, Eldridge F., of South Reading; a mason; enlisted as private for three years, in 35th Reg.

Anderson, Geo. W., of South Reading, son of John and Elizabeth, born at Lynnfield; enlisted for nine months in Co. E, 50th Reg.; private; died of consumption at South Reading, Sept. 16, 1863, of disease contracted in the service.

Arrington, Geo. B., of South Reading, son of William; joined Co. E, of 8th Reg., July, 1864, and served 100 days.

Ash, Robert, of 1st Heavy Artillery.

Atwood, Otis W., of South Reading; born in Lynn; private and cordwainer; enlisted Sept. 2, 1861, for three years, in 1st Co. of Sharpshooters; *deserted* Sept. 17, 1863.

Atwood, Parker S.; joined Co. E, 8th Reg., July, 1864, and served 100 days.

Aborn, Frederic W., of South Reading, son of Frederick and Joanna D.; born in Augusta, Me., in 1830; enlisted Aug. 1864, for one year, in Co. K, Heavy Artillery; private; cordwainer.

Adams, John W., seaman.

Batchelder, Jeremiah S., of South Reading, son of Jeremiah and Caroline; born in North Hampton, N. H., in 1834; private; carpenter; enlisted July, 1861, for three years, in Co. E, 16th Reg.; transferred to the Vet. Res. Corps, Sept. 1863.

Baldwin, Thomas; enlisted in Co. I, 28th Reg., March 21, 1864.

Barnard, Benj. F., of South Reading, son of Jacob and Grace; born in North Reading, 1829; merchant; enlisted and served with the Richardson Light Guard in the three months' campaign; joined Co. K, of 23d Reg., as 2d Lieut., for three years; promoted to 1st Lieut. in May, 1862; discharged in 1863; re-enlisted as Quartermaster in 59th Vet. Reg., and commissioned 1st Lieut., 1863.

Barber, Thomas, of South Reading, son of Abiel and Nancy; born 1832, in Wickford, R. I.; enlisted Sept., in Co. E, 50th Reg., for nine months; re-enlisted March, 1864, for three years in Signal Corps, and discharged Aug. 1865, when his services were no longer required.

Bancroft, Benj. F., of South Reading, son of Nathaniel and Sarah; born in Reading, Jan. 18, 1813; enlisted July, 1861, for three years, in Co. E, of 16th Reg., and was discharged Sept. 1861, for disability.

Batchelder, Geo. W., of Melrose; served in the three months' campaign; enlisted May, 1861, in Co. E, of 5th Reg.

Barker, Samuel S., of Andover, of Co. E, of 5th Reg.; served in the three months' campaign.

Baumister, George.

Beckwith, Robert S., of South Reading, son of George and Margaret S.; born in Edinburgh, Scotland, March 8, 1840; carpenter and cordwainer; enlisted April, 1861, in Co. E, of 5th Reg., and served in the three months' campaign; re-enlisted as Sergeant, for three years, in Co. H, of 20th Reg.; promoted July, 1862, to be 2d Lieut.; was wounded at Fredericksburg, Dec. 13, 1862; died of his wounds, Dec. 31, 1862, and was buried at South Reading; a talented young officer.

Blakney, Tho. B., of South Reading; born in 1838; enlisted July 1861, for three years, in Co. I, 11th Reg.; mustered out in 1864.

Bladden, Thomas, of South Reading; born in Ireland; enlisted in Co. E, of 69th Reg.

Bickford, Charles F., of South Reading, son of Charles and Mary; born in Wakefield, N. H., in 1830; enlisted July, 1861, for three years, in Co. E, 16th Reg.; re-enlisted April, 1864; transferred to Vet. Res. Corps in Sept. 1863.

Bixby, Hiram, of South Reading; served in the three months' campaign in Co. E, 5th Reg.; a private.

Bond, James, Jr., of South Reading; born in England in 1832; enlisted Dec. 1861, for three years, in Co. E, 16th Reg.; wounded at the battle of Gettysburg, July 2, 1863, and died in consequence of the wound, July 26, 1863; a private; farmer; married.

Brooks, Albert F., of South Reading, son of Franklin and Rebecca A.; born in Boston in 1835; married; a clerk; enlisted July, 1861, in Co. D, 13th Reg., for three years; transferred July, 1864, to 39th Reg.

Bruce, Clarence M., of South Reading, son of Nathaniel F.; born in South Reading in 1842; enlisted for three years, in Co. E, 16th Reg.; transferred to 11th Mass. Battalion; re-enlisted, 1864; a private and clerk.

Bruce, Jasper F., of South Reading, son of Nath'l; enlisted in 1862 for 9 months in Co. E, 50th Reg.

Brazell, Patrick, of South Reading; enlisted in 1864 for 3 years in 12th Battery.

Bryant, Wm. C., of South Reading, son of Ebenezer and Hannah; was b. at South Reading 1821; enlisted as an artificer in 1862 in Co. L, 1st Heavy Artillery; mustered out August, 1865, and re-enlisted.

Bryant, Wm. Wallace, of South Reading, son of Wm. C. aforesaid, and Ellen; b. in South Reading, March 12, 1845; a private; was mortally wounded at the battle of the Wilderness, and d. in hospital in Washington city; funeral at South Reading; single.

Brown, Wm. B., of South Reading; m.; b. in South Reading in 1815; enlisted in Co. B, of 24th Reg.

Bridger, Wm. J., of South Reading, son of Wm. and Mary, b. in England in 1832; private; cordwainer; enlisted 1861, in Co. C, 32d Reg., for 3 years; discharged 1862, for disability; re-enlisted in 12th Reg. Vet. Reserve Corps, in 1864; married.

Britton, Wm. B.; enlisted in 1st Battery of Heavy Artillery.

Burditt, James A., of South Reading, son of Aaron (Jr.) and Mary; b. in Providence, R. I., in 1837; enlisted in Co. E, of 5th Reg., for 3 months; re-enlisted for 9 months in the 50th Reg.; served with 100 days' men in Co. E, of 8th Reg.; was Corporal, Sergeant, and 2d Lieut.

Burditt, Geo. A., of South Reading, son of Geo. and Fidelia W.; b. in South Reading in 1844; private and cordwainer; enlisted for 3 months in Co. E, 5th Reg.

Burditt, John W., of South Reading, son of Nathan and Sophronia; b. in South Reading, 1829; enlisted for three years in Co. D, 13th Reg.; single; private; cordwainer.

Burditt, Aaron, of South Reading, son of Aaron and Sally; born in South Reading, 1841; enlisted for three years in Co. E, of 16th Reg.; died of fever in the hospital at Long Island, New York, July 12, 1862; was a private; single; cordwainer.

Burditt, Charles F., of South Reading, son of Aaron and Sally; born in South Reading, January, 1837; private; enlisted July, 1861, for three years in Co. E, 16th Reg.; died April 26, 1864.

Burditt, Geo., of South Reading, son of Michael and Polly; born in South Reading; was a Corporal; enlisted, September, 1861, for three years in 2d Co. (22d Reg.) of Sharpshooters; discharged for disability.

Burnham, James H., of South Reading, son of Joseph and Ruth; born in South Reading; farmer, and married; enlisted December, 1861, in Co. D, 24th Reg., for three years, and served his full time.

Buxton, Elijah; enlisted in Co. D, 1st Batt. of Heavy Artillery.

Butler, Wm., of South Reading; son of Aaron and Sally; born in South Reading, April, 1830; a private; enlisted August, 1864, in Co. K, of 4th Heavy Artillery.

Bryan, Nichols; a seaman, and substitute for John G. Aborn.

Butler, Henry; served with the 100 days' men; son of Aaron and Sally, of South Reading.

Bryant, Eugene C., son of Wm. C. aforesaid, of South Reading; born in South Reading; served with the 100 days' men.

Caldwell, Geo. H., of South Reading, son of Geo. M.; enlisted in 1861, in 11th Reg.

Carey, Daniel, of South Reading, son of Zenas and Susan; born in Bethel, Me., 1830; enlisted in 1865 in Co. C, of Cavalry, and served at the northern frontier; a private.

Carey, Geo. E., of South Reading, son of Gilman; served with the 100 days' men.

Carter, Geo., of South Reading, son of Charles; born in Baltimore, Md.; enlisted for three years in Co. E, 16th Reg.; discharged for disability; re-enlisted in 1862, in Co. E, 50th Reg., for nine months, and served also with the 100 days' men.

Cartwright, Joseph, of South Reading; a tinman; private; enlisted, 1862, in Co. E, of 50th Reg., for nine months.

Cassidy, Joseph H.; a seaman.

Chandler, Geo. H., of South Reading, son of James and Deborah; born in Duxbury in 1819; married; enlisted, 1861, for three years, in Co. I, 11th Reg., September, 1864; re-enlisted, Sept. 1864, in Co. A, 13th Regt., in Veteran Reserve Corps; died Feb. 19, 1865, at Galloupe's Island, in Boston Harbor.

Chandler, Geo. E., of South Reading, son of Geo. H. aforesaid, and Augusta M.; born in Duxbury in 1846; enlisted, 1864, for three years in Signal Corps; discharged, 1865, at New Orleans, La., for disability.

Chandler, Geo. D., of South Reading; drummer; enlisted for three years in 35th Reg.

Chambers, Wm., enlisted in Co. B, 17th Reg.

Chapman, Richard W., of So. Reading, son of Stephen and Hannah W.; born in Marblehead, July, 1834; enlisted July, 1861, for three years, in Co. E, 16th Reg.; was killed in battle May 3, 1863; a private; single.

Cheney, Charles H. R., of So. Reading; boot and shoe dealer; son of Daniel and Mahala; born in Bristol, N. H., Jan. 13, 1827; enlisted in Co. K, 4th Heavy Artillery, for one year; married.

Churchill, Henry D., of So. Reading; single; enlisted Aug. 1864, for one year, in Co. K, of 4th Heavy Artillery; discharged May, 1865, or disability.

Clark, John J., of South Reading; laborer; married; enlisted 1861, for three years, in Co. E, 11th Reg.

Clerk, Geo. W., of So. Reading, son of Samuel B. and Catherine D.; born in Boston, April 5, 1845; private; single; enlisted for three years, in Co. I, 20th Reg., and was discharged for inability; re-enlisted for three years in Co. B, 4th Cavalry.

Clemons, John H., of So. Reading, son of Robert M. and Olive T.; born in Deerfield, N. H., Jan. 1841; private; cordwainer; enlisted 1862, for three years, in Co. E, 16th Reg.; discharged Dec. 1862, for disability, and died at So. Reading, Aug. 4, 1863.

Clemons, Charles E., of So. Reading, brother of the last named; born in Andover; a private, and cordwainer; enlisted 1861, for three years, in 2d Co. of Sharpshooters in 22d Reg.; was discharged for disability.

Clifford, Leonard, of So. Reading; married to Eliza N. Hartshorn; enlisted July, 1861, in Co. E, 16th Reg.; died of disease Aug. 7, 1862.

Clifford, Shurburn, of 19th Reg.; a recruit.

Colby, Geo., of the 100 days' Volunteers.

Coleman, Stephen, of South Reading, of the 64th Col'd Reg. of U. S. Infantry; a representative recruit for Mrs. Betsey (Tho.) Emerson.

Collins, James, of South Reading; born in Ireland in 1833; enlisted July, 1861, in Co. F, 16th Reg., for three years; discharged in 1862 for disability; re-enlisted Dec. 1863, in Co. A, 59th Reg.

Collins, John, of South Reading; born in Ireland; enlisted in Co. K, 22d Reg., for three years; private; single; laborer.

Coney, John S., of North Reading; private; enlisted April, 1861, for three months, in Co. E, 5th Reg.; mustered out July, 1861; re-enlisted as 1st Lieut. in Co. D, of 50th Reg.

Conway, Daniel, of South Reading; born in Ireland; private; single; enlisted for three years in 28th Reg.

Conway, Arthur, of South Reading; born in Ireland; married; enlisted in Co. I, 16th Reg., for three years; was killed in battle.

Cook, Geo. F., of South Reading; single; drummer; born in 1846; enlisted in Co. G, 13th Reg., for three years; discharged in 1862 for disability.

Cook, Jona. J., of Reading; a private; enlisted for three months, in Co. E, of 5th Reg.

Coombs, Tho. W., of South Reading; enlisted as a Sergeant in 1861, in Co. F, 16th Reg.; born in England; cordwainer; was wounded in a skirmish at Woodlawn, near Fair Oaks, June 18, 1862; was hit three times; discharged for disability Feb. 1863; re-enlisted Dec. 1863, in Co. A, 59th Reg.

Coon, Wm. L., of South Reading, son of John and Phillippa; born in Charlestown, Dec. 25, 1842; a mechanic; single; enlisted 1862, in Co. E, 50th Reg., for nine months; served also with the 100 days' Volunteers.

Cooper, R. L., of South Reading; a private; married; enlisted 1862, in Co. E, 50th Reg., for nine months.

Corey, Henry H., of South Reading; private of 2d Cavalry.

Cowdrey, John, of South Reading, son of John and Sarah Cowdrey, of Stoneham; born in 1822; a cordwainer; enlisted 1861, in Co. E, 16th Reg., for three years, as Sergeant; was killed in battle, Aug. 29, 1862, at Kettle Run, near Bull Run, Va.

Cowdrey, Nathaniel, of South Reading, brother of last mentioned; a musician; married; enlisted in 1861, in 19th Reg., for three years; was discharged in 1864 for disability; re-enlisted in 4th Mass. Battery.

Cowdrey, Wm. F., of Stoneham; private; married; enlisted in 1864, in Co. K, 4th Heavy Artillery.

Craskie, Frank, of South Reading, of 4th Colored U. S. Infantry; representative recruit for Daniel Allen, of South Reading.
Currier, Horace P., of South Reading, son of John and Hannah; born at Lyman, Me., 1831; a grocer; married; enlisted 1861, as wagoner in Co. D, 13th Reg., for three years.
Danforth, Albert H., of South Reading, son of Stearns and Sophronia G.; born in Billerica, Sept. 17, 1835; private; cordwainer; enlisted Aug. 1864, for one year in Co. K, 4th Heavy Artillery; discharged June, 1865, for disability.
Danforth, Alfred W., of South Reading, a clerk; enlisted Sept. 1862, for nine months, in Co. E, 50th Reg.; served also with the one hundred days' volunteers in 1864.
Danforth, Robt. K., of South Reading, son of Stearns and Sophronia; born in Charlestown, 1833; enlisted 1864 for one year in Co. C, 1st Battery of Heavy Artillery; served also with the one hundred days' volunteers; was Corporal; served previously in 1st Massachusetts Infantry, from Woburn.
Davis, Charles Horton, of South Reading, son of Charles; enlisted 1862, for nine months, in Co. E, 50th Reg.; re-enlisted 1864, for one year, in Co. K, 4th Heavy Artillery; a carpenter; born in South Reading in 1827; was a Corporal, and married.
Davis, John, of South Reading, son of John and Margaret; born in Gloucester in 1829; enlisted 1864 in Co. K, 4th Heavy Artillery, for one year; was a Corporal, and married.
Day, Benj. I., of South Reading; served with the one hundred days' men.
Day, Joseph L., of South Reading; served with the one hundred days' men.
Day, John, of South Reading; born at Wilmington; a stable keeper; enlisted 1861, in Co. E, 16th Reg.; Sergeant; married; discharged 1862, for disability.
Day, Jerome, of South Reading, son of Benj. B. and Frances; born in Melrose; of 24th Reg., for three years.
Deadman, Wm. D., of South Reading; son of William, Jr., and Ruth; born in South Reading, 1843; private and butcher; enlisted 1862, in Co. E, of 50th Reg., for nine months; single; served also with the one hundred days' men in 1864.
Dearborn, Stanley B., of South Reading, son of Nathl. S. and Mary; born in Boston in 1845; private; single; enlisted 1863, in Co. L, 1st Heavy Artillery; wounded in the arm near Poplar Church, Va.
Dearing, John, of 9th Reg.
Dean, Martin P., of South Reading, of 4th Heavy Artillery.

Degen, H. D., of South Reading; son of Rev. Henry V. and Eliza J., born in New York city in 1832; a merchant; enlisted in 1862; for nine months in Co. E of 50th Reg.; was 1st Lieut. and Quartermaster; had been Capt. of the Richardson Light Guard.

Dickey, Neal G., of South Reading; enlisted in 39th Reg., for three years.

Dickson, A. L.

Dix, Joseph O, of South Reading; son of Benjamin and Susan; born in Salem 1809; enlisted for three months in Co. E, 5th Reg.; re-enlisted 1862, in Co. E, 50th Reg., for nine months, for Melrose; a private and carpenter; widower.

Dolan, Thomas, of South Reading; enlisted 1864, in 2d Cavalry.

Dow, Andrew, Jr., of Stoneham; son of David; born in Warren, N. H., 1829; married; a private; enlisted 1864, for one year, in Co. K, 4th Heavy Artillery.

Dow, Charles M., of South Reading, son of Milo; single; enlisted 1861, for three years, in Co. B, of 23d Reg.; died at Newburn, N. C., June 4, 1863.

Doyle, Cornelius, of South Reading; a laborer; born in Ireland; enlisted for three years in 35th Reg.

Draper, James D., of South Reading, son of Rufus F. and Polly; born Oct. 4, 1827 or 1828; cordwainer and married; served as 2d Lieut. in Co. E, of 5th Reg., in three months' campaign; enlisted 1862, for nine months, in Co. E, of 50th Reg., as 2d Lieut.; was wounded at siege of Port Hudson; re-enlisted in 1st Battalion of Heavy Artillery as Corp.

Draper, Rufus F., of South Reading; son of Rufus F. and Mary; born in South Reading in 1838; enlisted 1862, in Co. E, of 50th Regt., for nine months; was a Corporal; served also with one hundred days' men.

Drake, Alvin, Jr., of South Reading, son of Alvin; born in South Bosston, in 1832; cordwainer; drummer; enlisted 1861, for three months, in Co. E, of 50th Regiment; re-enlisted Dec. 1861, in 19th Regiment, for three years; discharged in April, 1864, for disability; re-enlisted 1864, in U. S. Signal Corps.

Duffin, Thomas, of South Reading; born in Ireland in 1841; enlisted 1862, for three years, in Co. H, of 20th Reg.; was discharged at Stevensburg, Va., March 28, 1864, by reason of re-enlistment; private; shoemaker; single.

Dunn, Edward D., of South Reading; son of Henry and Aurelia; born in South Reading in 1848; private; single; teamster; enlisted in

1865, in 19th Reg.; died at Galloupe's Island, Boston Harbor, Feb. 9, 1865.

Dunn, Horace H., of South Reading, brother of the last named, born at South Reading 1845; single; clerk; enlisted 1863 in 1st Battalion Heavy Artillery; transferred to the Navy in Sept. 1863; deserted.

Dyer, Wm. P., married; enlisted for three years (in 1863) in Co. B, 1st Battalion Heavy Artillery.

Eager, Alexander, of South Reading, son of James and Julia; born in Ireland; a seaman.

Eaton, Abijah A., of Reading; a private; enlisted 1861 for three months, in Co. E, 5th Reg.

Eaton, John Henry, of South Reading; son of Lt. John and Mary W.; born in South Reading; single; expressman; enlisted 1861 in Co. E, 16th Reg., for three years, and served his three years.

Eaton, Everett W., of South Reading, son of Lilley and Eliza N. Eaton; born in South Reading July 9, 1835; single; served as commissary clerk under Col. Beckwith, Commissary of the Army of the Potomac, under Capt. T. E. Berrier, Commissary of Subsistence; went with him to Centreville and Manassas; was at Fort Runyon three or four months; was at Alexandria when that place was headquarters of the Reserve Army Corps under Gen. Sturgis two months; went with Sturgis to the field, and was in Pope's retreat; then served with Capt. Knowles, Commissary Subsistence, in Maryland campaign, under Gen. Humphrey; accompanied the army on the march to the Rappahannock; was at the battle of Antietam; was taken sick and came home.

Eaton, John, of South Reading, son of Joseph and Sarah; born in South Reading, in 1813; married; expressman; enlisted 1861, as 2d Lieut. in Co. E, 16th Reg.; resigned and discharged 1862.

Eaton, John Smith, of South Reading, son of Zenas and Lois S.; born in South Reading, Oct. 30, 1827; enlisted for nine months in Co. E, 50th Reg., as Corporal; a cordwainer, and married.

Eaton, Chester Williams, of South Reading, son of Lilley and Eliza N., born in South Reading, Jan. 13, 1839; single; student at law; enlisted in 1862 for nine months in Co. E, 50th Reg.; served as Quartermaster's clerk; was at the taking of Port Hudson.

Eaton, Edward, of South Reading; son of Noah and Hannah W.; born in Cambridgeport in 1844; single; enlisted 1862, in Co. L, 1st Heavy Artillery; served as musician.

Eaton, Noah Martin, of South Reading; brother of the last named;

born in South Reading in 1832 ; married ; enlisted 1864, for one year, in Co. K, 4th Heavy Artillery.

Eaton, Victor, of South Reading, brother of the last named ; born in Cambridgeport in 1840; single ; enlisted 1862 for three years in Co. C, 24th Regiment, as a private ; re-enlisted 1864 ; wounded in the hand near Richmond, Oct. 14, 1864.

Eaton, David, of South Reading; brother of the last named ; served with the 100 days' men.

Eaton, Walter Sullivan, of South Reading, son of John Sullivan and Harriet W. ; born in South Reading, Aug 11, 1847 ; private and clerk ; single ; was detailed as clerk at Gen. Canby's head-quarters at New Orleans, La., Jan. 1865 ; was present at the taking of Mobile, Ala., April 11, 1865 ; now in Treasury Department, Washington, D. C.

Eaton, Jacob H., of South Reading, son of Zenas and Lois S.; born in South Reading, 1834 ; private ; married ; was of the 4th Cavalry.

Edmands, Consider, of South Reading, son of Rodney and Mary W. ; enlisted 1861, in Co. I, of 11th Reg., for three years ; was killed Aug. 29, 1862, near Bull Run ; was born in Saugus 1843.

Edmands, Rodney, of South Reading, son of Wm. and Ruth ; born in Chelsea ; enlisted 1861, for three years, in Co. I, of 11th Reg., and discharged in 1863, for disability ; re-enlisted in 1864, in Co. E, of 59th Reg.

Edwards, John, of South Reading ; single ; enlisted for three years in 11th Reg.

Ellis, Geo. W., of Co. G, 35th Reg. ; was killed Sept. 7, 1863.

Emerson, Charles Stillman, of South Reading; son of Abraham and Mary B. ; born in South Reading, Aug. 12, 1829 ; enlisted 1862, for nine months, in Co. E, 50th Reg. ; married about the time of enlistment, to Hannah Emmons.

Emerson, John Henry, of South Reading, son of John nd Lucretia ; born in South Reading, July, 1826 ; private and married ; enlisted in 1864, in Co. K, of 4th Heavy Artillery.

Emerson, Thomas Albert, of South Reading, son of Thomas, Jr., and Emily M. ; born in South Reading, Dec. 27, 1840 ; a graduate of Yale College ; enlisted 1863, as A. A. Paymaster, with rank of Lieut., on board U. S. brig "Perry" ; service at Port Royal, S. C., six months ; on blockade off Charleston, S. C., one month ; at Fernandina, Fla., sixteen months.

Estes, O'Neal J., of South Reading, son of Enoch and Betsey ; born in Bethel, Me., in 1836 ; private and single ; enlisted 1862, for nine months, in Co. E, 50th Reg.; died of fever at Baton Rouge, La., May 12, 1863.

Eustis, Henry W., of South Reading; son of James and Susan J.; born in South Reading, Feb. 27, 1835; married; a private; enlisted for three months in 1861, in Co. E, 5th Reg.; re-enlisted in 1864, for three years, in U. S. Signal Corps.

Eustis, Joseph S., of South Reading, brother of the last named; born in South Reading, Aug. 26, 1833; single; a private; enlisted for three months in 1861, in Co. E, 5th Reg., and was wounded at the battle of Bull Run; re-enlisted 1862, for nine months, in Co. E, 50th Reg.

Evans, Tho. Asaph, of South Reading, son of Asaph and Lucinda; born in South Reading in 1831; private; teamster; single; enlisted for three years in Co. E, 16th Reg.

Evans, Wm. O., of South Reading, brother of the last named; born in South Reading in 1834; private; married; enlisted for one year, in 5th Battery.

Evans, Charles A., of South Reading, brother of the last named; born in South Reading in 1838; private; mason; married; enlisted 1862, three years, in Co. K, of 23d Reg.

Evans, Henry H., of South Reading, brother of the last named; born in South Reading in 1841; drafted; married; was in Co. E, of 16th Reg.; transferred in 1864 to the 11th Mass. Battalion.

Fairbanks, Zephaniah F., of South Reading, son of Lewis and Martha; born in Chelsea in 1838; a saloon keeper; married; enlisted in 1861, for three years, in Co. G, 24th Reg.; acted as cook.

Fairbanks, James M., of South Reading, brother of the last named; born in South Reading in 1840; painter; private; enlisted in 1861 in Co. E, of 5th Reg., for three months; re-enlisted 1862, for three years, in Co. G, 24th Reg.; re-enlisted in 1864, and transferred to Co. D.

Fay, Patrick, of South Reading, son of Patrick and Margaret; born in Ireland in 1826; private and Sergeant; enlisted in 1861, for three years, in Co. I, of 16th Reg.; was transferred in 1864 to 11th Mass. Battalion; married.

Felton, A. P., of South Reading; married; enlisted for three years in Co. B, 22d Reg.

Flanders, Alexander, of South Reading, son of Levi; born in South Reading; enlisted in 1863 as a private in 1st Heavy Artillery; severely wounded at South Side Railroad, Va., at the battle of Poplar Spring Church, Oct. 2, 1864; was discharged for disability; re-enlisted in the Regular Army in 1865.

Fletcher, Charles N., of Reading; enlisted, 1861, for three months, in Co. E, 5th Regt.

Fogg, Lewis, of South Reading, son of Ransom and Hannah; born in South Braintree in 1839; enlisted, 1865, in Frontier Cavalry.

Folsom, Edward Channing, of South Reading, son of Peter and Emily; born in Grey, Me., 1845; a private and single; enlisted, 1864, for three years, in Signal Corps; discharged, 1865, for disability; now a physician in Washington, D. C.

Forbes, Patrick, of South Reading, son of Michael; born in Ireland, 1845; a private; enlisted, 1864, for one year, in 3d Heavy Artillery.

Forrest, John, of South Reading; served with the 100 days' men.

Foster, Aaron Augustus, of South Reading, son of Aaron and Abigail; born at South Reading, May 23, 1833; a printer; enlisted as a private, 1863, for three years, in Co. C, 2d Heavy Artillery; married.

Foster, Clarence P., of South Reading, half-brother of the last named; served with the 100 days' men.

Foster Davis, of South Reading, son of Russell and Sophia; born in South Reading; enlisted, 1861, in Co. E, 5th Reg., for three months; re-enlisted, 1861, for three years, in 24th Reg.; was 2d Lieut. in 1863; 1st Lieut. in 1864; Captain and Major.

Fowle, Clifford B., of South Reading; married; a private; enlisted, 1861, for three years, in Co. E, 16th Reg.; died July 3, 1864.

Freeman, Barnard, of South Reading; married; enlisted in 24th Reg.; was wounded by the accidental discharge of gun, and transferred to Vet. Res. Corps.

Fifield, Charles A., of South Reading, son of Abraham and Betsey; born in Lowell, 1834; single; a moulder; enlisted, 1864, for one year, in Co. K, of 4th Heavy Artillery.

Fisk, Joseph A., of South Reading; enlisted 1862, for nine months, in Co. E, 50th Reg.; discharged at New Orleans, 1863, for disability.

Foster, Franklin H., son of Aaron; enlisted in 9th N. H. Reg.; died in Salisbury prison Dec. 14, 1864.

Garland, Wingate, of South Reading; a private in 4th Cavalry; was taken prisoner and sent to Andersonville, where he died, Feb. 1865.

Gihon, Edward, of South Reading, son of John; born in Ireland in 1835; a cordwainer, and married; enlisted in 1861, for three years, in Co. D, 28th Reg.; re-enlisted.

Gilman, Geo. K., of South Reading, son of Joseph and Mary; born in

Tamworth, N. H., in 1835 ; was Corporal ; enlisted 1862, for nine months, in Co. E, 50th Reg. ; promoted to Sergeant.

Greggs, James H., of Reading ; enlisted for three months, in 1861, in Co. E, 5th Reg. ; was wounded and taken prisoner at the battle of Bull Run, July 21, 1861.

Green, Geo. Henry, of South Reading, son of Reuben and Lydia ; born in Malden in 1836 ; enlisted as corporal in Co. E, 5th Reg., for three months ; re-enlisted for nine months in Co. E, of 50th Reg. ; died at sea, while *en route* for New Orleans.

Green, Edward Isaac, of South Reading, son of Isaac ; born in South Reading ; enlisted in 2d Co., 22d Reg., Sharpshooters, fo three years.

Green, Patrick, of South Reading ; enlisted in 1864, for one year, in 3d Heavy Artillery.

Godfrey, Warren H., of South Reading, son of Enos and Leliance ; born in Brewster in 1833 ; enlisted 1864, in Co. K, 4th Heavy Artillery, for one year ; private ; married.

Goodwin, Andrew, of South Reading ; enlisted 1864, for one year, in Co. K, 4th Heavy Artillery ; married, and a private.

Hart, J. Frank, of South Reading, son of Charles and Martha S. ; born in South Reading in 1844 ; enlisted 1861, for three months, in Co. E, 5th Reg. ; re-enlisted in 1st Reg. of Heavy Artillery.

Hart, Howard C., of South Reading, son of Charles and Martha S. ; born in South Reading in 1841 ; enlisted in 1861, for three years, in Co. E, 16th Reg. ; transferred in 1864 to 11th Battalion ; re-enlisted 1865, in Co. D, Frontier Cavalry.

Hart, David A., of South Reading, son of Charles and Martha S. ; born in South Reading in 1846 ; enlisted in 1861, for three years, in the 24th Reg. ; transferred in 1863 to Vet. Res. Corps ; promoted to corporal ; re-enlisted in 1864.

Hart, Charles, of South Reading, son of Joseph and Betsey ; born in Lynnfield in 1807 ; father of the foregoing ; enlisted in Co. L, of 1st Heavy Artillery ; teamster.

Hartshorn, Oliver S., of South Reading, son of Thomas S. ; was of 8th Reg. ; died June 21, 1865, of disease contracted in the service.

Hart, John F., of South Reading ; son of Harfield ; born in South Reading ; enlisted in 1864, and served with the 100 days' volunteers.

Hartwell, Abner A., of Reading ; enlisted 1861, in Co. E, of 5th Reg., for three months.

Hartshorn Charles F., of South Reading, son of James and Mary ; born in South Reading in 1835; enlisted 1862, for nine months, in Co. E, 50th Reg.; was Corporal and Sergeant.

Hartshorn, Jeremiah W., of South Reading, son of Jeremiah and Caroline; born in South Reading July 4, 1832; enlisted in 1864, for three years, in Signal Corps.

Harnden, James, of South Reading, son of Samuel and Nancy; born in 1835; enlisted 1864, for one year, in Co. K, 4th Heavy Artillery.

Harmers, ——.

Harrington, Charles T., of South Reading, son of Peter and Caroline; born in Watertown in 1838; enlisted 1861, for three months, in Co. E, of 5th Reg.; re-enlisted for nine months, in 1862, in Co. E, of 50th Reg.

Hall, Frank, of South Reading, son of Prentice and Clarissa; born in South Reading; enlisted for three years in Co. H, 24th Reg., and re-enlisted; was a drummer.

Hangle, William, of South Reading; born in Ireland; enlisted 1861, for three years, in Co. D, 9th Reg.

Haggerty, Timo., of South Reading, son of Daniel; enlisted in Co. A, 35th Reg., for three years.

Hamilton, Robert, of South Reading, son of Hans and Mary; born in Brookfield, N. S., in 1840; enlisted in 1862, for nine months, in Co. E, 50th Reg.; died at South Reading, Sept. 27, 1864, of disease contracted in the service.

Hamblin, Wm. A., of South Reading; born in Boston; enlisted 1864, in Co. K, 4th Heavy Artillery, for one year.

Haskell, Henry L., of South Reading, son of George and Lucy E.; born in Gloucester in 1837; enlisted 1861, for three years, in Co. K, 23d Reg.

Hawkes, Francis, of South Reading, son of Davis W. and Lucretia; born in South Reading in 1836; enlisted in 1861, in 2d Co. of 22d Reg. of Sharpshooters, for three years.

Hawkes, John, of South Reading, son of Adam and Patty; born in South Reading in 1828; enlisted in 1862, in Co. E, 50th Reg., for nine months; re-enlisted in 1864, for one year, in Co. K, of Heavy Artillery.

Hawkes, Winfield S., of South Reading, son of Benj.; served with the 100 days' men in 1864.

Hayden, Frank W., of South Reading, son of Wm. H. and Elizabeth J.; born in Hallowell, Me., in 1835; enlisted in 1861, for three months, in Co. E, 5th Reg.; re-enlisted in Co. E, 5th Reg., for three years; promoted to 2d Lieut. in 1862; taken prisoner at Kelley's Ford, Va., in 1863, being injured by a horse falling on him; was kept a prisoner seven weeks; was promoted to 1st Lieut. and Quartermaster; served in Frontier Cavalry.

Hayden, Wm. H., Jr., of South Reading, son of Wm. H. and Elizabeth J.; born in Hallowell, Me., in 1827; enlisted for three months in Co. E, 5th Reg., in 1861; re-enlisted in 1862, as Sergeant, in Co. B, 1st Batt. of Heavy Artillery; appointed 2d Lieut. in 1863, in Co. A.

Hayward, Alex. N., of Reading; enlisted for three months in Co. E, 5th Reg.

Heath, Micah, of South Reading, son of Michael and Mary S.; born in Meredith, N. H., 1817; enlisted for three years, in 1861, in Co. E, 16th Reg.; transferred in 1864 to 11th Mass. Batt.

Hebbetts, James, of South Reading; born in Ireland; enlisted 1861, for three years, in Co. D, 28th Reg.; wounded Sept. 1, 1862, in second Bull Run battle, and died on Sept. 16, 1862, in the hospital at Washington, D. C.

Hilborn, Henry E., of South Reading; born at Minot, Me.; enlisted 1861, in Co. E, 16th Reg.; was a corporal; discharged for disability in 1863.

Hodgkins, Samuel P., of South Reading; served with the 100 days' men.

Holmes, George E., of South Reading, son of Elizabeth; enlisted in 1864, in 4th Cavalry.

Hosmer, Oliver S., of Woburn; enlisted 1861, for three months, in the 5th Reg.

Howe, Wm. C., of South Reading, son of Joseph W.; born in South Reading; enlisted for three years, in 1861, in 10th Reg.; re-enlisted, in 1863, in 4th Mass. Cavalry; musician.

Howe, Nathaniel H., of Charlestown; enlisted 1863, in Co. L, 1st Heavy Artillery.

Howe, Wm. F., of South Reading; enlisted 1863, in 31st Reg.

Hood, Tho. R. P., of South Reading, son of Asa and Martha; born in Salem, 1825; enlisted 1864, in Co. G, 59th Reg.

Hoyt, Henry D., of South Reading; born in Shorington, N. H.; enlisted in 1861, for three months, in Co. E, 5th Reg.; re-enlisted in 1861, for three years, in 22d Reg.

Hurd, Joseph L., of South Reading; enlisted in 16th Reg., and served also with 100 days' men.

Hurley, Timothy, of South Reading, son of Daniel and Ann; born in

Ireland in 1829; enlisted for three years, in Co. I, 1st Reg.; became a Corporal.

Hunt, George, of Stoneham; enlisted 1864, for one year, in Co. K, 4th Heavy Artillery.

Hunt, Henry, of Stoneham; enlisted 1864, for one year, in Co. K, 4th Heavy Artillery.

Harnden, James W., of South Reading; served with 100 days' men.

Jackson, George H., of Medford; enlisted in 1864, for one year, in Co. K, 4th Heavy Artillery.

Jameson, Edward T., of South Reading; born in Boston; enlisted for three years, in Co. D, 4th Battery.

Jennison, Williston, of South Reading; enlisted for three years in 35th Reg.

Johnson, Isaac, of South Reading; colored; was drafted.

Johnson, John, of South Reading, of 2d Cavalry.

Jones, Alden N., of South Reading; enlisted in 1861 in Co. B, 12th Reg., for three years; was born at Chelsea, Vt., 1835.

Jones, Geo. S., of South Reading; enlisted for three years in 35th Reg.

Jones, Nathan G., of South Reading, of 100 days' men.

Kaka, John, a recruit.

Kelley, Patrick, of South Reading; enlisted for one year in Co. K, 4th Heavy Artillery.

Kelley, Joseph, of South Reading; born in England; enlisted in 1861, for three years, in Co. A, 28th Reg.; married; died Dec. 17, 1861, at Camp Cameron, Cambridge, Mass., of typhoid fever.

Kenney, Thomas J., of South Reading, of Co. I, 11th Reg.; transferred to Veteran Reserve Corps.

Kennedy, Patrick, of South Reading; enlisted for three years in 35th Reg.

Kidder, George H., of South Reading; enlisted for three months, in 1861, in Co. E, 5th Reg.; born in South Boston in 1837; son of Daniel and Sarah; re-enlisted in 1861, for three years, in Co. E, 1st Mass. Cavalry.

Kingman, Wm. W., of South Reading, son of Samuel and Sarah R., born at South Reading in 1832; enlisted 1862, for nine months, in Co. E, 50th Reg.; afterwards served with 100 days' men.

Kinnerson, J. Henry, of South Reading; a seaman.

Kirley, Thomas, of South Reading; born in Ireland in 1831; son of Patrick and Deborah; enlisted in the naval service in 1864; fireman; was on board the U. S. Steamer "Tristram Shandy"; was on the blockading service off Wilmington, N. C.; was in the first and second engagements at Fort Fisher, N. C.

Knight, Jason H., of South Reading, son of Otis and Sally; born in Charlestown, 1838; enlisted for three months in Co. E, 5th Reg.; was a Sergeant; re-enlisted 1862, for nine months, in Co. E, 50th Reg.; afterwards served with 100 days' men as Lieutenant.

Knight, Henry C., of South Reading, son of Henry and Ruhamah; born in South Reading, 1829; enlisted in 1862, for nine months, in Co. E, 50th Reg.

Lane, John, of South Reading; seaman; enlisted 1862, on board the "Sebago."

Lane, Loammi C., of South Reading, son of Stephen and Ann; born in Gloucester in 1832; enlisted for one year in Co. K, 4th Heavy Artillery.

Lane, William, of South Reading, brother of last mentioned; born in Gloucester in 1834; enlisted in 1861, for three years, in Co. I, 11th Reg.; transferred in 1863 to Veteran Reserve Corps.

Lang, James, of South Reading, son of Wm. and Ellen; born in Ireland; enlisted in 1862 for three years, in 33d Reg.

Lawrence, Charles A., of South Reading, son of Daniel and Mary B.; born in Concord; enlisted for three years in Co. G, of 24th Reg.; died at Saxonville, Mass., Oct. 20, 1862, of disease contracted in the service.

Lawrence, Geo. B., of South Reading, son of Daniel and Mary B.; born in Concord; enlisted for three years in Co. G, of 24th Reg.

Lawrence, Edward R., of South Reading, son of Daniel and Mary B.; born in Concord in 1841; enlisted 1861, for three years, in Co. H, 25th Reg.

Leathers, Albert N., of South Reading; enlisted 1864, for one year, in Co. K, 4th Heavy Artillery.

Lee, John, of South Reading, son of John and Sally; born in Salem in 1813; enlisted in 1861, for three years, in the 24th Reg.

Lee, John F., of South Reading, son of Charles E. and Rhoda B. (and great-grandson of Gen. Benj. Brown, of Revolutionary memory); born in South Reading in 1843; enlisted in 1861, in Co. E, 16th Reg.; discharged 1863, for disability, and died at South Reading of disease contracted in the service.

Lewis, John; seaman; enlisted 1864.

Littlefield, Samuel F., of South Reading, son of Nath'l and Dorcas; born in Wells, Me., in 1826; enlisted for nine months, in Co. E,

50th Reg.; was Captain; re-commissioned as Captain of the 100 days' men.

Locke, John W., of South Reading, son of Josiah and Elizabeth W.; born at Ashburnham, 1831; enlisted 1861, for three months, as Captain of Co. E, 5th Reg.; commissioned in 1862, as Lieutenant-Colonel of 50th Reg., and served nine months.

Locke, Geo. L., of South Reading; enlisted 1861, for three years, Co. E, 16th Reg.; killed in battle near Bull Run, Va., August 29, 1862.

Long, Robert, of South Reading, of the 6th Colored Infantry; representative recruit for Thomas Emerson.

Lord, Byron, of South Reading, son of James and Marcia A.; born in South Reading in 1840; enlisted 1861, for three months, in Co. E, 5th Reg.

Lord, Geo. H., of South Reading, brother of last named; enlisted 1861, for three months, in Co. E, 5th Reg.

Lufkin, Stephen, of South Reading, son of Humphrey and Lois; born in Chester, N. H., in 1814; enlisted in 1862, for three years, in Co. G, 13th Reg., and discharged for inability in 1863.

Lufkin, Stephen W., of South Reading, son of the last named; born in Woburn in 1844; enlisted in 1862, in Co. G, of 13th Reg., for three years; was wounded severely at Gettysburg, July 1, 1862, and was taken prisoner; was re-taken the next day by Union troops, and discharged on account of the wound.

Lufkin, Frederick H., of South Reading, brother of the last named; born in South Reading in 1848; mother's name, Sarah G. W.; enlisted 1865, for one year, in Capt. Porter's Co., in 62d Reg.; was a Corporal; served also with 100 days' men.

Lyons, John W., of South Reading, son of William and Mary P.; born in Ireland in 1845; enlisted in 3d Heavy Artillery, Co. M, for one year.

Madden, Jerry, of South Reading, son of Cornelius and Maria; born in Ireland, 1822; enlisted 1862, for nine months, in Co. G, 48th Reg.

Madden, John W., of South Reading; enlisted in 1864, for one year, in 3d Heavy Artillery.

Magee, Edward, of South Reading; a seaman.

Mansfield, Wm. J., of South Reading, son of Wm. and Phebe; born in South Reading in 1845; enlisted in 1863, in Co. L, 1st Heavy Artillery.

Mansfield, James F., of South Reading, son of James J. and Martha

B.; born in South Reading in 1836; enlisted in 1861, for three years, in Co. E, 16th Reg., as Sergeant; promoted to 1st Lieut. in 1864; transferred the same year to the 11th Reg.; promoted to Captain, October, 1864, and afterwards to Major and Lieutenant-Colonel.

Mansfield, Joseph H., of South Reading, brother of the last named; born at South Reading, 1841; enlisted in 1861, in Co. E, of 16th Reg., for three years; died of fever in hospital, New York, Sept. 14, 1862.

Mansfield, Edward G., of South Reading, son of Edward, served with the 100 days' men.

Martin, John, of South Reading, served with the 100 days' men.

Marshall, Cyrus E., of South Reading, served with the 100 days' men.

Moulton, Erastus, of South Reading, served with the 100 days' men.

Mayo, Nath'l C., of South Reading, son of Josiah and Ruth; born in Eastham, 1831; enlisted in 1864, in Co. K, 4th Heavy Artillery, for one year.

McCabe, James M., of South Reading, son of Bridget; born in Boston; enlisted in 1861, for three years, in Co. K, 22d Reg.

McCarty, Timothy, of South Reading, of 6th Battalion.

McCleary, John E., of South Reading; born in Prince Edward Island; enlisted, 1862, for three years, in Co. H, 27th Reg.; re-enlisted in 1864; promoted to Sergeant in 1864; was principal musician of regiment in October, 1864; was wounded and taken prisoner at battle of Kingston, N. C., March 8, 1865; paroled March 26; promoted to 1st Lieut., May 15, 1865.

McDonald, George, of South Reading, of 38th Reg., for three years.

McGee, Edward, of South Reading, enlisted 1861, for three months, in Co. E, 5th Reg.; re-enlisted 1864, for three years, in Co. C, 24th Reg.

McKay, Tho. M., of South Reading, son of John and Elizabeth M.; born at Boston, Dec. 5, 1836; enlisted, 1861, for three months, in Co. E, 5th Reg.; re-enlisted for three years in Co. G, 20th Reg.; was Sergeant; was promoted Sept. 5, 1862; to be 2d Lieut., Dec. 18, 1862; to be Captain, July, 1863; was killed by a shot from a conscript, Oct. 5, 1863, at Culpepper, Va.

McKay, Gordon, from Melrose; served in the three months' campaign.

McKensie, John, from Boston; served in the three months' campaign.

McKensie, A., of South Reading, served in the Frontier Cavalry.

McPherson, David, of South Reading, son of Edward ; born in Scotland in 1840 ; was cook ; enlisted 1861, for three years, in Co. E, 24th Reg. ; re-enlisted in 1864 for some other town.

McLaughlin, Thos., of 19th Reg.

McQueeny, Wm., from Boston ; enlisted 1864, for one year, in Co. K, 4th Heavy Artillery.

McQuillan, Joseph, from Charlestown ; of Co. L, 1st Heavy Artillery ; killed June 16, 1864, near Petersburg, Va.

Miller, Charles, of South Reading ; enlisted 1862, for nine months, in Co. E, 50th Reg.

Moore, John L., Jr., of South Reading, son of John L. and Marie ; enlisted 1862, in Co. E, 50th Reg., for nine months ; died at Baton Rouge, La., April 6, 1863.

Morrill, James M., of South Reading, son of Manning and Merriam ; born in Danville, Me., 1837 ; a carpenter ; enlisted 1861, for three months, in Co. E, 5th Reg. ; re-enlisted in 1862, for nine months, as Corporal in Co. E, 50th Reg. ; served as Orderly Sergeant with 100 days' men.

Morton, Joseph, of South Reading, son of Joseph B. and Patience ; born in South Paris, Me., 1832 ; enlisted 1862, for nine months, in 50th Reg. (in the band) ; enlisted in 1864, for one year, in Co. K, 4th Heavy Artillery.

Moses, John F., of South Reading, son of Nath'l and Elizabeth ; born at South Reading, 1834 ; enlisted in 1862, for nine months in Co. E, 50th Reg. ; died at Baton Rouge, La., July 4, 1863.

Moses, George, of South Reading, brother of the last named ; born at South Reading, 1841 ; enlisted 1861, for three months, in Co. E, 5th Reg. ; re-enlisted in 1862 for nine months, in Co. E, 50th Reg., and in 1864, for three years, in Signal Corps.

Murkland, Robert L , of South Reading, son of John and Jane ; born at Lowell in 1837 ; enlisted in 1862, for nine months, in Co. E, 50th Reg.

Murray, Jeremiah, of South Reading ; seaman.

Newhall, Elbridge G., of South Reading, son of Benj. S. and Hannah S. ; enlisted for three years in Co. E, 16th Reg. ; discharged for inability ; born in South Danvers.

Newhall, David, of South Reading, brother of the last named ; born at South Danvers, 1841 ; enlisted in 1862, in Co. E, 50th Reg., for nine months ; served also with 100 days' men as Corporal.

Newhall, Wm., of South Reading ; son of James I. and Sally N Pease ; born in Lynnfield, 1809 (name had been altered from *Pease* to

Newhall); enlisted 1861, for three years, in Co. K, 23d Reg.; was wagoner and ambulance driver; discharged for inability.

Newman, J. Frank, of South Reading, son of John H.; enlisted 1862, for nine months, in Co. E, 50th Reg.

Nichols, Edmund, of South Reading; enlisted 1864, in 4th Cavalry.

Nichols, Geo. R., of South Reading, of 100 days' men.

Nichols, Geo. W., of Reading; enlisted for three months in Co. E, 5th Reg.

Nichols, G. Hannibal, of South Reading, son of Jona. and Elizabeth; born in South Reading, 1830; enlisted, 1861, for three years in Co. E, 16th Reg., and discharged for inability.

Nichols, Warren, of South Reading, brother of the last named; born in South Reading, in 1840; enlisted, 1861, in Co. E, 16th Reg.; was a Corporal; was wounded slightly at the battle of Gettysburg, taken prisoner, and paroled; was wounded severely at the battle of Coal Harbor, in 1864, and discharged.

Oliver, James, of South Reading, son of Ezekiel and Sarah; born at South Reading in 1820; enlisted as 2d Lieut. in Co. E, 16th Reg.; was promoted to 1st Lieut. in 1862.

Oliver, Alfred, of South Reading, son of the last named; served with the 100 days' men.

O'Reardon, Matthew (or Michael), of South Reading; enlisted for three years in 35th Reg.

Parker, Thos. A., of South Reading; born in 1831; enlisted in 1861 in Co. G, 13th Reg.; was taken prisoner at Kettle Run, Va., paroled, and in 1863 discharged for disability.

Parker, Thos. E., of South Reading, son of Thomas and Hannah; born in Salem in 1820; enlisted 1861, in Co. E, 24th Reg.; served as cook and butcher; discharged Sept. 25, 1862; died at South Reading, Oct. 29, 1862.

Parker, John Q. A., of South Reading, brother of the last named; born at South Reading, 1829; enlisted 1862, in Co. E, 50th Reg., for nine months, as Corporal, and served as butcher.

Parker, Nathan D., of Reading; enlisted 1861, for three months, in Co. E, 5th Reg.

Parker, Wm. Durant, of South Reading, son of William and Abigail; born in South Reading in 1826; enlisted 1861, for three months, in Co. E, 5th Reg.; re-enlisted in 1861, for three years, in Co. H, 24th Reg.; discharged for inability in 1863.

Parsons, Benj. W., of Lynnfield; enlisted 1861, in Co. E, 5th Reg., for three months, and discharged for inability.

Pasco, Wm. C., of South Reading; enlisted 1864, for one year, in Co. K, 4th Heavy Artillery.

Peterson, Leonard, of South Reading; enlisted 1861, in Co. E, 5th Reg., for three months.

Phipps, John W., of South Reading; son of John and Mary; born in South Reading in 1824; enlisted 1864, for one year, in Co. K, 4th Heavy Artillery.

Pierce, James H., of Stoneham; enlisted in 1864, for one year, in Co. K, 4th Heavy Artillery.

Pilling, Jonathan, of South Reading, son of Jonathan; enlisted 1862, for nine months, in Co. E, 50th Reg.; died at Baton Rouge, April 1, 1863, of disease.

Poland, Joseph Warren, of South Reading; a seaman; son of Joseph and Emily C.; born at South Reading 1845; was hospital steward; was at the bombardment of Fort Fisher.

Pope, J. Holman, of South Reading, son of John and Harriet; born at South Reading 1831; enlisted 1862, for nine months, in Co. E, 50th Reg.

Pratt, Benj. C., of South Reading; son of Sumner and Susan; born in South Reading; enlisted 1861, in Co. E, 16th Reg., for three years and served his full term.

Pratt, Edwin, of South Reading, son of David and Hannah; born in Reading in 1838; enlisted 1861, in Co. E, 5th Reg., for 3 months; re-enlisted 1862, in Co. E, 1st Battery of Heavy Artillery, and discharged for disability.

Proven, Charles, of South Reading; enlisted in 1861, for three years, in second Reg., as musician.

Rahr, Christian E., of Reading; enlisted for three months in Co. E, 5th Reg.; a native of Denmark; born 1840.

Ransom, Wm. E., of South Reading, son of Barzillia and H. J.; was Corporal; enlisted 1861 in Co. E, 5th Reg., for three months.

Ransom, Edward M., of South Reading, brother of the last named; born at Brooklyn, N. Y., in 1840; enlisted in 1861, in Co. E, 13th Reg., for three years; employed as clerk in Quartermaster's department; discharged Dec. 1861, by order of Gen. McClellan.

Ransom, Geo. W., of South Reading, brother of the last named; enlisted in the 1st Heavy Artillery, Co. L, for one year; was a Corporal.

Rayner, John, of South Reading; son of Jacob S. and Nabby; born at Townsend 1823; enlisted in 1861, for three months, in Co. E, of 5th Reg.

Rayner, Ozias, of South Reading, brother of the last named; born in Charlestown; enlisted in 1861, for three months, in Co. E, of 5th Regiment; re-enlisted in Co. H, 24th Reg.; was a Sergeant.

Reed, Silas L., of South Reading; a seaman; and of 35th Reg., for three years.

Reed, Washington, of Reading, son of Michael W. and Antisianna, born in Quincy in 1834; enlisted in 1864 in Signal Corps, for three years.

Resterick, Walter, of South Reading, son of Jane Resterick; enlisted 1862, for nine months, in Co. E, 50th Reg.; re-enlisted in 1865 in Frontier Cavalry.

Reynolds, Charles H., of South Reading; enlisted for three years in 35th Reg.

Richards, Frederick S., of South Reading, son of Joseph and Abigail W.; born in Searsport, Me., 1834; enlisted in 1861, in Co. E, 16th Reg.; was killed in battle before Richmond, June 18, 1862.

Richardson, J. Warren, of South Reading, son of Joseph and Elizabeth Richardson; born in South Reading; mustered into service 1864; served one year in Co. E, 1st Batt. Heavy Artillery, Fort Warren.

Ripley, Allen M., of South Reading, son of Asa P. and Mary C.; born in Londonderry, N. H., in 1844; enlisted in 1864 in Co. K, 4th Heavy Artillery.

Robinson, Charles H., of Reading; enlisted for three months in 1861, in Co. E, 5th Reg.

Robinson, John E., of Reading; enlisted 1863 in Co. L, of 1st Heavy Artillery; wounded May 19, 1864, and missing.

Roundy, John D., of Reading; enlisted 1861, for three months, in Co. E, 5th Reg.

Rowland, Thomas, of South Reading; enlisted for one year in 3d Heavy Artillery.

Royal, Dudley C., of South Reading, son of Robert and Miriam; born in 1827 in Pownal, Me.; enlisted 1861, for three years, in the 24th Reg.; re-enlisted 1864.

Rummery, Tho. J., of Co. I, 11th Reg.

Ryder, Andrew J., of South Reading, son of James and Cynthia; of Frontier Cavalry.

Ryder, Verenus H., of South Reading, son of James and Cynthia; enlisted 1864, for one year, in Co. K, 4th Heavy Artillery.

Scanlan, Anthony, of South Reading; of 2d Cavalry.

Seaver, Geo. A., of South Reading, son of Hammond and Amelia; born in Boston in 1827; enlisted 1864, for one year, in Co. K, of 4th Heavy Artillery.

Seaver, Howard M., of South Reading, brother of the last named; born in Boston in 1828; enlisted in 1861 in Co. A, 3d Maryland Reg.

Severns, Wm. H., of South Reading, son of Luther and Hannah R.; born in Brookline, 1842; was a Corporal in Co. G, 59th Reg.; enlisted for three years in 1864, and discharged for inability.

Shea, Michael.

Sheafe, John C., of South Reading; enlisted for three years in Co. A 1st Batt. of Heavy Artillery.

Shepard, Charles H., of South Reading; enlisted 1861, as 1st Lieut in Co. E, 5th Reg.; re-enlisted as 2d Lieut. in Co. L, 1st Heavy Artillery; promoted to 1st Lieut.

Sherman, Marcus M., of South Reading; enlisted in 1864 in Co. K, 4th Heavy Artillery, for one year.

Sherman, Wm. H., of Reading; enlisted 1861, for three months, in Co. E, 5th Reg.

Simpson, Charles L., of South Reading; enlisted 1863, in Co. B, 1st Batt. Heavy Artillery.

Skinner, Gustavus F. D., of South Reading, son of Thomas and Mary; born in South Reading in 1828; enlisted 1861, for three years, in Co. E, 16th Reg.; discharged for inability in 1862; re-enlisted in 1864 in 1st Cavalry.

Skinner, Geo. F., of South Reading, son of Abraham and Martha; enlisted 1862 in Co. B, 39th Reg.; was wounded severely.

Skinner, Thomas Judson, of Reading, son of Thomas and Phebe; served with the 100 days' men.

Skinner, Wm. G., 2d, of South Reading, son of Lilley E. and Rhoda J.; born in South Reading in 1845; enlisted in 1862 in Co. E, 50th Reg., for nine months.

Smalley, Leonard D., of South Reading; born in Yarmouth, Me., in 1832; married Ellen M., dau. of Jacob Tufts; was a seaman; was acting master on board the "Westfield"; was present at the taking of Forts St. Philip and Jackson; also at the taking of New Orleans, La., and Galveston, Tex.

Smiley, J. Henry, of South Reading, son of John and Priscilla; enlisted for three years in Co. H, 24th Reg.

Smith, Daniel, of South Reading, enlisted 1864 in Co. E, 1st Batt. of Heavy Artillery.

Smith, John, was a substitute for Wm. H. Atwell, Jr.; was a seaman.

Smith, Solon C., of South Reading, son of Porter and Sarah; born in South Reading, 1840; enlisted 1864; acting 3d assistant engineer; served on board the "Hibiscus"; died of fever at St. Andrews Bay, Fla., July 10, 1865.

Smith, Thomas, of Melrose ; enlisted 1861, for three months, in Co. E, 5th Reg.

Snell, Lewis A., of South Reading, son of Quartus and Lovice ; born at Charlestown, Mass , 1840; enlisted 1862 in Co. E, 50th Reg., for nine months.

Snell, Franklin L., of South Reading, brother of the last named ; enlisted 1862, for nine months, in Co. E, 50th Reg.

Somers, Joseph, of 7th Battery.

Spaulding, David, of South Reading ; of Frontier Cavalry.

Stephens, John R., of Stoneham ; enlisted 1861, for three months, in Co. E, 5th Reg.

Stetson, Everett, of South Reading, son of Melzar and Lucy; born in Maine ; enlisted 1861, for three years, in Co. K, 23d Reg.

Stimpson, James W., of South Reading, son of Geo. W. and Susan ; born in South Reading 1843 ; enlisted in 1861, for three years, in Co. E, 16th Reg. ; taken prisoner at Gettysburg July 2, 1863 ; died at Richmond, Va., about Jan. 1, 1864.

Stimpson, Wm. W., of South Reading, son of Alfred and Mary ; born in South Reading in 1839 ; enlisted for nine months, in 1862, in Co. E, 50th Reg. ; died of fever at Baton Rouge, La., May 19, 1863.

Stoddard, Geo. W., of South Reading ; served with 100 days' men.

Stone, Orin, of South Reading, son of Ambrose and Martha ; enlisted for three years in Co. E, 16th Reg.

Stowell, John D., of South Reading, son of Martin and Olive ; born in South Reading in 1841 ; enlisted 1862, for three years, in Co. K, 23d Reg. ; discharged in 1864 by reason of wounds.

Sunbury, Horace A., of South Reading, son of Daniel and Mary ; born in Canada 1833 ; enlisted for three years in 1st Mass. Cavalry ; promoted to 2d Lieut. ; transferred to 61st Reg. in 1864 ; promoted to 1st Lieut. in 1865.

Sullivan, John, seaman.

Swain, John P., of North Reading ; enlisted 1864 in Co. L, 1st Heavy Artillery ; re-enlisted.

Sweetser, Albert H., of South Reading, son of P. H. and Louisa ; born in —— ; enlisted as a soldier in 31st Mass. Reg. (Zouaves) ; was discharged at Ship Island, by Gen. Butler, for disability ; re-enlisted in the 57th Reg. (Veteran) under Col. Gould, and fought in the battle of the Wilderness.

Sweetser, James M., of South Reading, son of Moses and Fanny ; born in South Reading 1828 ; enlisted 1861, for three months, and served as Corporal in the 5th Reg.; re-enlisted in 1862, for nine months, in Co. E, 50th Reg.; served as Sergeant with the 100 days' men.

Sweetser, Oliver S., of South Reading, son of Tho. J. and Lavinia S.; born at St. Augustine, Fla., in 1832; enlisted in 1861 in Co. E, 5th Reg., for three months.

Sweetser, Thomas, of South Reading, brother of the last named; born in Florida in 1835; enlisted in 1861, for three months, in Co. E, 5th Reg.; re-enlisted as Sergeant in 1862, for nine months, in Co. E, 50th Reg., and discharged soon after for disability.

Sweetser, Luther, of South Reading, son of John and Sarah; born at South Reading, 1845; enlisted 1861, for three years, in Co. E, 16th Reg.; was taken prisoner at Gettysburg, July 2, 1863, and died a prisoner at Andersonville, S. C., Aug. 8, 1864.

Sweetser, Francis, of South Reading, son of Thos. J. and Lydia; born at South Reading, 1839; enlisted 1861, for three years, in Co. E, 16th Reg.; was killed at the battle of Fair Oaks, June 25, 1862.

Sweetser, Madison C., of South Reading, son of Madison and Phebe; born in South Reading in 1840; enlisted in 1861, for three years, in 2d Co 22d Reg. (Sharpshooters); re-enlisted for one year, in 1864, in Co. B, 1st Vet. Reg. (Hancock's Corps).

Sweetser, Jewett B., of South Reading, brother of the last named; born in South Reading, 1842; enlisted in 1865 in Frontier Cavalry.

Sweetser, John E., of South Reading, son of Stephen and Nancy; born in South Reading, 1839; enlisted for three years in Co. E, 1st Mass. Cavalry, and discharged in 1863 for disability.

Sweetser, Edmund, of South Reading, brother of the last named; born at South Reading, 1843; enlisted 1862 in Co. L, Heavy Artillery; re-enlisted in 1864 for Weymouth.

Sweetser, Stephen, of South Reading, brother of the last named; born in South Reading; served in the 5th Battery; previously served in the 4th Mass. for Taunton.

Sweetser, E. Leroy, of South Reading, son of Elbridge and Mary; born in South Reading in 1842; enlisted 1862, in Co. E, 50th Reg., for nine months.

Symonds, Artemas, served with 100 days' men.

Tackney, Patrick; enlisted 1864, for three years, in 6th Battery.

Talbot, H., of South Reading; of Frontier Cavalry.

Taylor, Augustus, of South Reading, son of Augustus and Elizabeth; born in Dedham in 1841; enlisted 1862, for three years, in Co. D, 4th Battery; died of fever at New Orleans, May 31, 1864.

Taylor, Henry W., of South Reading, son of Wm. H. and Roxanna; born at Cambridgeport 1843; enlisted 1861, for three years, in Co. C, of 3d Battery; afterwards enlisted in the Navy.

Thompson, Charles, of South Reading, son of Joseph and Susan; born at South Reading, 1838; enlisted, 1861, in Co. E, 5th Reg., for three months.

Thompson, John A., of South Reading; born in Boston; enlisted 1861, as drummer, in Co. E, 16th Reg., for three years; discharged in 1862 for disability.

Thompson, J. Frank, of South Reading, son of John A. and Mary B.; born at South Reading in 1832; enlisted April, 1861, for three months, in Co. E, 5th Reg.; in Dec. 1861, re-enlisted, for three years, in Co. B, 3d Reg. (Maryland Reg.); re-enlisted in 1864, in 4th Heavy Artillery; was a Corporal.

Thompson, Geo. A., of South Reading, brother of the last named; born at South Reading, 1844; enlisted 1862, for nine months, in Co. E, 50th Reg.; served also with 100 days' men.

Tibbetts, Charles H., of Reading; enlisted 1861, for three months, in Co. E, 5th Reg.; discharged on account of having shot off by accident the end of his finger.

Tibbetts, Frank L., of Reading; enlisted 1861, for three months, in Co. E, 5th Reg.; was taken prisoner at Bull Run, July 21, 1861.

Townsend, Geo. W., of South Reading, son of Jacob and Nancy; born at South Reading in 1827; enlisted in 1861, for three months, in Co. E, 5th Reg.; was Sergeant; re-enlisted Dec. 1861, for three years, in Co. E, 24th Reg., as Corporal; was wounded at the battle of Newbern, N. C., and lost two fingers of right hand; re-enlisted 1864, in 59th Vet. Reg.

Townsend, Jacob, Jr., of South Reading, brother of the last named; born at Lynnfield, 1821; enlisted 1864, for three years, in Signal Corps.

Townley, Benjamin, of South Reading, son of Calvin and Jane; born in Orange, N. J., 1812; enlisted 1861, for three years, in Co. E, 16th Reg.; discharged 1862, for disability; re-enlisted 1863, in Co. B, 1st Heavy Artillery, and again discharged, 1865, for disability.

Tucker, Chas. E., of South Reading, son of Peter and Nuamah; born at South Reading, 1842; enlisted 1862, in Co. E, 16th Reg.; discharged in 1863 for disability; re-enlisted in 1864, in Co. K, Veteran Reserve Corps.

Turnbull, Alexander, of South Reading, son of Robert and Annie; born in Scotland in 1825; enlisted 1861, for three years, in Co. E, 20th Reg.; carpenter and wagoner.

Turnbull, Robert, of South Reading, brother of the last named; born in Scotland in 1835; enlisted for three years in Co. E, 20th Reg.; died of consumption at South Reading, Aug. 14, 1863; disease contracted in the service; was unmarried.

Tufts, Albert C., of the 100 days' men.

Tuttle, H. Ballard, of South Reading, of the 100 days' men.

Twiss, Adoniram J., of South Reading, son of Nancy; enlisted 1861, for three months, in Co. E, 5th Reg.

Tyler, Wm. N., of South Reading, son of John A. and Marion L.; born at South Reading, 1834; enlisted 1861, for three months, in Co. E, of 5th Reg.; was Corporal; re-enlisted in 1861, in Co. E, 50th Reg., for nine months; served also with 100 days' men.

Tyler, Geo. L., of South Reading, brother of the last named; born in Andover in 1836; enlisted 1862, for nine months, in Co. E, 50th Reg.; re-enlisted in 1864, in Co. K, of 4th Heavy Artillery.

Tyler, Chas. W., of South Reading; enlisted for three years in 35th Reg.

Upham, Elbridge S., of South Reading; enlisted for three years in 35th Reg.

Upton, Eben Davis, of South Reading, son of Edward and Betsey; born in Lynnfield; enlisted 1861, in Co. B, 22d Reg.; was killed at the battle of the Wilderness, May 5, 1864.

Vaux, William, of South Reading, son of Thos. H. and Susan; born in New York city in 1837; served 1861, three months, in Co. E, 5th Reg.; a musician; re-enlisted in 1862, in Co. A, 1st Heavy Artillery; was Drum-Major.

Wadlin, Daniel H., of Reading, son of Daniel and Pamela; born in 1820; enlisted in 1864 in Co. K, 4th Heavy Artillery.

Walker, Charles R., of South Reading, son of Charles and Mary R.; born at South Reading, 1837; enlisted 1861, for three years, in 2d Reg. (as musician); discharged for disability the same year; re-enlisted in Maj. Cabot's unattached company of Heavy Artillery, 1st Battalion.

Walker, Wm. H., of South Reading, son of Levi and Laura; served in 1861, three months, in Co. E, 5th Reg.; re-enlisted 1862 for three years, in Co. G, 20th Reg.; promoted to 1st Lieut. in 1863; severely wounded in the thigh at the battle of Gettysburg, July 3, 1863; promoted to Capt., Aug. 1863; resigned in 1864.

Walton, Samuel L., of South Reading, son of Amos L. and Susan;

born in South Reading in 1842; enlisted 1861, for 3 years, in Co. I, 11th Reg.

Walton, Augustus L., of South Reading, son of Leonard and Nancy; born at South Reading, 1832; enlisted for three years in 19th Reg.; discharged; re-enlisted in 11th Battery.

Walton, Solon, of South Reading, brother of the last named; born at South Reading, 1830; enlisted for three years in Co. E, of 1st Massachusetts Cavalry; was Corporal and Orderly Sergeant.

Walton, Oliver, 2d, of South Reading, son of Jotham and Sarah; born at South Reading 1837; enlisted 1862, for nine months, in Co. E, 50th Reg.

Walton, Geo. K., of South Reading, son of Joshua and Harriet M.; born at South Reading in 1843; enlisted in 1862, in 16th Battery.

Walton, Frank O., of South Reading, son of Oliver and Sarah; born at South Reading in 1840; enlisted 1864, in Co. E, 16th Reg.; transferred, 1864, to 11th Mass. Battalion.

Waitt, John N., of South Reading, son of John; born at South Reading, 1842; enlisted for three years in Co. B, 13th Reg.

Waitt, Aaron H., of South Reading, brother of the last named; born at South Reading; enlisted in Co. B, of 22d Reg.; was bugler.

Waitt, Henry B., of South Reading, son of David and Nancy L.; born at South Reading in 1834; enlisted 1861, in Company B, 22d Reg., for three years.

Warren, Horace M., of South Reading, son of Edwin R. and Mary H.; born in Topsham, Me., July 8, 1841; enlisted 1861, for three years, in Co. E, 20th Reg., and was chosen Sergt., having previously served three months in Co. E, 5th Reg.; was severely wounded in the arm, body, and leg, at battle of Ball's Bluff; re-enlisted 1862, in Co. E, 50th Reg., for nine months, and was chosen 1st Lieut.; re-commissioned as 1st Lieut., and Adjt. of 59th Veteran Reg., and promoted to Major 1864; mortally wounded in battle at Weldon Railroad, Va., Aug. 19, and died Aug. 27, 1864; funeral and burial at South Reading.

Warren, Alvin S., of South Reading; brother of the last named; born in Augusta, Me., Nov. 24, 1843; enlisted 1861, for three years, in Co. E, 16th Reg.; was Corporal; died at Fortress Monroe, June 12, 1862, of fever, and was interred at South Reading.

Warren, Edwin R., Jr., of South Reading, brother of the last named; born in Topsham, Me., 1838; an Acting Ensign and Lieut. in the Naval service; was on board the "Bermuda" and "Wamsutta"; was present at the bombardment of Charleston, S. C., 1864; on special service in South Atlantic Squadron.

Washington, George, of South Reading, of 48th Colored Reg.; a representative recruit for Thos. Emerson.

Weston, Robt. H., of Reading; enlisted 1861, for three months, in Co. E, 5th Reg.

Whitehead, Jeremiah, of South Reading; son of Geo. and Eliza, born in Charlestown; enlisted 1861, for three years, in Co. C, 14th Reg.

Whitehead, George H., of South Reading, brother of the last named; born in Charlestown; enlisted in Co. E, 17th Reg.; was killed in action, Feb. 1, 1864, near Newbern, N. C.

Whitehead, John E., of South Reading, brother of the last named; born in Charlestown; enlisted in Co. B, 17th Reg., for three years; discharged for inability in 1863.

Whitford, John, of South Reading, born in England; enlisted 1861, in Co. E, 16th Reg., for three years; discharged for inability in 1863.

Wheeler, Morris P., of South Reading; son of Philip C.; served with the 100 days' men.

Wheeler, T. Edward, of South Reading, born in 1837; enlisted 1861, for three years, in Co. G, 13th Reg.; discharged in 1862, for inability.

Winegar, Wm. H., of South Reading; enlisted for three years in 33d Reg.

Winship, Samuel, of South Reading, son of Joel and Eliza; born in South Reading 1822; enlisted in 1862, for nine months, in Co. E, 50th Reg.

Winthrop, Alexander M., of South Reading; enlisted for three years in 20th Reg.

Wiley, Joseph E., of South Reading, son of Peter and Nancy; born at Royalston 1838; enlisted 1861, for three months in Co. E, 5th Reg.; re-enlisted 1862, in Co. L, 1st Heavy Artillery; promoted to Sergeant; re-enlisted 1864, as a veteran.

Wiley, John, 2d, of South Reading, son of Peter B.; born at South Reading; enlisted in Co. E, 16th Reg., a company he was instrumental in recruiting and of which he was Captain; he resigned in 1863.

Wiley, Wm., of South Reading, son of Capt. John and Elizabeth; was born at South Reading, 1836; enlisted in 1861, for three months, in Co. E, 5th Reg.; re-enlisted 1862, for three years, in Co. A, 17th Reg.; was 1st Sergeant; died at Newbern, N. C., Oct. 12, 1862, of fever; funeral at South Reading, Dec. 16, 1862.

Wiley, Wm. H., of South Reading, son of Ira and Lucetta; served with the 100 days' men.

Wiley, Ira, Jr., of South Reading, son of Ira and Lucetta; served with the 100 days' men.

Wiley, Baxter I., of South Reading, son of Ellis; served with the 100 days' men.

Wiley, J. Barnard, of South Reading, son of Ebenezer and Jane; served with the 100 days' men.

Wiley, Geo. H., of South Reading, born in Amherst, N. H.; enlisted in 1861, in Co. E, 16th Reg., and discharged 1864, for inability.

Wiley, Samuel A., of South Reading, son of Samuel S. and Rebecca N.; born in South Reading in 1841; enlisted 1861, for three years, in Co. H, 23d Reg.; died of measles at Hatteras Inlet Hospital, Feb. 7, 1862.

Wiley, Augustus T., of South Reading; born at Lynn; enlisted for three years, in 1861, in Co. E, 1st Mass. Cavalry; killed near Kelley's Ford, Va., June 9, 1863.

Wiley, Albert S., of South Reading, son of John and Harriet; born in South Reading, 1832; enlisted 1861, in Co. E, 1st Mass. Cavalry, for three years; severely wounded at Poolesville, Sept. 5, 1862; discharged by reason of wounds; re-enlisted 1862, for three years, in Co. E, 1st Cavalry.

Wiley, Herbert A., of South Reading, son of Adam and Eunice; born at South Reading, 1839; enlisted 1862, for three years, in Co. K, 23d Reg.; died of typhoid fever, at Newbern, N. C., Nov. 19, 1862.

Wiley, Alonzo E., of South Reading, son of Enos and Susan C.; born at South Reading, 1839; enlisted 1864, for three years, in Signal Corps.

Wiley, Caleb S., of Stoneham, son of Caleb and Susanna, born in Stoneham, 1827; enlisted 1864, for one year, in 4th Heavy Artillery.

Williams, Leonard T., of South Reading; born in Stoneham, 1839; enlisted 1861, for three years, in Co. G, 13th Reg.; discharged 1862, for disability.

Williams, Henry, of South Reading, son of Phebe D.; enlisted in 4th Cavalry.

Williams, James E., of South Reading; enlisted in 5th Cavalry.

Williams, Alexander, of South Reading, representative recruit for Peter Folsom; enlisted in 5th colored Heavy Artillery.

Williams, Francis E., of South Reading, son of Francis and Laura; born in South Reading, 1847; enlisted 1864, for one year, in 4th Heavy Artillery.

Williams, Chas. B., of Boston; enlisted 1864, for one year, in 4th Heavy Artillery.

Wilder, Geo. W., Jr., of South Reading, son of Geo. W.; born at South Reading 1823; enlisted 1864, for three years, in 1st Cavalry; discharged 1862, for disability.

Willan, Thomas, of South Reading, son of John and Agnes, born in England, 1836; enlisted in 1863, in Co. L, 1st Heavy Artillery; taken prisoner at Petersburg, Va., June 22, 1864, and kept at Andersonville; paroled Nov. 20, 1864.

Wilkins, Edward L., of South Reading; enlisted 1861, for three months, in Co. E, 5th Reg.; re-enlisted 1864, in 4th Heavy Artillery.

Woodfin, John H., of South Reading, son of Moses and Joanna; born in Marblehead, 1833; enlisted as 1st Sergeant, in Co. E, 16th Reg.; promoted to 2d Lieut., May, 1863, and to 1st Lieut., Aug. 1863; was killed at the battle of Wilderness, May 6, 1864.

Woodis, Hiram, of South Reading, son of Josiah C. and Lois; born at Bartlett, N. H., in 1820; enlisted 1861, in Co. E, 16th Reg., for three years; was Corporal; wounded at Bull Run 1862; re-enlisted in 1864, and transferred to 11th Reg.

Woodward, Thomas T., of South Reading, son of Thomas and Esther; born at South Reading, 1827; was a seaman.

Woofindale, Geo. H., of South Reading; enlisted for one year in Co. D, 3d Heavy Artillery.

Wright, Joseph T., of South Reading, son of Hiram and Lydia; born at Middleton, 1831; enlisted 1861, for three years, in Co. E, 16th Reg.; re-enlisted in 1864 (for Marblehead), and transferred to 11th Mass. Battalion; wounded in arm at battle of Wilderness, and died in consequence in 1865.

Wright, Dexter C., of South Reading, son of Nathaniel C. and Judith; served with the 100 days' men.

Wyman, Wm., of South Reading; enlisted for three years, in 24th Reg.

Wyman, Wm., of Melrose; enlisted 1861, for three months, in Co. E, 5th Reg.

Warey, James, of South Reading; born in 1833; enlisted in 1861, for three years, in 11th Reg.

Whole number of men furnished by South Reading during the war, including re-enlistments, was 505
Number killed in battle 18
Number died of disease contracted in the service . . . 42

VOLUNTEERS.

Alphabetical list of all persons who have been in the Military or Naval Service of the United States, and credited on the quota of Reading, during the late Rebellion; also residents of Reading who have been in said service as a part of the quota of any other town.

Names.	Term of Enlistment.	Reg.	Co.	Mustered into U. S. Service.	Mustered out or Discharged.	Remarks.
Abbott, Oramel G., Lieut.	9 mos.	50	D,	Sept. 19, 1862.	Aug. 24, 1863.	Formerly in Co. B, 5th Reg.
Aborn, Sylvester,	3 yrs.	2		Aug. 12, 1862.		Died.
Adams, Oliver S.		1				R. I. Cavalry. Formerly in 5th Reg, Co. B.
Albert, George,	3 yrs.	5		June 16, 1864.		Cavalry.
Allen, George S.	"	1		Feb. 16, 1864.		Andrew Sharpshooters.
Allen, Jules R., Corp.		33	D,	Aug. 5, 1862.		Killed at Gettysburg, July 3, 1863.
Appleton, Thomas,	3 mos.	8	E,	July 19, 1864.	Nov. 10, 1864.	
Arnold, Marcus P.	3 yrs.	1		Feb. 16, 1864.		Andrew Sharpshooters.
Austin, Alpheus,	"	33	D,	Aug. 5, 1862.	Jan. 18, 1864.	Transferred to Co. K, 3d Mass. Cav.
Baker, Adelbert,	1 yr.		D,	Dec. 29, 1864	June 30, 1865.	Frontier Cavalry.
Balink, Herman,	3 yrs.	33	D,	Aug. 5, 1862.	June 11, 1865.	
Bancroft, George,	"	59	D,	Jan. 28, 1864.	July 30, 1865.	
Bancroft, Haskel K.	9 mos.	50	D,	Sept. 19, 1862.	Aug. 24, 1863.	
Bancroft, John M., Lieut.	3 yrs.	4		June 20, 1861.		Mich. Vols. Promoted Sept. 28, 1862. Trans. to Co. H, same Reg. Enlisted as Sergt.
Bancroft, Thomas E.	3 yrs.	13	G,	Aug. 12, 1862.		Killed at Spottsylvania, Va., May 8, 1864.
Barnes, John A.	9 mos.	50	D,	Sept. 19, 1862.	Feb. 16, 1863.	For disability. Died in Reading, March 24, 1863.
Bartlett, George J., Sergt.	"	50	D,	" "		Died at Baton Rouge, La., July 2, 1863.
Battelle, Charles P., Sergt.	3 yrs.	59	A,	Dec. 5, 1863.	July 13, 1865.	Wounded at Petersburg, Va., March 25, 1865, and had left leg amputated. Formerly in 50th Reg., Co. D, for 9 mos.

VOLUNTEERS.—Continued.

Names.	Term of Enlistment.	Reg.	Co.	Mustered into U.S. Service.	Mustered out or Discharged.	Remarks.
Battelle, George W.	3 yrs.	40	B,	June, 1861.	Sept. 24, 1864.	N. Y. Vols.
Beatie, William, Corp.	"	24	H,	Oct. 2, 1861.		Wounded at Newbern, N. C., Mar. 14, '62.
Bell, Henry,	1 yr.	29		June 16, 1864.		
Bemis, E. Eugene,	1 yr.		E,	Aug. 11, 1864.	June 28, 1865,	1st Bat. H. A., Ft. Warren.
Bemis, Horace C.	"		E,	" 10, 1864.	" " "	"
Berry, Daniel,	3 yrs.	14	H,	July 5, 1861.	Jan. 20, 1862.	Died in Reading, Jan. 26, 1862.
Berry, Daniel W.	"	24	H,	Sept. 30, 1861.	Jan. 24, 1866.	Re-enlisted about Jan. 1, 1864, for 3 years more.
Berry, William B.	"	33	D,	Aug. 5, 1862.		Frontier Cavalry. Formerly in 8th Reg. [Co. E, 3 months.
Bessey, Charles A.	"		B,	Dec. 29, 1864.	June 30, 1865.	Formerly in 13th Reg., Co. G.
Bessey, George A.	1 yr.	59	B,	Jan. 5, 1864.	July 30, 1865.	Wounded at Gettysburg, July 2, 1862. A bullet passed through one arm.
Bessey, Seth,	3 yrs.	59	A,	Dec. 5, 1863.		
Blanchard, Sylvanus,	"	33	D,	Aug. 5, 1862.	June 3, 1865.	Navy. Credited by the State.
Borden, Hiram C.	9 mos.	50	D,	Sept. 19, 1862.	Aug. 24, 1863.	H. Artillery. Formerly in 13th Reg., Co. G. Wounded at Antietam, Sept. 17, 1862, and discharged on account of wound, Nov. 29, 1862. Promoted to Lieut. July 27, 1864.
Boyce, Charles M.	3 yrs.	3	8	Aug. 1, 1863.		
Boyce, George P., Lieut.						
Brett, John,	3 yrs.	9	B,	June 11, 1861.	Sept. 9, 1861.	For disability.
Bridger, William J.	"		D,	Dec. 3, 1864.	Nov. 14, 1865.	Veteran Reserve Corps.
Brien, Michael O.	"	33	E,	Aug. 5, 1862.		
Brooks, Orlando M.	1 yr.		E,	Aug. 8, 1864.	June 28, 1865.	1st Bat. H. A. Ft. Warren.
Brown, Henry M.	"		E,	" "	" " "	1st Bat. H. A. Ft. Warren. Formerly in band of 14th Reg.
Bruce, George G.	9 mos.	50	D,	Sept. 19, 1862.	Aug. 24, 1863.	Died at Baton Rouge, La., April 19, 1863.
Buck, Asa C., Serg.	"	50	D,	" "	" "	

Name	Term			Enlisted	Discharged	Remarks
Buck, William, Corp.	9 mos.	50	D,	Sept. 19, 1862.	Aug. 24, 1863.	Wounded at Port Hudson, June 30, 1863. [A bullet passed through both legs.
Bunker, Noble,	"	50	D,	"	"	
Butters, Willie R.	3 yrs.	13	G,	Dec. 28, 1863.	June 23, 1865.	
Campbell, Samuel G.	"		1st,	Sept. 2, 1861.	Sept. 2, 1864.	Andrew Sharpshooters.
Carney, Joseph,	"	13	G,	Dec. 9, 1863.		
Carter, George H.	"	25	H,	Oct. 24, 1861.	Sept. 26, 1862.	For disability.
Carey, Jeremiah,				1861.		Regular Army.
Cate, John M.	3 yrs.	33	D,	Aug. 5, 1862.	June 11, 1865.	
Caughlin, Daniel,	"					[from since.
Chapman, Orrin J.	"	56	D,	Dec. 29, 1863.		Taken prisoner Sept 30, 1864. Not heard Maine Reg. Re-enlisted Dec. 31, 1863, for 3 years.
Cleaves, Calvin H.	"	9	F,	Sept. 8, 1861.	Dec. 15, 1864.	1st Bat. H. A., Ft. Warren.
Clement, William,	1 yr.	50	E,	Aug. 8, 1864.	June 28, 1865.	
Coburn, Josiah W., Capt.	9 mos.		D,	Sept. 19, 1862.	Aug. 24, 1863.	1st Bat. H. A., Ft. Warren.
Coffin, William E.	1 yr.	50	E,	Aug. 8, 1864.	June 28, 1865.	1st Bat. H. A., Ft. Warren.
Coney, George A.	9 mos.	50	D,	Sept. 19, 1862.	Aug. 24, 1863.	Afterwards in 5th Reg, Co K, for 3 mos.
Coney, George C.	"			"	"	
Conway, James,	4 yrs.	13	G,	Dec. 6, 1864.	Sept. 25, 1862.	Marine Corps.
Cook, George F.	3 yrs.	33	G,	Aug. 12, 1862.	June 11, 1865.	For disability.
Cook, Henry,	3 yrs.		E,	Aug. 5, 1862.	Sept. 18, 1865.	[of 2d Reg.
Cook, Jere. C.	"			Dec. 28, 1863.		3d unattached H. A. Formerly in Band
Cook, John F.		13	D,	July 16, 1861.	Aug. 1, 1864.	Wounded at Gettysburg, July 3; 1863.
Cook, Geo. W.	1 yr.			Aug. 8, 1864.	June 28, 1865.	1st Bat. H.A., Ft. Warren.
Cook, J. Warren, Lieut.	3 yrs.	2	A,	May 25, 1861.	May 23, 1864.	Wounded May 3, 1863, at Chancellorsville. Enlisted as private. Promoted to 2d Lieut. March 19, 1863, and to 1st Lieut. Sept. 13, 1863.
Cook, Jonathan, Jr.	3 yrs.	24	H,	Sept. 30, 1861.		Re-enlisted for three years about Jan. 1, 1864. Taken prisoner at Rams Station, Va., June 30, 1864. Died at Annapolis, Md., Dec. 5, 1864, while on his way home, from the effects of starvation while a prisoner. Formerly in 5th Reg, Co. B.

VOLUNTEERS.—*Continued.*

NAMES.	Term of Enlistment.	Reg.	Co.	Mustered into U. S. Service.	Mustered out or Discharged.	REMARKS.
Cook, Orange S.	3 yrs.	21	G,	Aug. 16, 1861.	Jan. 6, 1863.	On account of wounds received Sept. 1, 1862, at Chantilly, Va. A bullet passed through one leg.
Copeland, Ellis,	3 yrs.	59	I,	April 2, 1864.	Sept. 6, 1865.	For disability.
Copeland, Sydney,	"	22	D,	Aug. 28, 1861.	" 28, "	Killed at Gains's Mills, Va., June 27, '62.
Corrie, John H.	1 yr.		E,	Aug. 8, 1864.	June 28, 1865.	1st Bat. H. A., Ft. Warren.
Cox, James P.	"			Dec. 1, 1864.	" 6, "	" "
Crosby, Thomas,				" 17, "		" "
Crouch, Charles L.	3 yrs.	2	G,	July 16, 1861.	M'ch 17, 1863.	Cavalry.
Crowe, William,	"	13	G,	" "	May 7, 1863.	For disability. Died Sept. 25, 1863, in [Reading.
Cleaves, John H.	"	13	D,	Aug. 28, 1861.	Jan. 29, 1863.	"
Damon, Albert,	3 yrs.	22	E,	July 12, 1861.		Re-enlisted for three years about Jan. 1, 1864. Taken prisoner June 4, 1864, and died of starvation in Millen, Ga., Nov. 17, 1864.
Damon, Amos,	3 yrs.	33	D,	Aug. 5, 1862.	June 11, 1865.	
Damon, Edgar,	1 yr.		E,	Aug. 8, 1864.	" 28, "	1st Battalion H. A., Ft. Warren.
Damon, Henry,	3 mo.	8	E,	July 19, 1864.		
Damon, Henry, 2d,	3 yrs.	33	D,	July 12, 1861.	Nov. 10, 1864.	
Damon, John, Jr.	1 yr.		E,	Aug. 8, 1864.	June 28, 1865.	Killed May 3, 1863, at Chancellorsville, Va.
Damon, Otis,	3 yrs.	25	K,	Sept. 20, 1861.	July 13, "	1st Bat. H. A., Ft. Warren.
Dana, David, Dr.	"	14		July 5, 1861.	Oct. 30, 1862.	Surgeon.
Davis, James A.	1 yr.		E,	Aug. 10, 1864.	June 28, 1865.	1st Bat. H. A., Ft. Warren.

Name	Term	Age	Co.	Date of Enlistment	Date of Discharge	Remarks
Davis, William W.	3 yrs.	13	G,	Aug. 12, 1862.	Aug. 22, 1863.	For disability, on account of a wound received at Gettysburg, July 1, 1863. A bullet passed through wrist of right arm. Enlisted again in 59th Reg, Co. A, Dec. 5, 1863, as Sergeant. Promoted to 2d Lieut. June 22, 1864, and to 1st Lieut. Oct. 7, 1864. Wounded at Petersburg, July 30, 1864. Left hand amputated. Discharged Nov. 29, 1864.
Deadman, Henry,	3 yrs.	13	G,	Aug. 12, 1862.	Dec. 23, 1863.	For disability. Wounded at Gettysburg, July 1, '63, by bullet passing through one leg.
Delay, Jeremiah,	9 mos.	50	D,	Sept. 19, 1862.		Died at Mound City, Ill, Aug. 10, 1863. Formerly in 22d Reg., Co. D.
Delay, Patrick,	3 yrs.	26	D,	Dec. 1, 1864.		Died at New Orleans, La., Sept. 8, 1862. 1st Battalion Heavy Artillery.
Dewhurst, Joseph W.	1 yr.					
Dinsmoor, Chas. A., Corp.	3 yrs.	56	D,	Dec. 29, 1863.		Wounded at Petersburg, July 30,'64, taken pris'r, died of his wounds at Petersb'g, Aug. 5, '64. Formerly in 8th Battery.
Dorr, Henry,	3 yrs.	33	D,	Aug. 5, 1862.	June 11, 1865.	Navy, credited by the State.
Eastman, James,	"	R. I.				Formerly in 5th Reg'r, Co. B, Mass. Vols., [for three months.
Eaton, Alvin A.	"					
Eaton, Benjamin,	"	16	E,	July 12, 1861.	April 12, 1863.	Navy, credited by the State.
Eaton, Joseph,	"	50	D,	Sept. 19, 1862.		For disability.
Eaton, Moses F.	9 mos.					Died Feb. 18 1863, at New Orleans.
Edson, John W.	3 yrs.					Navy, credited by the State.
Ellis, Samuel,	"					"
Elwell, John W.	"					"
Emerson, Albert B.	"	22	D,	Aug. 28, 1861.	Aug. 24, 1863.	Kld. in the Wilderness, Va., May 5, '64.
Evans, Charles A.	9 mos.	50	D,	Sept. 19, 1862.	Oct. 19, 1864.	
Evans, George,	3 yrs.			Aug. 28, 1861.		Porter's Battery.
Evans, Thomas A.	"	16	E,	July 12, 1861.		
Farmery, Daniel G.	"			Dec. 16, 1864.		6th Battery.

VOLUNTEERS.—Continued.

NAMES.	Term of Enlistment.	Reg.	Co.	Mustered into U.S. Service.	Mustered out or Discharged.	REMARKS.
Farwell, John L.	9 mos.	50	D,	Sept. 19, 1862.	Aug. 24, 1863.	Navy, credited by the State.
Farming, William F.	3 yrs.				June 28, 1865.	1st Bat. H. A.
Fitzpatrick, William D.	1 yr.		E,	Aug. 12, 1864.	Sept. 18, 1865.	Heavy Artillery.
Flannigan, Michael,	3 yrs.		15,	May 30, 1864.		Navy, credited by the State.
Flaxington, Samuel,	"					
Fleig, Ferdinand,	"	20		Feb. 16, 1864.	March, 1863.	For disability. Died at Fortress Monroe Aug. 2, '63. Formerly in 5th Reg., [Co. B.
Fletcher, Charles N.	3 yrs.	22		Aug. 28, 1861.		
Fletcher, Nathan B.	9 mos.	50	D,	Sept. 19, 1862.	Aug. 24, 1863.	
Flint, Geo. H.	3 yrs.	1				R. I. Cavalry. Re-enlisted about Jan. 1, [1864, for three years more.
Flynn, John,	"	20	H,	Feb. 17, 1864.		Cavalry.
Fonde, Patrick,	"	2		Dec. 17, 1864.		For disability. Wounded and taken prisoner near Richmond, June 26, 1862.
Foss, Edward A.	"	22	D,	Aug. 28, 1861.		Heavy Artil. Formerly in 13th Reg, Co. G. Wounded at Antietam, Sept. 17, 1862. Discharged on account of wound, Jan. 14, 1863. Promoted to 2d Lieut. in H. A., Sept. 2, 1864.
Foss, Henry M., Lieut.	"	3	8	Aug. 1, 1863.		
Foster, William E.	"	13	G,	July 16, 1861.	Aug. 1, 1864.	Wounded in hand, Aug. 31, 1862, at Bull [Run, Va.
Francis, Henry A.	"					Navy, credited by the State.
Francis, James,	"					" " "
French, Francis O.	"					" " "
Frost, Jonathan,	"					By representative recruit.
Frost, Charles C.	9 mos.	50	D,	Sept. 19, 1862.	Aug. 24, 1863.	
Gambell, Mathias,	3 yrs.	33	D,	Aug. 5, 1862.		Died Oct. 7, 1862, in Hospital, at Alexandria, Va.

OF THE TOWN OF READING. 639

Gerritson, Henry C.	3 yrs.	12	A,	June 26, 1861.	July 8, 1864.	Wounded at Culpepper, Aug. 9, 1862, and taken prisoner Aug. 30, 1862, at [Bull Run.
Gerry, Jonas,	3 yrs.	12	A, 2	"	"	For disability. Andrew Sharpshooters.
Goldthwait, Ebenezer G.	"	16	D,	Oct. 3, 1861.	Feb. 16, 1862.	"
Goodhue, Amos,	3 yrs.	50	H,	Dec. 2, "	March 4, 1863.	N. Y. Reg.
Goodwin, George H.	9 mos.	99	G,	Sept. 18, 1862.	Aug. 24, 1863.	
Green, Andrew J.	3 yrs.	13	D,	Feb. 19, "	Feb. 17, 1865.	For disability. Formerly in 5th Reg., Co. B. Wounded and taken prisoner at Bull Run, July 21, 1861. Released in June, 1862.
Green, Orne,	"	33		Aug. 12, "	Aug. 1, 1864.	
Griggs, James H., Sergt.				Aug. 5, "	Mar. 19, 1863.	
Grover, Charles A.	9 mos.	50	D,	Sept. 19, 1862.	Aug. 24, 1863.	1st Bat. H. A, Ft. Warren.
Hall, Charles E.	1 yr.		E,	Aug. 13, 1864.	June 28, 1865.	
Hall, Frank J.	3 mos.	8	E,	July 19, "	Nov. 10, 1864.	
Hall, William,	3 yrs.	2		Dec. 17, "		Cavalry.
Harborn, John H.	"	29		June 16, "		
Harriman, Isaac,	1 yr.		⁻E,	Aug. 8, "	June 28, 1865.	1st Bat. H. A., Ft. Warren.
Hartshorn, Oliver S.	3 mos.	8	E,	July 19, "	Nov. 10, 1864.	Died in Reading, June 21, 1865.
Hartwell, Albert A.	1 yr.		E,	Aug. 13, "	June 28, 1865.	1st Bat. H. A., Ft. Warren. Formerly in 5th Reg., Co. B.
Harvey, Marshall C.	"		E,	" "	" "	1st Bat. H. A., Ft. Warren.
Hayward, Alex. M., Capt.	3 yrs.	24	G,	Sept. 30, 1861.	Jan. 24, 1866.	Re-enlisted about Jan. 1, 1864, for 3 yrs. Promoted to 2d Lieut. Jan. 4, 1864, and to 1st Lieut. June 11, 1864, and to Capt. Sept. 24, 1864. Formerly in 5th Reg., [Co. B.
Hennesey, James,	3 mos.	8	E,	July 19, 1864.	Nov. 10, 1864.	
Heselton, Jonathan,	"	8	E,	" "	" "	
Heselton, Richmond,	3 yrs.	13	G,	Aug. 12, 1862.	Nov. 22, 1862.	For disability.
Hetler, Adam,	"	16	E,	July 12, 1861.		Died in Hospital at Annapolis, Md., Oct. 27, 1862.
Hetler, Thomas,	3 mos.	5	F,	June 20, "		Killed in the battle of Bull Run, Va., July 21, 1861. The first Reading volunteer killed.

VOLUNTEERS.—Continued.

Names.	Term of Enlistment.	Reg.	Co.	Mustered into U.S. Service.	Mustered out or Discharged.	Remarks.
Holbrook, George W.	3 yrs.	25	C,	Sept. 20, 1861.	July 13, 1865.	Re-enlisted about Jan. 1, 1864, for 3 yrs.
Holt Charles,	9 mos.	50	D,	Sept. 19, 1862.	Aug. 24, 1863.	Died at Mattoon, Ill., Aug. 9, 1863, on his [way home.
Holt Squares,	"	50	D,	"	"	
Hopkins, George W.	"	50	D,	"	"	
Hopkins, Joseph B.	"	50	D,	"	"	
Horton, Charles C.	3 mos.	8	E,	July 19, 1864.	Nov. 10, 1864.	
Housemann, Charles H.	3 yrs.	32	A,	Nov. 25, 1861.		Re-enlisted for 3 years more about Jan. 1, 1864, and killed near Poplar Grove Church, Va., Sept. 30, 1864.
Houseman, John M.	"	16	E,	July 12, "	Sept. 22, 1862.	For disability.
Hoyt, David W.	1 yr.		E,	Aug. 13, 1864.	June 28, 1865.	1st Bat. H. A., Ft. Warren.
Hunt, George W.	3 yrs.	33	D,	Aug. 5, 1862.	Jan. 20, 1864.	For disability.
Hyde, Daniel F.	"	12	A,	June 26, 1861.	April 1, 1862.	"
Jeffrey, John, Capt.	"	56	K	Sept. 5, 1863.	July 30, 1865.	Formerly Serg. in 12th Reg., Co. A. Promoted to 2d Lieut. Sept. 5, 1863, and transferred to Co. K, 56th Reg. Promoted to 1st Lieut. March 10, 1864, and to Capt. March 15, 1865.
Jeffrey, Robert,		50	D,			Captain's boy; was also captain's boy in Co. D, 22d Reg.
Jenkins, Forrest,	3 yrs.	16	E,	July 12, 1861.	April 20, 1864.	For disability.
Jenkins, Henry, Sergt.	"		I,	Sept. 2, "	Oct. 2, 1863.	" Andrew Sharpshooters.
Jones, Charles W.	"	22	D,	Aug. 28, "	Oct. 17, 1864.	Died in Reading, Dec. 1, 1864.
Jones, Eliab C.	"	22	D,	"	Jan. 18, 1863.	For disability. Wounded and taken prisoner near Richmond, June 27, 1862. Enlisted again Dec. 30, 1864, for 1 yr. in Co. D, Frontier Cav. Also enlisted in 8th Reg., Co. E, July 19, 1864, for 3 mos.

Name	Term	Age	Co.	Enlisted	Discharged	Remarks
Jones, William S.		22	D,	July 22, 1862.	Oct. 17, 1864	Died at Fairfax, Va., June 23, 1863.
Keefe, David O.	3 yrs.	9	A,	June 16, 1864.		By representative recruit.
Kelley, James,	"	29				"
Kendrick, Rufus,	"					1st Bat. H. A., Ft. Warren.
Knight, Francis H.	1 yr.		E,	Aug. 8,	June 28, 1865.	Frontier Cavalry.
Kimball, James D.	"		D,	Dec. 30,	June 30, "	For disability.
Kummer, Frederic,	3 yrs.	41	E,	Sept. 20, 1862.	Jan. 18, 1864.	Killed at Antietam, Sept. 17, 1862.
Kummer, Henry W.	"	12	A,	June 26, 1861.		
Kummer, Henry W., Jr.	"	20	A,	Feb. 16, 1864.		
Lamson, Levi,	"	11	L,	June 13, 1861.	June 13, 1862.	For disability. Enlisted again Sept. 19, 1862, in Co. D, 50th Reg, for 9 months.
LaClaire, William,						
Lang, Charles H., Lieut.	"	13	G,	July 16, "	May 15, 1865.	Enlisted as private. Wounded at Antietam, Sept. 17, 1862. Promoted to Corporal, Sept. 1, 1863, and to 2d Lieut. April 19, 1864, and transferred to the 59th Reg. Was taken prisoner July 30, 1864, and released March 1, 1865. Was promoted to 1st Lieut. Aug. 24, 1864, while a prisoner.
Leathe, Charles B., Capt.	3 yrs.	11	I,	June 13, 1861.	Dec. 1864.	Enlisted as a private. Promoted to Corp. May 5, 1862. To 2d Lieut. Aug. 23, 1862, and transferred to Co. A, 40th Reg. Promoted to 1st Lieut. June 9, 1863, and to Capt. April 21, 1864. Was wounded in Florida, Feb. 20, 1864, left arm broken, and discharged in Dec. 1864. Enlisted in Frontier Cavalry, Co. D, for 1 year, Jan. 2, 1865; was com'd 2d Lieut. and soon after Capt.
Leathe, George E., Jr.	3 yrs.	11	I,	June 13, 1861.	June 24, 1864.	
Lee, John H.	1 yr.			May 27, "		
Lewis, John B, Jr.	"		E,	Sept. 12, 1862.	June 18, 1863.	In Navy. Ship Colorado.
Lewis, William,	"	44	E,	Aug. 8, 1864.	June 28, 1865.	1st Bat. H. A., Ft. Warren.

VOLUNTEERS.—Continued.

NAMES.	Term of Enlistment.	Reg.	Co.	Mustered into U.S. Service.	Mustered out or Discharged.	REMARKS.
Lincoln, Freeman B.	1 yr.	8	E,	Aug. 8, 1864.	June 28, 1865.	1st Bat. H. A., Ft. Warren.
Loring, Gustavus,	"	8	E,	"	"	"
Lovejoy, Jeremiah G.	3 mos.	3	E,	July 19, "	Nov. 10, 1864.	"
Loyd, Francis,	3 yrs.	32	H,	July 23, 1862.	Dec. 1, 1862.	Heavy Artillery. For disability.
Macdonald, William,	"	32	H,	July 23, 1862.	Dec. 1, 1862.	For disability.
Marshall, William H.	9 mos.	50	D,	Sept. 19, 1862.	Aug. 24, 1863.	Enlisted again in Nim's Bat, Jan. 8, 1864, for 3 years on the quota of Chelsea.
Massey, Isaiah,	1 yr.		E,	Aug. 8, 1864.	June 28, 1865.	1st Bat. H. A., Ft. Warren.
Massey, Leverett,	1 yr.		E,	Aug. 13, 1864.	June 28, 1865.	"
Masury, Lawrence,	"		E,	" 9, "	"	"
Maurizo, Nicholas,	3 yrs.	29	I,	June 16, "		
McAllister, Benjamin,	"	11		" 13, 1861.	June 15, 1864.	Wounded at Gettysburg, July 2, 1863, in both shoulders.
McAlear, Joseph,	9 mos.	50	D,	Sept. 19, 1862.	Aug. 24, 1863.	
McIntire, Amos,	"	50	D,	"	"	
McAllistor, Benjamin F.	3 mos.	8	E,	July 19, 1864.	Nov. 10, 1864.	
McGann, John,	3 yrs.	4	G,	Dec. 16, 1864.	Nov. 14, 1865.	Cavalry.
McKay, James,	"	13	15	Aug. 12, 1862.	Aug. 1, 1864.	
McMillan, Michael,	"	16	E,	June 17, 1864.	Aug. 30, 1861.	Heavy Artillery.
Mellen, C. Alonzo,	"	59	D,	July 12, 1861.	July 3, 1865.	For disability.
Messer, John A.	"	12	A,	Jan. 28, 1864.	" 8, 1864.	
Moor, Robert P.	"	58	G,	June 26, 1861.	" 14, 1865.	
Munroe, Charles W.	"	58	G,	Mar. 26, 1864.	April 5, 1865.	For disability.
Munroe, Isaac,	"					Veteran Reserve Corps.
Murphy, John,	9 mos.	50	D,	Dec. 15, 1864.	Aug. 24, 1863.	
Myers, Charles,	"	50	D,	Sept. 19, 1862.	"	
Nash, William H., Corp.	"	50	D,	"	"	
Nelson, George W.	3 yrs.	59	D,	1864.		Killed near Petersburg, Va., July 4, '64.

Nichols, Edward E.	9 mos.	50	D,	Sept. 19, 1862.	Came home sick, and died Aug. 20, '63.
Nichols, George W., Capt.	3 yrs.	24	H,	" 30, 1861.	Re-enlisted about Jan. 1, 1864, for 3 years more. Promoted to 2d Lieut. Jan. 8, 1864, to 1st Lieut. June 16, '64, and to Capt. Sept. 28, 1864. Formerly in Co. B, 5th Reg, for three months.
Nichols, George W. 2d,	3 mos.	8	E,	July 19, 1864.	Nov. 10, 1864.	Enlisted again in 62d Bat., which was mustered out a few days after.
Nichols, John W.	3 yrs.			Nov. 6, 1863.		Regular Army.
Nichols, Parker,	3 yrs.			May 18, 1864.		Drafted and put in substitute.
Nichols, Richard B.	"			July 14, 1863.		Drafted and paid commutation.
Nichols, William R.	"	59	C,	Jan. 14, 1863.	July 30, 1865.	Chief Musician. Formerly in 50th Reg, Co. D.
Noble, George W.	"		D,	Dec. 14, 1863.		Veteran Reserve Corps.
Nolan, John,	"	33	E,	Aug. 5, 1862.	June 28, 1865.	Killed May 5, 1864.
Norris, Charles W.	1 yr.			Aug. 8, 1864.		1st Bat. H. A, Ft. Warren.
Norris, Henry L.	"	17				
Norris, James T.	3 yrs.	13	G,	Aug. 12, 1862.	Aug. 1, 1864.	U. S. Cav. Died in Reading, Dec. 3, 1862. Formerly in 5th Reg, Co. F.
Nichols, Robert F.	"	1				1st Bat. H. A, Ft. Warren.
O'Connell, Dennis,	1 yr.	50	E,	Aug. 8, 1864.	June 28, 1865.	
Parker, Clarkson,	9 mos.	12	D,	Sept. 19, 1862.	Aug. 24, 1863.	For disability.
Parker, Edmund B.	3 yrs.	50	A,	June 26, 1861	" 12, 1862.	
Parker, Edward,	9 mos.		D,	Sept. 19, 1862.	" 24, 1863.	1st Bat. H. A., Ft. Warren.
Parker, Frederick H.	1 yr.		E,	Dec. 1, 1864.	June 28, 1865.	Wounded at Antietam, Sept. 17, 1862. Also at Fredericksburg, Dec. 14, '62.
Parker, George H.	3 yrs.	13	G,	July 16, 1861.	Aug. 1, 1864.	
Parker, Horace A.	"	22	D,	Aug. 28, 1861.	Oct. 17, "	Wounded in the head in the Wilderness, Va., Oct. 17, 1864.
Parker, Nathan D.	"	9		Jan. 3, 1862.		Hospital Steward. Wounded near Richmond, Va., July 27, 1862. Formerly in 5th Reg.
Parker, Henrie K.	3 yrs.	1	L,			Colorado Cav. Killed near Fort Larned, Kansas, Sept. 25, 1864.

VOLUNTEERS.—Continued.

NAMES.	Term of Enlistment.	Reg.	Co.	Mustered into U.S. Service.	Mustered out or Discharged.	REMARKS.
Parker, Thomas A.	1 yr.		E,	Aug. 8, 1864.	June 28, 1865.	1st Bat. H. A., Ft. Warren. Formerly in 13th Reg., Co. G.
Parker, Walter S.	3 mos.	8	E,	July 19, "	Nov. 10, 1864.	
Parker, William C.	"	8	E,	"	"	
Peabody, Charles G.	3 yrs.	4	D,	Oct. 8, 1861.	July 19, 1865.	Minnesota Vols. Re-enlisted for three years, Jan. 1, 1864.
Peasley, George M., Corp.	9 mos.	50	D,	Sept. 19, 1862.	Aug. 24, 1863.	
Penney, Andrew J.	3 yrs.	22	D,	Aug. 28, 1861.	April 1, "	For disability.
Penniman, Nathaniel W.	"			Feb. 16, 1864.	Aug. 29, 1864.	Andrew Sharpshooters.
Perkins, Belmont, Lieut.	"	6	K,	Sept. 19, 1861.		Missouri Vols.
Perkins, Nelson A.	"		2,	Oct. 3, "		Andrew Sharpshooters.
Perkins, Walter G.	"	59	A,	Dec. 5, 1863.	July 30, 1865.	Killed at Gettysburg, July 2, '63. Formerly in 5th Reg, Co. B.
Peterson, Leonard,	"	33	D,	Aug. 5, 1862.		
Phillips, William M.	1 yr.	4	E,	Aug. 8, 1864.	June 28, 1865.	1st Bat. H. A., Ft. Warren.
Pierce, Edward F.	3 yrs.	2	E,	Jan. 27, 1864.		Cavalry, on the quota of Chelsea.
Pinkham, Charles B.	"		G,	Aug. 28, 1861.		N. H. Vols.
Pinkham, Orlando C.	"	3	8,	July 29, 1863.	Nov. 10, 1864.	For disability, H. A.
Pinkham, Tobias, Corp.	9 mos.	50	S,	Sept. 19, 1862.	July 30, 1865.	Died at Baton Rouge, May 28, 1863.
Porter, George H.	3 yrs.	59	B,	Jan. 5, 1864.	Aug. 1, 1864.	Taken prisoner at Bull Run, Va., Aug. 30, 1862. Enlisted again for one year in Co. B, Frontier Cav., Dec. 29, 1864.
Pratt, Charles S.	"	13	G,	July 16, 1861.		
Pratt, David, 2d,	1 yr.		E,	Aug. 8, 1864.	June 28, 1865.	1st Bat. H. A., Ft. Warren.
Pratt, Edward E.	9 mos.	50	D,	Sept. 19, 1862.		Died Oct. 13, 1863, in Reading.
Pratt, Edwin,	1 yr.		E,	Aug. 8, 1864.	June 28, 1865.	1st Bat. H. A., Ft. Warren. Formerly in 5th Reg., Co. B.

OF THE TOWN OF READING.   645

Pratt, Harland P.	1 yr.	50	E,	Aug. 8, 1864.	June 28, 1865.	1st Bat. H. A., Ft. Warren.
Pratt, Stillman M.	9 mos.	13	D,	Sept. 19, 1862.	Aug. 24, 1863.	Enlisted again Dec. 29, 1864, for one year, in Frontier Cavalry.
Pratt, Wilmot K.	3 yrs.		G,	July 16, 1861.	Aug. 1, 1864.	
Prentiss, Harley, Sergt.	9 mos.	50	D,	Sept. 19, 1862.	Aug. 24, 1863.	Enlisted again Aug. 8, 1864, for one year, in 1st Bat. H. A., Ft. Warren.
Prentiss, Samuel,	"	50	D,	"	"	Died in Reading, March 19, 1865. Formerly in Co. G, 13th Reg.
Preston, Charles B., Corp.	3 yrs.	1	E,	Jan. 4, 1864.		Mass. Cavalry.
Putnam, Henry E.	1 yr.		D,	Aug. 8, 1864.	June 28, 1865.	1st Bat. H. A., Ft. Warren.
Putten, John Van,	3 yrs.	33	D,	Aug. 5, 1862.	June 11, "	
Quigley, James,	"	56	G,	Jan. 19, 1864.		
Rahr, Christian E., Corp.	"	32	F,	Mar. 18, 1862.	Oct. 12, 1865.	For disability. Re-enlisted Jan. 4, 1864, for 3 years. Wounded at Petersburg, Va., July 29, 1864. A bullet went in at the backbone and out at the hipbone. Formerly in 5th Reg, Co. B, for 3 mos. Andrew Sharpshooters.
Randall, Lot J.	"		1	Feb. 16, 1864.		For disability.
Reed, William B.	"	33	D,	Aug. 5, 1862.	Oct. 20, 1863.	Formerly in Co. F, 47th Reg.
Richardson, Charles A.	1 yr.	50	E,	Aug. 8, 1864.	June 28, 1865.	
Richardson, David G., Corp.	9 mos.	50	D,	Sept. 19, 1862.	Aug. 24, 1863.	
Richardson, Horace A.	"		D,	"	"	
Richardson, J. Warren,	1 yr.		E,	Aug. 8, 1864.	June 28, 1865.	1st Bat. H. A., Ft. Warren.
Robinson, Charles H, Sergt.	3 yrs.	20	G,	Aug. 27, 1861.	Aug. 29, 1864.	Formerly in 5th Reg., Co. B, for 3 mos. Navy; ship "Ino.," Enlisted again Nov. 30, 1863, in 1st Reg. H. A., and killed at Spottsylvania, Va., May 19, 1864.
Robinson, John E.	1 yr.			Aug. 1, 1862.	Sept. 1, 1863.	
Rogers, George,	9 mos.	50	D,	Sept. 19, 1862.	Aug. 24, 1863.	
Ronde, John D. De, Corp.	3 yrs.	33	D,	Aug. 5, 1862.	July 6, 1865.	Formerly in the 5th and 20th Regts.
Ronde, Martin J. De.	"	12	A,	June 26, 1861.	July 7, 1862.	For disability.
Rowe, Henry J.	"	33	D,	Aug. 5, 1862.	Feb. 9, 1863.	"
Ruggles, Edwin O.	3 mos.	8	E,	July 19, 1864.	Nov. 10, 1864.	
Ruggles, Emily, Miss,	3 yrs.					By representative recruit.
Ruggles, Ira W.	"	14		Oct. 21, 1861.	Aug. 14, 1862.	Regimental band.

VOLUNTEERS.—Continued.

Names.	Term of Enlistment.	Reg.	Co.	Mustered into U. S. Service.	Mustered out or Discharged.	Remarks.
Sanborn, Benjamin C.	3 yrs.	22	D,	Aug. 28, 1861.		Died at Washington, Feb. 19, 1863.
Sanborn, Otis S., Corp.	"	33	D,	Aug. 5, 1862.		Died at Alexandria, Va., Oct. 22, 1862.
Sargent, Charles U.	3 mos.	8	E,	July 19, 1864.	Nov. 10, 1864.	
Schager, William J.	1 yr.			Dec. 17, "		1st Bat. Heavy Artillery.
Sherman, William H.	3 mos.	5	B,	May 1, 1861.	Aug. 1861.	Enlisted again in fall of 1862, in Co. E, 6th Reg, for 9 months.
Shuster, Christian,	3 yrs.	20	B,	Feb. 15, 1864.		For disability. H. A., formerly in band 28th Reg.
Simes, George W.	"		3	Dec. 8, 1863.	July 26, 1864.	For disability.
Smith, Charles B.	"	22	D,	Aug. 28, 1861.	Dec. 7, 1862.	1st Bat. H. A., Ft. Warren.
Smith, Emerson,	1 yr.		E,	Aug. 8, 1864.	June 28, 1865.	For disability.
Smith, Franklin H.	3 yrs.	33	D,	Aug. 5, 1862.	Nov. 19, 1862.	Died at Baltimore, Md., Feb. 24, 1865; Mortally wounded at Weldon R. R., Va., Sept. 30, 1864; died at City Point, Va., Oct. 6, 1864.
Smith, Josiah,	"	18	K,	Jan. 4, 1864.		
Smith, Solon B.		18	K,	"		
Smith, Sydney L.						Navy; ship "Kearsarge." Assistant Engineer, and was in the action with the "Alabama."
Somes, Gardner G.	3 yrs.	13	G,	July 16, 1861.	Oct. 22, 1862.	For disability.
Stevens, Charles H., Capt.	"	15	A,	" 12, "		Enlisted as Corp. Was promoted to 2d Lieut. July 19, 1862, to 1st Lieut. Nov. 21, 1862, and to Capt. July 4, 1862. Was wounded at Gettysburg, July 2, 1863, and mortally wounded at Bristow's Station, Oct. 14, 1863, and died at Alexandria, Va., the next day.

Stone, Horace E.	3 yr.	13	G,	Aug. 12, 1862.	Jan. 3, 1863.	For disability. Enlisted again July 19, 1864, in Co. E, 8th Reg, for 3 mos.
Stowell, Frank S.	"	33	D,	" 5, "	June 11, 1865.	Navy, credited by the State.
Stimpson, Patrick,	2 yrs.			Dec. 23, 1864.		B Battery.
Sullivan, John O.	3 yrs.					Navy, credited by the State.
Sullivan, Patrick,	2 yrs.					
Sweetser, Samuel T.	9 mos.	50	D,	Sept. 19, 1862.	Aug. 24, 1863.	For disability. Enlisted again Aug. 8,'64, for 1 year in 1st Bat. H. A., Ft. Warren.
Symonds, Thomas S.	3 yrs.	22	D,	Aug. 28, 1861.	Oct. 2, 1862.	Enlisted again Dec. 29, 1864, in Co. B, Frontier Cavalry, for 1 year.
Taylor, Charles,	9 mos.	50	D,	Sept. 19, 1862.	Aug. 24, 1863.	Navy, credited by the State.
Taylor, James R.	1 yr.					By representative recruit.
Temple, Mark M.	3 yrs.					Veteran Reserve Corps.
Terry, John,	"	12	A,	Dec. 14, 1864.	July 8, 1864.	
Thompson, Eben P., Corp.				June 26, 1861.		
Thompson, William H.	1 yr.					Navy, credited by the State.
Tibbitts, Asa P., Corp.	9 mos.	50	D,	Sept. 19, 1862.		Died June 8, 1863, at Baton Rouge, La.
Tibbitts, Charles H., Corp.	3 yrs.	33	D,	Aug. 5, "		Deserted March 30, 1863. Formerly in 5th Reg., Co. B, for 3 months.
Tibbitts, Frank L.	3 mos.	5	B,	May 1, 1861.		Taken prisoner at Bull Run, July 21, 1861. Released in June, 1862.
Tibbitts, Harrison, Serg.	3 yrs.	12	A,	June 26, "		Died at Alexandria, Va., Oct. 19, 1862.
Tibbitts, Warren V. B.	"	33	D,	Aug. 5, 1862.		Died March 15, 1863, near Stafford Court House, Va.
Tobin, William,	2 yrs.					Navy, credited by the State.
Totten, Robert C.	3 yrs.	13	G,	Aug. 12, 1862.	Aug. 1, 1864.	"
Tucker, John,	1 yr.					
Tucker, Thomas E.	"					
Turner, Naaman H., Capt.	3 yrs.	33	D,	Aug. 5, 1862.	June 11, 1865.	Promoted to 1st Lieut. March 3, '63, and to Capt. March 9, 1864. 1st Bat. H. A., Ft. Warren.
Tweed, Charles O.	1 yr.		E,	Aug. 8, 1864	" 28, "	For disability. Enlisted again Aug. 8, 1864, in Co. E, 1st Bat. H. A., Ft. Warren, for 1 year.
Vaughn, Samuel,	3 yrs.	13	G,	July 16, 1861.	Jan. 3, 1863.	

VOLUNTEERS.—Continued.

NAMES.	Term of Enlistment.	Reg.	Co.	Mustered into U. S. Service.	Mustered out or Discharged.	REMARKS.
Wadlin, Daniel H.	1 yr.	4	K,	1864.		
Wakefield, Wendall P.	3 yrs.	59	G,	March 4, 1864.	July 30, 1865.	
Walsh, James N.	"	9	B,	July 22, 1862.	Oct. 30, 1862.	For disability.
Washington, George H.	1 yr.					Navy, credited by the State.
Wardwell, Henry F.	3 yrs.	33	D,	Aug. 5, 1862.		Died at Washington, Feb. 15, 1863. Formerly in 5th Reg., Co. B, for 3 months.
Weary, James,	1 yr.		E,	Aug. 10, 1864.	June 28, 1865.	1st Bat. H. A., Ft. Warren. Formerly in 11th Reg., Co. I, for 3 years.
Weeden, Chester,	1 yr.					Navy, credited by the State.
Weeks, John E.	"					"
Welch, John F.	3 yrs.	2		Sept. 2, 1861.	Mar. 17, 1863.	For disability. Andrew Sharpshooters.
Weston, George T.	"	22	D,	Aug. 28, 1861.	Feb. 6, "	"
Weston, John H.	9 mos.	50	D,	Sept. 19, 1862.	Aug. 24, "	Enlisted again July 19, 1864, in 8th Reg. for 3 months. Died in Reading, Oct. 26, 1865.
Weston, Charles P.	3 yrs.	20	E,	Feb. 17, 1863.	June 28, 1865.	Navy, ship "Water Witch." Taken prisoner June 3, '64. Paroled Oct. 18, '64 1st Bat. H. A., Ft. Warren.
Weston, Milton P.	1 yr.		E,	Aug. 8, 1864.		
Weston, Robert H., Corp.	3 yrs.		A,	Aug. 30, 1861.		Taken prisoner at Ball's Bluff, Oct. 21, 1861. Died at Falmouth, Va., Jan. 13, 1863. Formerly in 5th Reg., Co. B, for 3 months.
Weston, S. Nelson,	9 mos.	50	D,	Sept. 19, 1862.	Aug. 24, 1863.	Died in Reading, Sept. 6, 1863.
Whitman, Albert H.	3 yrs.	22	D,	Aug. 28, 1861.	Feb. 21, 1862.	For disability. Enlisted again Sept. 19, 1862, in Co. D, 50th Reg., for 9 months.
White, Lorenzo D.	"	22	D,	"	Oct. 17, 1864.	Wounded May 8, 1864, at Spottsylvania Court House, Va.
Wight, Ephraim,	"	18	K,	July 14, 1863.	July 13, 1865.	Drafted and went.

Name	Term		Co.	Enlisted	Discharged	Remarks
Wiley, Elbridge A.	1 yr.		E,	Aug. 10, 1864.	June 28, 1865.	1st Bat. H. A., Ft. Warren.
Wiggins, John R.	3 yrs.			Jan. 5, 1864.		Nims' Battery, on the quota of Chelsea.
Williams, Charles,	"			"		"
Williams, Joseph F.	9 mos.	50	D,	Sept. 19, 1862.	Aug. 24, 1863.	
Willis, Ethan,	3 yrs.	18	K,	Jan. 2, 1864.	July 13, 1865.	Navy, credited by the State.
Wilkins, Theodore L.	1 yr.					"
Williams, Lawrence,	"					"
Wilson, Edward,						
Wilmarth, Augustus A.	3 yrs.	13	C,	July 16, 1861.		Died in Washington, Jan. 4, 1863.
Winn, George B.	"	33	G,	Aug. 5, 1862.		1st Bat. H. A., Ft. Warren.
Wood, Albert A.	1 yr.		E,	Aug. 8, 1864.	June 28, 1865.	"
Wright, Henry D.	"		E,	"	"	"
Wright, Hiram F.	9 mos.	50	D,	Sept. 19, 1862.	Aug. 24, 1863.	
Young, Charles O.	3 yrs.	12	A,	June 9, 1864.		Died Sept. 8, 1863, at Rappahannock, Va.
Young, Edward B.	"			June 26, 1861.		Drafted, and put in a substitute.
Young, Sumner B.	"	12	A,			Taken prisoner July 2, 1863. Supposed to have died at Belle Isle.
Youre, Robert,	1 yr.					Navy, credited by the State.

Total, including re-enlistments 411

Number killed in battle 15

Number died of disease contracted in the service 33

NORTH READING.

NAMES OF PERSONS WHO WERE IN THE MILITARY OR NAVAL SERVICE DURING THE WAR OF THE REBELLION FROM NORTH READING.

Allen Charles, 1st Reg.
Abbott, Joseph H., 1st Batt'y, Ft. Warren.
Burrell, Elbridge W., 1st Batt'y and 11th Reg.
Bradford, D. B., Sharpshooters.
Bentley, Noah, 15th Reg.
Burditt, Charles J., 33d Reg.
Burditt, Charles, 2d Reg.
Burditt, John N., 33d Reg.
Barker, Henry C., 33d Reg.
Bartlett, Joseph H., 32d Reg.
Batchelder, Josiah, 16th Reg.
Batchelder, Joseph T. (Sergt.), 50th Reg.
Buxton, Edmund, 1st Batt'y.
Buxton, Elijah, 1st Batt'y.
Brien O. John, 1st Batt'y.
Crane, Dennis, 26th Reg.
Carleton, Geo. W., 22d Reg.
Chapman, Ezra W., 22d Reg.
Coney, Chas. W. H., 33d Reg.
Cross, Samuel B., 33d Reg.
Curmick, James M., 32d Reg.
Carr, Arthur W., 33d Reg.
Cook, Augustin P., Signal Corps and 50th Reg.
Coney, John S. (Lieut.), 50th Reg.
Coney, Edward S., 1st Batt'y.
Case, Daniel W., 50th Reg.
Collins, Patrick, 2d Reg.
Doe, Geo. W., Batt'y.
Dane, James O., 33d Reg.
Davis, William, 32d Reg.
Dean, Bradley (Lieut.), 33d Reg.
Damon, Christopher C., 50th Reg.
Dixon, John H., 2d Reg.
Dame, James A., 1st Batt'y.
Eaton, Daniel W., Sharpshooters.
Eaton, Appleton P., 50th Reg.
Eaton, Edwin (Ft. Warren), 1st Batt'y.
Eaton, Thomas, 2d Reg.
Eaton, Geo. W., Signal Corps.
Flint, Henry E., Sharpshooters.
Flint, Henry C., 26th and 59th Reg.
Flint, Frank S., 11th Reg.
Flint, Chas. A., 1st Reg.
Flint, Asa A., 50th Reg.
Flint, Wm. W., 50th Reg.
Flint, C. H., Batt'y.
Flint, W. Scott, 2d Reg.
Fairbanks, James E., 26th Reg.
Fry, William, 33d Reg.
Foster, Sumner, 2d Reg.
Gerry, William, 11th Reg.
Green, Geo. W., 50th Reg.
Gates, Henry A., 50th Reg.
Goodwin, Samuel, 2d Reg.
Grant, John, 28th Reg.

Hinman, Edward P., 11th Reg.
Harris, Thos. W., 50th Reg.
Holt, Milton G., 50th Reg.
Hunter, Wm. A., 50th Reg.
Haynes, Geo. H., Rifle Corps.
Jones, John, 22d Reg.
Jenkins, F., 16th Reg.
Jones, Wm. H., Frontier Cavalry.
Kelly, Wm., 33d Reg.
King, Andrew G., 33d Reg.
Keawley, Joseph, Batt'y.
Little, Moses, Batt'y.
Munroe, Brigham A., 2d Reg.
Munroe, George, 1st Reg.
McIntire, Wm. C., 39th Reg.
McIntire, John, 11th Reg.
McIntire, Ezra, 12th Reg.
McIntire, Chas. H., 26th Reg.
McIntire, Geo. E., 2d Reg.
McIntire, David P., 35th and 1st Reg.
McIntire, Charles W., 35th and 1st Reg.
McIntire, Horace M., 35th and 1st Reg.
McIntire, Eliab P., 1st Reg.
McIntire, Dexter, 1st Reg.
McIntire, Daniel D., 1st Reg.
McIntire, Caleb, 1st Reg.
McIntire, Fred. C., 15th Reg.
McIntire, Sylvester H., Frontier Cavalry.
Munroe, Chas. M., Sig. Corps and 50th Reg.
Mason, Osro (Ft. Warren), 1st Batt'n.
Morton, Chas. H., 51st Reg.
Munroe, Wm. H., 2d Reg.
McMunus, John, Rifle Corps.
Nichols, Geo. W., 22d Reg.
Nichols, Moses E., 3d Reg.
Nichols, Wm. W., 11th Reg.
Nichols, Elijah, 33d Reg.
Nichols, Nathaniel, 59th and 50th Regs.
Nichols, Amos B., 50th Reg.
Norwood, George A., 31st and 42d Regs.
Norwood, James, 39th and 42d Regs.
Orcutt, Joseph C., Sharpshooters.
Proctor, George W. N., 2d Reg.
Poole, John F., 33d Reg.
Platts, Chas. B., Sig. Corps and 50th Reg.
Platts, George H., 1st Batt'n.
Powers, William, 1st Batt'n.
Quailan, J. W., Artillery.
Rayner, Walter, 1st Batt'n, Fort Warren.
Rayner, Warren G., Illinois Reg.
Rice, Chas. W., 35th Reg.
Snith Joseph A, 1st Reg.
Smith, Chas. H., 2d Reg.
Smith John P., 14th Reg.
Simpson, George F. 11th Reg.
Sheldon, George F., R. I. Reg.

Sheldon, Rufus, 1st Batt'y.
Sidelinker, G. W., 50th Reg.
Swan, Daniel, 1st Reg.
Stearns, C. E., 59th Reg.
Sweetser, Oliver S., 1st Reg.
Stewart, J. A., Battery.
Travis, Nathan F., Sharpshooters.
Tileston, G. H., 33d Reg
Thompson, William, 30th Reg.
Watts, Ruggles T., 33d Reg.
Weston, Frank C., 50th Reg.

Weston, Justin M., 50th Reg.
Whitehouse, Chas. E., 50th Reg.
Walls, Paschal A., Sig. Corps and 50th Reg.
Walls, George S., 42d Reg.
Wright, Thomas, 59th Reg.
Walsh, Robert B., 40th Reg.
Whipple, Calvin, 1st Reg.
West, Thomas P., Frontier Cavalry.
Hammond, Harrison B., Signal Corps.

N. B. — Some of the following named persons served in both military and naval warfare : —

Donnell, James O., Jr., Navy.
Gilchrist, Frank C., Navy.
Hunter, Needham, Navy.
Holt, William P., Navy.
McIntire, Caleb, Navy.

Morris, John, Navy.
Reynolds, John, Navy.
Weston, Francis C., Navy.
White, William L., Navy.

ROLL OF CO. E, SIXTEENTH MASSACHUSETTS REGIMENT.

REGULAR SERVICE. — THREE YEARS' ENLISTMENT.

Captain. — John Wiley, 2d, South Reading.
First Lieutenant. — James R. Darracott, Boston.
Second Lieutenant. — James Oliver, South Reading.
Sergeants. — John H. Woodfin, John Cowdrey, James F. Mansfield, John Day, Joseph T. Wright, South Reading.
Corporals. — Henry Goodell, Woburn ; Jeremiah S. Batchelder, South Reading ; Clifford B. Fowle, Woburn ; Alvan S. Warren, Hiram Woodis, Warren Nichols, Henry E. Hilborn, South Reading ; Hollis M. Gilman, Lowell.
Musicians. — John A. Thompson, South Reading ; Joseph L. Daniels, Bellingham ; Alonzo S. Norris, Ellenburg, N. Y.
Wagoner. — G. F. D. Skinner, of South Reading.

Privates.

Aborn, Warren, Reading.
Allen, John F., Reading.
Ansorge, Alfred E., Winchester.
Adams, Samuel H., South Reading.
Babcock, Chas. F., Sherburne.
Batchelder, Josiah, Jr., North Reading.
Bruce, Clarence M., South Reading.
Bancroft, Benj. F., South Reading.
Bancroft, Wm., Woburn.
Bickford, Chas. F., South Reading.
Burditt, Chas. F., South Reading.
Burditt, Aaron, South Reading.
Bent, Amos R., Bellingham.
Bermingham, John, New Braintree.
Bowen, Geo. E., North Attleboro'.
Bond, James, Jr., South Reading.
Cutler, Benj. S., Woburn.
Campbell, Wm. M., East Abington.
Carter, George, South Reading.
Chapman, Richard W., South Reading.
Clifford, Leonard, South Reading.
Caldwell, Samuel P., Cambridge.

Cutter, Albert, Woburn.
Cutter, Samuel B., Woburn.
Corcoran, Thomas H., Boston.
Davis, Royal A., Winchester.
Damon, Albert, Reading.
Damon, Henry, Reading.
Darling, Edward C., Lynn.
Danforth, Edwin S., Woburn.
Day, John A., Woburn
Eaton, John H., South Reading.
Evans, Thomas A., South Reading.
Eaton, James, Saugus.
Eaton, Joseph, Reading.
Farnum, William, Somerville.
Flagg, Warren F., Concord.
Foster, Henry L., Stoneham.
Flint, Herman, Concord.
Fairbern, George H., Somerville.
Freeman, William T., Boston.
Gates, Samuel, Woburn.
Heath, Micah, South Reading.
Hettler, Adam H., South Reading.

Houseman, John M., South Reading.
Howard, Charles, Boston.
Holbrook, Amos A., Upton.
Hunnewell, William H., Winchester.
Hutchinson, John A., Waltham.
Hurd, Joseph L., South Reading.
Hart, Charles H., South Reading.
Jenkins, Forrest, North Reading.
Jennison, Luther P., Holliston.
Joy, Henry, South Randolph.
Kelsey, E., Chatham Four Corners, N. Y.
Knowlton, William H., Hopkinton.
Kennison, Daniel S., South Reading.
Kidder, Daniel W., Saugus.
Lee, John F., South Reading.
Locke, George L., South Reading.
Marshall, Charles H., Holliston.
Mellen, Charles A., Reading.
Mansfield, Joseph H., South Reading.
Martin, William H., Chicopee.
Newhall, Elbridge G., Lynnfield.
Newhall, Lucius E., Lynn.

Nichols, Geo. W., Southboro'.
Nichols, Hannibal, South Reading.
Nichols, Joseph, Jr., Cambridgeport.
Perry, Charles H., Woburn.
Pratt, Benj. C., South Reading.
Richards, Fred. S., South Reading.
Rogers, Peter M., Stoneham.
Safford, Edward P., South Boston.
Snow, Robert F., Chelsea.
Stimpson, James W., South Reading.
Sweetser, Luther, South Reading.
Sweetser, Francis, South Reading.
Smith, Charles H., Woburn.
Simmons, John N., Woburn.
Stone, Orrin, South Reading.
Symmes, Rufus, Limerick, Me.
Taber, Thomas, Sherburne.
Townley, Benjamin, South Reading.
Wiley, George H., South Reading.
Whitford, John, South Reading.
Wrin, Edward, Roxbury.

ROLL OF CO. D, FIFTIETH MASSACHUSETTS REGIMENT.

NINE MONTHS' SERVICE, 1862-3.

Captain. — Josiah W. Coburn, Reading.
First Lieutenant. — John S. Coney, North Reading.
Second Lieutenant. — Oramel G. Abbott, Reading.
Sergeants. — Stephen P. Rowell, Melrose ; Levi Swain, Jr., Wilmington ; Harley Prentiss, Reading ; Edmund D. Pearson, Wilmington ; Joseph T. Batchelder, North Reading ; George J. Bartlett, Asa C. Buck, Reading.
Corporals. — James P. Morton, Wilmington ; Geo. M. Peaslee, Wm. Buck, Wm. H. Nash, Reading ; Justine M. Weston, North Reading ; Samuel T. Sweetser, Daniel G. Richardson, Reading ; Augustine P. Cook, North Reading ; Tobias Pinkham, Asa P. Tibbetts, Reading.
Musician. — John L. Farwell, Reading.
Wagoner. — George Rogers, Reading.

Privates.

Bunker, Noble, Reading.
Battelle, Chas. P., Reading.
Boyce, Chas. M., Reading.
Bruce, Geo. G., Reading.
Bancroft, Henry L., Wilmington.
Bancroft, Geo., Wilmington.
Blanchard, Edwin, Wilmington.
Bancroft, Haskel K., Reading.
Barnes, John A., Reading.
Cook, Geo. W., Salem.
Coney, Geo. A., Reading.
Coney, Geo. C., Reading.
Carr, Daniel W., Wilmington.
Damon, Christopher C., North Reading.
Delay, Jeremiah, Reading.
Evans, Chas. A., Reading.
Eames, Henry W., Wilmington.
Eaton, Appleton P., North Reading.
Eaton, Moses F., Reading.

Fortiss, Wm., Wilmington.
Frost, Charles C., Reading.
Fletcher, Nathan B., Reading.
Flint, George B., North Reading.
Fulton, Joseph W., Andover.
Flint, Wm. W., North Reading.
Flint, Asa A., North Reading.
Gowing, Charles, Lawrence.
Green, Geo. W., North Reading.
Goodwin, George H., Reading.
Grover, Charles A., Reading.
Gowing, Gayton, Wilmington.
Gale, Henry A., North Reading.
Harnden, George W., Andover.
Hunter, William A., North Reading.
Harris, Thomas W., North Reading.
Holt, Squire, Reading.
Hopkins, Joseph B., Reading.
Hopkins, Geo. W., Reading.

Howard, John L., Wilmington.
Harnden, Otis, Wilmington.
Holt, Milton G., North Reading.
Holt, Charles, Reading.
Jenkins, Charles, North Reading.
Jones, Loring, North Reading.
Kendall, Waldo T., Charlestown.
LaClair, Wm., Reading.
Marshall, Wm. H., Reading.
Munroe, Chas. M., North Reading.
Myers, Chas., Reading.
McIntire, Amos, Reading.
McAleer, Joseph, Reading.
Miligan, George, Wilmington.
Nichols, Amos B., North Reading.
Nichols, Nathaniel, North Reading.
Nichols, Wm. R., Reading.
Nichols, Edward E., Reading.
Pearson, Daniel N., Wilmington.
Parker, Edward, Reading.
Parker, Clarkson, Reading.

Pratt, Stillman M., Reading.
Pratt, Edward E., Reading.
Platts, Chas. B., North Reading.
Perkins, Walter G., Reading.
Prentiss, Samuel, Reading.
Pearson, Geo. O., Wilmington.
Richardson, Horace A., Reading.
Sidelinker, Geo. W., North Reading.
Taylor, Chas., Reading.
Trull, John A., Andover.
Upton, Russell, Wilmington.
Upton, Ambrose, Wilmington.
Williams, Joseph F., Reading.
Weston, Nelson S., Reading.
Weston, Francis C., North Reading.
Walls, Paschal A., Reading.
Wright, Hiram F., Reading.
Weston, John H., Reading.
Whitman, Albert H., Reading.
Whitehouse, Charles E., North Reading.

ROLL OF CO. E, FIFTIETH MASSACHUSETTS REGIMENT.

NINE MONTHS' SERVICE, 1862-3.

Captain.— Samuel F. Littlefield, South Reading.
First Lieutenant. — Horace M. Warren, South Reading.
Second Lieutenant. — James D. Draper, South Reading.
Sergeants. — Jason H. Knight, James M. Sweetser, James A. Burditt, Charles F. Hartshorn, George K. Gilman, Geo. H. Green, Thos. Sweetser, South Reading.
Corporals. — Joseph S. Eustis, James M. Morrill, John Q. A. Parker, W. N. Tyler, Rufus F. Draper, Geo. Carter, South Reading ; Myron H. Whittredge, Lynnfield; Chas. S. Emerson, South Reading.

Privates.

Anderson, Geo. W., South Reading.
Aborn, Henry, South Reading.
Bruce, Jasper F., South Reading.
Brown, John C., Saugus.
Brown, Benjamin V., Lynnfield.
Barber, Thomas, South Reading.
Brown, Charles H., Hingham.
Butterfield, Francis M., Saugus.
Barron, Elliot F., Melrose.
Bent, John S., Boston.
Brown, Jonas G., Melrose.
Cox, Geo., Lynnfield.
Cox, James P., Melrose.
Crow, Wm. L., South Reading.
Cartwright, Joseph, South Reading.
Cooper, Reuben L., South Reading.
Dix, Joseph O., Melrose.
Danforth, Alfred W., South Reading.
Deadman, Wm. D., South Reading.
Davis, Chas. H., South Reading.
Dodge, Ignatius, Topsfield.
Degen, Chas. F., Watertown.
Donoghue, John J., Melrose.
Eustis, Wm. C., Cambridge.
Eaton, John Smith, South Reading.

Eaton, Chester W., South Reading.
Emerson, Justus, Lynnfield.
Estes, O'Neal J., South Reading.
Farrell, Michael, Melrose.
Fisk, Willard L., Saugus.
Fisk, Joseph A., South Reading.
Fuller, George P., Melrose.
Hamilton, Robert, South Reading.
Harrington, Chas. T., South Reading.
Hawkes, John, South Reading.
Knight, Henry C., South Reading.
Kingman, Wm. W., South Reading.
Lyman, Henry H., South Reading.
Moses, Geo., South Reading.
Murkland, Robt. L., South Reading.
Miller, Chas. C., South Reading.
McAllister, Geo. H., Melrose.
Morton, Joseph, Wilmington.
Moses, John F., South Reading.
Moore, John L., South Reading.
Newman, J. Frank, South Reading.
Newhall, David, South Reading.
Place, Franklin C., Charlestown.
Pope, Jacob H., South Reading.
Prentice, Chas., Melrose.

Pilling, Jonathan, South Reading.
Resterrick, Walter, South Reading.
Randall, Howard, Raynham.
Richardson, Osborne, Jr., Lynnfield.
Richardson, Irving, Lynnfield.
Snell, Franklin L., South Reading.
Snell, Louis A., South Reading.
Skinner, Wm. S., South Reading.
Shelton, Thos., Melrose.
Stafford, Wm. C., Saugus.
Symonds, Chas. H., Malden.
Sweetser, Elbridge L., South Reading.
Stimpson, Wm. W., South Reading.
Trefethen, Benjamin, Saugus.
Thompson, Geo. A., South Reading.
Tibbetts, Geo. E., South Reading.
Tyler, Geo. L., South Reading.
Upton, Augustine, Danvers.
Unrah, Geo. R., Malden.
Winship, Samuel, South Reading.
Walton, Oliver, 2d, South Reading.
Wellman, Henry B., Lynnfield.

LIST OF THE ENROLLED MEN OF SOUTH READING,

AND THE AMOUNT THAT EACH PAID IN AID OF FILLING THE QUOTA, UNDER THE CALL OF JULY 18, 1864.

[Those marked with a star * denote they were in the service at the time of the call, or absent from the Town.]

Name	Amount	Name	Amount	Name	Amount
Aborn, John G.	$150 00	Burditt, Joseph T.		Dager, Thomas	$30 00
Atwell, William H.	120 00	Burditt, William		Dager, Alfred A.	25 00
Adams, J. W.	65 00	Burditt, Henry		*Deadman, Wm. D.	25 00
Armour, William L.	30 00	*Burditt, James A.		Dean, J. W.	25 00
Adams, Charles W.	25 00	Cutter, George W.	$125 00	Dunn, H. B.	25 00
*Aborn, Henry		Coombs, S. G. B.	110 00	Daland, George A.	20 00
Arrington, Geo. B.		Cardell, E. Lyman	75 00	Davis, John	10 00
Aborn, F. W.		Cheney, Chas. H. R.	60 00	Davis, C. Horton	10 00
*Allen, Richard W.		Chapman, Amos W.	55 00	*Danforth, A. H.	
Blanchard, Abner J.	150 00	Currier, Samuel E.	50 00	*Day, Joseph L.	
Bicknell, Alfred	150 00	Currier, A. A.	50 00	*Danforth, N. F.	
Brown, James, Jr.	100 00	Cowdrey, Waldo E.	50 00	Drake, Alvan, Jr.	
Bailey, Isaiah W.	60 00	Coombs, A. B.	50 00	*Dunn, William A.	
Buck, Aaron D.	60 00	Clark, Asaph	25 00	Doe, Albert	
Britton, Richard	55 00	Clark, Sylvanus	25 00	Davis, Talbert C.	
Beach, Horace H.	55 00	Cash, William L.	25 00	Dennett, John F.	
Blanchard, Abner N.	50 00	Cash, J. T.	25 00	Day, John	
Bancroft, Joseph W.	50 00	Carter, Charles S.	20 00	*Draper, Rufus F.	
Brown, Charles B.	50 00	Chadwick, Joseph	15 00	Emerson, James F.	150 00
Bullen, George	50 00	Carter, Charles, 2d	10 00	Evans, Montello C.	55 00
Bliss, Charles R.	50 00	Carey, Gilman	10 00	Emerson, John H.	50 00
Burrill, Alonzo P.	50 00	Churchill, L. O.	10 00	Emerson, Chas. S.	50 00
Bishop, James H.	50 00	Carey, Daniel		Emerson, Putnam	50 00
Burbank, B. B.	25 00	Colby, George		Eames, Joshua	50 00
Boardman, Moses B.	25 00	Cox, Timothy		Eaton, Henry L.	50 00
Brierly, J., Jr.	25 00	Clements, Chas. E.		Eaton, Isaac F.	50 00
Burditt, M. B.	20 00	*Carey, George E.		Eaton, John Sullivan	50 00
Barker, H. F.	10 00	*Carter, George		Emerson, James E.	35 00
Burgess, Edwin B.	10 00	*Coon, William L.		Eaton, Levi B.	25 00
Bayrd, C. L.	10 00	*Carr, Thornton B.		Eaton, Chester W.	25 00
Butler, William	5 00	Copp, John H.		Eaton, Everett W.	25 00
Butterfield, E. A.	5 00	Dole, William	50 00	Evans, George W.	25 00
Burditt, Sylvester	3 00	Dole, John	50 00	Eager, John	10 00
Boardman, John T.		Degen, H. D.	50 00	Emerson, D. W.	10 00
Butler, Henry		Draper, James D.	50 00	*Emerson, Rufus H.	
Butler, Aaron, Jr.		Dearborn, George E.	50 00	Emerson, Howard	

OF THE TOWN OF READING.

Emerson, L. N.		Kidder, C. E.	$10 00	Oliver, David B.	$10 00
Evans, William O.		*Knight, Albert M.		Oliver, Charles M.	
Eames, Daniel		Kirby, Thomas		Oliver, John	
Eaton, Henry		Kennedy, Patrick		Oliver, John G.	
Eaton, S. A.		*Knight, Jason H.		Oliver, Ernest E.	
Eaton, John B.		*Kingman, William W.		Philpot, Cyrus A.	75 00
Eustis, Joseph S.		Lewis, William W.	100 00	Packard, George	65 00
Fields, H. G.	$25 00	Locke, John W.	75 00	Pierce, James M.	60 00
Flint, Luther W.	25 00	Le Baron, Ziba	50 00	Peacock, Frank R.	60 00
Fifield, Charles A.	25 00	Leighton, Jacob	25 00	Parker, Samuel, Jr.	50 00
Fairbanks, David S.	20 00	Lane, Loami C.	25 00	Patch, Charles	50 00
Flint, Silas W.	5 00	Lord, George	15 00	Phipps, J. W.	40 00
Fogg, Lewis		Leathers, Albert N.	10 00	Pratt, George	35 00
Farnsworth, C. P.		*Lucas, Edward		Parker, James E.	25 00
*Foster, Albert A.		*Lucas, James H.		Porter, Elam	25 00
Goodwin, Andrew	60 00	Lawrence, Henry		Putney, Samuel	20 00
Godfrey, Warren H.	50 00	Lowe, Joseph K.		Pope, J. Holman	20 00
Gilman, George K.	15 00	Leavitt, Freeman		Phillips, Joseph A.	10 00
Gammon, Orlando	15 00	Mansfield, A. A.	60 00	Perkins, David	10 00
Grey, Israel	10 00	Martin, William	50 00	Pillings, Joseph	10 00
Griffin, Francis J.	5 00	Martin, Frederic	50 00	Parker, W. D.	5 00
Gould, Thomas		Mansfield, Benjamin	50 00	Phillips, Micah	5 00
Griffin, Woodbury		Merrill, Greeley	50 00	Pitman, Lawrence J.	
Hartshorne, Jacob C.	75 00	Morton, Joseph	50 00	Plummer, William	
Hart, Everett	75 00	Mayo, N. C.	50 00	Plummer, William J.	
Hawkes, Albert	60 00	Mason, D. P.	50 00	Parker, Henry	
Harrington, C. T.	55 00	Murkland, Robt. L.	30 00	Perkins, Zenas	
Hutchinson, A. J.	55 00	McCarty, J. B.	25 00	Putney, George H.	
Harrington, Wm. H.	50 00	Morton, J. R.	25 00	Parker, John Q. A.	
Haskell, Daniel F.	50 00	Merrian, A. E.	20 00	Ripley, Thomas W.	50 00
Hartshorne, John W.	50 00	Moody, L. J.	15 00	Rayner, William E.	50 00
Hartshorne, H. G.	50 00	McMahan, Thomas	15 00	Rayner, James	50 00
Hartshorne, Jona. F.	50 00	McMasters, Samuel	10 00	Reed, John J.	50 00
Hutchinson, Oscar	50 00	Magner, William	10 00	Reagan, P. J.	30 00
Hawkes, L. B.	50 00	Maxim, Charles R.	10 00	Richardson, Warren	25 00
Hollis, John B.	50 00	Mayo, Samuel	5 00	Ryder, Verenas H.	25 00
Holt, F. J.	50 00	*Marshall, Cyrus E.		Ripley, A. N.	10 00
Hart, Henry J.	25 00	*McKay, Joseph C.		Rayner, John	5 00
Hill, Hiram P.	25 00	*Mansfield, Edward G.		Ripley, Daniel S.	
Hamblin, Wm. A.	25 00	*Morse, John S.		Rand, John	
Hartshorne, Chas. F.	15 00	*McAllister, David		Russell, George W.	
Hartshorne, W. H.	10 00	Martin, Harvey		Richardson, S. O., Jr.	
Hopkins, E. G.	5 00	*Mayson, James		*Ransom, E. M.	
Hawkes, Adam A.		*Marshall, Benjamin		Reed, Luther	
*Heath, William S.		Mansfield, Eugene E.		Rimrey, Jonathan C.	
*Hartshorne, Jere. W.		*Morrill, James M.		Riley, P.	
Hewes, Edwin L.		*Moulton, Erastus		Stevens, John	100 00
Hoyt, Henry D.		Niles, Charles E.	50 00	Swain, S. O.	100 00
*Hilbourn, Henry E.		Newhall, William J.	50 00	Savage, J. G.	60 00
Hill, G. S.		Newhall, John S.	25 00	Stoddard, Wm. O.	60 00
*Hanglin, William		Nickerson, S. H.	20 00	Sweetser, John E.	50 00
*Hart, John F.		Nichols, Everett	20 00	Stowell, Issachar, 3d	50 00
Harding, James		Nichols, James	10 00	Stowell, H. W.	25 00
*Hurd, Joseph L.		*Newhall, Elbridge		Spear, William	25 00
Hawkes, John		Nichols, George R.		Stearns, Charles H.	25 00
Jenkins, J. W.	50 00	*Nichols, George H.		Sweetser, E. Felton	25 00
Jameson, James	35 00	Nickerson, Franklin		Seaver, R.	20 00
Jones, A. N.	10 00	Newhall, David		Sawin, Lyman	10 00
Jordan, Charles		*Newman, J. Frank		Strong, W. G.	10 00
Jameson, Edward		Oliver, B. W.	30 00	Sheldon, Isaac F.	10 00
Keene, Lorenzo D.	60 00	O'Leary, Richard	15 00	Stimpson, Geo. W. Jr.	10 00
Knight, H. C.	20 00	O'Niel, Michael	15 00	Spaulding, Frank	5 00

656 GENEALOGICAL HISTORY

*Stoddard, Geo. W.		Thomas, G. W.	$10 00	Williams, Leonard T.	$5 00
Skinner, Benjamin D.		Twisden, Thomas	10 00	White, Cyrus N.	5 00
Sweetser, Thomas		*Tibbetts, Albert H.		*Wiley, William H.	
*Spaulding, John W.		Thompson, John F.		Wiley, Joseph L.	
Sweetser, Jewett B.		Twiss, A. J.		*Wiley, J. Barnard	
*Smilie, John H.		Tucker, John P.		*Wheeler, Morris P.	
*Simons, Artemas		Tarbox, Charles W.		*Wright, Frank M.	
Sharpe, Daniel W.		*Tuttle, H. B.		*Wilkins, E. L.	
Smith, Thomas		Tuttle, Joseph		Walker, Charles R.	
Seaver, George A.		Tibbetts, George E.		Whitney, Edward W.	
Simms, John		Trask, Charles		*Wright, Dexter C.	
*Sheafe, Joseph P.		Upton, E. A.	25 00	*Walton, Samuel L.	
*Sawyer, Sylvester		Upton, E. P.	10 00	Walker, James	
Smith, Frederic		Unknown,	4 00	*Wiley, Baxter J.	
Stowell, Elbridge W.		Varney, Charles		Wiley, Enos	
Simons, John A.		Walker, Thomas B.	110 00	*Wiley, Ira, Jr.	
Sweetser, Oliver S.		Woodward, Jas. F.	75 00	Wiley, David	
*Sweetser, James M.		Winship, John	65 00	Walton, James C. W.	
Sweetser, E. Leroy		Wiggin, Samuel J.	60 00	Weldon, William	
Toppan, Charles	$200 00	Walton, E. H.	50 00	*Wiley, Elbridge A.	
Tasker, Lyman H.	100 00	Walton, J. Dunn	50 00	Woodward, Thomas T.	
Tasker, Eben	100 00	Welch, Michael	25 00	Winship, Samuel	
Trow, Charles	55 00	Woods, Albert C.	25 00	Walton, Oliver, 2d	
Townsend, Warren	50 00	Wiley, James M.	25 00		
Travis, Henry H.	25 00	Wright, J. W.	15 00	Total,	$8,472 00
Taylor, Marcus C.	20 00	Williams, F.	10 00		
Tyler, George L.	15 00	Wiley, Warren	10 00		

AMOUNT RECEIVED FROM CITIZENS NOT ENROLLED.

Allen, Daniel	$125 00	Greene, Thomas	$25 00	Oliver, Daniel S.	$10 00
Atwell, John	35 00	Gardner, Samuel	20 00	Oliver, William	10 00
Beebe, Lucius	50 00	Greene, C. W.	10 00	Oliver, E. S.	3 00
Baker, F. M.	5 00	Gammon, Nelson	10 00	Parker, Samuel T.	10 00
Boswell, James O.	2 00	Gammon, H. W.	5 00	Richardson, S. O.	200 00
Coffin, N. R.	50 00	Hurd, F. P.	200 00	Raddin, R. H.	10 00
Cowdrey, Jonas	25 00	Hardy, George A.	50 00	Sweetser, P. H.	50 00
Coffin, A. H.	10 00	Hill, C. H.	5 00	Sweetser, A. G.	25 00
Crocker, L.	10 00	Kingman, Samuel	15 00	Sweetser, A. N.	15 00
Clifford, Curtis	5 00	Knight, Manasseh	50 00	Swift, S. B.	10 00
Dolliver, Horatio	15 00	Kimball, J. H.	10 00	Upham, E. S.	10 00
Dager, Haley F.	15 00	Knowles, H.	5 00	Walton, Daniel G.	75 00
Donnavan, Timothy	5 00	Lane, D. P.	20 00	Winship, Thomas	75 00
Emerson, Thomas	125 00	Loring, Thomas D.	10 00	Waite, R. P.	25 00
Evans, L. B.	50 00	Mansfield, Edward	100 00	Waite, W. B.	25 00
Eaton, Lilley	25 00	Mansfield, J. D.	25 00	Wheeler, P. C.	25 00
Folsom, Peter	125 00	Nash, Stephen G.	125 00	Wiley, Leonard	20 00
Fairbanks, Lewis	10 00	Newhall, William	12 00	Wheelock, D. B.	20 00
Ford, Edward	10 00	Newman, J. H.	10 00		
Gould, Samuel	25 00	Norcross, Daniel	3 00	Total,	$2,077 00
Greene, Jeremiah	25 00	Nichols, Hero	2 00		

TREASURER'S REPORT.

CONTRIBUTORS TO THE RECRUITING FUND IN ACCOUNT WITH GEORGE W. CUTTER, *Treasurer.*

CR.

Amount received from Contributors	$10,549 00

DR.

Amount paid 43 Recruits ($175.00)	$7,525 00
Amount paid 6 Recruits ($200.00)	1,200 00
S. O. Richardson, Jr., aid in procuring Substitute for 3 years	200 00
James F. Emerson, " " " " "	200 00
J. G. Aborn, " " " " "	200 00
S. O. Swain, " " " " "	200 00
T. B. Walker, " " " for 1 year	175 00
William H. Atwell, " " " " "	175 00
Printing and Stationery	40 00
Uncurrent Money	10 00
Amount deposited at State House for 1 representative Recruit	125 00
Balance on hand	499 00
	$10,549 00

RECAPITULATION.

Amount received from Enrolled Men	$8,472 00
" " " Citizens not enrolled	2,077 00
	$10,549 00

NAMES OF VOLUNTEERS

WHO ENLISTED TO FILL THE QUOTA OF SOUTH READING, UNDER THE CALL OF JULY 18, 1864.

Charles B. Williams.
William McQueeney.
Nathaniel C. Mayo.
John Davis.
C. H. R. Cheney.
Daniel H. Wadlin.
Charles W. Adams.
Charles B. Davis.
John W. Phipps.
William Butler.
George L. Tyler.
Warren H. Godfrey.
Albert N. Leathers.
John Hawkes.
F. C. Williams.
Andrew J. Dow.
A. H. Danforth.

Charles A. Fifield.
Henry Hunt.
John H. Emerson.
W. C. Pasco.
Patrick Kelley.
L. C. Lane.
W. F. Cowdrey.
Caleb S. Wiley.
Edward L. Wilkins.
William A. Hamblin.
James H. Pierce.
Allen M. Ripley.
James Harnden.
John F. Thompson.
Andrew Goodwin.
Henry D. Churchill.

Noah E. Eaton.
George A. Seaver.
George H. Jackson.
George Hunt.
Frederick W. Aborn.
Joseph Morton.
Marcus M. Sherman.
Varenus H. Ryder.
James D. Draper.
D. C. Smith.
Thomas Kirby.
John W. Lyons.
Patrick Green.
Patrick Forbes.
John W. Madden.
Thomas Rowland.

CHAPTER XV.

IN MEMORIAM.

" So shalt thou rest.
    Yet not to thine eternal resting-place
Shalt thou retire alone, — nor couldst thou wish
Couch more magnificent. Thou shalt lie down
With patriarchs of the infant world, — with kings,
The powerful of the earth, — the wise, the good, —
Fair forms, and hoary seers of ages past,
All in one mighty sepulchre.

            " As the long train
Of ages glide away, the sons of men —
The youth in life's green spring, and he who goes
In the full strength of years, matron and maid,
And the sweet babe, and the gray-headed man —
Shall, one by one, be gathered to thy side
By those who in their turn shall follow them."

Bryant.

DR. NATHAN RICHARDSON,

Son of Nathan and Mary (Belknap) Richardson, was born in Brookfield (Worcester County), Mass., Nov. 16, 1781.

His early education was limited to the town school, which was usually kept about seven months of the year, and during the remainder he assisted on his father's farm, which comprised many acres in extent. As a boy, he was very fond of books, and read everything that came in his way. His mother used to relate many anecdotes of his love of reading, — as, when sent to the post-office, several miles distant, he would buy a book with the money given him to purchase his dinner, and on his way home would let the horse stroll leisurely along at will, while he was absorbed in his newly acquired volume. His father, becoming exasperated at his over-fondness for reading, and the neglect of his labor on the farm, threatened to burn every book he possessed. This compelled him to conceal his books in the barn, and while pitching

Nathan Richardson

down hay from a loft one day, his father was surprised at the sudden appearance of a shower of books.

This love of reading continued through life. Poetry seemed to possess the most attraction. His memory of what he read enabled him to repeat the whole of Pope's "Essay on Man," Milton's "Paradise Lost," and the "Book of Job." Although never a disputant, yet he would not hesitate to measure weapons with any minister who chose to argue with him. His general information was extensive, and he had a large fund of humorous anecdotes in constant readiness.

In what year he commenced the study of medicine it is not recollected; but he was a student of the famous Dr. Kittredge, in company with Dr. D. A. Grosvenor, who settled in Reading.

Nov. 28, 1805, when twenty-four years of age, he married Asenath Rice, of Brookfield, and went to North Reading, where he began the practice of a physician. That he possessed a peculiar aptitude for his calling was immediately apparent. He soon had the custom of that entire community, and also of the neighboring towns. While residing in North Reading, two sons were born, — Winslow and Solon Osmond. Winslow died at the age of eighteen, in South Reading; and Solon Osmond was educated as a physician, became eminent, and died Aug. 31, 1873.

After several years' residence in North Reading, Dr. Richardson removed to Reading, and occupied the house now owned by Mr. Appleton, on the road leading to Woburn. His wife died here Sept. 8, 1820. He then determined to remove to Cambridge, sold his place and practice to Dr. John Hart, of South Reading, for the occupancy of his son, and pledged himself in the sum of two hundred dollars not to practise within ten miles of Reading; but on the eve of his departure from Reading, some of the prominent citizens of South Reading, headed by the late Burrage Yale, unwilling to have so excellent a physician leave their neighborhood, prevailed upon him to remove to South Reading, and sacrifice his bonds, offering him, as a special inducement, the large tract of land on a part of which his residence was built; the estimated value of the land, at that time, being $1,500. He thereupon removed to South Reading, occupying what was known as the "old Prentiss House" while his own residence was building, which was subsequently that of his son, and is now occupied by his grandson.

Perhaps some of the present inhabitants of Wakefield remember the occasion of the "raising" of the frame-work of the Doctor's house. It was a general holiday for the town; every man, woman, and child participated, and gave a helping hand. Cider, lemonade, "Medford," crackers, cheese, and salt-fish, all played prominent parts on that occasion. The Doctor's hospitality was the theme of conversation for a long time. It was considered the most extravagant "raising" that ever took place. This was in 1822.

In the mean time (Sept. 4, 1821) he had taken for his second wife, Betsey Alden, of Saugus, with whom he had seven children, three of whom are now living. Nathan went to Europe and studied music, became quite celebrated as the author of "Richardson's New Method for the Piano-Forte," and died in Paris in 1858. Of the six children of the first wife, three are living, and reside in Wakefield.

Dr. Richardson became identified with South Reading, and during the remainder of his life was one of its most active citizens. He was foremost in every project for the improvement and welfare of the town; would subscribe liberally to everything he was asked to, — moral, intellectual, and political. Poverty and misfortune won his immediate friendship: he would empty his pockets to any person who touched his sympathies. Although in receipt of a munificent income, he was so indifferent to the value of money that he would never present a bill for his professional services; if a patient paid him, it was simply from his own choice. His ledger was a curiosity in bookkeeping, showing nothing on the debit side. If he wanted money, he never hesitated to borrow it, and frequently of those who were indebted to him. His professional fee for cases where a popular physician of the present day would obtain an hundred dollars or more, would be a sum so insignificant as to invariably cause a smile. Probably no physician of that time had so large a practice, among all classes, as Dr. Nathan Richardson. Although not connected with the Massachusetts Medical Society, he was frequently invited to consultations with its members.

As a physician, particularly in pulmonary complaints, he was without a rival. A word of hope or encouragement from him gave life and renewed vigor to the despairing; and his diagnosis of disease was marvellously accurate. He would frequently be affected to tears when he saw there was no relief for his patient.

The magnitude of the practice of Dr. Richardson, and his eminence as a physician, will be better appreciated when it is stated that it extended throughout the New England States, and obliged him to erect a private hospital for his patients at his own home, which is still standing, though converted to other uses. It is stated by old residents that, during his practice-days at home, the carriages of patients used to line both sides of the main street of old South Reading, near his residence.

Dr. Richardson's second wife died Dec. 5, 1832; and Nov. 24, 1834 he married Mrs. Grace Barnard, of North Reading, who survived him thirty-five years, and died Nov. 26, 1872.

Dr. Richardson died very suddenly, of apoplexy, Sept. 17, 1837, in the fifty-sixth year of his age. He was buried in the cemetery at Reading, by the side of his two wives. A monument erected to his memory by his son, Dr. S. O. Richardson, marks his burial-place.

HON. JOHN PRENTISS.

Mr. Prentiss was the son of Rev. Caleb Prentiss, and his youthful days were passed in what is now the town of Wakefield, to which cherished locality he frequently returned during the later years of his extended life, with an interest therein which ceased only with his life.

His entertaining reminiscences of early scenes and impressions will be found elsewhere in this history. He died at Keene, N. H., June 6, 1873.[*]

We copy the following extracts from the "New Hampshire Sentinel," of June 12, 1873: —

"Hon. John Prentiss, the founder of this paper, and for forty-eight years its editor, died at his residence in Court Street on Friday afternoon, June 6, at the age of ninety-five years and three months. Up to within two or three weeks of his decease he had enjoyed excellent health, and though weak and feeble, was able to walk about the streets daily, and to superintend the management of his fine homestead, in addition to doing considerable work in his garden. The immediate cause of his last sickness it is perhaps difficult to define; it seemed to be a general wearing out of the system. During the last two weeks of his life he was confined to his room, and suffered considerable pain, — more than he had experienced, as he himself declared, during his previous ninety-five years of life. His mind was unclouded to the very last, and he conversed upon general subjects with all the apparent interest and enthusiasm that ever characterized his conversation, giving minute directions in regard to private business matters, and manifesting a lively interest in the news of the day At the same time he was conscious of the fact that his time was very short, and talked of his fast approaching dissolution with perfect freedom and astonishing calmness, remarking that he had long been ready to go, and was every way prepared. For years, in fact ever since he retired from business in

---

[*] See Prentiss Genealogy, page 193.

1847, he has contributed almost weekly to the editorial columns of this paper, the last of which contributions appeared in our last issue over his well-known signature (¶), and which was simply a correction of an erroneous idea conveyed in a somewhat lengthy religious article of the preceding week. This correction was written on Tuesday, three days previous to his death, in a clear and steady hand, and was probably the last paragraph ever penned by him. From that time he continued to grow weaker, and on Friday afternoon he sank into an easy slumber, from which he never awoke.

"In the death of Mr Prentiss, Keene loses one of the citizens who connected her present history to her past, and whose name was a byword for merit and deserved fame. He came to this town in March, 1799, at the age of twenty-one, and established the 'Sentinel,' under many embarrassments, and with a list of subscribers numbering only seventy. His first printing-office (as we learn from the 'Prentiss Family Genealogy') was in a low building standing where S. W. Hale's house now stands, and for some time afterwards in the new building south of Dr. Edwards' tavern. Subsequently (in 1825) he erected a fine block on the west side of the square, where he, in connection with his son, John W., carried on the printing, publishing, and book business up to 1847, when he retired. In 1808 he built his homestead and planted the fine elms in front, and has since enjoyed under their shade a sufficiency of this world's goods, acquired by his own industry and exertions. During his half century of active business life, he held various offices of trust, having been town clerk, town treasurer, representative in the legislature, and a member of the Senate. He was also for many years president of the New Hampshire Historical Society, and during his whole life was prominently identified with religious and educational matters. After retiring from business in 1847, at which time he was one of the oldest editors in the United States, he presented to each of the fourteen school districts of this town a set of the Massachusetts School Library of thirty-eight volumes; and his love for and interest in the schools never abated. In 1850 he travelled over Great Britain and the European continent, attending the peace convention at Frankfort-on-the-Main, as delegate from New Hampshire. His interesting letters from abroad were published in the 'Sentinel,' attracting much attention and interest. For sixty-seven years he was a prominent member of the Masonic fraternity, having been made a Master Mason in 1806, Royal Arch Mason in 1813, and a Knight Templar in 1867.

"The influence for good which Mr. Prentiss exercised upon the community in which he so long and prominently figured, cannot be over

Thos Emerson

estimated. Strictly temperate in all things, cheerful, kind, and benevolent, with a disposition to encourage and aid every individual, local, and general enterprise, he was ever a leading and popular citizen. He was the fearless champion of every good cause, and unqualifiedly denounced wrong and oppression wherever they existed. He was firm and outspoken on all questions of public policy, and at the same time treated with deference the opinions of those who opposed him.

"Mr. Prentiss survived all the members of his family except his daughters Corinna (wife of Judge Hopkinson of Lowell, deceased), and Pamela (wife of Judge French of Concord, Mass.). His son's widow, Mrs. John W. Prentiss, has had the superintendence of his home since the death of her husband in 1863, and has ministered to his wants and necessities with untiring devotion. He was surrounded with every comfort which wealth and filial affection could bestow, and his life closed peacefully, and without a groan."

HON. THOMAS EMERSON.

Among the worthy sons of Wakefield who have recently died, none received a larger measure of respect than the honored citizen whose name is given above. Descended from a Puritan ancestry, among whom were clergymen, patriots of the Revolution and of former wars, and leading men of this and other towns, he illustrated in his own life and character the principles for which the founders of New England are justly famed. He was born Oct. 2, 1785, and died Nov. 29, 1871, reaching the advanced age of 86 years.

Obliged from very early years to work at the bench or on the farm, and enjoying but the most limited means for gaining knowledge, he showed the native force of his mind by rising above all the difficulties of his lot, and taking a leading part in the affairs of the town. He was advanced to almost every office in the gift of his fellow-townsmen, and always discharged his duties with exact punctuality, sound wisdom, and inflexible integrity.

He was chosen to represent the town in the Legislature eight years, and filled the office of Senator two years. He was prominent in the formation of the South Reading M. & A. Institution in 1833, was made its first vice-president, and for many years was its president. In 1844, at the organization of the bank, he was elected its president, which position he held until his death. One associated with him for many years, once said of him, " In financial matters he was long considered an oracle, a safe counsellor and adviser."

In the year 1810, he formed a partnership, with Ebenezer Nelson, for the manufacture of shoes, which continued with a fair measure of success, till Mr. N., thinking it his duty to become a preacher, it was amicably dissolved. Mr. Emerson took the business and increased it from year to year till it more than equalled that of all the other manufacturers in town. To him was given the main credit of inaugurating a system of cash payments to workmen, in place of barter, as was the early system. By the frequent introduction of improved machinery and methods, he was able to furnish profitable occupation to large numbers of people.

His personal traits of character were such as to gain for him the respect and affection of all who knew him. Affable, sympathetic, and kind to the poor, he had numerous friends in all ranks of society. He was a liberal contributor to many philanthropic and missionary enterprises. He was youthful in his feelings, even in his old age, and many a young man derived from him not only the help of kind words, but the more effective assistance of generous deeds. He retained his energies to the last year of his life, and with a clear mind and an elastic step attended to his daily duties at the bank. He was a trusted and leading member of the Congregational Church, and fulfilled his duties in that relation with great zeal and discretion. An extract from the records of that body, showing the esteem in which he was held by his Christian brethren, may properly be inserted here. It was made soon after his death, and is as follows: —

" Few members of this church have ever filled a larger measure of usefulness. Successful in business, he employed his wealth for purposes that reflected the highest honor upon his judgment and his heart. Honored by his fellow-townsmen with official position and duties, he guarded with entire faithfulness every public interest. Intrusted during many years with the management of important financial matters, he always merited and received the most thorough confidence of all men. As a member of this church he was faithful, earnest, liberal, and devout. Scrupulously exact in the discharge of every duty, strongly attached to the house of God and to its worship, a constant teacher in the Sabbath school, attentive to the truth, and keenly alive to those portions of it which relate to personal piety, he was a Christian whose sincerity was never doubted, and whose example was a source of perpetual instruction."

Mr. Emerson was married in early life to Miss Betsey Hartshorn, who survived him less than two years, departing this life Sept. 26, 1873.

HON. LILLEY EATON.

An honorable and useful life is a precious legacy. Such a life was that of Mr. Eaton. He was born Jan. 13, 1802, and at his death had completed his seventieth year. His ancestors were among the early settlers of this town, and during successive generations were distinguished for many public and private virtues. In early manhood Mr. Eaton showed a remarkable aptitude for public business, and during a long series of years the confidence of the people in his capacity and integrity was manifested by intrusting to him almost every public office. He was selectman twenty-five years, and a member of the school board nearly as long, and generally chairman in each. He was town clerk twenty years, representative seven years, senator two years, justice of the peace thirty-eight years, and a member of the Constitutional Convention in 1853. He is said to have shaped, to a great extent, the policy and action of the town upon almost all subjects, during a long period of time. The practical wisdom which he brought to the solution of public questions gave great weight to his counsels, and often an opinion from him was sufficient to decide any matter. Thoroughly conversant with the laws, in their application to the various interests of business and to town affairs, and also with the opinions and spirit of the people, he was able to suggest the best measures for their consideration and decision. There was nothing dictatorial in his nature. He always appealed to the judgment of the people, and advocated nothing for which he could not give sound reasons. Progressive in his spirit, he was a friend of all improvements. He introduced system in the mode of conducting town business, and officers of other towns adopted some of the features which he devised. He was deeply interested in the schools, and it was mainly to his suggestions, ably seconded and carried out by his associates, that the town is indebted for the admirable system upon which its schools have for many years been conducted.

His well-known integrity and ability gave him great influence in private affairs. Those who were in trouble, the poor and the destitute, found in him a safe counsellor and friend. The settlement of estates, the investment of money, and the temporary control of funds, were often intrusted to him, and never did any one have reason to say that he ever failed to manage the business committed to him in the most upright and honorable manner. He had much to do with financial affairs. In conjunction with Mr. Thomas Emerson, he was mainly instrumental in establishing the Mechanic and Agricultural Institution. He was its first, and till his death, only treasurer. At the formation of the South Reading Bank he was elected cashier, and held the position till he died. In these stations he was methodical, careful, and accurate, and in all respects worthy of the confidence which was abundantly reposed in him.

Mr. Eaton, although enjoying but few advantages not possessed by others, found time to cultivate a literary taste, and various addresses, showing both research and ability, were delivered by him. With those *public* addresses our citizens are quite familiar, and we here insert an extract from a private letter, addressed to his eldest sister, on the reception of the news of the death of an only and cherished son, for the purpose of rendering this description of his style more complete: —

"Your letter of the 23d instant, with its ominous seál, — sad token of its grievous contents, — has come to hand; its tidings have cast a gloom over our family circle, for we all loved the little, amiable Rowland. Not ten minutes, perhaps, before the reception of your letter, I was thinking of our friends at Worcester, that it was long since we had heard from them, and that I would write immediately.

"While musing on my friends away, —
 The loved ones of the earth, —
And fancying how their lot might be,
 In sorrow or in mirth,
I seemed to hear a mournful tone
 Come sighing on the breeze,
The wind, it had a startling moan,
 While whistling through the trees;
I hark'd — and on the air's vibration,
 I caught the sounds of woe,
They told of grief and lamentation,
 Of death, that cruel foe.
Again I lent my anxious ear,
 To catch distincter tones,
A father's sounding sigh I hear,
 A mother's sobbing moans;
The whispering winds' peculiar strain,
 So fearful in their lay,
Remind me, in a language plain,
 Of relatives away.

"'T was so; for on the next sad blast
 That came with solemn roar,
Was heard the voice, — ' He 's breathed his last,
 Our Rowland is no more;

> The little, lovely, prattling boy,
>   So patient and so bright,
> His father's and his mother's joy,
>   No more shall greet our sight.'
>
> "Again I hark'd; and from the air,
>   The heavenly arch midway,
> A song celestial struck my ear,
>   And thus it seem'd to say:
> 'Rise, spirits, rise! our upward way
>   With swifter wing pursue,
> We 'll 'scort to realms of endless day,
>   Where bliss is ever new,
> This little seraph, snatched from earth,
>   From sorrow and from pain,
> To dwell with those of heavenly birth,
>   And with his Saviour reign.'"

March, 1840.

Mr. Eaton was much given to antiquarian studies, and this history gives abundant evidence of his patience in tracing the genealogy of families, and in exploring ancient records for important facts and instructive events. He possessed skill in delineating character, was fond of humor, and had a fund of anecdotes drawn chiefly from characters of early New England history, which made both his written productions and his conversation interesting.

The personal traits exhibited by Mr. Eaton were very attractive. A perpetual urbanity disarmed opposition to the plans he might be at any time urging. He had the faculty of imparting his views, not so much by direct iteration as by quiet suggestion. He rarely expressed half-formed opinions, but when a controverted subject was presented, gave himself time for reflection, and then expressed his opinion and the reasons for it so courteously that those who could not agree with him were never offended with him. This urbanity was not a skilfully woven garment to cover, and enable him to prosecute, selfish designs, but it was the natural expression of his character; his heart was kind and gentle, and his manners were but the language in which it uttered its real feelings. Though Mr. Eaton never connected himself with any church, he was a constant attendant upon public worship, and accepted the truths of the Gospel in their more direct and personal meaning.

The death of Mr. Eaton occurred but two months after that of Mr. Emerson, with whom he had been joined in many relations of business and friendship for fifty years. On the Saturday upon which he was smitten with the disease which terminated his life, he had prepared, at the request of his pastor, a brief account of the life of his lamented friend, Mr. Emerson. The kind and truthful words with which that account closed, *the last words which he ever penned*, as they described the character of his friend, so also do they describe his own. These are the words: "His was an unblemished reputation for honesty, integrity, and uprightness. He was patriotic, wise, liberal, kind, peaceable."

HON. P. H. SWEETSER.

Hon. P. H. Sweetser, the eldest son of Paul and Sarah Sweetser, was born Sept. 23, 1807, and died June 11, 1872. During his boyhood, like most of the boys of South Reading, he learned the shoemaker's trade, at which he worked during his minority.

At about the time that he attained his majority, the South Reading Academy was opened, and he was one of the first to enter it. He was a quick scholar, and after a brief term at the academy, he taught school in one of the districts in town, with marked success. From this time he attended the academy, teaching school winters, till he had taught in nearly every district in town. His first permanent school was in Saugus, where he taught one or two years, leaving there to take an ushership in Boston. While teaching in Saugus, he married Louisa Foster, of Danvers, a daughter of Capt. Aaron Foster.

This union was in all respects fortunate and happy, and gave him a home to which he was most devotedly attached. Of seven children born to them, one died in infancy, and six survive him. That the education of his children was not neglected will appear from the fact that two of his sons are now successful preachers, one preparing for the medical profession, and the daughters had the best opportunities that could be obtained by public or private instruction. Often, in his later years, while not engaged in active business, he spoke of his strong desire to educate his children, and expressed his willingness to incur any expense, even beyond his income if necessary, to promote the end he had so much at heart.

In 1838 he was appointed master of the Harvard School in Charlestown, where he remained till 1847. As a teacher, he was uniformly successful, and took a deep interest in education generally. A good disciplinarian, always having control of his school, he was on good terms with his pupils, and admitted them to a familiarity which rendered school pleasant and school exercises interesting; this familiar-

F.T. Stuart Sc. Boston

ity, and a playful humor in which he indulged, always made him popular with his pupils. He was prominent in the enterprise of forming the Massachusetts Teachers' Association, and establishing the "Massachusetts Teacher" as its organ. For several years he acted as one of the editors of this journal, and the numbers prepared by him were uniformly interesting and able.

Nor did his interest in popular education cease when he was no longer a teacher. He was for many years a member of the school committee of Wakefield, and many of the annual reports for the last twenty years are from his pen, and attest his interest in the schools and his ability as a writer.

One of the last articles that he wrote was the school report for 1871-2, an exceedingly interesting document; and I remember telling him, after reading it, that I thought it the best of the numerous and excellent reports he had written. From an early period he had been deeply interested in the antislavery cause and the temperance movement, and a frequent contributor to the journals in the interest of these and other reforms. Nor with his pen alone. Mr. Sweetser was a very ready and effective speaker. His temperament, always impulsive, imparted an earnestness to his utterance which was sure to secure the attention, and his habits of thought and feeling prevented him from ever becoming wearisome. During the time of the Washingtonian movement, although engaged through the day in teaching, he was yet one of the most acceptable and efficient lecturers, and labored with great earnestness to organize and direct the movement.

Some of his last years were also devoted, to a considerable extent, to the promotion of the same object, and many of the ablest articles in the "Nation," a temperance paper published in Boston, were from his pen. He wrote also many hymns of great excellence, for general or special occasions, not a few of which have taken a permanent place in our sacred poetry. He was for several years a member of the examining committee for Tufts College, the duties of which he performed with fidelity and ability. After leaving the profession of teaching, Mr. Sweetser was twice elected county commissioner for the County of Middlesex, which office he held for six years. He also held almost every office in the gift of the town. As an officer, he was prompt and efficient, and his decisions in all matters in controversy were ready, and in the main judicious. He was a man of remarkably quick perception, and moved forward to a judgment so readily as not unfrequently to give an impression of haste, and to render him impatient of the slower movements of others. He was, perhaps, as is apt to be the case with persons of a nervous temperament, hasty sometimes in his expressions, but seldom so in his actions; they were marked by a caution and careful consideration which did not always manifest themselves in his ordinary conversation.

Mr. Sweetser was just and prompt in all his business affairs, and, whether personal or official, they would have borne the most thorough examination. It was a favorite maxim with him to "owe no man," and it is safe to say that no one ever lost a cent by him that was justly his due.

The writer of this brief sketch was of nearly the same age as Mr. Sweetser, was a boy with him, being a near neighbor, labored in the same profession and the same place for many years, and was brought into still nearer relations with him by marriage; and the friendship that began almost with his life continued to its end.

It would seem sometimes that what would apparently fit us especially for the performance of a duty is, after all, almost a hinderance. I confess that I have felt this in what I have written. In the intimacy of personal intercourse and friendship, we often fail to estimate and weigh character as we do when the object is at a greater distance. What is seen at too short a range is seen only in its parts, and a longer perspective is necessary to view the object as a whole. Death has now given us such a view of our friend, and I am sure that his memory will be dearer, and his character will appear more marked and estimable, as we look at him from a point more favorable to observe the constant and permanent qualities of his character. For some years previous to his death he had not enjoyed perfect health; and to one of his intense activity of mind, joined with a temperament not too hopeful, it is not strange that he should have been sometimes inclined to look on the dark side of things. But his sympathies were always with the right, though he might not be so sanguine of its speedy success as some. Few men felt an intenser interest in whatever concerned the welfare of humanity, or were more uniformly on the side of progress and justice.

He had a strong attachment to his native town, and was always prominent in any enterprise for its improvement; especially so in whatever related to education, the public library, and the schools.

In his death his family has lost one whose life was bound up in its welfare, the town has lost a good citizen, and the cause of education, one whose experience rendered him invaluable as a member of the school committee, and whose vote and voice were always given for whatever promised to extend and improve the means of education. He will be remembered with gratitude by many now in the morning of life, who

H. W. Smith

Solon O. Richardson

have listened to his words of advice and encouragement in his frequent visits to the schools, as he now is in his native town and elsewhere by those who sat under his instructions. Such is a brief and imperfect sketch of the events in the life of an honored citizen; and an estimate of his character, — which, though dictated by the hand of friendship, is, I believe, truthful and just.

DR. SOLON OSMOND RICHARDSON

Was the second son of Dr. Nathan and Asenath (Rice) Richardson, and was born at North Reading, July 19, 1809, on what was formerly known as the "old Dix Place," and there spent the earliest years of his childhood.

Being but a few years of age when his father removed to Reading and established himself in practice there, the greater part of his boyhood and youth were spent in that town and South Reading, to which his father subsequently removed (1821). The holes to the dove-cote, cut out by him when a lad, are still observable upon the place then occupied by his father on the road from Reading to Woburn, since owned by Mr. Appleton, ex-county-commissioner for Middlesex.

As a lad at Reading and South Reading, Dr. Richardson received his education at the academy kept by a Mr. Wm. Coffin, of Nantucket, at North Reading, in the public schools of Reading, the academy at Atkinson, N. H., and the Pinkerton Academy at Derry, N. H., where he had as classmates his life-long friends and associates, Dr. Aug. Grosvenor, of Danvers, and Hon. Horace P. Wakefield, M. D., now of Monson. Always better than average in his general studies, he was especially noted at school for his fair, distinct, and graceful chirography, which, coupled with his genial courtesy and manner, secured for him, when a lad in his teens, a clerkship in the Charlestown Post-Office, then under Paul Willard, Esq.; and while there his clerkly abilities and general popularity prompted a proposal which was made to him to become assistant clerk of the House of Representatives, which was, however, declined.

The eminence and extent of practice of his father was such that his professional engagements led him from home the major portion of the time, and Solon, being the eldest of his large family of children (his older brother having died at an early age), was intrusted with much of the care of his father's affairs and family. When not at school he was often employed in the preparation of medicines for his father, and thus became early familiar with the science and practice of pharmacy. Finding this pursuit congenial to his inclination and taste, he very readily acquiesced in his father's wish that he should adopt the profession of medicine, and shortly before attaining his majority he entered the medical school of Dartmouth College, from which he received his medical degree, graduating with honors Nov. 30, 1831, and immediately taking up practical study with his father.

He held for a time the position of assistant surgeon at the State Prison, and became a member of the Massachusetts Medical Society, from which he afterwards retired, in conformity with usage, on establishing a proprietary medicine. He soon entered general practice with his father, an arrangement that proved, for the short time it was enjoyed, highly satisfactory and successful with both. Besides that at home, offices were established in Lowell, Salem, and Boston, each of which places Dr. Richardson visited on certain days of the week, driving to and from in a carriage, an amount of professional riding that in these days would be considered a grievous hardship.

On the 3d day of April, 1837, Dr. Richardson was married at the "Old parsonage" (recently removed to Salem Street), by Rev. Reuben Emerson, to Susan Barnard of North Reading. Their children have been, a daughter who died in infancy, at Nahant, during a summer's residence of the family there, and an only son, S. O. Richardson, Esq., of Wakefield.

During the studies and novitiate of Dr. Richardson, he had given much attention to diseases of the heart and lungs, and his thesis upon these subjects when he graduated from college was able, and received the commendation of the profession, as displaying much research and original thought. In his treatment of these diseases he was eminently successful, and the number of those who sought his advice in complaints of this character induced him to make them a specialty, and to abandon general practice.

In 1808 his father, Dr. Nathan Richardson, had introduced into his practice a remedy which he called "Sherry Wine Bitters," which proved an effective agent, the favorable results of which, as ascertained from a prolonged and extensive use thereof among his patients, gave it his repute, the demand becoming such that instead of supplying it in powdered form, as for many years he had prescribed it, for convenience' sake he prepared it in common quart wine bottles. Soon after engaging in practice with his father, Dr. Richardson observed with satisfaction the beneficial effects of these "Bitters," and naturally made extensive use of them in cases to which they were adapted.

In the September following his marriage, his father suddenly died, his extensive practice and business thus devolving upon him. To this he gave his best energies, but it soon became evident that his health, which was never very robust, could not long withstand the stress of the duties he had assumed. Reluctant as he was to abandon thus early in life a profession which was endeared to him by many pleasant associations, in which he was gaining note, and which was in every particular congenial to his taste and aspirations, his perceptions indicated clearly to him an early grave or an abandonment of his pursuit.

Deciding in favor of the chance of prolonged life, he resolutely decided to abandon practice, and from this period he confined himself to the manufacture and sale of the "Sherry Wine Bitters," which had for so long a period been satisfactorily employed in his father's and his own practice.

At this time proprietary medicine was a branch of trade unknown in the New England States, and there had never been introduced for sale in the country such a compound as medicated bitters, the idea of preparing medicine in that form originating therefore with Dr. Richardson. The labor and expense of preparing and introducing this medicine in proper and convenient form, cannot be imagined by any inexperienced in its details: first, the common wine bottles were ill-shaped for packing and were too heavy; a new form was designed, and moulds prepared, but the manufacture of suitable bottles had not been accomplished in this Commonwealth, and the many experiments and failures of the manufacturers to produce a light bottle that would withstand pressure and secure safe transportation were vexatious, expensive, and discouraging. Nearly every sale in the early period of using new bottles was attended with more or less breakage in every package, but this difficulty was finally overcome by manufacturers in Philadelphia. Numerous obstacles also were presented in originating and preparing various plates for printing and in creating the embellishments requisite for perfect arrangements. The express business had not then been established, railroads were almost unknown, and private means of transportation for orders, throughout the country, had to be created. To accomplish this Dr. Richardson was obliged to provide several expensive teams, which were constantly employed in transporting his medicine to different parts of the New England States. Nor did he fail to make his medicine known by liberal advertising, and very soon after its introduction to the public, its merits were universally appreciated and the demand increased beyond even the most sanguine anticipations. To meet the requirements of this wide and unexpected demand, a large capital was needed, a laboratory had to be erected, a large number of horses and carriages supplied for transportation, and every facility for manufacture established, notwithstanding the employment of which at certain seasons the demand was such as to render prompt supply of orders impossible.

Dr. Richardson's success being now fully established, he was enabled to indulge liberally in expenditures which it was his ambition to enjoy. He never entertained a desire to acquire wealth except to promote the comfort and welfare of his family and the community in which he lived. He had been a close observer of the evils attending the acquisition of extreme wealth, and was convinced that unhappiness was the too frequent associate thereof. It was an early resolve with him that after gaining a competency, any overplus should be devoted to such charitable and benevolent purposes as comported with his judgment and pleasure; and in after life he adhered to this resolve, in most cases desiring and enjoining that his benefactions should not be made public. He was always needlessly prodigal in all expenditures connected with his business, in which every department evinced the most thorough organization. The horses used for his medicine wagons were selected without regard to expense, and his wagons were elaborately constructed and highly finished by the best makers. He always kept in his stables for his personal use five or six of the best horses that could be procured, possessing great love for and fine taste and judgment in horses, in the ownership of which he for many years aspired to excel.

His benevolence and liberality extended to every commendable object brought to his notice. Becoming interested in the maintenance of the citizen-soldiery of the Commonwealth, he favored the creation of a local military company; and on the formation of the organization in this town, in 1851, of the Richardson Light Guards, on the intimation of the founders of the company that it was their wish that it should be so designated, Dr. Richardson, in accepting the honor, testified his appreciation thereof by a most generous gift, which he yearly supplemented with others of kindred nature, manifesting at all times the most lively interest in whatever pertained to the welfare of the Guards, and having unceasingly at heart, as one of his dearest objects, their highest prosperity and success. For years the expenses of parades, target practice, etc., was borne by him, — furnishing music, and often a bountiful collation on his premises, and aiding them by means and influence in any measures for their advantage. This cherished interest never abated anything of its zeal, and to his last hour was continued in all its original strength and vigor; and he remained to the end of life what he became at its birth, its faithful and beneficent foster-father and friend.

To Dr. Richardson also belongs the honor of having been the original mover in the publication of the town history.

In 1852 Dr. Richardson was elected Town Treasurer, though not desiring the office, which he retained but one year, discharging its duties and trusts to universal satisfaction. He became engaged some years since with a half-brother, Mr. Nathan Richardson, in the music business, but abandoned the business after a brief time. In 1869 he suffered, while attending to business in Boston, an attack of paralysis, the results of which seriously impaired his health and activity, though by the exercise of the most rigid care of himself he was enabled to maintain a degree of comfort and ability. Even when in enfeebled health his concern for the prosperity and progress of our town continued active, and within the last few months of his life he inaugurated and carried to most successful culmination an enterprise of enduring value and benefit to all. Believing alike in the refining and educating influence of art, and the helpfulness of beneficial surroundings, and that his town ought to preserve in secure form for the benefit of our posterity the features of her greatest benefactor, and that the influence of the faces of men who had benefited mankind is advantageous and encouraging, he set on foot a movement for the purchase and presentation to the town of the valuable portraits of George Washington and Cyrus Wakefield, which now adorn the walls of our town hall, and became himself responsible for the greater part of the attendant expense, thereby leaving with us another monument to his philanthropy and generosity.

While making a social call at the residence of Cyrus Wakefield, Esq., on Sunday evening, Aug. 31, 1873, Dr. Richardson was seized with apoplexy, and lived but a few hours. His death occasioned universal sorrow.

Said the "Wakefield Citizen," in its issue following his death: —

"Having lived for more than forty years in this community, his name intimately associated with not a few of its prominent institutions, his home ever renowned for its hospitality and his hand for its generosity, Dr. Richardson had become so much a part of the town and its history, that his loss becomes a public sorrow; and though illness and age had in late years impaired his vigor, and prevented his active participation in the affairs of the day, his interest in the welfare of the various local organizations whose well-being he had long made his care, and his wide-reaching liberality, continued unabated.

"The frosts of age had no power to chill, or the infirmities of body disposition to weaken the characteristic kindness and benevolence of the man, and to the latest hours of his life he continued to place both institutions and community under frequently renewed obligations.

"Quietly and peacefully his life was spent, unostentatiously the wide bestowal of his bounty was accomplished, and his every undertaking was characterized by rare good taste and completeness of execution. Success in his efforts seemed with him a duty, and nothing he attempted was ever done slightingly.

"His fondness for home, friends, children, music, and animals was strongly noticeable, and the open hospitality and abounding good cheer of his home, his wide circle of affectionate friends, the happy relations that plainly existed between himself and the little ones he was wont to meet on our streets, his hearty delight in and liberal patronage of good music, and the keen satisfaction he had in the fine points and qualities of, and the real love he had for his horses, thoroughly attested the genuineness of his enjoyment therein.

"A public-spirited citizen, a good neighbor, the kindest and most indulgent of husbands and fathers, a true friend, his regard for the interests of the friends and objects he held dear was most deep and sensitive, and the last hours of his life were marked by characteristic efforts at lessening the annoyances and increasing the happiness of others. Possessed of ample fortune, his hand stayed not at giving; prompted by the warmth of his heart, his energies were directed in the gratification of those about him; and his name and memory are deservedly dear in the hearts of the community in which the greater part of his life was spent. His end was like his life, peaceful and composed, and he has entered into rest."

He was followed to his grave by a large and mourning company, — the Richardson Light Guard, whose benefactor he had so long been, returning from camp at Framingham to perform escort duty for the remains of their honored and beloved friend. His remains were laid to rest in Mount Auburn Cemetery.

Dr. Richardson was through life a member and liberal supporter of the Universalist society of his town, and was always ready to cheerfully assist in every good word and work. Though the evening of his days was clouded by infirmity, the current of his life was peaceful and serene, and it is unfailing pleasure to remember him as when, in the days of his full health and vigor, he adorned society and upheld his work among men.

Cyrus Wakefield

CYRUS WAKEFIELD.

Cyrus Wakefield was born in the town of Roxbury, New Hampshire, on the fourteenth of February, 1811. His parents were James Wakefield and Hannah Heminway Wakefield, of that town. His father was a citizen of marked integrity and of considerable prominence, serving at the same time as town clerk, selectman, and representative.

His father's occupation was that of a farmer, and thus his early associations were those connected with the rugged discipline of a New England farm-boy.

The school was a mile and a half away over the hills, and it was no easy task in winter with the snow over the fences to reach it. Yet the New England boy lingers not by the fire, even in the severest storms, but with his books under his arm, and his cap well tied about his ears, he resolutely goes on to his place at school. And well he may, because there are but two terms a year of ten weeks each, one in winter, the other in summer; and when he is twelve years of age, he will not be allowed the privileges of the summer term, since his help is required on the farm. Young Cyrus seems to have realized the importance even of these slight educational advantages, and by applying himself with great zeal to his studies, mastered the rudiments of the common school.

The executive and administrative qualities of his mind began to develop very early in life. There were numberless projects in his busy child-brain, to the accomplishment of which he bent not only his own but also the abilities of his brothers. He would induce his father to lay out work in advance for himself and younger brother, sometimes having plans which required a month's time for their execution. At one time, it would be the construction of a fish-pond; at another, the building of coal-pits, the product of which he sold to the neighboring blacksmiths.

He was an enthusiastic lover of nature, delighting in nothing so much as in taking long tramps through the forest in search of game, or in following the course of the running brook for fish. The boys of his acquaintance were not fond of joining him in these excursions, as his powers of endurance were unusually great, and he had but little conception of distance. He was also an acknowledged leader in all athletic sports.

At an early age he grew restive. Some of his relatives had gone to other States, and at times would return to tell what they had seen and done in the great cities. His father's farm would seem now too small for his growing ambition. The successes of his friends kindled in his own bosom a generous emulation. He too would try his fortune in the great world outside.

At last, after much urging, his father consented, and Cyrus went to Peterboro', N. H., to enter a cotton mill as a picker-boy. This was a most excellent position to dissipate the rosy hues which had gathered about his ideal world, and to discover to him the cold, stern reality.

Only a short time elapsed, and he was back at the old homestead, still determined to realize his fondest hopes of one day becoming a merchant. He had heard of the fame of Mr. Appleton, of Dublin, who had emerged from obscurity like his own, but who was then widely known as a successful and an honorable merchant. What others had done he could do, and he incessantly urged his views upon his father, who as constantly presented the other and darker side, showing how many who went to the city lost health, time, and even character, in their pursuit of wealth, and were ultimately obliged to return in disgrace to their native towns. His father at length sent him to live with a clergyman in a neighboring village, who, in return for his taking care of his horse and cow, should give him suitable books to read, and, if possible, lead his mind into theological studies. This good man, however, was not apt to teach. On the first day he put him down before a large book containing the history of the controversy between Calvin and Arminius. The book was dry and uninteresting. After a trial of several days the boy gave up in despair, convinced that if Calvin and Arminius could not settle the theological matters in dispute, he certainly could not hope to do it. He returned again to his father's house, more resolutely determined than ever to go to Boston and try his luck in the great world of trade.

After a few more futile attempts to find congenial employment for him near home, at the age of fifteen years, with his parents' consent, he came to Boston, declaring that he would achieve success, and make a name of which his friends would be proud.

Arriving in Boston, he at first entered the retail grocery store of Messrs. Wheeler & Bassett, on Washington Street, but soon after secured a clerkship with Messrs. Stearns, Cobb & Winslow, on India Street. While in their employ, he conceived the plan of doing business on his own account, since he had some time at his command not required by his employers. His aim was, to secure, if possible, a sufficient sum of money to allow him to pursue his studies in some established school, for he felt the need of a better education.

His employers gave him the liberty to buy and sell empty barrels and casks. They also assisted him in other ways, in small business transactions.

At length he had saved one thousand dollars in hard cash. But with the thousand dollars came a still stronger desire for money. He saw the path to wealth opening before him, and instead of pursuing a course of study at some college, he bent his energies more strongly than ever to the accumulation of property. This step he regretted in after life, feeling that he had made a serious mistake. Yet he did not wholly lose sight of his original purpose. He attended evening schools both of an academic and mercantile nature; he visited the various debating societies and churches; observed carefully the habits of the people; listened, so far as his time would allow, to the various courses of scientific lectures, for which his mind had a keen relish; and thus laid the foundation of what general knowledge he possessed. During his business engagement with Messrs. Stearns, Cobb & Winslow, he made shipments to Valparaiso and to South America, with indifferent success.

In 1834 he entered the grocery business under the firm name of Foster & Wakefield, on Commercial Street, opposite Commercial Wharf. In 1836 the firm was dissolved, and Mr. Wakefield sent to New Hampshire for his younger brother, Mr. Enoch H. Wakefield, with whom, two years after, he formed a co-partnership under the name of Wakefield & Co. This firm was continued until 1844. During the latter part of this co-partnership, a small lot of rattan, thrown out of a ship as refuse matter, was accidentally purchased, and sold at a profit to a few chair-makers, who, working the raw material by hand, used the outside of the cane in seating chairs. This favorable purchase led to others, until, at the dissolution of the firm, Mr. Wakefield opened an office at the corner of Commercial and Cross Streets, where he carried on a jobbing trade in rattans.

The demand for split rattans in seating chairs now increased. The great cost of preparing the rattan in this country without the aid of machinery, caused Mr. Wakefield to look abroad for a supply; and as he had a brother-in-law in the house of Messrs. Russell & Co., Canton, China, he forwarded to him samples of the cane most in demand. In a few years his importations of Canton Split Rattan were known throughout the United States. But upon the breaking out of the Opium War between the Chinese and European powers, this branch of the trade received a sudden check and was for a time suspended. In the mean time the use of rattan in its manufactured form had greatly increased, and Mr. Wakefield, in the year 1856, resolved to begin the manufacture of cane in this country, and to utilize, so far as possible, the whole of the material. The American Rattan Company were at this time the only party cutting cane by machinery, and they used the cane only for seating chairs. The remainder of the rattan was wasted. But Mr. Wakefield determined to make the whole of the rattan — cane, pith, and shavings — valuable. He began with one or two machines worked by hand in Boston. A fortunate speculation gave him both credit and capital, so that he could enlarge his business. Learning that there were several large lots of rattan in the New York market, the article at this time being much depressed, Mr. Wakefield, with all the ready money he could command, went to that city, established his quarters quietly at the Astor House, and put his brokers at work to obtain the lowest price at which the entire stock could be purchased, enjoining upon them not to name the purchaser. Having obtained the desired information, he decided to take all the available lots, for which he paid sufficient cash to make the material subject to his order. This gave him the whole control of the rattan stock of the country. Prices soon advanced, and he was enabled to sell, so that he realized a handsome profit. This single operation not only put money and credit at his disposal, but also gave him a prestige in the business, which he ever after maintained. Soon after this he removed his works from Boston to South Reading. Water power took the place of hand power, and as the business rapidly increased, steam power was soon added. The mill at South Reading in which he first began, soon became too small for him, and building after building was erected, until at the time of his death his manufactories and store-houses covered an area of ten acres of flooring.

Nor was this wonderful increase in his business the only remarkable feature. There was a corresponding advance in utilizing the whole of the rattan, so that nothing was lost. From a comparatively small jobbing trade in an article at that time of little value, he advanced to the manufacture of reeds for hoop skirts, then to cane for seating chairs, then to the manipulation of the waste, and finally to the use of all the small pieces, and even shavings, in making various beautiful and useful articles. His original idea was thus realized, and probably no one ever succeeded, in the face of so many difficulties and with such a stubborn material as rattan, in so nearly accomplishing his object.

In 1865 Mr. Wakefield sent his nephew and namesake, Mr. Cyrus Wakefield, 2d, to Singapore, since which time they have imported nearly the whole stock of rattan for the country. The Indian trade also included the importation of tin, gambier, pepper, coffee, spices, and all the products of the Straits Settlement and Java. This department increased in importance up to the time of his death.

About the year 1851, Mr. Wakefield made his first purchase of real estate in South Reading. In July of that same year he bought the larger part of the land comprising his homestead, and in place of the mansion house, which then stood upon it, he built in 1861 a magnificent residence. About this time he fully realized that the town was destined to become a very important place. And now he seemed never to have enjoyed a moment, so long as he knew that there was a piece of real estate in the vicinity of his house or factories which could be purchased. He would not rest till he had a deed of it in his own name on record. Many of these purchases were of low swamps and meadows, which he cleared, filled up, and drained, making valuable building lots of what had been waste land.

While in the spring of 1867 the citizens of South Reading were considering the propriety of erecting some suitable memorial to the brave men who had gone from their number to the War of the Rebellion, and had perished, Mr. Wakefield came forward and voluntarily offered to give to the town a lot of land, and a cash contribution of $30,000 for a new Town House, in which provision should be made for a Soldiers' Memorial Hall. In accepting this munificent offer, the town at once decided to change its name, and on the 20th day of January, 68, by acclamation, voted that it should henceforth be Wakefield. On the 4th of July, 1868, the new name was adopted by appropriate and interesting exercises.

Mr. Wakefield more than fulfilled his promise to the town. He more than quadrupled the cost of the edifice, and on Feb. 22, 1871, in the presence of an audience completely filling the new and beautiful hall, he surrendered the keys of the building to the proper officers of the town. But this act alone does not fully reveal his great interest in the town.

In order that people might be induced to settle in Wakefield, he was active in the organization of the Real Estate and Building Association; at first assuming nearly the whole of the capital stock, besides turning into the Association a large tract of valuable land, then unoccupied, but which has since been built upon. He also had a strong desire to improve the opportunities for education, and favored every project for better school-houses and enlarged facilities for instruction. His mind dwelt so much upon this subject, that he was not only eager to assist worthy students individually, but he inaugurated a course of free lectures on scientific subjects for the masses.

Although Mr. Wakefield never held a position where elevation was due to political influence, yet he was a leader in all local enterprises and improvements, and sometimes led the way where few were ready to follow.

He was one of the corporators of the Savings Bank, director in the Citizens' Gas Light Company, president and largest stockholder in the Ice Company, member of the School Board, of the Agricultural Association, and National Bank of South Reading.

The plan of furnishing the town with an abundance of pure water was among his last projects. Indeed, he had so far developed it as to organize the Quannapowitt Water Co.

His whole thought was thus centred upon the town which had honored him by assuming his name. He expected to live to see it famed for its institutions of education, distinguished by its beauty of landscape and architecture, an honor to its citizens, an enduring monument to his name. But Mr. Wakefield's plans reached beyond his adopted town. It is interesting to trace the growth of his conceptions as regards the future of Boston, the city in which he had labored so vigorously and successfully. In 1863 he purchased an estate in Hanover Street, afterwards a second in North Street, both of which were situated between Cross and North Centre Streets. Subsequently he bought and consolidated seven estates at the corner of Hanover and North Centre Streets, and two in Cross Street. In 1864-5 he became the owner of three estates on Canal Street; then in 1868 of the Hall Distillery estate in Prince Street; in 1868 of the tenement houses in Friend Street Court, which he replaced with a fine brick block in 1870-1871. These large purchases were not made at random. He believed in the future of Boston. He saw that Washington Street must come to Haymarket Square, and to the accomplishment of this object he bent his energies for a year. Although he did not live even to see the work begun, yet to him is largely due the credit of its successful completion. In 1871, when he knew that Washington Street would be extended, he purchased the Brattle Square Church, the Quincy House, and adjoining estate on Hanover Street. In 1872 the Studio Building was purchased, the Central House, and an estate adjoining in Brattle Square.

In June, 1873, he made his last purchase of real estate, on the line of the Washington Street extension. His object in becoming so large a real estate owner was to improve and develop the northern part of Boston, according to the ideal which was ever before his mind. In addition to his other duties he was a director in the Boston and Maine, Fitchburg, Nashua, Acton and Boston, and Middlesex Horse Railroads, in the first two of which he was the largest stockholder. The plans which he had conceived, but was prevented by death from fully executing, show the breadth and scope of his mind. He had projected the levelling of Copp's Hill so as to form a great freight depot and docks for the use of a railroad in which he was interested; the purchase of the Music Hall property; the erection of a noble edifice at Harvard, in which there should be rooms for the "Wakefield Library," and for other educational purposes; the founding of a college at Wakefield (the plans of which were known only to a few intimate friends), where the children of the poor might enjoy the benefits of superior training. These unfinished schemes reveal the intention and heart of Mr. Wakefield much better than words could do.

Mr. Wakefield was married on the thirty-first day of October, 1841, to Miss Eliza A. Bancroft, the only daughter of Captain Henry Bancroft, who survives him.

Mr. Wakefield was a man of iron will and resolute purpose, combined with great physical endurance. Energy, perseverance, and an indomitable courage in the face of almost insuperable obstacles, were his prominent characteristics.

He had a keen perception, and results that other men reached by hard thought seemed to intuitively come to him.

He knew human nature thoroughly, and could read a man at a glance. To those who knew him best he revealed at times a warm, genial, and tender nature, though to a stranger he might seem distant.

He was charitable, giving not only in large sums to public enterprises, but cheering the hearts of the poor with his generous gifts. Many students struggling for an education remember with gratitude his timely aid. As a merchant, he was shrewd, industrious, persistent, and careful in the details of his business. His character and deeds are thus epitomized in the resolutions adopted by his fellow-citizens on the evening after his death: "The valuable citizen, the prosperous merchant, the progressive leader in ornamental and architectural improvements, the friend and helper of education, the chief promoter of our local industrial pursuits, our munificent namesake, whose numerous and generous benefactions will remain his enduring memorials."

Mr. Wakefield died very suddenly on Sabbath morning, Oct. 26, 1873, at a quarter before 8 o'clock, at the age of sixty-two years and eight months. His funeral was attended at his late residence on the following Wednesday.

"The silver cord is loosed and the golden bowl is broken."

APPENDIX.

APPENDIX.

A.

INDIAN DEED OF LYNN AND READING.

"To all Christian People, to whom this present Deed of Confirmation and Alienation shall come, David Kunkshamooshaw, who, by credible intelligence, is grandson to old Sagamore George-No-Nose, so called, alias Wenepowweekin, sometime of Rumney Marsh, and sometimes at or about Chelmsford of ye colony of ye Massachyets, so called, sometimes here and sometimes there, but deceased, ye said David, grandson to ye said old Sagamore George-No-Nose, deceased, and Abigail Kunkshamooshaw, ye wife of David, and Cicely, alias Su-George, ye reputed daughter of said old Sagamore George, and James Quonopohit of Natick, alias Rumney Marsh, and Mary his wife, send greeting, &c. : —

"Know ye, that the said David Kunkshamooshaw, and Abigail his wife, and Cicely, alias Su-George aforesaid, and James Quonopohit aforesaid, with his wife Mary, who are the nearest of kin and legal successors of ye aforesaid George-No-Nose, alias Wenepowweekin, whom wee affirme was the true and sole owner of ye land, that the towns of Lynn and Reading (aforesaid) stand upon, and notwithstanding ye possession of ye English dwelling in those townships of Lynn and Reading, aforesaid, wee, ye said David Kunkshamooshaw, Cicely, alias Su-George, James Quonopohit, the rest aforesaid Indians, doe lay claim to the lands that these two towns aforesaid, Lynn and Reading, stand upon, and the dwellers thereof possess, that ye right and title thereto is ours, and belong to us and ours; but, howsoever, the townships of Lyn and Reading, having been long possessed by the English, and although wee make our clayme, and ye Selectmen and Trustees of both towns aforesaid, pleading title by graunts of Courts and purchase of old of our predecessor, George Sagamore, and such like matters, &c., wee the Claymers aforesaid, viz.: David Kunkshamooshaw and Abigail, his squaw, Cicely, alias Su-George, the reputed daughter of old Sagamore George, alias Wenepowweekin, and James Quonopohit and Mary his wife, all and every of us, as aforesaid, and jointly together, for and in consideration of ye summe of sixteen pounds of current sterling money of silver, in hand paid to ye Indians clayming, viz.: David Kunkshamooshaw &c. at or before the ensealing and delivery of these presents, by Mr. Ralph King, William Bassett, Senr., Matthew Farrington, Senr., John Burrill, Senr., Robert Potter, Senr., Samuel Johnson, and Oliver Purchas, Selectmen in Lynn, in ye County of Essex in New England, trustees and Prudentials for and in behalf of ye purchasers and now proprietors of ye townships of Lynn and Reading, well and truly payd, the receipt whereof, wee, viz.: David Kunkshamooshaw, Abigail his wife, Cicely, alias Su-George, ye reputed daughter of old Sagamore George, and James, alias Rumney Marsh, and Mary his wife, doe hereby acknowledge themselves to be fully satisfied and contented, and thereof and every part thereof, doe hereby acquit, exhonerate and discharge ye said Mr. Ralph King, Wm. Bassett, Senr., with all and every of ye Selectmen aforesaid, trustees and prudentials, together with the purchasers and now proprietors of ye said townships of Lyn and of Reading, their heirs, executors, administrators and assigns, forever, by these presents have granted, bargained a full and a firme confirmation and ratification of all grants of Courts, and any former alienation made by our predecessor or predecessors, and our own right, title and interest, clayme and demand whatsoever, and by these presents doe fully, freely, clearly and absolutely give and grant a full and firme confirmation of all grants of Courts, and any sort of alienation made by our predecessor or predecessors, as also all our owne clayme of right, title, interest and demand, unto them ye said Mr. Ralph King, Wm. Bassett and the rest, Selectmen aforenamed, trustees and prudentials for ye town of Lyn,— ye worshipful Mr. John Browne, Capt. Jeremiah Sweyn and Lt. Wm. Harsey, trustees and prudentials for ye towne of Reading, to their heirs and assigns forever, to and for ye sole use, benefit and behoof of ye purchasers and now proprietors of ye townships of Lynn and Reading aforesaid, and all ye said townships of Lynn and Reading, joyning one to another, even from the sea, where the line beginneth, between Lynn and Marblehead and so between Lynn and Salem, as it is stated by those towns and marked, and so to Ipswich river, and so from thence, as it is stated betwixt Salem and Reading, and as the line is stated and runne betwixt Will's Hill, and as is stated and runne betwixt Reading and Andover, and as it is stated betwixt Oburne and Reading, and as it is stated and runne betwixt Charlestowne, Malden, Lynn and Reading, and upon the sea, from ye line that beginneth at Lynn and Marblehead and Salem, to divide the townes aforesaid, so as well from thence to ye two Nahants, viz.: ye little Nahant and ye great Nahant, as ye sea compasseth it almost round, and so to the river called Lynn river, or Rumney Marsh river or Creek, unto the line from Bride's Brook to the said Creek, answering ye line, that is stated between Lynn and Boston, from said Bride's Brook up to Reading. — This said Tract of land, described as aforesaid, together with all houses, edifices, buildings, lands, yards, orchards, gardens, meadows, marrishes, feedings, grounds, rocks, stones, beach Flats, pastures, commons, and commons of pasture, woods, underwoods, swamps, waters, watercourses, damms, ponds, fishings, flowings, ways, easements, profits, privileges, rights, commodities, royalling, hereditaments and appurtenances whatsoever, to ye said townships of Lynn and Reading, and other the premises belonging or in anywise appertaining, or by them now used, occupied and enjoyed as part, parcel or member thereof; and also all rentes, arrearages of rentes, quitrents, rights and appurtenances whatsoever, nothing excepted or reserved; and also all deeds, writings and evidences whatsoever, touching ye premises, or any part or parcel thereof.

To have and to hold all ye said townships of Lynn and Reading, as well as ye two Nahants aforesaid, ye little and ye great Nahant, as they are encompassed by ye sea, with their beaches, from ye great Nahant to ye little, and from ye little Nahant homeward where Richard Hood now dwelleth, and so to Mr. King's, with all ye above granted premises, with their and every of their rights, members and appurtenances, and every part and parcel thereof, hereby given, granted, confirmed, ratified unto ye said Mr. Ralph King, Wm. Bassett and the rest, Selectmen in behalf of Lynn, and ye worshipful Mr. John Browne, and ye rest aforenamed for Reading, all trustees and prudentials for the townships of Lynn and Reading, to them and their heirs and assigns forever, to and for ye sole use, benefit and behoof of ye purchasers and now proprietors of ye said townships of Lynn and Reading; and they, ye said David Kunkshamooshaw and Abigail his wife, and Cicely, alias Su-George, ye reputed daughter of George-No-Nose deceased, and James Quonopohit, and Mary his wife, Indians aforesaid, for themselves, their heirs, executors, administrators and assigns, jointly, severally and respectively, doe hereby covenant, promise and grant to and with ye said Mr. King, Wm. Bassett, Senr, and ye rest of Lynn and ye worshipful Mr. John Browne, and ye rest of Reading, trustees and prudentials for ye towns of Lynn and Reading, as aforesaid, their heirs and assigns, and to ye purchasers and now proprietors of yᵉ said townships of Lynn and Reading, etc., in manner and forme following (that is to say), that at the time of this graunt, confirmation and alienation, and until the ensealing and delivery of these presents, their ancestor and ancestors and they, the above-named David and Abigail his now wife, and Cicely, alias Su-George, and the rest aforenamed Indians, were yᵉ true, sole and lawful owners of all yᵉ aforebargained, confirmed and aliened premises, and were lawfully seized off, and in yᵉ same and every part thereof in their own propper right, and have in themselves full power, good right and lawful authority to grant, alien, confirm, and assure yᵉ same as is afore described in this deed unto Mr. Ralph King, Wm. Bassett, Senʳ, and yᵉ rest, Selectmen of Lynn, and yᵉ worshipful Mr. John Browne and yᵉ rest aforenamed agents for Reading, all trustees and prudentials for yᵉ two townships of Lynn and Reading, to them, their heirs and assigns forever, for yᵉ use aforesaid, viz : yᵉ benefit and behoof of yᵉ purchasers and now proprietors of yᵉ two townships aforesaid, as a good, perfect and absolute estate of inheritance, in fee simple, without any manner of condition, reversion or limitation whatsoever, so as to alter, change, or make void yᵉ same, and that yᵉ trustees aforesaid, and yᵉ purchasers and now proprietors of yᵉ said townships of Lynn and Reading, their heirs and assigns, shall and may, by virtue and force of these presents, from time to time, and at all times forever hereafter, lawfully, peaceably, and quietly, have, hold, use, occupy, possess and injoy, yᵉ above-granted, aliened and confirmed premises, with yᵉ appurtenances and benefits thereof, and every part and parcel thereof, free and clear, and clearly acquitted and off and from all and all manner of other gifts, grants, bargains, sales, leases, mortgages, jointures, dowers, judgments, executions, fforfeitures, and off and from all other titles, troubles, charges, incumbrances whatsoever, had, made, committed, done, or suffered to be done by yᵉ said David and Abigail his wife, Cicely, alias Su-George, and the rest, Indians, aforenamed, them or any of them, or any of their heirs or assigns, or any of their ancestors at any time or times.

And further, that yᵉ said David Kunkshamooshaw and Abigail his wife, Su-George, James Quonopohit and Mary his wife, &c., their heirs, executors and administrators, &c., jointly and severally will and shall by these presents, from time to time, and at all times hereafter, warrant and defend yᵉ aforegranted and confirmed premises, with their appurtenances, and every part and parcel thereof unto yᵉ said trustees, or prudentials aforenamed, for yᵉ townships of Lyn and Reading, against all and every person or persons whatsoever, anywaies lawfully clayming or demanding the same or any part or parcell thereof.

And lastly, that they, ye said David and Su-George and James Quonopohit, their wives, or any of their heirs, executors, or administrators, shall and will, from time to time, and at all times hereafter, when thereto required, at ye cost and charges of said trustees and prudentials, their heirs or assigns, or ye purchasers and proprietors of ye townships of Lynn and Reading, etc., doe make, acknowledge, suffer all and every such further act and acts, thing and things, assurances and conveyances in ye law whatsoever, for ye furthermore better surety and sure making of the abovesaid townships of Lynn and Reading, with ye rights, hereditaments, benefits, and appurtenances, above, by these presents, mentioned to be bargained, aliened, confirmed, vnto ye aforesaid trustees and prudentials, their heirs and assigns, for ye use aforesaid, as by ye said trustees aforesaid, their heirs or assigns or ye said proprietors, or by their *Council*, learned in the law, shall be reasonably devised, advised, or required.

In witness whereof, ye said David Kunkshamooshaw, and Abigail his wife, and Cicely, alias Su-George, and James Quonopohit and Mary his wife, have hereunto set their hands and seals, ye day of ye date being ye fourth day of September, one thousand six hundred eighty and six, annoque regni regis Jacobus Secundi Anglice.

DAVID "ψ" KUNKSHAMOOSHAW.
his mark.

ABIGAIL "ψ" KUNKSHAMOOSHAW.
her mark.

CICELY "η" alias SU-GEORGE.
her mark.

"JAMES QUONOPOHIT."

MARY "Χ" QUONOPOHIT.
her mark.

All the persons hereunto subscribed, acknowledged the within written to be their act and deed, May 31, 1687.

(as certifies) BARTHO. GEDNEY, one of ye Council.

The above deed is copied from Lewis and Newhall's "History of Lynn," and was by them, or rather by Mr. Newhall, found among the records at Salem.

B.

At a General Court of Election, held at Boston, 23d of May, 1666,—

Whereas, the Honorable General Court having formerly granted to the town of Reading a Tract of Land of two miles, lying between their Grant of four miles and Mr. Bellingham's farme and the great (Ipswich) river, and also ordered them to have it laid out sometime before this Court sate;— at the request of the Town that this Platt of Land is laid out and returned, butted and bounded as followeth, running from a Pine tree at A, north by the compass, Six hundred rods, joynes to the Town of Reading land unto B, to the top of a Rocky hill; and from B, East two hundred sixty-eight rods to an Oak tree at C, marked R. B., and joynes the Andover land; and from C, South South East 8 deg. = 30 — to E five hundred seventy six rods, this joynes upon the Governor's farme to a black oak tree at D, marked R. B., and this line joynes upon Mr. Bellingham's farme; the fourth line runs from D, E. B. N., two hundred thirty six rods to a walnut tree at E, and joynes also on Mr. Bellingham's farme; the fifth line from E, South East and be (by?) South, two hundred and four rods to a black oak in Salem line at F, which joynes upon the farme of Thomas Fuller; the sixth line runs from F, west South West, $2^{d.}$ S. four hundred and twenty rods to a black oak at G., the which line is Salem bounds. The 7th line from G., West by North, $7^{D.}$ No:, five hundred and sixty eight rods to a Pine tree at A (the place of beginning), alongst the river (Ipswich) side.

Pr. me, ELISHA HUTCHINSON.

The Court allows of this returne, Provided it intrench not on any former Grant.

A true Copy as appears of Record.

Exam'd Pr. JAS. ADDINGTON, *Sec'r'y.*

C.

At the second Session of the General Court held at Boston, 8th of October, 1662.

Laid out by order of the General Court, the Deputy Governor, Richard Bellingham Esq., his farme, now in the occupation of Bray Wilkinson, the 23^{d} of September, 1662.

The first line runs from a white Oak marked R. B. northwesterly to a Rocky point, where a white Oak is marked; and from thence by the Southerly corner of Beachy meadow to a white oak marked, the length about a mile and a quarter. The second line from the last marked white oak upon a west and by South Point, about a mile to an Oak marked R. B.

The third line from the said Oak upon a South and by East point a mile and quarter to a Tree marked on the South West side of the Pond, taking in a meadow of about twenty-five acres, lying without the said line and adjoining to it, towards the northerly end thereof.

The fourth line from the last marked Tree, upon an East and by North point to the first white Oak marked R. B., in length one mile and a quarter.

Also, One hundred acres lying square on the plain before the Dwelling house of Bray Wilkinson; beginning at the brook that runs into Price's meadow, and running in length down to a white oak marked, about 160 rod, and in breadth at both ends 100 rods to a Tree marked, at either end; the lower or South East angle being a Pine Tree marked; the upper or North West angle being an oak marked, standing near a great Rock, — Provided, that part of the Pine Swamp, that lieth within the said Bounds, shall be free and common for any to take off the timber growing thereon.

       , WM. HAWTHORNE,
        THOMAS HOWLET.

The Court allowes and approves of this Return.
   A true Copy, as appears of Record,
     Exam'd Pr. JAS. ADDINGTON, *Sec'y*.

D.

A LIST OF THE SOLDIERS OF THE REVOLUTION FROM READING.

It is not presumed that this is a perfect list, but as nearly so as we had time and ability to make it.

Ephraim Abbott.	Jonas Bancroft.	David Batchelder.
Josiah Abbott.	Jonas Bancroft, Jr.	Wm. Beers.
Jonas Adams.	Edmund Bancroft.	Joshua Burnham, Fifer and Drummer.
Joseph Bancroft, Lt.	Job Bancroft.	Sampson Blackman, col'd.
Caleb Bancroft,	John Bancroft.	Primus Blackman, "
James Bancroft, Captain.	John Batchelder.	Amos Boardman.
Sam'l Bancroft.	John Batchelder, Jr.	Elias Boardman.
Joshua Bancroft.	Nat'n Batchelder.	

APPENDIX.

Benj'n Boardman.
Moses Boardman.
Joseph Boutwell.
John Boutwell.
Kendall Boutwell.
James Boutwell.
John Brooks.
Joseph Brooks.
Jona. Brooks.
Benj'n Brown.
Charles Brown.
Jacob Brown.
Jona. Brown.
Joseph Brown.
Amos Bryant.
Timothy Bryant, Jr.
James Bryant.
John Bryant.
Elias Bryant.
—— Butters.
John Brooks, Capt.
John Buxton.
John Buxton, Jr.
Ebenezer Buxton.
Jeduthun Buxton.
Stephen Buxton.
Benja. Buxton.
Jona. Buxton.
Wm. Buxton.
Jacob Burnap.
John Burnap.
Geo. Burnap.
Isaac Burnap.
Joseph Burnap.
John Balley.
Joseph Barrett.
Stephen Barrett.
—— Bacchus, col'd.
Abijah Beard.
Cleaveland Beard.
Wm. Beard.
Zachariah Bragg.
Michael Baldwin.
Jeremiah Baldwin.
Samuel Bodge.
Samuel Badger.
Joseph Burditt.
John Cutler or Cutter.
Ephraim Carter.
Benja. Carter.
Jabez Carter.
Stephen Carter.
Enoch Carter.
Robert Convers.
Josiah Convers.
Nathan'l Cowdrey.
Nathan'l Cowdrey, Jr.
Reuben Coombs.
Reuben Camp (or Kemp).
Peter Calley.
Stephen Curtis.
Samuel Cory.

Elijah Cory.
Samuel Clapp.
Siers Cook, Ens.
David Damon.
Benja. Damon.
Ezra Damon.
Samuel Damon.
Daniel Damon.
Joseph Damon.
Ebenezer Damon.
Wm. Deadman.
John Dix.
Robert Douglas.
Robert Daland.
James Davis.
Daniel Davis.
Benja. Dutton, Corp.
Samuel Ellenwood.
Joseph Eberdon.
Thomas Edmands.
James Emerson.
Peter Emerson.
Wm. Emerson.
Thomas Emerson.
Ebenezer Emerson.
Elias Emerson.
John Emerson.
John Emerson, Jr.
Benja. Emerson.
Joseph Emerson.
Aaron Emerson.
Daniel Emerson.
Kendall Emerson, Sergt.
Natha'l Emerson.
Joshua Eaton, Sergt.
Joshua Eaton, Drum Maj.
Reuben Eaton.
Lilley Eaton.
Abraham Eaton.
Timothy Eaton.
Charles Eaton, Fifer.
Samuel Eaton.
Nathaniel Eaton.
Jonathan Eaton.
Thomas Eaton.
Thomas Eaton, Jr.
Wm. Eaton.
Nathaniel Eaton, Jr.
Eliab Eaton.
Jeremiah Eaton.
Sampson Eaton.
Samuel Evans.
Daniel Evans.
Nathaniel Evans.
Andrew Evans.
Chester Freeman, col'd.
Doss Freeman, "
Primus Freeman, "
Sharper Freeman, "
Peter Freeman, "
Cato Freeman, "
John Fowle.

Benja. Flint.
Levi Flint.
Ebenezer Flint, Sergt.
Sam'l Flint.
Edmund Flint.
Daniel Flint.
John Flint.
George Flint.
Wm. Flint.
Jona. Flint.
Hezekiah Flint.
—— Farley.
Edward Farmer.
John Farmer.
Nathan Foster.
Abraham Foster, Capt.
Benja. Foster.
Edmund Foster.
Wm. Foster, Corporal.
Andrew Foster.
Sam'l Frothingham.
John Farrar.
Nathan Felch.
John Felch.
Parker Felch.
Sam'l Felch.
Sam'l Felt.
Daniel Gould.
Reuben Gould.
Jona. Gould.
Wm. Gould.
Benja. Gould.
Wm. Green.
Thomas Green.
Jeremiah Green.
Daniel Green.
Jonas Green.
John Green, Serg.
Daniel Graves.
Nathaniel Graves.
Benj. Gleason.
Stephen Greenleaf.
Thaddeus Goodwin.
John Goodwin.
Nathaniel Goodwin.
Samuel Goodwin.
Thomas Goodwin.
John Hart.
Asa Hart.
Jeremiah Hartshorn.
Thomas Hartshorn.
Jona. Hartshorn.
Wm. Hartshorn.
John Hartshorn.
Nathaniel Hartshorn.
Timothy Hartshorn.
Thomas Hatson or Hudson, Fifer.
Joel Holden.
John Holden.
Joseph Holden.
Thomas Hay.

APPENDIX.

William Hay.
Samuel Hutchins.
Joseph Hopkins.
Joseph Hill.
James Hill.
John Hill.
Paul Hill.
Asa Hill.
Alpheus Hill.
John Hatson.
Benj. Hunt.
Benja. Herrick.
Jacob Herrick.
Nicholas Holt.
Joseph Holt.
Wm. Holt.
John Hutchinson (Naval).
Henry Hawkes.
Joseph Hawkins.
A. Johnson.
Joseph Johnson.
Benja. Johnson.
Seth Johnson.
Wm. Johnson.
Daniel Killom, Corp.
Archelaus Kenney.
Enoch Kidder.
Seth Leviston (Livingston), Sergt.
John Lambert (Naval).
Davis Lambert.
Jonas Lewis.
Samuel Lewis.
Samuel Lamson.
Sampson London.
Phineas McIntire.
Benja. McIntire.
Daniel McIntire.
Wm. McIntire.
Eben'r McIntire.
Elijah McIntire.
Elias McIntire.
Nathan Mason.
Rob't Mason.
Richard Mason.
Wm. Melendy.
Wm. McMillian.
Peter McAllister.
—— Nick.
Thomas Nichols.
Ebenezer Nichols.
Jesse Nichols.
Jona. Nichols.
Benja. Nichols.
Jeremiah Nichols.
Joseph Nichols.
John Nichols.
Jephthah Nutting.
Jona. Nutting.
Elisha Newhall.
Aaron Nurse.
David Parker.

Wm. Parker.
Joseph Parker.
Daniel Parker, Jr.
Jonas Parker.
Aaron Parker.
Ebenezer Parker.
Nathan Parker.
Edmund Parker.
Benja. Parker.
Elisha Parker.
Ichabod Parker.
Caleb Parker.
Amos Pearson.
Seward Poland.
Jonathan P. Pollard.
John Pike.
Ebenezer Pike.
John Pratt.
Ephraim Pratt, Left.
Daniel Pratt.
Benja. Pratt.
Silas Pratt.
Wm. Pratt.
Ezra Pratt.
Joseph Perry.
Edward Pratt.
Eleazer Flagg Poole.
Samuel Poole.
Daniel Poole.
James Poole.
Titus Potamia, col'd.
Isaac Ridgway.
Thos. Richardson, Left.
Wm. Richardson.
Edmund Richardson.
Peter Richardson.
Herbert Richardson.
Luke Richardson.
Benja. Roaff.
Jonas Rice.
Wm. Raddin.
Wm. Russell.
Thos. Sawyer.
Wm. Sawyer.
Eben'r Smith.
Isaac Smith.
Ezra Smith.
Abraham Smith.
Benj. Smith.
Wm. Stimpson.
Wm. Stimpson, 2d.
Ebenezer Stimpson.
Phineas Stimpson.
Enoch Stocker.
Cornelius Sweetser.
John Sweetser.
Wm. Sweetser.
Benja. Sweetser.
Jona. Stearns.
Isaac Stearns.
James Symonds.
Thomas Symonds.

Isaac Symonds.
Samuel Seagrave (Naval).
Ebenezer Stone.
Russell Sheldon.
Jesse Snow.
Elisha Tottingham.
Elisha Tottingham, Jr.
Thomas Thoyt.
Wm. Tarbox.
Jona. Thompson.
Wm. Thompson.
Israel Taylor.
Samuel Taylor.
John Taylor.
Samuel Temple.
Nath'l Upton.
Amos Upton.
Ebenezer Upton.
Isaac Upton.
John Upton.
Paul Upton.
Abraham Upton.
Jeduthan Upton.
Jethro Upton.
Timothy Vinton, Jr.
Oliver Walton.
Benja. Walton.
Jacob Walton.
Ebenezer Walton.
Josiah Walton.
James Walton.
Nathan Walton.
Isaac Walton.
Jotham Walton.
Israel Walton.
Timothy Wakefield.
Eben'r Wakefield.
Wm. Winship.
Jacob Wait.
Thomas Wait.
David Wright.
Nathan Woolley
David Watson.
Abel Whiting.
James Wilson.
Leonard Wilson.
Wm. Wilson.
Benja. Williams, Corp.
Asa Williams.
Eben'r Williams.
Nathaniel Wiley.
Wm. Wiley.
Eben'r Wiley.
James Wiley.
John Wiley.
Timothy Wiley.
Phineas Wiley.
Samuel Wiley.
Jona. Weston.
Nathaniel Weston.
James Weston.
Reuben Weston.

Daniel Weston.	Benj. Welch.	Nathaniel Wiley, Jr.
John Walker.	Sam'l Woodward.	Benja. Wiley.
Samuel Walker.	Timothy Wiley.	Benja. Young.
Joseph Walker.	Jona. Wiley.	Wm. Young.

E.

"Reading, May 7, 1719.

A petition of ye assessors of ye north presinct in Reeding, in ye behalf of ye foresaid presinct to ye towne of Reeding, that whareas by an act of ye Genneral Cort we ware made a presinct and thair by obliged to setil a minister, and to see him comfortably suported ; and thair being savrail parsels of madow, which the towne has devoted to a minesteral use, altho' we are two distinct presincts, yet we are but one towne, hoping yt you will one us for a part of the Towne by granting us, ye North presinct, ye emprovement of ye one half of ye minesteral madows, which we hope you Readely Doe, which will be a halp to us and an incorigment to ye Reverand Mr Putman to continue amonst us, a man in whome we tak much satisfaction ; — which we hop you rejoyc in ; which we have Reson to think you do, by what we have heard yt there is a considrable number that has subscribed fifteen pounds annually for five years to incorig the satilment of the gospel amongst us ; and also the Towne in General afterward by a free and voluntary Contribution, which was a great halp to us, and no doubt but a great incorigment to the Revrand Mr. Putman, for which we thank god for opning your harts thus bountifully to us in our beginings to incorig the gospel amongst, for w^c we Render you harty thanks.

So we remain your Frinds and humble pettioners, by the Request of presinct and in behalf of the presinct.

"THOMAS TAYLOR.
JOHN HARNDEN.
JOHN EATON."

F.

"To ye freehold^{rs} & inhabitants of Reading (peticularly those belonging to this parish) convened May 14, 1719, Grace, mercy and peace unto you be multiplyd, amen. Brethren, I lately received of Constable Ed: Brown £9 2s. 1d. in full for my Sallary for ye year 1718, wth my thanks to you, yt tis so early come in. Twas seasonable to me. But I confess twas much too scant for my necessity. You are not insensible yt allmost everything is strangely raised of late. Brethren, I am sensible of the charge this parish has lately been at, both in incourageing y⁰ North precinct, at wᵉ I have rejoyced, and moveing yᵉ pulpit wʳin I find help and benefit. It is not yʳfore wᵗʰout sensible trouble, yt I feel a necessity to tell you my sinking circumstances. I have recᵈ my Sallary, and yet find myselfe more than £20 in debt for necessaries received yᵉ last year, besides what is advanced in ys, wᶜ is more yn half of yt sum. And yet I have pay'd my money, rec'd of you, as far as it would go, reserving but a short pittance to myselfe. In other years yt I have been wᵗʰ you, when I was in Straits (as wᵗ I have had of you has never maintained me), I helped myselfe out of my own estate, &c., more than 20 pounds, and yt most cheerfully; for I came not here to make a prey of you, nor an estate among you; but because I thou't God call'd me here: But of late such has been, & yet are the circumstances of my proper estate, yt I cant do as I have done; could I, I had done it still wᵗʰout troubling you now. In short, *Brethren*, if to have no cheese, buttʳ, malt, nor stock of meal, no more yn one bushel of corn, nor money to buy, be to be in want, I am so. But I will not faint, yᵉ Earthe is yᵉ Lord's and the fullness yʳof. *Brethren*, If you can considʳ me and raise my Sallary in time to come, I leave it with you & commit myselfe to yᵉ Lord, & under him to you, while I am among you; Being willing to my utmost to serve you so long as yᵉ Ld shall enable me, and you willing to suport me.

"I am yr Soul's frind and Servant,

"RICH'D BROWN."

"May 11, 1719."

G.

SOLDIERS IN THE FRENCH AND INDIAN WARS OF 1745 TO 1759–'60.

Col. Eben'r Nichols.
Capt. Wm. Flint (died at Lake George in 1756 or '7).
Lieut. Benj. Foster.
" Samuel Hartshorn.
" Jacob Bancroft.
Corp. Benj. Parker.
" Joseph Hill.
Wm. Stimpson, clerk.
Caleb Bancroft.
Jeremiah Bancroft.
Kendall Flint.
Cornelius Calnon.
Elijah Dennis.
Lt. Benj. Flint.

Samuel Graves.
John Batt.
John Jeffrey.
Thos. Gould.
Thos. Hart.
Eben'r Lewis.
Joel Morgan.
Timothy Nichols.
Phineas Richardson.
Thos. Thoyts.
Wm. Winchester.
Thos. Richardson.
Green Parker.
Abraham Foster.
Isaac Walton.
Didymus Nichols.

Stephen Knight.
John Brown.
Joshua Eaton.
Kendall Goodwin.
Lemuel Jenkins.
Thos. Rayner.
Ebenezer Parker.
John Weston.
Nathaniel Eaton.
Jona. Foster.
Jona. McIntire.
Ens. James Poole.
Wm. Sheldon.
Richard Melendy.
Timo. Hartshorne (died).
Timo. Bryant.

APPENDIX.

Capt. David Greene.
Sergt. Joshua Nichols.
James Hartshorne.
John Emerson, Jr.
Benj. Batchelder.
John Boutwell.
Michael Sweetser.
James Williams.
Capt. Jonathan Poole.
Daniel Gardner.
Capt. Thos. Flint.
Abraham Sheldon.
James Flint.
Wm. Sawyer.
Timo. Russell.
Ephraim Pratt.
Jona. Dix.
Eben'r McIntire.
Timothy McIntire.
Benj. McIntire.
Jona. Tower.
Daniel Graves.
Timothy Eaton.
Samuel Marbel.
John Buxton.
Solomon McIntire.
Ephr'm Holt.
Timothy Stimpson.
Jacob Upton.
Nathan Phelps.
Asa Barker.
Jeremiah Richardson.
Timo. Bancroft.
James Woodward.
Wm. Pelsue.
James Walton (died in the service).
Joseph Felch (died in the service).
Asa Buck.
Capt. Sam'l Bancroft.
Phineas Lovejoy.
Ephraim Parker.
Benja. Nichols.
Joseph Bancroft.
Jona. Weston.

Jacob Townsend.
John Atwell.
Nath'l Cowdrey.
Phineas Parker.
Isaac Noyes.
Sam'l Smith.

Troop of Horse.

Capt. Jona. Eaton.
Capt. John Bryant.
Q. M. James Weston.
Corpl. Jabez Damon.
Francis Kendall, Jr.
Thos. Eaton.
Eben'r Smith.
Peter Emerson.
Timo. Nichols, Jr.
John Weston.
Wm. Bryant, Jr.
Jacob Upton.
Abraham Upton.
Jonah Parker.
Elijah Upton.
Wm. Winchester.
Archelaus McIntire.
Eph'm Sheldon.
Collins Hartshorn.
Jacob Pierce.
Daniel Sheldon (died in service).
Jona. Batchelder.
Thos. Nichols.
Mingo, servant of Jere'h Swain.
Sergt. Nathan Walton.
Capt. John Dix.
Thos. Brown (son of Jere.).
John Kimball.
Sam'l Smith.
Josiah Walton, Jr.
Nathan Flint.
Jesse Richardson.
Jere'h Richardson.
John Lilley.
Nath'l Eaton.

Lemuel Jenkins.
Thos. Rainer.
John Brown.
Stephen Knight.
James Stimpson, Surgeon's mate, in His Majesty's ship "King George."
Phineas Parker, Jr.
Nath'l Swain (son of John).
Wm. Coggin.
Eben'r Damon.
Daniel Foster.
Samuel Foster.
John Nichols (escaped by flight from the massacre at Fort Edward).
Jona. Person (2d Lt.).
Sergt. John Swain.
Nath'l Batchelder.
Jonas or Jona. Parker.
Thos. Boutwell.
Samuel Brown (son of Jere.).
John Boutwell (son of John).
Samuel Farley.
Benj. Batchelder.
Tim. Damon.
Amos Green.
Jere'h Bryant, Jr.
Reuben Boutwell.
Amos Flint.
Wm. Upton.
Eben'r Lewis.
Sam'l Damon.
Samuel Sheldon.
Benj. Curtis.
Sam'l Reed.
Wm. Buxton.
Benj. Swain.
Kendall Townsend.
Nath'l Sawyer.
Asa Parker.
Eben'r Flint.
Wm. Bickford.

H.

ROLLS OF THE THREE COMPANIES OF MILITIA,

In the Town of Reading, belonging to the Regiment commanded by Col. David Green, of Reading, as they stood April 19, 1775.

1st Parish Co.
John Walton, Captain.
John Pratt, Lieut.
Thomas Green, Ens.
John Brown, Sergt.
John Vinton,   "

Wm. Green, Sergt.
Daniel Gould,   "
James Smith, Corp'l.
James Bennett,   "
Thomas Poole, Drummer.
Thos. Hudson, Fifer.

Aaron Green.
John Fowle.
Isaac Smith.
Michael Sweetser.
Nathan'l Wiley.
David Smith.

APPENDIX.

Benj. Boardman.
Reuben Eaton.
Wm. Gould.
Wm. Gould, Jr.
James Wiley.
Amos Boardman.
Nathan Green.
Wm. Tarbox.
James Johnson.
John Pratt.
Nath'l Gerry.
Isaac Green.
Jonas Green.
Josiah Bryant.
Jeremiah Bryant.
Jonathan Evans.
Thomas Evans.
Jonas Evans.
Eben'r Smith.
Sam'l Felch.
Nathan Felch.
John Farrier.
Nathan Wolley.
Cornelius Sweetser.
Daniel Lewis.
Timothy Bryant.
Samuel Evans.
Eben'r Parker.
John Colman.
John Lambert.
Eben'r Williams.
Tho. Damon.
Benja. Hartshorn.
Jonathan Hartshorn.
Eben'r Stimpson.
Eben'r Hopkins.
Wm. Bennett.
John Goodwin.
Benja. Emerson.
Jacob Walton.
Benj. Butters.
Sam'l Hitchens.
Peter Emerson (died in the army, Nov. 16, 1783).
Tho. Davis.
Jona. Eaton.
Benja. Brown.
Wm. Brown.
Joseph Emerson.
Joseph Gould.
Thos. Parker, Jr.
Thos. Emerson.
Thos. Emerson, Jr.
Aaron Nurse.
Lille Eaton.
Jonathan Foster.
Jere'h Brown.
Wm. Walton.
Eben'r Walton.
Oliver Walton.

John Hawkes.
Brown Emerson.
Jabez Carter.
James Hartshorn.
John Green.
Elias Boardman.
Tho. Parker, Sen'r.
Jacob Emerson.
Josiah Green and Tho. Hay, from Stoneham.

2d Parish Co.
John Flint, Captain.
John Dix, 1st Lt.
*Eph'm Pratt, 2d Lt.
Timothy Russell, Sergt.
Geo. Flint,   "
Benja. Upton,   "
Jabez Upton,   "
Jonathan Batchelder.
Job Bancroft.
John Burnap.
Mr. John Bragg.
John Clummons.
Stephen Curtis.
Mr. Ezra Damon.
Mr. David Damon.
Dea. Jeremiah Eaton.
Timothy Eaton.
Israel Eaton.
Nath'l Eaton, Jr.
Nath'l Evans.
Sam'l Ellenwood.
Lt. Eleazer Flint.
Lt. Benj. Flint.
Mr. Jona. Flint.
Mr. James Flint.
Eben'r Flint, Jr.
Benj. Flint, Jr.
Benj. Flint, 3d.
Benj. Flint, 4th.
Jona. Flint, Jr.
Wm. Flint.
James Foster.
Benja. Foster.
Nathan Foster.
Abraham Foster.
Martin Herrick.
Samuel Herrick.
Jacob Herrick.
Benj. Holt.
John Hayward.
Daniel Hart.
Asa Hart.
Ens. Joseph Lewis.
Benj. McIntier.
Benja. McIntier, Jr.
Nath'l McIntier.
Hezekiah McIntier.
Eben'r McIntier.

Eph. McIntier.
Solomon McIntier.
Mr. Jacob McIntier.
Wm. Nichols.
Henry Putnam.
Joseph Phelps.
David Parker.
Sam'l Parker.
Isaac Tinkcom.
Wm. Russell.
Sergt. Abraham Sheldon.
Ens. Wm. Sawyer.
John Stack or Slack.
Nath'l Sheldon, Jr.
Zack'h Sheldon.
Wm. Stone.
Thos. Taylor, Jr.
Samuel Taylor.
Joseph Upton.
Jacob Upton.
Amos Upton, Jr.
Amos Upton, 3d.
Eben'r Upton.
W. Upton.
Nath'l Upton, Jr.
John Upton.
David Upton.
Dr. Amos Upton.
Capt. Hezekiah Upton.
Wm Whittredge.
David Wright.

3d Parish Co.
Thomas Eaton, Capt.
Jonas Parker, Lieut.
John Emerson, Ens.
Amos Pearson, Sergt.
Joseph Bancroft,   "
Wm. Parker,   "
John Boutwell,   "
John Temple, Corpl.
Asa Parker,   "
Isaac Pratt,   "
Wm. Nichols, Drummer.
Edmund Bancroft.
Samuel Emerson.
Samuel Damon.
Abraham Eaton.
John Nichols.
Daniel Parker, Jr.
Benja. Parker.
John Pratt.
Richard Nichols.
Thos. Symonds.
Jethro Richardson.
Wm. Foster.
Eben'r Richardson.
Nath'l Weston.
Jonathan Poole.
Aaron Emerson.

---

* Took the small-pox at Ticonderoga, and died at the Lake George Hospital.

Caleb Parker.	Aaron Parker.	Jona. Nichols.
Wm. Temple.	Isaac Parker.	Jona. Weston, Jr.
Wm. Beard.	John Hartshorn.	John Stimpson.
Timothy Pratt.	Timothy Wakefield.	Jacob Townsend.
Jeremiah Nichols.	John Farmer.	Andrew Beard.
James Boutwell.	John Buxton.	Daniel Parker, Sen'r.
James Eaton.	Joseph Boutwell.	Ephraim Parker, "
Jonas Eaton.	Richard Mason.	Jos. Hill.
Edm'd Parker.	Reuben Weston.	Jonathan Weston, Sen'r.
Sam'l Pratt.	Benja. Young.	Jabez Damon.
Ephraim Parker, 2d.	Wm. Tompson.	Eben'r Emerson.
Abijah Weston.	Jeduthun Buxton.	John Weston.

HH.

REMINISCENCES OF THE REVOLUTION.[*]

Among the men of note who formerly belonged in Reading, the name of Dr. John Brooks, afterwards Governor of the State, stands prominent. He lived here for some time before the breaking out of the War of the Revolution, residing in the house formerly belonging to Mr. Samuel Damon, on John Street. He m. Lucy Smith, of Reading, in 1774, and was in practice here the same year, though only twenty-two years of age. His sister, Elizabeth, m. Rev. Jacob Burnap. Was Major in Bridge's regiment, and active in intrenching Breed's Hill June 16, 1775, but was not in the battle of the 17th. Feb. '76, made Major in Col. Webb's regiment, 19th, and went with it to Long Island. In '77, promoted to Lieut.-Col. of Eighth Massachusetts Regiment. In '78 made Col. of Seventh Massachusetts Regiment; appointed by Washington Marshal and Inspector of the Revenue in '95. In War of 1812 was Adj.-Gen. of the State, and Governor from 1816 to '23. A company of minute-men was formed here before the breaking out of hostilities between the colonies and the mother country. Dr. Brooks was chosen its Captain. Not being accustomed to military drill and tactics, he watched the military evolutions of the British at Boston, where he frequently resorted, perhaps for that object, and put the knowledge thus gained into immediate practice in drilling his company here. He was in Boston on the afternoon of April 18, 1775, the day before the battle of Lexington, and saw the preparatory movements of the British. In the night following he received a message that they were moving towards Concord. He had a patient at the Hartshorn house on Haverhill Street, then called "Pratt Row," whom he visited about midnight, and took the opportunity to notify the men of his company in that part of the town of the movement of the British.

---

[*] Furnished by Hiram Barrus, of Reading.

It appears that some of his company lived in what is now North Reading. Ephraim Pratt lived about a mile north of the meeting-house there, and belonged to the company, with his son Ephraim. It is said that Capt. Brooks galloped into the yard fronting his house, calling out in a stentorian voice, " Stand to your arms! stand to your arms!" Father and son arose, picked their flints, saw that their powder was dry and their bullets ready, and hastened to the field of strife.

C. P. Judd, Esq., relates that he had the information from reliable sources that this company was in constant preparation for such an emergency. The members had loaves of bread baked, and a supply of cheese ready to take with them at a moment's warning. They had a preconcerted signal by which they might be summoned together in the shortest possible time, but as they had the night before them in which to make preparation, it does not appear that the signal was required. It is understood that the chief part of the company were together in the latter part of the night near Weston's Corner, and under command of Capt., then Lieut. James Bancroft, set out upon their march in season to be at Bedford early in the morning of the day of the battle.

Edward Everett says, "Every cross road opened a new avenue to the assailants. Through one of these the gallant Brooks led up the minute-men of Reading." From this it appears that Gov. Brooks assumed command of his company when they reached the scene of action, if not before.

Hudson, in his History of Lexington, says, " The British commenced their retreat from Concord about noon. For the first mile they were unmolested; but when they arrived at Merriam's Corner they encountered a party of minute-men from Reading under Major Brooks, — Col. William Thompson, with a body of militia from Billerica and the vicinity, coming up about the same time. The Provincials on the high grounds near the North Bridge, seeing the British leaving the village, went across the 'great field' to the Bedford road, and arrived in time to support the troops brought up by Brooks and Thompson. Here may be said to have commenced the *battle* of the 19th of April. At Lexington Common and at Concord North Bridge but few guns had been fired by the Americans, and though ten Americans had fallen, only one of the king's troops had been killed. But now all restraint seems to have been removed, and every true patriot felt at full liberty to fire without the bidding of any superior. Rev. Edmund Foster, then a young man and a private in the Reading company, gives a graphic account of what occurred at this point : 'A little before we came to Merriam's Hill, we discovered the enemy's flank guard of about eighty or a hundred men, who, on the retreat from Concord, kept the height of land, the main body being in the road. The British troops and the Americans at that time were equally distant from Merriam's Corner. About twenty rods short of that place the Americans made a halt. The British marched down the hill with very slow but steady step, without music or a word being spoken that could be heard. Silence reigned on both sides. As soon as the British had gained the main road and passed a small bridge near the corner, they faced about suddenly and fired a volley of musketry upon us. They overshot, and no one to my knowledge was injured by the fire. The fire was immediately returned by the Americans, and two British soldiers fell dead at a little distance from each other in the road near the brook. The battle now began, and was carried on with little or no military discipline or order on the part of the Americans, during the remainder of the day. Each sought his own place and opportunity to attack and annoy the enemy from behind trees, rocks, fences, and buildings, as seemed most convenient. . . . We saw a wood at a distance, which appeared to lie on or near the road where the enemy must pass. Many leaped over the walls and made for that wood. We arrived just in time to meet the enemy. There was on the opposite side of the road a young growth of wood filled with Americans. The enemy were now completely between two fires renewed and briskly kept up. They ordered out a flank guard on the left to dislodge the Americans from their posts behind the trees; but they only became better marks to be shot at. A short but sharp contest ensued, in which the enemy received more deadly injury than at any other place from Concord to Charlestown.'"

This account shows that the Reading men were in the hottest of the fight, and among the first, if not the first, to begin the *battle*. It is remarkable that none of them were killed, and this fact probably is the reason why the part performed by the Reading men has not received more notice.

It appears that some of the minute-men did not go with their company to the scene of action. Among these were Timothy Wakefield, Esq., Capt. Joseph Bancroft, Col. Nathan Parker, Capt. Jonathan Weston, and possibly others, who started later in the day, direct for Lexington, and encountered the British on their retreat. Capt. Weston related to his grandson, Sumner Weston, that he was employed near where the Lynnfield Hotel now is, and that a man rode up on the morning of the 19th, and gave the alarm. He immediately went to his house, which then was the last house in Reading on the way to Stoneham, took his gun, and, accompanied by Mr. Thomas Sweetser, who lived in the first house in Stoneham, they proceeded on their way, till they reached the retreating redcoats. Shielding themselves behind a rock near a stone fence, they commenced firing upon the regulars. They were so intent upon their patriotic work that they did not observe the approach of the enemy's flank guard till they were almost upon them. Mr. Sweetser discovered their approach, and with a word of warning to Weston, who sat with his ammunition in his hat before him, started for a place of safety. Weston was so absorbed in his business that he did not recognize the note of alarm till it was repeated and emphasized by Col. Nathan Parker, who came up at that moment, when the trio, mid the whistling balls of the guard, made their escape unharmed to the woods near by.

Whether our men who had been engaged in the fight during the day returned to their homes that night, or remained in camp, we have no positive information, but it is said they returned. An account-book that formerly belonged to Lieut. Joseph Bancroft has this item, which implies that some of our men continued in the service from the day of the battle: "April 19, 1775. I was in the Province service ten days." Another item follows, indicating further service for the cause: "May 5, 1775. I carted eight barrels of pork from Reading to Watertown Bridge."

An obituary notice of Capt. James Bancroft, published in the "New England Magazine," Vol. I, July, 1831, mentions that "he became a subaltern officer in a company of minute-men, and was engaged in the skirmishes at Lexington. He then with his regiment took post at Cambridge." The town records of May 18, 1775, within a month after the Battle of Lexington, show that at that date, Dea. Jacob Emerson was chosen "selectman in the room of James Bancroft, who is gone into the army." It is evident from this act of the town and the statement referred to, that he soon, if not at once, gave up his time to the common cause. On the day of the Battle of Bunker Hill, June 17, his company was on guard at head-quarters. Gen. Washington took command of the army under the famous Cambridge Elm, July 3, 1775. The Reading minute-men, under Capt. Bancroft and Major Brooks, were assigned one of the most honorable positions on that occasion. The company had provided themselves for use on special occasions at home a cheap paper cap that resembled those worn by the British Grenadiers. Major Brooks desired Capt. Bancroft to procure, if possible, a sufficiency of them to supply the company, in order to give the commander-in-chief as respectful a reception as possible. But the requisite number could not be had, and the august General was received by citizen soldiers in citizens' apparel.

It would be gratifying to know the name of each person belonging to this Reading company of minute-men, but it is extremely doubtful whether they can ever be obtained. It is possible that the papers of Gov. Brooks, the first captain of the company, or those of Rev. Edmund Foster, who was a member of it, and who wrote that portion of the account of the battle at Concord which has been quoted, may yet furnish the desired information, but the probabilities are against it.

Gen. Lafayette, in his visit to this country in 1825, passed through this town on his way to Concord, N. H. He stopped at the hotel that then stood where the bank building now stands, for half an hour or so. He made a short address to a crowd of the citizens that came to see and welcome him. Rev. Mr. Sanborn responded, and in the course of his remarks he claimed that the company of minute-men under Dr. Brooks was the first company formed. He also stated that the company was accustomed to meet in the kitchen of his house (where Mr. Grouard now resides) for drill in the use of their muskets, and that the abrasion of the plastering in the upper parts of the room, caused probably by shouldering their arms, was then visible. The marks can still be seen where they were pointed out by Mr. Sanborn.

The General was attended by another French gentleman, and several carriages containing other distinguished parties. Rev. William Wakefield, then quite a lad, was present, and still retains a vivid recollection of the interesting scene.

The sound of the guns discharged in the Lexington fight was heard, it is said, here in Reading. Mr. William Parker, father of Mrs. William Wakefield, early in the morning heard what he believed to be the first volley fired on that memorable occasion. As he lived on the high land in the south part of this town, it is quite probable that his belief was well founded. Capt. John Parker, who had command of the Lexington militia and participated in the first skirmish with the British, was a son of Josiah, who was born in Reading in 1694, who was son of John, born 1664, son of Hananiah, born 1638, son of Thomas Parker, born 1609, who came from London 1635; was made freeman 1637, and became deacon of the first church in Reading. Jonas Parker, one of those first killed by the British on Lexington Common, was a cousin of John, the captain; his father also was a native of Reading. It will be remembered that the two muskets in the Massachusetts Senate chamber, presented by Rev. Theodore Parker, formerly belonged to this Capt. John Parker, one of which was used by him in the battle, and the other was the first fire-arm captured in the war for Independence.

APPENDIX.

It is impossible to obtain, at the present time, full accounts of the time and place of service of many of the heroes of the Revolution who belonged here. The date of the death and the ages of several buried in the cemetery here are as follows: —

NAME.	WHEN DIED.	AGE.
Aaron Parker,	April 28, 1841,	84.
John Emerson,	Feb. 19, 1803,	72.
Tim. Wakefield, Esq.,	April 19, 1849,	94.
Wm. Parker,	May 13, 1850,	90.
Daniel Damon,	Sept. 9, 1844,	87.
Daniel Pratt,	Sept. 18, 1816,	61.
Jeremiah Nichols,	Feb. 12, 1813,	58.
Lieut. Jonas Parker,	Jan. 9, 1800,	72.
Joseph Boutelle,	July 4, 1840,	84.
Lieut. Thomas Eaton,	June 18, 1787,	35.
Jas. Bancroft, Esq.,	May 17, 1831,	92.
Col. Nathan Parker,	July 30, 1815,	67.
Thomas Symonds,	June 31, 1836,	91.
James Weston,	Dec. 27, 1811,	61.
Capt. Abraham Foster,	Feb. 4, 1792,	57.
John Bachelder,	July 31, 1846,	84.
Joseph Damon,	Feb. 18, 1843,	84.
Maj. Josiah Barton,	April 18, 1827,	79.
Lieut. Jonathan Pool,	Sept. 1799,	79.
Timothy Eaton,	Oct. 27, 1822.	
Nathaniel Eaton,	March 11, 1823.	

Joseph Boutelle was in the Battle of Bunker Hill.

Aaron Parker was in service at Ticonderoga and West Point. He received a pension. Daniel Damon, Joseph Damon, Timothy Wakefield, Daniel Parker, Ephraim Pratt, were among those who were at Ticonderoga. Daniel Damon was also at the taking of Burgoyne. Benjamin Damon, brother of Daniel, at the age of sixteen, went into the service at Winter Hill, as one of the guard over Burgoyne's soldiers during the winter after their surrender. He continued to serve in the army till the close of the war.

Capt. Abraham Foster was in the service probably for several years. A memorandum in the account book of Lieut. Joseph Bancroft, Aug. 17, 1777, reads, "Mr. Haven preached a sermon from Luke 3: 14, to Capt. Foster and others going to the service."

His daughter Rebekah exhibited her patriotism by running bullets for the use of our troops.

It appears from the testimony of many who remember the narratives of the old soldiers, that quite a large number of the Reading men were at "Ti," as they called Ticonderoga. The fort there commanded the passage into Lake George. On the receipt of the news of the Battle of Lexington, Col. Ethan Allen made his memorable capture of the fort, May 10, 1775. It was held by our forces till what was considered the ignoble surrender of July 5, 1777. It is said on the authority of Capt. Joseph Bancroft, who was there, that our troops suffered greatly for want of provisions. This indicates that he must have been there as early as 1776. A letter written from there by Capt. Thomas Weeks, of Hampshire County, in this State, dated March 28, 1777, says, "We live with the major in a good barrack, have good pork and beef, good bread and peas, and sometimes beans that grew in Massachusetts. We have but few troops, but expect more daily. The Indians are about us. They have killed four men and taken twenty more prisoners." From an abstract of the mileage of Capt. James Bancroft's company in Col. Read's Regiment from Fort Edward to Reading, numbering seventy-six men, it appears they had arrived here in Reading, Jan. 30, 1777, or previously. It is suggested, as Fort Edward was near Ticonderoga, that these men may have been those who had been at "Ti," where they had previously suffered on the short allowance of food, which it would seem, from the letter of Capt. Weeks, could not subsequently have occurred.

. Capt. Bancroft continued at Cambridge during 1775 and '76, and twice in the latter year received commissions signed by the Council of the Massachusetts Bay as captain. Under date of Jan. 1, 1777, he received another commission as Captain in the 8th Mass. Reg. of the Continental Army, of which Col. Michael Jackson was Colonel, which was at West Point in 1780. This commission was given "By order of Congress," and signed by John Hancock, President, and Charles Thomson, Secretary. All these commissions are still preserved. He was at Ticonderoga and at Saratoga, where he was personally engaged in the conflict with Burgoyne, and at the head of his company stormed the British works in the regiment under the command of Col. Brooks. It was here that Sergeant Joshua Eaton fell mortally wounded, the only Reading soldier that was killed in battle during the war. Col. Brooks saw him fall, and called Capt. Bancroft's attention to it, saying, "Our brave Sergeant Eaton is gone." Eaton lived on the Ivory Murray farm, near Squire Prescott's.

The following copy of a letter from Capt. Bancroft contains many interesting facts, some of which are not generally known.

"CAMP VALLEY FORGE, January 5, 1778.

"*Dear Sir*,— While in my tent these cold long evenings, I often think of Reading, and should think myself very happy could I step in and spend a few hours with you and take a pipe and mug of cider, both which are very scarce here, and perhaps it would not be very disagreeable to you to hear something of our fatigues and dangers. Had I had opportunity to write before I came from the northward, I should liked to have written something particular of northward affairs, but it has got too old to write about. I could write nothing new. As we have had some trying times, perhaps you will ask how my courage held out. If you should, I can't say, as some have done, that they have no fear; but I can say, I had not so much fear but what I could go where I was ordered; and if it had been *much worse* I believe I should have tried to go.

We have a very good corps of officers (one excepted). If the regiment was full of officers and soldiers as good as what we now have, and should be ordered to storm Philadelphia, I am apt to think we should make one bold push for it. The whole campaign has been very hard and fatiguing, but in general healthy. I have not missed one tour of duty since I joined the army.

As to affairs here at the southward, I am at loss what to write. I don't find anything as I expected. I believe the enemy's strength is greater, and ours less, than you imagine. So far as I can judge by the movements, both armies are a little afraid to engage under any disadvantage. There has been, I believe, some misconduct this way among officers, and our army, in most, if not all actions, have retreated, though in that of Germantown it is said they *retreated from victory*, and that without Gen. Washington's order. I have often heard he has offered a large sum to any that would inform him who gave the orders; but since we arrived, though we have not fought much, we have not run away any. Though the enemy have threatened to drive us off, they have not ventured to make any attack on us; but when we have been about to attack them, they incline to march to Philadelphia. The Battle of Germantown was before we came. I find since that time it has been very sickly here among our officers; more than a hundred have been confined, and some of them broke, one of them a Major-General. The most of the inhabitants here are Friends, or Quakers, who, you know, never bear arms. I believe they are Tories, which is no small damage to us; but being Friends, or Tories, does not save them from being plundered by the King's troops when they have an opportunity. I hope the enemy's having some opportunity to plunder will have the same effect here that it had last year in the Jerseys, and make the Tories become good Whigs.

I hope, sir, if my family should stand in need of your assistance, you will be ready to afford it. It has been out of my power to do anything for them, even so much as to send home any money. The officers, in general, in the regiment, have been obliged to do without or borrow. The army is at present a poor place to get money. Everything is so dear we are obliged to spend considerable for provision or live very poorly. I have been obliged to give half a dollar for one pint of bread and milk; three or four shillings for a fowl; two shillings for one pound of pork. Spirits are three or four dollars a quart, but I seldom use any. Sweetening, butter, or cheese, I have not had for near three months. I expect soon to receive seven or eight months' pay, when I hope to be able to send home some considerable to my wife. I hope the time will come when I shall have the opportunity of seeing you and my friends at Reading; but when that will be God only knows. We have some hard trials to meet yet. If I should tell you what is believed here, that the enemy are more in numbers than we, perhaps you would disbelieve me. The regiments not being full is very great damage to the cause. Had they all been filled up I don't believe Howe would have had any footing in America at this time. They are more deficient this way than with you. Please to give my compliments to Mrs. Bancroft. If you could write to me it will be gladly received by

Your humble servant,

JAMES BANCROFT."

"*To Mr. Joseph Bancroft, Reading.*"

From a "Return of the 4th Mass. Brigade, commanded by Col. Michael Jackson, at West Point, May 27, 1780," found among the papers of Capt. Bancroft, it appears that 504 men, rank and file, constituted a regiment. This 4th Brigade was made up of three regiments: the 2d Mass., Col. Bailey; 8th Mass., Col. Jackson, to which Capt. Bancroft belonged; 9th Mass., Col. Wesson. Two of the colonels are reported absent on furlough. Of the 18 captains only 8 are reported as present fit for duty; 2 are on furlough; 3 recruiting; 2 on the staff; 2 vacancies. The brigade, when the regiments were full, should have had, rank and file, 1,512 men, but the return shows a vacancy of 1,140 men, leaving only 378 men actually belonging to it. Of these only 162 are reported as "Present fit for duty"; 19 present are sick; 1 is sick at Boston, 3 at Fishkill, 2 at other places; 99 are "on command," 32 on furlough, 54 on extra service ; of this last-named class 23 are assigned as artificers, 8 wagoners, 1 butcher, 1 baker, 3 foraging, 3 colliers, 2 with Gen. Gates and Heath (the latter in command at West Point), 3 in the country tending horses, and one with Col. Kosciusko. This officer superintended the construction of the military works at West Point, and at other places. He was the brave and noble Pole who, after his return to Europe, engaged in the Polish revolution of 1794, and became generalissimo. It was of him, after his hopeless defeat, that the poet Campbell wrote the familiar lines, —

> "Hope for a season bade the world farewell,
> And Freedom shrieked as Kosciusko fell."

Capt. Bancroft seems to have been intimately acquainted with Gen. Washington, who spoke of him as his "faithful Bancroft." He expected promotion to higher official position, but it was so long deferred that he finally resigned, and in 1780 left the army and returned home. He was often employed by his fellow-citizens to manage their public interests, and for many years he was an influential member of the popular branch of the State government. During the Shay Rebellion, his sound judgment and long experience gave him an important influence over public measures.

He drew a pension of twenty dollars per month during the last years of his life, and it was subsequently increased to full pay, forty dollars per month, and continued to his widow.

Capt. Bancroft, or as he was more generally known in later years, "Squire" Bancroft, was held in great respect by all who knew him. When he left the army, the officers of his regiment accompanied him to the line, expressing their regret at his resignation ; and we are told by his grandson, Mr. Edmund Eaton, that he ever afterward spoke of his own action in the matter with regretful feelings.

He was once met in the night, near Winter Hill, in Somerville, by a man who demanded his money. As he was about to give it up, the man recognized him, and refused to take it, saying he would not take from him a single farthing. Mr. Bancroft related the incident, but kept the name a secret.

He was an excellent marksman. While in the army, an eagle was discovered upon a tree-top a half mile away. About twenty men fired at it without frightening it from its perch. The captain brought it down at the first shot. He preserved some of the quills for many years, which persons now living remember to have seen. Like many another good soldier he never directly admitted that he knew of killing any of the enemy's men, though he remembered seeing men fall at whom he fired, but he suggested that others might have fired at the same object at the same moment. The gun he used till the time of the battle at the taking of Burgoyne was a poor one. But at that time, finding a good one lying on the battle-field, belonging probably to the British, he took it for his own use, and threw away his old one.

For some time during the War of the Revolution, Mr. Thomas Sweetser was engaged in carrying supplies to the army. When our troops were stationed near Boston, the soldiers suffered for want of fuel. Mr. Sweetser, with others, carried wood from this vicinity for their relief. They went twice, at least, to the "North River" — Hudson — with supplies for the army stationed in its vicinity. On one of these journeys the loading was powder and liquors. Mr. Caleb Parker, a brother of Col. Nathan, had a man to assist him. He found this man one night busily but thoughtlessly employed with his lantern in close proximity to the powder casks. The suddenness with which the two dangerous elements were put at a safe distance apart, was a caution to the assistant that did not need a repetition. Mr. Sweetser's team was two yokes of oxen and a horse. On returning from one of these expeditions, the river was found to be open for a short distance on its opposite shore, and most of the company declined to cross. Mr. Sweetser being anxious to return, went forward upon the ice, as far as he could, and then made his team swim the open part, and safely reached the other bank. He arrived home nearly a fortnight in advance of his party. The whiffle-tree used by Mr. Sweetser on these occasions is still preserved by his son, Thomas Sweetser, Esq.

Joseph Bancroft was commissioned 2d Lieut., May 6, 1776, and 1st Lieut. Aug. 20, 1777. He probably spent the winter of 1778 at Winter Hill. A paper dated Feb. 21, 1778, signed by Col. Jacob Gerrish, permits him "to be absent from the garrison five days and then return." His papers and accounts show that he was subsequently engaged in hiring and paying men for army service. Among his papers is found a summary of statistics pertaining to Reading, taken in 1784 by the assessors. The whole number of acres of land granted to, or surveyed for, any person, is given by them as 13,290, "not including 150 acres of land owned by the ministers of the town." The number of dwelling-houses, 205; other buildings, 184; number of white inhabitants, 1,402; blacks, 12. Another paper contains an Act of the Legislature passed in 1779, requiring each town to furnish shirts, shoes, and stockings equal to one seventh of the number of males in town above the age of 16 years. Reading is required to furnish 58; Cambridge, 56; Charlestown, 35; Malden, 33; Boston, 407; Salem, 166; Andover, 102; Worcester, 62; Hull, 5.

J. Brooks Leathe, Esq., whose labors have greatly aided in supplying the historical facts and incidents relating to Reading, has the original notice sent to this town, written the day after the Battle of Bunker Hill, of which the following is a copy: —

IN COM'TEE OF SAFETY, CAMB., June 18, 1775.

To the Selectmen of Reading:

Gent., — You are desired to provide provision sufficient for the militia of your town now here, and send it forward to Camb. as soon as may be.

Per order,
JONA. HASTINGS, *Clerk.*

I.

COPY OF A LETTER

WRITTEN BY COL. (AFTERWARDS GENERAL) BENJAMIN BROWN, OF READING, WHILE HE WAS ABSENT IN THE ARMY, ADDRESSED TO HIS WIFE.[*]

"TICONDEROGA, Aug. 31, 1776.

"*My dear Spous*, — I received yours, dated Aug. 15, with no small (satisfaction?) — which was in ten days after the date, in which you Express your Ernest desire that I may enjoy the light of God's countenance in a distant land. Truly, a distant land it is, but nevertheless, there is such a din and noise and company that I am almost a stranger to retirement. I can enjoy no other religious exercise then ejaculatory, excepting morning and evening Public Prayers, and on the Sabbath a sermon or two by Mr. Emerson of Concord and Mr. Hitchcock of Beverly, — very agreeable gentlemen. I am glad to hear you are calm and resigned to your lonesome lot, and yet not alone, but enjoy the Comforter; may his presence attend you in this dark world, until you arrive to eternal day. It gives me unspeakable satisfaction to hear that peace and harmony is householder in my family; and that the morning and evening sacrifice is constantly ascending to heaven, by the mouth of my well beloved son, in its stated seasons. May the best of heaven's blessing rest on you and all my family and friends, til I return or am gathered to my people in peace with God and my own conscience.

You tell me you have purchased some Hemlock bark; I am glad to

---

[*] It is copied *verbatim et literatim.*

hear it, and hope that the tanning and currying may be done well and seasonably, which will greatly contribute to the support of the family. You may send word to Mr. Nathan Newhall that his son is well and looks hearty. I told him his mother was concerned for him; he smiled and passed by me. I understand by you that the little General (referring probably to an infant son, then about ten months old, who was named for Gen. Joseph Warren) is your bedfellow; I hope you will norish him and make a fine fellow of him, til I return and take part of your soft bed, with him and you; for the softest bed I have is boards, and sometimes hemlock boughs. Through divine goodness, I am now in good health, but want many things, which I used to enjoy, viz.: Cider, and sauce and butter, if you please; I have had but one drink of Cider since I came to this place. I think I am tolerably respected, — have dined with Gen. Gates several times, and have been *swore* at by him, as many; but no bones broken at present. I have often to go on fatigue, commanding three or four hundred men, who are fortyfying the place; but we have been retarded from the work, from Monday last to Thursday afternoon, on account of rainy weather. We have seen nothing of the enemy, nor hear their sittuation, since I have been in this place, so as to be depended upon. Gen. Gates tells me he expects a *warm* attack from Burgoyne; — that soon. I hope we shall be ready to give them a *warm* reception. I see no fear or intimidation in the camp. I understand we are going to be joined by Col. Phinis and Whitcom's regiments from Boston. A number of our friends are taken with the Small Pox, and a number of others have colds and fever and ague. As to the Geography of this place, where I now am encampt it is surrounded by water, except the Norwest part; and there is redoubts and brest works to defend that part, it being the place where many of the bones of our ―― lay above ground to this day, that were slain in the year 176(9).

I have left my tent at present and live in the fort with Mr. John (Winzer) Paymaster, who treats me very corteous. My sincere duty to my honored mother, and love to all my children, kind respects to my Brothers and Sisters and all friends; in particular, Mr. Prentice, Doct. Swain, and that brother Bachellor, brother Emerson, Peter Emerson, John Pratt, Mr. (Bachellor), Wm. Gould, Samuel Poole, Capt. Goodwin, Thomas Damon and their Spouses; and let them know that a line from either of them would be very acceptable.

James (probably James Wiley, his wife's son by a former husband) has been very poor (ly?) for sum days, but is on the mending hand. By what I can learn from those that have the Small Pox, they are mostly like to recover. Those from Reading that have it is Ephraim Pratt, Kemble (Kendall?) Emerson, and poor old (Clafter?). We are in great danger of it; but no enoculation is allowed of. When we find any break out, we send them off immediately to fort George, which is 30 miles distant. Give my kind respects to Mr. Nutting and his Spous, and tell them that (J.) is well; and also tell Mr. Carter that his son Benja. is neighbor to me and is in good health and wants to come home. My dear Spous, — I often think on you with pleasure and delight, and flatter myself I shall once more imbrace you in my affectionate arms, in some cold night next winter, when I shall be willing to relate to you the hardships I have endured in this campaign, which will sweeten our innocent imbraces and heighten our matrimonial delights, at which happy circumstance, let our brests not only glow with gladness, but with treu thankfulness to our kind and beneficent Preserver, but if otherwise, be content with the will of heaven, rather than I should flee my colors, and fall into the lowest contempt; especially when I am engaged in so noble and good a cause. I write no more at this time, but take the liberty to subscribe myself your effectionate husband till Death,

"BENJA. BROWN.

" N. B. This is the fourth letter I have sent to you, and when you write to me again, be so obliging as to put your name to it.
"B. B."

J.

Capt. James Bancroft, of the third parish in Reading, had the reputation of being a prompt, brave, and able officer while in the army. He commanded a company in the regiment commanded by Col. John Brooks. When Col. Brooks was elected Governor, on the day of Inauguration, in 1816, Capt. Bancroft, then 77 years old, went down to witness the ceremony; and on his way through Medford, passing the house of the Governor elect, the Governor, while at breakfast, saw him passing with his cocked hat and long cane, and sent out and invited him in to take a cup of coffee. The Governor then said to him, "There is no man living I am more glad to see on this occasion than yourself." To whom the Capt. replied: "There is no one, Col. Brooks, who rejoices in it more than I do. I breakfasted in Reading, and came down on purpose to witness the ceremonies of the occasion. The choice of Governor which the people have made delights my heart. If you make as good Governor as you did Colonel of a Regiment, I shall be satisfied." Tears flowed down the cheeks of both of them as they clasped each other's hands.

Gov. Brooks explained afterwards why the meeting was so affecting: said he, "On the day of the last battle with Gen. Burgoyne (Oct. 7) I was dining with Generals Gates and Arnold. Firing commenced. I went in, commanding the 8th or Jackson Regiment. After the discharge of the enemy's volley, a company on the left flank went suddenly down. I thought the volley had shot them all down, and I rode to the extreme left in great haste, to ascertain what was the matter. I was greatly agitated, and there met Capt. Bancroft, who commanded the left wing. He also had quit his place to see what disaster had occurred. At this moment the company all rose up and we were relieved from our apprehensions. I was yet however greatly agitated, and speaking sharply to Capt. Bancroft, said, 'What business have you here, Sir?' The Captain said, 'I came out to see what had happened to the company on the left.' I then said, 'You are out of your place, Sir.' With the submissive spirit of the good soldier, the Captain replied, 'I am ready to obey your orders, Colonel.' With great perturbation, I responded, 'My orders are that you advance and enter those lines, Sir.' The Captain smarting under the reproof, quickly gave the word, 'Come on, my boys, and enter that fort!' (Breyman's Fort.) Then leading the way himself, he made a rapid movement forward, and the whole company ascended the parapet. Surprised at the suddenness of the assault, the enemy retired from the fort, and the whole regiment entered it."

Capt. Bancroft's wife (who was Sarah Pierson) was a lady of intelligence, education, and piety.

The following extract from a letter written by her to her husband while he was in the army may be interesting, to her descendants at least:—

"My Dear, we received yours, in which you mention the capture of Lt. Gen. Burgoyne. We congratulate you, Sir, upon the large success, in which your Regiment was distinguished for their valor and conduct.

Dr. Hay desires especially to present his compliments of congratulation upon the great success attending the American arms, under Gen. Gates, in which you had an active part.

The children all present their duty and express their joy to learn that you endure the fatigues of war with so much spirit and so little prejudice to your health. As you take a particular concern for your domestic affairs, we have the satisfaction to acquaint you that the crop of corn turned out remarkably well. We have cider enough for our family, and our work goes on well. Gen. Burgoyne's officers are quartered principally in Cambridge, — the men on Prospect Hill, the German troops upon Winter Hill. All your friends desire their respects may be given you, and that you would embrace every opportunity to acquaint us with the situation of the army.

No more at present to add, but an earnest desire that you may prosper in arms as long as your country shall require.

Honor ever be the concomitant of your actions; and in due time you be returned to your loving family in health and laden with divine mercy.

I remain your loving wife,

SARAH BANCROFT."

READING, Dec. 18, 1777.

K.

NAMES OF SOME OF THE PERSONS BELONGING TO BOSTON AND CHARLESTOWN, WHO WERE RELIEVED AND ASSISTED AT READING BY THE TOWN, IN 1775.

These people were called "Donation People."

Margaret Bodge, aged 35, of Charlestown.
Samuel Bodge, " 6, " "
Henry Bodge, " 4, " "
David Bodge, " 2, " "
Vietta Blair, " "
Jonathan Carey, " 76, " "
Sarah Carey, his wife, aged 76, of Charlestown.
John Carey, " "
Mrs. Coverly, " "
Sarah Capen, aged 63, " "
John Doak, of Boston.
Hannah Doak, his wife, of Boston.
Two Doak children, " "
Sarah Edes, aged 45, of Charlestown.
Grace Edes, " 16, " "
Jonathan Edes, " 14, " "
Hulda Edes, " 8, " "
Abigail Edes, " 7, " "
David Edmands, " "
Mary Fosdick, " "

Mary Fillebrown,	of	Boston.
Elizabeth Hiler,	"	"
Thomas Jarvis,	"	Charlestown.
Mary Kella, aged 58,	"	"
Ebenezer Leman (a cripple), aged 44, of Charlestown.
Elizabeth Leman (his wife),	" 36,	" "
Four Leman children (8, 6, 4, 2),	"	"
Abiah Larkin,	aged 22,	" "
Ann Larkin,	" 3,	" "
Thomas Larkin,	" 1½,	" "
Elizabeth Orr,	" 37,	" "
Jane Orr,	" 16,	" "
Elizabeth Orr,	" 11,	" "
Mrs. Elizabeth Osborn,	"	"
Jane Page,	"	"
Mrs. Pool, wife of Benja.,	"	Boston.
Stephen Pierce,	" 71,	" Charlestown.
His daughter,	" 45,	" "
Ann Rand,	" 53,	" "
Thomas Sargent,	"	"
Ann Shepard,	" 33,	" "
Thos. Shepard,	" 9,	" "
Anna Shepard,	" 5,	" "
Asa Shepard,	" 3,	" "
Elias Stone (Paralytic),	" 67,	" "
Wm. Stone,	" 12,	" "
Bethiah Stone,	" 8,	" "
Samuel Stone,	" 6,	" "
Anna Symmes (blind and deaf), " 64,	" "
Mrs. Tree,	"	"
Mrs. Way,	"	"
Sarah Widdefield,	" 39,	" "

Children of do.; Sarah, aged 10; John, 9; Hugh, 7.

L.

COPY OF LETTER FROM DR. SAMUEL HART.

"My father, Dr. John Hart, was born in Ipswich, Mass. Octr. 23rd, 1851. His father, John Hart, was a lawyer; and our paternal ancestry, as nearly as I can trace it, emigrated to this country and settled in

Ipswich as early as 1636. His mother I believe was also a native of Ipswich; her maiden name was Mary Knowlton.

"Of my father's boyhood, I know but little. Educational advantages, in that period of our Country's history, were far less generally extended than now. But we record it to the honor of the early settlers of New England, that having established themselves upon the soil, and having escaped from the persecutions and narrow bigotries of the Old World, they consecrated their adopted country to Religion, Education, and Human Liberty. Harvard University was established in 1636, sixteen years only after the Landing on Plymouth Rock. Dear New England, how I love and honor you! even your stony hills I esteem and venerate. And my native town, the place of my family sepulchres, and its inhabitants, I love and regard more than any other locality on earth.

"My father must have enjoyed a good share of educational opportunities, and acquired some knowledge of languages, particularly Latin, which is indispensable to entering upon the study of a scientific profession. At the age of fourteen, he entered the office of Dr. John Califf, an eminent physician, who had enjoyed all the advantages of medical education in England, came to this country, and settled in Ipswich. This gave him rare advantages, for in those days, Medical Colleges and Schools had no existence in the Colonies. At the age of nineteen, Dr. C. pronounced him qualified to enter upon the arduous duties and formidable responsibilities of practical life. His extreme youth led him to conclude that no one who knew him would intrust themselves to his care; and he went to Maine, then a District of Mass., and settled in Georgetown, now Bath. Possessed of an active mind, indomitable energy, and untiring, persevering zeal, he there received, boy-physician as he was, a respectable share of patronage and success.

"When it became evident that the misunderstanding between the Colonies and the home government could only be decided by an appeal to the sword, my father returned to Mass., received a commission of Surgeon in the Army, and joined Col. Prescott's regiment in Cambridge. This Col. Prescott was a man distinguished for bravery, courage, and military skill. I have heard my father speak of his activity and influence in the battle of Bunker Hill over the minds of the Soldiers; he wore a long frock coat, and seemed, with his sword flying, to be in every part of the line almost at the same instant, imparting to them his own fearless activity and courage. After the enemy obtained possession of the Hill, the inquiry was made, who that d—d Ban Yan fellow was, alluding to Prescott, saying that his activity had cost them a great deal of British blood. He was grandfather of the late historian Prescott, who has contributed so largely to elevate the character of the historians of our country abroad.

"After the evacuation of Boston by the British troops in 1776, he accompanied Col. Prescott's Regiment to New York, and was stationed on Staten Island, until the enemy took possession of Long Island, and was then driven to the Highlands. Many mementos of the fierce struggle for the possession of Long Island now exist in Brooklyn, the city of my adoption. Tradition points out the house which Gen. Washington occupied while our army was stationed in Brooklyn: it is a small building of brick and stone, dilapidated and unoccupied, standing on the corner of Fifth Avenue and Third Street, and was erected in 1696. This is now being removed to give place to a modern block of buildings.

"At this time Col. Prescott's Regiment was disbanded; and my father was appointed Surgeon of the 2d Mass. Regiment, and continued this connection with it to the close of the war in 1783. This regiment was commanded by Col. John Bailey.

"During the whole war my father was in active service. I heard him say that he accompanied his regiment in every battle, attended by his Assistant Surgeon, provided with instruments, bandages, and every appliance necessary for smaller operations, and for the dressing of such wounds as could properly be done on the field. I am now happily in possession of two cases of instruments he thus appropriated, and prize them highly as revolutionary relics.

"I am unable to furnish the date or the locality of some of the incidents and events of interest I have heard him relate, and in which he participated; some of which I have never seen recorded in history. The ruse by which Gen. Arnold (afterwards the Arch Traitor) succeeded in raising the siege of Fort Schuyler, often called Fort Stanwix, I have heard him relate more particularly than any account I have seen of it, except as related by Col. Stone in his Life of Brant. This Brant was a Mohawk Indian and chief Sachem of the Six Nations; was educated at Dartmouth College, and was the master-spirit of the Indian expeditions into the Valley of the Mohawk and other points during the revolutionary struggle. Col. Willett, accompanied by Major Stockwell, in the night of the 10th of August, 1777, escaped from the fort, successfully eluded the besieging forces of British and Indians, and gave notice of the straitened condition of the Garrison. Gen. Schuyler ordered Gens. Arnold and Larned with the Massachusetts Brigade, which were joined by some New York troops, to advance to the relief of the fort.

Gen. Herkimer had previously, with the militia under his command, marched to its relief, had fallen into an ambush, his army severely handled, himself wounded, and subsequently died of his wounds. Gen. Arnold commanded the expedition ; fearing his force insufficient to raise the siege, he adopted the following stratagem. At Fort Dayton, Arnold found a strange being, Hon Yost Schuyler, who seemed little above an idiot, yet somewhat shrewd, under sentence of death for treason. His mother and brother begged the Gen. to spare his life. This he consented to do, on condition that he would perform a certain act, which he required of him ; and in case of failure his brother should be executed in his stead. This was agreed to, and his brother put in prison. Hon Yost, having had several balls shot through his clothes, was dispatched to the camp of St. Leger, and fulfilled his part of the contract faithfully. He was to state to that officer, that Gen. Arnold was at Fort Dayton, with two thousand troops and several pieces of Cannon, and was to commence his march at daylight the next morning, to attack the besieging army. In proof of this, he stated that he was on his way to the gallows to be hanged as a traitor ; but not being closely guarded, he thought he might as well be shot as hanged ; that he ran, was fired upon, and showed the holes in his clothes as evidence of its truth. At the same time, an Oneida Indian entered the Indian camp, giving mysterious hints of an immense army advancing upon them. This had the intended effect. Arnold, upon the supposition that it would put the besieging army to the rout, commenced his march ; and when he reached the fort, found the enemy had fled, leaving behind their tents, a great part of their artillery, camp equipage, and baggage. This was achieved by Benedict Arnold, afterwards the prince of traitors. My father always entertained the opinion, that this success essentially aided in the capture of Burgoyne's army at Saratoga the following October. He also related that when Washington fully ascertained the treason and escape of Arnold, he said at the table, addressed to all present, that he always felt averse to appointing to an important position any one who was dissipated, unprincipled, or reckless ; that he knew Arnold to be such, a spendthrift and a high liver, but that the ability, activity, success, and seeming patriotism he had displayed in the war had been such as to secure him from any such terrible, deliberate conduct ; and that in future no such character would receive any appointment from him. My father mentioned a stunning rebuke Arnold afterwards received from a soldier, who accompanied a flag to the British Commander in New York. Arnold was present, and, supposing himself unknown to the soldier, inquired of him what was said of Gen. Arnold in the American camp. The soldier recognized him, and replied, 'Sir, they say in the American camp that, could they get Gen. Arnold, they would hang him till he was rotten; but the leg which was wounded in their service, they would bury with all the honors of war.' The sacrifice of poor André was the result of Arnold's treason. Gen. Washington appointed forty-one Officers to attend his execution; my father was one of them. I have heard him say, it was the most awful scene he ever witnessed. Major André desired to be shot. When the procession reached the gallows, and the truth flashed upon him, he said to the officer who had him in charge, 'You ought to have told me of this before.' After the rope was adjusted, he was asked if he wished to say anything; he raised the cap, looked upon all with a pleasant smile, and said, 'Nothing more than this, gentlemen: in a few moments I shall know more than you all.' All present were affected to tears. He was a noble and accomplished young officer; but this sacrifice of him was regarded as indispensable to the salvation of the American cause. I believe, my father participated in almost every important battle during the war; and interesting incidents of many of them I have heard him relate. But they are the record of history with which your readers are familiar, and in this sketch I have designed to state only those which are not so generally known. He frequently remarked, that after the Battle of Monmouth, N. J., June 28, 1778, he suffered discomforts from high temperature that he never experienced before; that the heat that day was intense; and that he saw many British soldiers lying dead at brooks and creeks from the severity of the heat and from unwisely satisfying intense thirst.

"On one occasion, Gen. Washington appointed my father to go to Boston, and bring to him three thousand dollars in Gold, which was deposited there for his special use. The journey was hazardous, and must necessarily be performed on horseback. He packed it in a valise, at every stopping-place took it into the house with him, every night put it under his pillow, piled chairs, &c., against the doors and windows of the room, cocked his pistols, laid them in a chair at the head of his bed, and his drawn sword beside them; slept soundly till morning; and returned to the camp with it in safety. At what period of the war, or where the army was at this time encamped, I do not recollect to have heard him say. He enjoyed some intimacy with the Commander in Chief, and I have seen notes inviting him to Washington's table. Indeed, it was his habit to invite all the officers of the Army in turn to his table.

"At the close of the war in 1783, my father was appointed to a regiment under the command of Col. Henry Jackson, and was not discharged till July, 1784. Our family are in possession of many letters he wrote to my mother, dated at West Point, during this period, from which it seems he was the principal surgeon there, and which we highly prize.

"My Grandmother, a lady highly intellectual and social, and with whom my earliest recollections are associated, was very proud of her son; and in my childhood often told me of his personal, manly beauty and gracefulness. She said, that when he first came to Ipswich, after he entered the army, he went to meeting and wore his military dress, (that an officer's uniform was then much more showy than when she related it), and that this and his handsome person, it was said, captivated a great many young ladies' hearts. If this be so, it only proves that young ladies in those days, as truly as since, were attracted by a sword knot, a sash, and a feather. She died suddenly at my father's residence, in July, 1812, in the ninetieth year of her age.

"My father married Miss Mary Gould, only child and daughter of Capt. Abraham Gould, of Stoneham. I can find no record of its date, but presume it took place in the year 1777. She was born May 1, 1753. Her father commanded a company in a body of troops raised for a limited period in the Revolutionary War, and at the close of this period retired from the army. When a boy, I often played with a cannon ball which was fired at him during his service in the army; he was riding alone at a distance from a British encampment, and being discovered by his uniform to be an American officer, this ball was aimed at him, it passed him, and fell in the road; onr eaching it he dismounted and put in his pocket. This ball, I regret to say, is now lost.

"This union was a long and happy one, extending to nearly or quite sixty years. They survived six of their nine children. My mother, of precious, blessed memory, was a kind, gentle, affectionate parent; she faithfully trained us all up in the way we should go, daily led us all to the throne of grace, and we all have risen up and called her blessed. To others, she was kind and benevolent, and truly sought the good of all; always diffident and retiring, a true follower of Him who went about doing good. She died Novem[er] 15, 1838.

"After my father was relieved from the army in July, 1784, he settled in Reading, now South Reading, purchased his residence near the north end, and in front of Smith's Pond; but which in these refined days is called, perhaps, by the more classic name, Crystal Lake. Well, be it so; locomotive momentum is the watchword of our day. Here he resided some fifty years, until his death, May 27, 1836. Those lofty elms, one of which now stands, spreading its long branches over the spot where his dwelling once stood, were planted and reared by his own hands.

"He was the firm friend and liberal supporter of religious, educational, and benevolent institutions, and contributed freely to sustain them. He conscientiously embraced the faith of the Puritans, but was not sectarian in his opinions.

"He was warmly attached to the principles of the Revolution, and regarded the Society of the Cincinnati well suited to keep alive and perpetuate those principles. I believe he was never absent from one of its meetings, and filled some office in the Society from my earliest recollection, and until his death. As his only surviving son, I became his successor, and can well appreciate the reasons of his great attachment and interest in it. With this attachment and interest I perfectly harmonize.

"The active part he took in the revolutionary struggle gave him strong political opinions; these were purely republican, and this interest in public affairs continued through life. He was elected eight times to the House of Representatives, and five times to the Senate of Massachusetts. He was a justice of the peace and of the quorum, and also of the Court of Sessions.

"I feel a delicacy in speaking of my father's professional life, but cannot well avoid such an allusion. He must have been a practising physician some sixty-five years, and few medical men have lived, who have performed so large an amount of business as he has done. He was a close observer of disease, and the effects of remedial agents; and predicated his treatment mainly upon his own observation and experience, though a constant reader of Medical Literature. My own experience corroborates their accuracy, and even at this period of my professional life, I, or rather my patients, derive essential benefit from them. He thought highly of medical associations, as adapted, by an interchange of experiences and observations among the members, to enlarge the sphere of knowledge, and increase their practical usefulness. He was a member of the Middlesex Association, which was organized in 1790, and a Fellow of the Massachusetts Medical Society, of which he was many years a Councillor. He regarded the Medical a Scientific profession, as it truly is, and sternly frowned upon every thing dishonorable or empirical.

"In this sketch I have said nothing of myself, or of my three brothers and five sisters; you know their history, and for the most part my own. My life has been an active one; it has ever been m y aim to make my life practical and useful, and have received an ample share of professional patronage. I have never aspired to professional honors and distinctions, but have received a larger share of them than my humble merits deserved. I am a member of the American Medical Association, the Massachusetts and New York State Medical Societies, of three other Medical Societies, and two other Medical Associations; have been honored with the Presidency of the Medical Societies of the Counties of Oswego and Kings, and a Curator of the Medical Department of the University of Buffalo.

"The great interests of the nation, the extending and elevating our educational institutions, have largely engaged my attention, with my best efforts for their welfare. My father's political opinions I have fully embraced, but political preferment has formed no part of my desires. Religion, inspiring and animating the pure motives of conduct and affection, and elevating and sustaining above all earth's sorrows, I have endeavored should incite and influence every act of my life, that I may honor Him who died for me, and fulfil the lot He has appointed me."

M.

PROCEEDINGS AT THE INAUGURATION OF THE TOWN OF WAKEFIELD, JULY 4, 1868.

PRELIMINARY ACTION OF THE TOWN.

At a meeting of the qualified voters of the town of South Reading, in due form convened on the twentieth day of January, 1868, the following report was submitted: —

REPORT.

To the Town of South Reading:

The Committee who were appointed to consider the matter of erecting a Soldiers' Monument or Memorial Hall, herewith submit a final report, as follows: —

It will be remembered that the Committee have already, at a former meeting of the town, submitted a partial report, and obtained leave longer to consider the subject; that in said *partial* report the Committee represented that a majority of their number was in favor of a Memorial Hall, — first, as being cheaper, if, in the erection of a new Town

House, provision should be made for such a hall therein; and second, as being more useful, sentimental, and historic than a simple granite or marble monument; that said Committee also represented that intimations had been given that liberal donations towards the expense of erecting a new Town House, sufficiently spacious to furnish, in addition to other conveniences, a room for a Memorial Hall, might be expected; and further, that your Committee asked of the town more time to consider the matter, in order that such intimations might take shape and become definite realities.

The Committee have the pleasure to report that the expectations based upon the intimations aforesaid have been abundantly realized. The Committee are now in the possession of the assurance, ample and satisfactory: First, that a lot of land and a cash contribution of $30,000 to $35,000 (as may be needed) for a new Town House (and such further sum of money as may be necessary in order to build a house satisfactory to the town), the same being the gift of CYRUS WAKEFIELD, Esq.; and, secondly, that $1,000 for furnishing and adorning the rooms in said proposed Town House, the gift of SOLON O. RICHARDSON, Esq., now await the town's acceptance.

Your Committee would therefore recommend the acceptance by the town of the aforesaid offers, and that in accepting them, the town tender their hearty thanks and lively congratulations to Cyrus Wakefield, Esq., for his princely proposal, and to Solon O. Richardson, Esq., for his munificent offer, and proffer to both these gentlemen the assurance that the town most highly appreciates these splendid gifts, and will hold the donors of them in honorable and perpetual remembrance.

The Committee would also unanimously recommend the passage of the following votes: —

First, That instead of building a granite or marble monument to the memory of those gallant soldiers from South Reading who gave their lives for their country, whenever a new Town House shall be built, provision shall be made for a suitable room therein that shall be set apart for a "Soldiers' Memorial Hall," and which shall be furnished and adorned, and supplied with portraits, relics, and other memorials of the lives and services of the living, and especially of the departed brave.

Second, That a Building Committee of seven persons be now appointed (to serve gratuitously), who shall have authority to erect in behalf of the town, during the present year, upon such part of the "Noah Smith House Lot," on Main Street, in South Reading, as said Committee shall agree upon, a new Town House of sufficient capacity to furnish a suitable Hall for Town Meetings and Public Lectures, a Soldiers' Memorial Hall, rooms for the Town Library, Town Officers' rooms, and rooms for Military and other Municipal purposes, to cost, in addition to the land for a site, not less than $30,000; the size, plan, materials, and all the details and surroundings to be left to the discretion of said Committee, provided that a deed conveying to said town a site of suitable size, and located on said "Smith Lot," shall be secured; and provided also, that a sum not less than $30,000 shall be gratuitously furnished.

Third, That the Building Committee aforesaid shall be also authorized to appropriate and expend, at their discretion, in furnishing and adorning the rooms in said Town House, such sums of money as are or shall be given for such specific purpose.

All which is respectfully submitted by order, and in behalf of, the Committee.

LILLEY EATON, *Chairman.*

South Reading, January 20, 1868.

At the same meeting, Daniel Allen, from Committee on Change of Town's Name, submitted the following

REPORT:

The Committee, chosen by the town to take into consideration the subject of changing the name of the town, and also to designate a new name for adoption, would respectfully report: —

In consequence of the action of the town, at their meeting in November last, upon this subject, — then voting, unanimously, to *change* the name, — the Committee do not deem it necessary to go into any argument, or to present facts upon that subject; still, we are happy to state, that in all our investigations, and in all our consultations with our fellow-citizens, and in all that has come to the knowledge of the Committee, *all* are in confirmation of the action of the town upon the subject.

One of the most prominent objections to our present position is, that, outside of our immediate vicinity, we have no personal identity as an independent and separate town, which leads to constant inconvenience.

The First, or South Parish, of Reading, was incorporated as the Town of South Reading, in 1812, containing then a population of eight hundred, and a valuation of $100,000.

From 1850 to 1855, the town of Old Reading lost in population

$17\frac{15}{100}$ per cent, while in the same period, South Reading gained $27\frac{86}{100}$ per cent.

In 1860 Old Reading contained 2,662 inhabitants, and South Reading, 3,207.

It is also worthy of remark, that in the settlement of the town of what is now Reading, North Reading, and South Reading, the first settlements were in South Reading, near our present Common.

The Committee, therefore, are of the opinion that we are old enough and large enough to be independent, and to have an identity as an active and independent town.

It only remains for the Committee to suggest a name for the consideration of the town.

Under ordinary circumstances the proposition to change the name of the town might be met with a variety of opinions; but under the circumstances of to-day, and in view of the Report of the Committee just presented, and the general expressions made to the Committee, we take great pleasure in recommending that the name of the Town of South Reading be changed to WAKEFIELD.

All of which is respectfully submitted.

DANIEL ALLEN,
S. O. RICHARDSON,
J. D. MANSFIELD,
Committee.

Both these reports were, with great unanimity and enthusiasm, accepted and adopted; and Cyrus Wakefield, S. O. Richardson, P. H. Sweetser, Lilley Eaton, Daniel Allen, J. D. Mansfield, and Thomas Emerson, Jr., were chosen a Building Committee, with authority to superintend the erection and furnishing of the proposed new Town House.

In accordance with a vote of the town, the Selectmen prepared and presented to the Legislature, then in session, a petition requesting the passage of an Act in conformity with the above expression of the town.

Said petition received prompt attention, and no person appearing in opposition thereto, the following act was approved by the Governor, Feb. 25, 1868: —

Be it enacted, etc.

SECTION I. The Town of South Reading, in the County of Middlesex, shall take the name of Wakefield.

SECTION 2. This Act shall take effect from and after the thirtieth day of June, in the year one thousand eight hundred and sixty-eight.

Subsequently, it was decided to make the occasion of the assumption of the new title a day of general festivity and enjoyment, and to mark its advent with appropriate public ceremonies.

The town having selected the anniversary of American Independence as the day for the proposed celebration, and having voted, also, a generous appropriation to defray its expenses, intrusted the arrangement and superintendence of the exercises of the occasion to the following

Committee.

CYRUS WAKEFIELD,	S. O. RICHARDSON,
DANIEL ALLEN,	LILLEY EATON,
P. H. SWEETSER,	J. D. MANSFIELD,
JAMES F. EMERSON,	LUCIUS BEEBE,
JOHN S. EATON,	JAMES OLIVER,
P. C. WHEELER,	J. F. MANSFIELD,
N. S. DEARBORN,	JOHN WINSHIP,
WM. H. ATWELL,	THOMAS WINSHIP,
EDWARD MANSFIELD,	WALDO E. COWDREY,
J. C. HARTSHORN,	CHESTER W. EATON,
JOHN F. HARTSHORN,	JOHN G. ABORN,
E. H. WALTON,	T. J. SKINNER,
M. P. WHEELER,	J. WHITTEMORE,
T. A. EMERSON,	JOHN WILEY, 2D,

RICHARD BRITTON.

This Committee labored with diligence and faithfulness in the arrangement of the various details, — and very *successfully*, also, as the smoothness with which the programme was executed abundantly testified. Especial credit is due to DANIEL ALLEN, Chairman; EDWARD MANSFIELD, Treasurer; T. J. SKINNER, Secretary; and to CYRUS WAKEFIELD and SOLON O. RICHARDSON, for their liberality and labors in aid of the celebration.

THE DAY

Opened brilliantly, to the music of pealing bells, and through all its shining hours from a cloudless sky was poured a perfect blaze of sunlight, rendering the shadows of the graceful elms peculiarly grateful and refreshing.

A national salute, at sunrise and at sunset, awoke the hillside echoes, and helped to swell the mighty anthem of rejoicing which, on that day, rose heavenward from a free and peaceful republic.

The town of Wakefield, always beautiful, on this day presented unusual attractions, the brilliant hues of fluttering flags and decorated arches mingling charmingly with its emerald lawns and leafy avenues, which throughout the day were filled with a happy and *perspiring* company.

The Committee secured the services of Col. William Beals, of Boston, who furnished the various arches, mottoes, and flags, for decorating the streets and public buildings; while many of the citizens placed upon their dwellings beautiful and appropriate embellishments, and extended to their thronging visitors a welcome, — *warm*, cordial, and refreshing.

At eight o'clock, the regular exercises of the day commenced with a morning concert, on the Common, by the Boston Brigade Band, which performed a selection of popular airs.

The concert assembled a large collection of people, and the beautiful music of the band was heartily applauded.

At nine o'clock a procession was formed under the marshalship of Major John Wiley, 2d, and moved in the following order: —

Detachment of Police.
Aid.   Chief Marshal.   Aid.
Brown's Brigade Band.
Richardson Light Guard, Capt. J. F. Emerson.
Yale Engine Co., No. 1, Capt. Richard Britton.
Carriages, containing the President of the Day and
CYRUS WAKEFIELD, Esq.;
The Historian and Poet; Chaplain of the Day;
Reader and Toast-Master;
Committee of Arrangements;
Aid.   Invited Guests;   Aid.
Town Officers and Clergymen of Reading, North Reading, and Wakefield.
Employees of Wakefield Rattan Works.
Employees of Emerson's Sons Shoe Manufactory.
Citizens.
Children of the Public Schools, in Carriages.

The procession commenced to move at about ten o'clock, passing over the designated route through the principal streets, and reaching the High School Grounds soon after noon.

The streets along the route, at many points crowded with spectators from this and the surrounding towns, were exceedingly dusty, and the march in the intense heat was relieved by halts, frequent and refreshing.

The procession presented a fine appearance, and the presence of the school children, in large numbers and in appropriately decorated carriages, added much attractiveness to this portion of the ceremonies.

The exercises on the hill were conducted in a large tent, erected for the purpose, where seats had been prepared for the invited guests, aged citizens, etc., and under the guidance of Daniel Allen, Esq., President of the Day.

Rev. Charles R. Bliss opened the exercises with prayer; after which, the President said : —

It becomes my pleasant duty, in behalf of the Committee of Arrangements and the town of Wakefield, to bid you to our new relations a cheerful welcome. In the order of exercises I shall be followed by those who will give you the interesting facts and details in regard to our town, and the relation which we have this day assumed.

We heartily bid you welcome to our new town, and to the new relations we assume to-day among the towns of the Commonwealth. Welcome to our beautiful hills and valleys. Welcome home, — those of you who were former residents of this town. To all of you, welcome again, not to South Reading, but to the Town of Wakefield. We bid you welcome, on this national holiday, to the scenes of your early days, and hope the exercises of this occasion will bring no discredit to the time-honored town of South Reading.

In conclusion the President introduced Mr. B. P. Snow, Principal of the High School, of Wakefield, who read, in a very acceptable manner, the Declaration of Independence.

The band played "Hail Columbia," when Hon. Lilley Eaton was introduced, who read the following

HISTORICAL ADDRESS.

Mr. President, and Ladies and Gentlemen :

On this most interesting and joyful occasion, this national birthday anniversary, this new and memorable era in our municipal history, — the stirring memories of other days, the gallant deeds of our ancestors, in the acquisition and defence of freedom and independence, and more recently, of our brothers and sisters, and sons and daughters, for the preservation of that freedom and independence; the interesting story of our town's early settlement, its progress in population, resources, knowledge, and refinement, its present bright and auspicious prospects, all the exciting considerations to which this twofold celebration of our national freedom and local prosperity gives rise, come thronging before the mental vision in such profusion as to be wellnigh overwhelming. As I look around upon this numerous and expectant assembly, composed of the strength and beauty and *élite* of the vicinity, and find myself standing among the venerable and hoary fathers of the ancient town of Reading, in the presence of the professional talent and official dignity of the town, of the neighboring towns, and of other States, I would fain preserve that golden silence which is far more precious than any language of mine, and I would be silent, not for the want of thoughts, *kindling* thoughts, for of such I am full, but for the want of *burning* words and animating sentences with which suitably to express the sentiments and emotions of this eventful opportunity.

But a duty has been assigned me as the historiographer of the occasion, that I must proceed to perform as I may be best able. The half hour allotted for this service will permit me to do scarcely more than simply to glance at a few of the more striking events and incidents of our national or municipal story.

It is natural, honorable, and appropriate that at this advanced date and prosperous condition of our village life, we should first revert to our day of small things, — to the early settlement of our village; seek acquaintance with those men who first located upon these pleasant plains and swelling hills, and around these lovely lakes, in the midst of what was then a lonely, howling wilderness, — those men

> "— who did, for conscience' sake,
> Their native land forego,
> And sought a home and freedom here
> Two hundred years ago."

It is good for us often to visit our ancient cemeteries, and meditate upon life's evanescence among those mossy monuments, where,

> "Beneath those rugged elms, that yew tree's shade,
> Where heaves the turf in many a mould'ring heap,
> Each in his narrow cell forever laid,
> The rude forefathers of the hamlet sleep."

The settlement of this village was commenced in 1639, under a grant of land from the General Court to the town of Lynn of "four miles square," and was called "Lynn Village."

This grant included substantially the present towns of Wakefield and Reading.

In 1644, seven houses having been erected, and seven families settled, and a little church edifice built, the village was made a town corporate by the name of "Reading."

This little meeting-house stood on the Common, near where is now our post-office, and in it the Rev. Messrs. Green, Haugh, and Brock, men eminent for their learning and piety, successively ministered up to the time of their respective deaths.

In 1651, twelve years after the first grant, a second grant of territory was made to the town of Reading of "two miles square."

This latter grant constituted substantially what is now "North Reading."

The early settlers of our township were rude, but heroic, industrious, and pious men,

> "Witty and wise, grave, good, among the best
> Were they, — the mem'ry of the just is blest."

We desire to pay to their memory this day the tribute of our gratitude for their wisdom and sagacity in selecting this spot so beautiful for situation, the constant joy of its successive inhabitants; for their justice in purchasing it by peaceable negotiation of its former Indian possessors, as appears by a deed thereof, duly signed and executed by their chief men and women, which is still on record; for their valor and labor and hardships in defending and subduing this then uncultivated wild, and changing it to smiling fields, and a safe and happy abode; for their decided moral character, their stern integrity, their virtuous habits, and their early support of liberty, learning, and religion, the valuable influences of all which have been ever felt and enjoyed by their successors down to the present day.

Our early fathers were valiant men as well as good and industrious ones. For although they themselves made peaceable purchase of their lands of the Indians, and were on friendly terms with their immediate Indian neighbors, yet there were many hostile tribes around them, who made frequent forays upon the English settlements; and the settlers for many years were obliged to labor with the axe or spade in one hand and a musket in the other; to maintain watch-houses and garrisons for their protection; and were often called upon to join in expeditions against the savage foe. They thus became a brave and martial people, and during the first century of our history were frequently engaged in wars with the Indians and French. The names of some of these early citizens became renowned as warriors and leaders.

Richard Walker, their first captain; Jonathan Poole, their second captain; Major Jeremiah Swain, who was commander-in-chief of all the Colonial troops; Captain Thomas Bancroft, a noted officer in King

Philip's Indian War, and others that might be named, shine out on the page of our early record, as eminent for their ability and bravery.

In 1688 the humble meeting-house, erected in 1644, having become too small for the convenience of the people (for all the people attended public worship in those days), was sold, and the sum which it brought may give some idea of its size and value: it was sold for twenty-five shillings and a "watch-house frame," and the money was appropriated for *the school*, showing that our ancestors thus early were mindful of the importance of schooling, — a mindfulness which their successors have ever manifested in a commendable degree, and never more so than at the present time.

Our fathers then proceeded to erect their second meeting-house. It was located a few rods northwesterly of the present Congregational meeting-house, in the easterly part of the present town burial-ground. It was a quaint, unique, and curiously-formed structure. Our accomplished architect, John Stevens, Esq., who is projecting a plan thereof, finds it more difficult to sketch than he does the more spacious and splendid edifice whose lofty walls and tower, and elegant halls, are soon to add grace, convenience, and honor to our town. This old church was of moderate size, with a roof not exactly like a modern *French* one (but may have been the original idea of one), and was a sort of cross between a "regular pitch," a "hipped," and a "gambrel" or "*surd*," with dormers on at least three sides, and a turret in front, with a bell therein; its windows contained glass of very small size, diamond-shaped, set in lead. Within was a gallery on one side; and on the floor, in front of the pulpit, were long body seats, in which the adult male worshippers sat, who were seated by a committee, chosen annually for that purpose, — the oldest, richest, and most hoary in front, and so back in regular gradation, according to age and real estate. The adult females also occupied seats by themselves, on either side, as arranged by the committee, on the same principle. The boys and girls were on the back side of the room, the young men and the tything-men with the singers in the gallery, and the dog-whippers where most convenient to exercise their vocation. There were here and there in the house pews which, by special permission of the town, had been built by some of the more aristocratic and wealthy citizens, at their own expense. This house served the people eighty years, and in it preached the Rev. Messrs. Pierpont, Brown, and Hobby, all liberally educated and distinguished men.

In 1706 the house of John Harnden, situated in the northwesterly part of the town, was attacked by a party of Indians. The family of

Mr. Harnden consisted of himself, wife, and eight children. Mr. Harnden was absent at the time. The Indians killed Mrs. Harnden and three children, burned the house, and carried the remaining children into captivity.

In 1713 the inhabitants of that part of Reading lying north of Ipswich River and Bare Meadow, "having," to use the language of the record, "become of sufficient and competent numbers to call, settle, and maintain a godly, learned, orthodox minister," were set off and incorporated as a distinct parish by the name of the "North Precinct of Reading," being the same territory, mainly, that now constitutes the *town* of *North* Reading.

Until this date (1713), all parochial matters had been transacted by the *town* in its *municipal* capacity. After this, until 1770, the residue of the town, including what is now Wakefield and Reading (then termed respectively the "Old Parish" and "Woodend"), constituted one parish designated as the "First Parish of Reading." In 1768, exactly one hundred years ago, the third church edifice in this part of Reading was built, having the same frame as that which now upholds the main body of the present Congregational remodelled church. It stood on a site near its present location, and for the time in which it was erected was a large and handsome structure. In 1769 the Rev. Caleb Prentiss, of Cambridge, a graduate of Harvard College, became the pastor of the First Parish. He was a liberal divine, of respectable talents, mild and persuasive as a preacher, patriotic and upright as a citizen.

This same year, 1769, the northwesterly part of the First Parish, the part then termed "Woodend," after several years of earnest effort, and in spite of a most determined opposition from the First Parish, were incorporated as a separate parish, by the name of the "West Parish of Reading." I have given the dates of these parochial incorporations, because that although they created simply religious bodies corporate, yet these parishes were the nucleus or foundation of those associations and affiliations that subsequently resulted in the municipal corporations of Reading, South Reading, and North Reading. In 1775 commenced the War of the Revolution. Into the spirit of that war in defence of American liberty and rights against the obnoxious acts and growing encroachments of British tyranny, the people of Old Reading entered with great unanimity and with all their hearts; to its support they not only *pledged*, but they freely *paid* their lives, their fortunes, and their sacred honor.

In 1776, July 4, was adopted that immortal document, that "Magna Charta" of our rights and glorious Declaration of American Inde pendence which has just been so impressively pronounced in our hearing, and the anniversary of the adoption of which, ninety-two years ago, we are now celebrating. In reference to that declaration, the town of Reading voted unanimously " to adhere to its sentiments and stand by it to the last, with their lives and their fortunes."

The town of Reading at this time occupied relatively among the towns of the State a position of much importance.

By a census of Massachusetts proper, taken in 1776, the town of Reading was the *second* town in population in the county of Middlesex, and the *thirty-third* in the State proper, and contained about 2,000 people. Boston at the same time contained only 2,700 inhabitants, and Charlestown only 360.

It is probable, however, that some 500 of the population of Reading at that time were refugees from Boston, Charlestown, and other places. The North and South Parishes then contained about 700 inhabitants each, and the West Parish about 600. The records of the town and of each parish, during the continuance of the war, breathe the most earnest and devoted patriotism and the most determined resolution; and are full of votes for raising and providing men, money, provisions, clothing, and fuel, in cheerful response to all the calls of the Government. It appears that the town of Reading sent to the Continental army, for longer or shorter terms, more than four hundred men; and that, without counting minute-men, or men drafted from time to time to guard prisoners, or privateersmen, of all which there were many, there were constantly in the field from Reading, on an average, one hundred men during the war.

Among these enlisted men were officers of talent and bravery; of whom we will mention Colonel David Green, Colonel Benjamin Brown (afterwards General), Captain John Walton, Captain William Flint, Daniel (afterwards Colonel) Flint; Captain James Bancroft, Surgeon John Hart, Captain John Brooks, afterwards Colonel in the army and Governor of the Commonwealth; and there were many others. From the close of the War of the Revolution to 1810, the onward progress of the town was slow, pursuing the even tenor of its way, — witnessing few important or extraordinary changes in its condition, and gaining only about two hundred inhabitants over the census of 1776, but seven hundred over the census of 1765.

In 1812 *two* memorable events occurred to vary the monotony of its municipal life. In the first place, in February of that year, " The Old Parish," so called, exclusive of " Woodend," was set off from the town of Reading, and incorporated as a distinct town by the name of " South Reading."

And in the second place, in the same year, war with England was declared by the United States.

The same general causes and considerations which resulted *directly* in the declaration of that war had *indirectly* led to the separation of the South Parish from her sister parishes.

The people of the South Parish, ever true to the government of the American Union, were *Republicans*, almost unanimously; were supporters of the National Administration then in power, and were in favor of fighting Old England for her insults to our seamen and our flag: while the people of the other parishes, not less honest or patriotic, we would charitably believe, but with different views of political expediency, were, with like unanimity, *Federalists*, unfavorable to the National Administration, and violently opposed to a war with England. Political feeling rose to a high pitch, and parties were very bitter towards each other. The Republicans of the South Parish were a minority in the town, and were excluded in a great measure from influence in municipal affairs or share in town offices. These considerations impelled to a separation.

The town of South Reading, at the time of its incorporation, contained a population of about eight hundred, and the valuation of all its real and personal estate, upon the assessors' books, was only $100,000.

This newly-made town, although small in territory, in numbers, and in resources, was very spirited and enthusiastic.

It contained among its citizens at this time an unusual proportion of able and gifted men, — men who loved liberty and independence, were qualified to speak for them and to act for them, and were ready, if need required, to fight for them; who appreciated the value of sound learning, and were liberal in its support; and who earnestly sustained religious institutions and religious freedom.

I well remember these men. Nearly all of them have gone to that land "from whose bourne no traveller returns."

I should be pleased to speak particularly of many of them, but time, at present, forbids. Suffice it to say here, that under their influence the town was earnest and efficient in sustaining the government in the war; cheerfully responded to all the calls of the War Department; sent numbers of its young men to the field and on the sea; mourned sadly over the defeats of its armies and navy, and rejoiced jubilantly over their victories.

At the close of the war, the citizens had a grand celebration, in thankfulness for the triumph of the American Arms, and for the return of peace, with an oration, civic feast, and other demonstrations of joy.

Some toasts given on the occasion, which were received with loud acclamation and swallowed with *ardent* satisfaction, will show somewhat the temper of the people at that time.

The first, by the orator of the day, Charles G. Haines, Esq., —

" *The British Lion* — We have hunted him, — we have hunted him to his den ! "

The second, by Benjamin Badger, Sen., a Revolutionary veteran, —

" *John Bull, the Pope, and the Devil,* — May they never control this happy land ! "

The progress of our town, from the time of its incorporation in 1812 to 1844, although not rapid, yet was more marked and considerable than in any previous period of like extent. Its population and valuation nearly doubled in the time. The increasing resources of its inhabitants had enabled them to grant a more liberal support to its public institutions, to its schools, and to various public improvements. The present Town Hall, soon to be so totally eclipsed, was erected during this period, and was considered a handsome and spacious building in its early days.

The South Reading Academy, established in 1829, on this very spot,[1] had flourished a while, gave an impetus to the pursuit of literature among us ; educated some of our sons, who have since become eminent in professional and industrial life, and induced, by its example, an improved condition of our common schools ; and as the common schools improved, the Academy declined, and was at length discontinued. Thus went on our town affairs until 1844, — the year bi-centennial.

In this year, as in 1812, two memorable events occurred, again to vary the monotony of our village life. One, instead of being a *separation*, as before, of the various corporations of Old Reading, was a *union* of them, in a bi-centennial celebration of the old town's incorporation, and was a most agreeable and interesting *re*union of the inhabitants of the old parishes, their descendants and friends.

The other event, instead of being, as before, a declaration and effort for the victories of *war*, was an effort for the victories of *peace*, in the chartering and construction of the " Boston and Maine Railroad," which was laid through our town in this year, and was to our village a most important event. It opened to the eye of the public these fertile lands, these pleasant plains and hillsides, and our unrivalled water scenery ; it superseded, in a great measure, those toll-bridges that sepa-

---

[1] The Address was delivered in the High School yard.

rated us from our metropolis, and were a hinderance to our increase; it brought the merchants of distant cities, in search of goods, to the doors of our manufactories; it has induced the traders and mechanics of Boston to seek homes for their families in this central and convenient location; and it has thus brought among us enterprise, wealth, and liberality. Since its establishment, the town has rapidly improved in population and resources. And while there is not so much that is *fair* and *high* in its Wakefield station-house as some of us would desire, there certainly is enough of the *fare* and *high* in the privilege of riding in its cars; but we would freely acknowledge its great importance to us, notwithstanding, and hope for greater kindness at less cost in the future.

Among the new-comers were men of wealth, talent, and activity, who, in conjunction with our native-born citizens of like gifts and character, have given new life to our business and to all our institutions.

In 1861, when the fearful War of the Rebellion burst upon us, it found us not only patriotic and true to the government and the Union, as always heretofore, but also able, from the multiplication of our numbers and resources, to meet, and to exceed even, all the calls of the nation for men and means, and to raise, during the war, some $50,000, and to send some five hundred men to the army and navy, — men brave, patriotic, and devoted, "who helped open the Mississippi who were present at Vicksburg, Port Hudson, New Orleans, and Mobile, who saw the starry flag as it ascended Missionary Ridge, and witnessed the flight of Bragg and his host; who marched from Atlanta to the sea, and who were among those who so long struggled between Washington and Richmond, and who at last saw the rebel flag go down upon the Appomattox."

Of these brave men, more than *sixty*, either in battle or hospital or prison pen, gave their lives for their country. High up in the temple of liberty and of their country's fame will be the niches that they wil occupy; in bold relief, upon the tablets of our Memorial Hall, will their names be engraved, and sweet will their memory forever be in the hearts of freemen.

I have said that this increase of population and enterprise has given new life and impulse to the various institutions of our town. And here let me say, that we have been and still are singularly fortunate in having among us men of ample means and generous souls, who have taken pleasure in contributing, from time to time, to those particular moral, social, literary, and municipal enterprises among us which needed encouragement, and they have given liberally. Hence we find that very properly their names are stamped upon our Library books and school diplomas; are sounded forth, sometimes in merry peals and sometimes in solemn tones, from our balconies; that we are reminded of them every hour, by day and by night; that they shine in golden letters from the frontal of the repository and head-quarters of our Fire Department; are heard in the martial strains and measured tread, and are seen upon the armorial escutcheon of our Infantry; and stand out in living characters upon our local record. There let them stand and shine, for they are worthy.

These various auspicious influences have caused our population to increase from eight hundred in 1812 to fifteen hundred in 1840, and to nearly four thousand in 1868; and our valuation to rise from $100,000 in 1812, to $280,000 in 1840, and to nearly $2,000,000 at the present time.

Since 1840 our meeting-houses have all been enlarged, remodelled, and improved; the value of our school-houses has been enhanced from $2,000 to $30,000; our annual school appropriations have risen from $1,000 to more than $6,000; a Public Library of three thousand volumes has been established, and many other valuable improvements have been made; our town is still prosperous and growing, — its star is still in the ascendant.

Under all these favorable circumstances of advancement and progress, our people came to the conclusion that they were entitled to a distinctive, uncompounded, municipal *name* of their own; not because they disliked the name of Reading; for, on the contrary, they love and venerate it for its antiquity and as the name of their own and their fathers' home; and if they could have had a clear and separate title to it, they would have been content. But we foresaw that our town was destined to occupy an important position upon the future page of history, and we desired that whether that position was one of honor or dishonor, that this town alone should have the credit or discredit of it. We wished therefore that its name and its portrait should so correspond that it should not be liable to be mistaken for what it was not.

We remembered the honorable pride of him, who, hailing from the "Eternal City," when absent from his native land, could exclaim, "I am a Roman citizen," and have his character at once recognized and respected; and we desired that our own townsmen, when absent in another State or nation, and being asked from whence they came, should be able to answer with equal pride and clearness, and commanding equal recognition and respect, not only "that they are American citizens," but also "that they hail from a town or city whose name and identity are clear and manifest." While our people were revolving this matter in their minds, and looking about for a name on which all might unite, our respected fellow-citizen, Cyrus Wakefield, Esq., came forward, and voluntarily and unconditionally, out of the abundance of his heart and of his regard to the town of his adoption, and the dwelling-place of his ancestors, and from the overflowings of his liberality and his purse, proffered to the town the free gift of a lot of land, and of a building to be erected thereon, for a Town Hall, Soldiers' Memorial Hall, Library and Armory Rooms, Town Officers' Rooms, Withdrawing Rooms, and all other conveniences, of such ample and sufficient capacity for all these purposes, and of such permanence and beauty of architecture and finish, as should satisfy the utmost reasonable wishes of the inhabitants, regardless of cost. In accepting this magnificent gift, the town at once decided for a change of its name, and what that name should be ; and forthwith, with unprecedented unanimity, and by acclamation, voted that its name should be changed to *Wakefield*.

And now, to-day, having obtained the requisite authority so to do, we lay aside the old corporate name of Reading, which we have worn, in whole or in part, for more than seven generations, and assume from this day forward the new name of *Wakefield*.

There is this very pleasing coincidence connected with this change of name.

The town of Reading was originally so named from the city of Reading, in England, for the reason, it is said, that John Poole, one of our earliest and wealthiest settlers, came from that city. This John Poole, in honor of whose birthplace the name of Reading was adopted, was the first settler upon that identical spot now owned by Cyrus Wakefield, Esq., his successor, in honor of whom we this day assume our new name, and is the place now occupied by the extensive " Rattan Factory." This John Poole was a glover and miller ; built the first grain and saw mills of the town, and, like his latest successor, was its richest citizen.

There is another coincidence, furnishing an additional appropriateness in our new name, viz. Hon. Horace *Poole Wakefield*, recently of Reading, is a lineal descendant of this same John Poole.

It is proper also to mention, in this connection, that our patron and namesake is of Reading and *South Reading* descent. It seems that an emigrant from France by the name of Wakefield was an early settler of Boston, — a goldsmith by profession ; that he soon buried his young wife, who left an infant son, Thomas Wakefield by name; that said infant son was put to nurse with the Gould family, on the farm recently known as the " Jenkins Place," then situated partly in Stoneham and partly in Reading. The father soon returned to France, and the son Thomas was adopted by the Gould family. He subsequently became an apprentice to Timothy Pratt, of Reading, to learn the trade of a carpenter. This Timothy Pratt, who was the ancestor of Nathan P. Pratt, Esq., the present Representative in the Legislature from Reading, lived on the easterly side of the "Great Pond," in the old Garrison house, that stood on land now owned by Lucius Beebe, Esq., and was the same house that has been recently purchased and removed by Mr. Zenas Perkins. This young Wakefield married, in 1750, Dorcas Pratt, the daughter of his master, and succeeded to the homestead; and here, in that old Garrison house, was born Thomas Wakefield, Jr., the grandfather of our worthy namesake.

And now, in conclusion, on this day sacred to liberty, to independence, and to victory, let me congratulate my fellow-citizens that we are now free and independent in *name*, as well as otherwise; that we now have a municipal appellation of our own, the reputation and good character of which are committed to our keeping. Let us then resolve, at this auspicious hour, that all our future municipal acts shall be such as shall promote good order, intelligence, humanity, freedom, and righteousness among this people, and shall make the town and the name of "Wakefield," "a joy, an honor, and a praise in the land."

I will improve this opportunity, in the name and behalf of this people, to thank Heaven for inspiring the heart of our munificent friend to be thus generous to his fellow-citizens, and to thank our friend sincerely for his most princely gift. We would likewise remember, in this connection, that our acknowledgments are also due to that other generous and respected friend, who, in addition to his former liberality, has proffered the sum of $1,000 for the purpose of furnishing and decorating the halls and other rooms of the new building. Our gratitude, therefore, to both of them, we would express and tender, with our invocations for their future welfare and happiness.

And may he whose name we this day adopt, amid these imposing ceremonies, and may we who have adopted it, — may we all remember that a new and mutual obligation has been assumed by us, never to perform any act that shall demean either party in the eyes of the other, or bring a stain upon the now fair character of the name of *Wakefield*.

And as our town and *future city* shall go onward and upward, increasing in population, in resources, in intelligence, in virtue, and an honorable fame, as we hope and pray that she may, let her never forget the illustrious citizen who has done so much to enrich and adorn the place of our abode. May he long live to enjoy the sweet reward of reflecting that he has performed a noble and a useful work. May our historians make fair and enduring record of his acts, and our poets, from this day forward,

> "To all the world his deeds rehearse,
> And praise him in harmonious verse."

May the name he this day secures "be better to him than that of *sons and daughters*"; may he ever have "that good name that is better than *great riches*," and be found among those whose names are written on high ; and at length,

> "Serus in cœlum redeat."

At the close of the address, — which was finely delivered and highly enjoyed by the numerous assembly, — the band again played an appropriate air ; after which Mr. John S. Eaton delivered the following

POEM.

> With joyful voices join, to greet
>   This birthday of the free ;
> Each glad return, more dear and sweet, —
>   The Nation's Jubilee !
>
> On all the winds her banner plays,
>   Star-gemmed, with folds of light ;
> A nation's hopes are in its rays -
>   The red, the blue, the white.
>
> Her brilliant flag, whose matchless hues
>   Float 'neath the Southern Cross,
> And o'er the whaler's daring crews,
>   On icy waters toss ;
>
> Her sacred flag, whose azure field
>   The lightest zephyr sways,
> And cheers, when flying squadrons yield,
>   The hero's dying gaze.
>
> The polished guns, from plain and peak
>   Opening their brazen throats,
> A people's gladness grandly speak
>   In all their echoing notes.
>
> Let the wild tones, unhindered, fly
>   From North to Southern wave ;
> Our flag, unfolding, gem the sky, —
>   Bright banner of the brave !

Thrice blest *this* day, whose breath of balm
    Refreshing blows, and free :
No slave-step 'neath the Southern palm,
    No slave-ship on the sea ;

Whose peaceful breath, o'er fragrant groves
    Where battling columns met,
Only the orange blossom moves,
    And lifts the violet.

That sacred turf, as emerald bright,
    So rudely torn and red,
Closing o'er leaders in the fight,
    Enshrines heroic dead.

Brave souls ! with martyrs' zeal endowed,
    'Neath battle's fiery crest,
With triumph flashing from the cloud,
    Secured the victor's rest.

Bright, starry wings adorn our sky,
    From out the war's eclipse,
Bless*é*d, as met the prophet's eye
    In the apocalypse.

As this fair angel sweeps the spheres, —
    Angel with spotless wing, —
The glories of the coming years
    What prophet-bard will sing ?

Our brotherhood of mighty States !
    Firm on a truer plan, —
For them a clearer day awaits,
    With brotherhood of man.

Stretching afar their gleaming lines
    'Neath Freedom's ample shields,
Triumphal art above them shines,
    Achieved on bloodless fields.

Westward the star of empire leads
    With most enticing ray ;
And all the Prairie's fruitful meads
    Are blossoming to-day.

Plains rolling boundless as the seas,
    Whose rich, uncultured sod
Withholds broad harvests from the breeze,
    By the fierce Indian trod.

Those flowery wilds — it is decreed —
　　A mightier tread must feel ;
The thunder of the fiery steed,
　　Steam-winged and shod with steel.

From East to West, with tireless feet,
　　Shall flaming coursers bear
To dwellers 'neath the torrid heat,
　　Products of Northern air ;

Through rocky tunnels, cold and grim,
　　Marvels of modern skill,
Along the steep Sierras' rim,
　　Reach Californian hill ;

From West to East, 'neath giant pines,
　　And mountain summits o'er,
Bear golden treasure from her mines
　　To the Atlantic shore ;

Along the firm and shining rails,
　　The wealth of Orient seas,
Above the Indian's fading trails, —
　　Immense, shall roll to these.

So, Progress, with unfettered limb,
　　And bold, adorning hand,
Shall cities build in forests dim,
　　With temples deck the land :

Her bands of steel surround the zone ;
　　Her conscious wires, the seas ;
To stainless triumph marching on,
　　And grander destinies.

So, down the ages, as they sweep
　　Unmarred by clashing sword,
Swells the blest anthem, strong and deep, —
　　Anthem of Earth's accord !

Here, on the bright, rejoicing day
　　Such hopeful omens crown,
We come, a pleasant word to say
　　For our dear, native town.

Fair town, whose legends, strange and old,
　　Wrought from her bending bowers,
By nobler bard have been enrolled,
　　In fairer lines than ours.

His graceful pen, with wondrous skill,
　　Traced those ancestral scenes,
And showed where dwelt, on plain and hill,
　　The ancient Browns and Greens.

Nor these alone : — with nicest tact
　　Those hardy settlers limned ;
Custom and form and word and act,
　　In flowing numbers hymned.

For *us*, an easier task remains,
　　Befitting humbler powers :
We sing the beauty of her plains,
　　The fragrance of her flowers.

No soft Italian scenes we boast,
　　Our summer skies less clear ;
But prized, the grandeur of our coast,
　　Our rocky hillsides dear.

No notes of foreign praise we swell,
　　Not, " Naples view, and rest ! "
Our invitation is, — " Come, dwell
　　In Wakefield, and be blest ! "

The native Indian, dull and rude,
　　Threading the forest wild,
Beside our lakes enchanted stood,
　　Where the Great Spirit smiled.

His wigwam's shield along these streams
　　In rustic beauty sprang :
Here, in the twilight's shadowy gleams,
　　His dusky daughters sang.

And later, here, our ancient sires,
　　By the same waters cheered,
Over the Indian's smouldering fires,
　　Their scanty dwellings reared ;

Fought for their title to the soil
　　With hungry wolf and bear ;
And where the savage sought his spoil,
　　Erected house of prayer.

All honor to those rugged men,
　　The coming needs foresaw,
And laid foundations firmly then,
　　Of liberty and law.

Their children here, and children's sons,
    O'erspreading hill and glen,
Have crowned with grace the work begun
    By those uncultured men;

With stately dwellings decked the slopes,
    With neat, attractive homes;
And crested the fair mountain-tops
    With Learning's ample domes.

Her classic sons, from thence sent forth,
    Superior place to claim,
Attest their rich, unfailing worth,
    With ripe, scholastic fame.

Sons, absent long, this day returned
    To childhood's rural seat,
Where kindling fires of genius burned,
    With welcome true, we greet.

From this smooth, academic ground,
    Whence streams of knowledge pour,
On smiling valley look around,
    The waving heights explore!

Broad, fertile fields and greenest shores,
    With sparkling rim of light,
To generous feast from Nature's stores,
    Our willing feet invite.

From rounded Cedar's airy crest,
    View lake, with leafy hem,
Two fairy islands on its breast,
    Shining a crystal gem, —

The sparkling waters of Smith's Pond
    (As olden records say),
While the green hillside steeps, beyond,
    In verdure stretch away.

Or climb to Castle's grander cone,
    Firm as the mountains be;
Around — the forest's swaying zone,
    Beyond — the restless sea.

Broad lines of woodland, bending down
    O'er smooth and yielding turf,
Touch the bold headland, rough and brown,
    Swept by the ocean surf;

White sails, far o'er the spires of Lynn,
   In the blue distance melt;
On rocky coast, the waves roll in
   And clasp with shining belt.

Elate, our western mount ascend,
   Haloed with golden beams:
Like silver shields the lakes extend,
   Like silver threads the streams.

Drink beauty there, at day's sweet close,
   While the bright vision waits,
And the celestial splendor glows
   At sunset's purple gates!

Northward, the flowery meadows rest
   Soft in the summer air;
Beyond, with sunshine on her crest,
   Our mother, Reading, fair,

Calm and sedate, as mother may,
   Over the lake's clear tide,
Watches her daughter's prosperous way,
   Arrayed as blooming bride, —

Bride, on whose flower-encircled brow
   No mark of years we trace;
Clad in her youthful beauty now,
   With added lines of grace.

And when, complete, her bridal gift,
   Munificent and fair,
Heavenward its massive towers shall lift
   In the caressing air

To greet the mornings, still and bright,
   Through many coming days,
Shall all the people, with delight,
   Award its donor praise.

His gift, for whom, from burning plains,
   O'er stormy billows rolled,
Are sent those slender, magic canes,
   His touch transmutes to gold;

His crowning gift, whose lavish hands,
   And fresh, persistent powers,
With verdure vests our level lands,
   Our thorny wastes, with flowers;

Who answers well that question old —
    "*What is there in a name?*"
An answer, clearly, grandly rolled,
    And mounts therewith to fame!

With smiles go forth the youthful brides,
    Circled with fairest flowers,
Afar from home, to tempt life's tides:
    Not thus we offer *ours!*

Our town beloved, our cherished pet,
    Our darling and our pride,
n golden ring her name is set,
    We keep ourselves the bride!

Our pine-clad hills and shadowy brakes,
    And flower-enamelled lawns,
O ur rocky peaks and rippled lakes,
    Bright in the rosy dawns;

Our darkling dells and forest plumes,
    Our sprays of brilliant leaves,
Our arching elms and garden-blooms,
    Fair in the golden eves;

Our spotless blossoms, floating fair
    Upon the crystal waves,
Our glitt'ring spires in sunlit air,
    Our fathers' hallowed graves,

And all the wealth our records bear
    Of old historic fame, —
All these we hold with strictest care,
    And yield, alone, *our name!*

'Neath the bright Future's glowing arch
    Of soft, unclouded skies,
What grand processions gayly march!
    What startling visions rise!

When fifty added years shall bring
    Their gifts of fair renown,
A sweeter bard their praise shall sing,
    And nobler works shall crown!

The city, from her triple hills,
    With ocean-girdle bound,
Already looks towards mountain rills,
    Selecting ampler ground;

Has gathered, now, rich highland farms,
    And, overcrowded thus,
Northward may stretch embracing arms,
    And Boston come to us!

Within that shining circle bound,
    Whose polished "*Hub*" we boast,
Our rustic charms no more be found,
    And our new name be lost!

From this clear summit, looking on
    Towards crowning heights of grace,
Our thoughts revert to pleasures gone, —
    The vanished years retrace.

From out the shadowy haunts of eld,
    From ancient roofs, moss-grown,
Arise the forms those years beheld,
    And swells aërial tone;

Forms, lost to sight, to memory dear,
    Those mystic chambers fill;
Tones, lost to earth, from purer sphere
    Our waiting spirits thrill!

As the fond lovers linger long,
    Nor haste to *say* farewells,
As the swan's sad, expiring song
    In sweetest cadence swells, —

So, on memories fond, intent,
    We linger with the past;
And the fair name, with childhood blent,
    Seems sweetest at the last!

Dear name, farewell! Our task is o'er;
    The coming glories see!
South Reading, henceforth, nevermore, —
    And Wakefield let it be!

At the termination of the literary and musical exercises, on Academy Hill, a procession, consisting of those persons who were intending to participate in the Celebration Dinner, was formed, and marched to the dining tent which had been erected upon the Common.

At the same time the children belonging to the several schools of the town were furnished with a collation in the Town Hall.

The "Mammoth Tent," in which the dinner was served, covered sufficient space to accommodate, at table, two thousand guests; and the dinner, furnished by Mr. A. A. Currier as caterer, proved to be an ample, satisfying, and enjoyable entertainment to its thousand participants.

Many of the former residents of South Reading, — now widely separated, and holding honorable positions in the various professions, — on this day revisiting the scenes of their boyhood as guests, surrounded the table, thereby adding as much to their *own* enjoyment, let us hope, as did their presence to the interest and success of the celebration.

N.

READING SOLDIERS' MONUMENT.

The Trustees of the Soldiers' Monument respectfully submit their doings to the town, with the action the town have taken in the matter; also the clause of the Will of the late Abiel Holden, Esq., making a bequest for the same, and such other matter in relation to the Monument as they thought might be of interest to the public.

It is well known to the citizens of Reading generally that Mr. Holden took a lively interest in our soldiers.

In the early stages of the Great Rebellion, he was very anxious to have a monument erected, while he lived, to the memory of those who were killed in battle or died of wounds received, or of disease contracted while in the line of their duty. He offered at that time to subscribe one hundred dollars for that purpose, but it being suggested to him that it would be better to wait till the close of the war, he reluctantly dropped the subject with the remark that he should not live to see a monument erected to the memory of our soldiers.

But he was so strongly impressed with the justice of having the monument at some future time, that he made in his will the generous gift of $500 for that purpose, in case of his death before the proper time arrived for erecting it.

Mr. Holden did not live to see the monument erected. He died Nov. 4, 1863, aged 65 years, 7 months, and 25 days.

At a town-meeting held March 7, 1864, the following communication received by the Selectmen was read: —

To the Honorable Board of Selectmen, — In executing the Will of the late Abiel Holden, we hand you the following: —

" I appropriate of my funds, not especially bequeathed by my said will, the sum of five hundred dollars, and give the same to said town of Reading, in trust, and for the purpose of procuring and erecting upon that part of the cemetery in said Reading called Round Hill, a monument to commemorate the deeds and perpetuate the memories of the soldiers of Reading who have been killed in battle or otherwise, or died from disease contracted, or wounds received, while in the service of the United States and in line of duty during this present War of Rebellion, provided that within two years next after my decease the said town of Reading, or the citizens thereof, shall raise the further sum of five hundred dollars, and with the said one thousand dollars shall procure a shaft of Italian marble, of suitable form and dimensions, and lay the foundations, and commence the erection of the same upon a pedestal of granite on said Round Hill, and shall without unnecessary delay finish the erection thereof, and cause the names of all said soldiers to be engraved thereon, with their ages and deaths, and also appropriate memorials of their military service, commencing at the lower part of the shaft and proceeding upwards. And I further appoint the selectmen of said town of Reading trustees, to take charge of procuring and erecting the said monument, until said town shall, at a lawful town meeting called by a warrant, having a special article relating to this matter, by ballot, choose a Board of Trustees whose duty it shall be to complete said monument."

ARKAID T. HOLDEN,
CLINTON B. HOLDEN,
WILLIAM J. HOLDEN,
Executors of the will of Abiel Holden.

On motion of William J. Wightman, —

Voted, That a Committee be raised to investigate the subject of the aforesaid proposition, and report to the town at a subsequent meeting, the best manner of fulfilling the requirements in said will, either by subscription or an appropriation by the town.

Thomas Sweetser, James S. Campbell, Jonathan Frost, Henry G. Richardson, and Joel M. Howard were chosen.

At a town-meeting held March 6, 1865, the Committee presented the following report:—

The Committee chosen March 7, 1864, to investigate the subject of erecting a monument to commemorate the deeds and perpetuate the memories of soldiers of Reading, respectfully recommend that the town accept the legacy of five hundred dollars, bequeathed by the late Abiel Holden, Esq., for that purpose, and would also recommend that the town appropriate a sum not less than five hundred dollars, nor exceeding $1,000, for the purpose of complying with the provisions of the will of the said Abiel Holden, Esq., in relation thereto.

>THOMAS SWEETSER,
>JAMES S. CAMPBELL,
>JONATHAN FROST,
>HENRY G. RICHARDSON,
>*Committee.*

On motion of William J. Wightman,—

Voted, That the town accept and adopt the report.

At a town-meeting held May 25, 1865, the following article was inserted in the warrant:—

ARTICLE 4. To see if the town will choose trustees to take charge of erecting the Monument to Soldiers, in accordance with the will of the late Abiel Holden, Esq., or what they will do in relation thereto.

On motion of William J. Wightman,—

Voted, To choose a Board of Trustees.

James S. Campbell, Solon A. Parker, and Joseph L. Pratt were chosen.

The Trustees visited several cemeteries for the purpose of seeing the monuments erected in them. And they also had a number of new designs presented to them.

After they had selected the design, the principal marble-workers in Boston and vicinity brought in proposals for building the monument. The contract was given to William Johnson, of Malden, for the sum of $1,500, which included the lettering and putting the monument on the lot designated. There were forty-six names put on the monument, with appropriate inscriptions.

In justice to Mr. Johnson, the Trustees will state that he fulfilled his contract to their entire satisfaction.

APPENDIX.

The following notice was printed and circulated: —
The Soldiers' Monument will be dedicated on Thursday, October 5, 1865.

PROGRAMME FOR THE OCCASION.

A procession, accompanied by the band from Fort Warren, will be formed on the Common at 1.30 P. M., arranged as follows: President of the Day, Selectmen, Public Speakers, Committee of Arrangements, a Choir of Singers, Families of deceased Soldiers, Returned Soldiers, Schools and Citizens, which will move at 2 o'clock.

ROUTE OF PROCESSION.

From the Common, through Woburn, Chute, High, Main, Pleasant, Manning, Salem, and Main Streets, through the Cemetery to the Monument, where an original ode by Mrs. P. H. Hanaford will be sung, thence to the Old South Church, where the dedicating Services will commence by a voluntary on the organ, followed by singing an original hymn composed by Miss Eliza Evans; other appropriate singing will be interspersed throughout the services. Reading of Scripture by Rev. W. W. Hayward, prayer by Rev. William Barrows, address by Rev. W. H. Willcox, concluding prayer by Rev. H. P. Guilford.

President of the Day. — Edward Appleton, Esq.
Chief Marshal. — William J. Wightman, Esq.
Aids. — Capt. John H. Jeffrey, Capt. J. Warren Cook, James McKay, Stillman E. Parker, J. Brooks Leathe, William M. Titus, Albert Nichols, B. M. Hartshorn, Oliver A. Swain, and Solon Bancroft.

COMMITTEE OF ARRANGEMENTS.

James S. Campbell, Solon A. Parker, Joseph L. Pratt, Capt. John H. Jeffrey, Capt. J. Warren Cook, Andrew Howes, William Proctor, and Daniel B. Lovejoy.

READING, Sept. 30, 1865.

The services were mainly conducted in accordance with the above programme.

Chaplain A. H. Quint, of the 2d Regt. Mass. Vols., and C. C. Coffin (Carleton) were present and took part in the services.

Address by Rev. William H. Willcox, delivered at the dedication of the Soldiers' Monument, in Reading, Oct. 5, 1865: —

ADDRESS.[1]

We are gathered here to-day, my friends, to dedicate, not merely a monument to the dead, but also a monitor to the living. That marble shaft is not simply the permanent embodiment of our admiration and gratitude for the forty-six patriots whose names it enshrines. It shall be also, through all coming years, a silent, but most impressive, preacher of patriotism to the successive generations of our town. Erected by the generous forethought of the late Abiel Holden, and the grateful co-operation of the citizens of Reading, — the gift of the dead and the living, to commemorate departed worth, — it shall ever stand between the living and the dead, not only to perpetuate the memory of the fallen, but also to rouse and stimulate the living to whatever of achievement or endurance our country may demand.

But to-day it speaks to us emphatically of the past. It reminds us of the four years of strife and blood through which, at last, the God of our fathers has triumphantly brought us. It reminds us of the brave men who so nobly turned their backs, at their country's call, upon the safety and comfort of home, and exposed themselves so cheerfully to all the toils and privations of the camp and the march, and to all the hazards of the battle-field. It reminds us of the untold sufferings they have endured in our behalf. It tells us of some wounded and dying upon the bloody field, with no sympathizing friend to alleviate their anguish, or bear their parting message ot the loved ones at home. It tells of some cast, by the fortunes of war, as prisoners into the hands of a merciless foe, by whom the simplest necessaries of life were denied them, until starvation freed them from their tormentors. It tells of some lingering long, through weary days and sleepless nights, in the soldiers' hospital; and of some, returning at length to home and friends, in the fond hope of years of health and prosperity, sinking under the assaults of disease, which they had brought with them from the swamps of the South. Their bodies slumber in far distant fields, some around us amid the graves of their fathers, and some in the soil which they baptized and made sacred with their life-blood. And thus they have in common with the thousands of their comrades who sleep, upon every battle-field, consecrated to a new life the whole land for which they died. Those Southern States, that in their madness would

---

[1] When this address was written, it was with the expectation that it was to be delivered in the open air. The request was made that it should not exceed twenty minutes in length. This must account for the absence of historical and biographical facts which otherwise the writer would gladly have presented.

have broken away from the nation, have not only failed in the suicidal attempt, — they are bound to us now more strongly and tenderly than ever before. Millions of Northern hearts feel to-day an interest in those States such as they never felt before the war, — such as they probably never would have felt had not the war arisen; for those States have become a vast cemetery, sacred with hallowed and tearful associations. Myriads of homes, all through the loyal States, have their choicest treasures deposited in the valleys of Virginia and Tennessee, and on the bloody plains of Georgia and Mississippi; and thus North and South are henceforth bound together, not only by mountain chains and navigable rivers, not only by a common Constitution and a common flag, but also by such unseen but indissoluble ties as bind the sorrowing heart to the sacred spot where rest the bones of its honored and beloved.

But it is not of the dead alone that this monument speaks, but also of the mourning kindred, of the widows and the orphans they have left behind them. Some of these are with us still, some within the sound of my voice to-day. In the name of the citizens of Reading, for whom I speak, I tender them our sincerest condolence and sympathy over their loss and ours. They have been called to suffer more deeply than we; for the war has entered their homes and their hearts, and inflicted wounds which no business prosperity, and no lapse of time, can ever wholly heal. To the loved care and blessing of Him who hath promised to be the widow's God and the Father of the fatherless, would we prayerfully commend them, with the fervent hope that their grief may be blended and softened with something of patriotic joy that they have been permitted to offer such precious sacrifices upon their country's altar.

But while this voiceful marble speaks to us thus, my friends, of what our fallen soldiers have done and suffered for you and for me, for your children and for mine, may it also speak and speak to willing ears of what we owe to the families they have left behind them. It has been said that "Republics are proverbially ungrateful." Citizens of Reading, let not the taunt find any support whatever in our treatment of the families of our fallen soldiers. We ought most cheerfully to regard them as a sacred trust, put under our guardianship by the noble men who have gone forth to battle and to die in defence of our common liberties and our common country. And it is due to ourselves, not less than to our fallen townsmen, — it is due to the patriotism of coming generations, which we ought not to stifle, but to encourage and develop, — that we do everything that can consistently be done to secure the comfort, the education, the prosperity in life of those whose natural guardians have laid down their lives for us. I know not how it may be with others ; but for myself, I can truly say that I scarcely ever see a soldier in his war-worn uniform of blue without a sense of personal indebtedness, and a feeling of personal gratitude, arising in my heart towards him. I feel somewhat as I should if he had rushed through the flames of a burning house, and at the risk of his own life saved my children from a horrible death. And so, in a measure, ought we all to feel towards the widows and the children of our unreturning soldiers, showing at once our gratitude to the heroic dead, and our own manhood in our treatment of the dependent ones they have left to our sympathy and protection.

But not of the dead alone, nor of the families of the dead, does this monument speak. Though none but the names of the fallen are chiselled upon its sides, and though it is "dedicated to the sons of Reading who died for their country in the Great Rebellion," yet should it speak to us of the living also ; of those who have borne the same burdens and exposed themselves to the same dangers, and yet have returned to us safe from amidst them all. For it is owing to no lack of courage, to no shrinking from the post of duty or of danger, that these too were not numbered among the dead. They have marched the same long and weary marches ; they have bravely and often faced the same stubborn foe ; they have fought side by side upon the same battle-fields with their fallen comrades. They are as worthy of our gratitude and praise as if their bones were now resting upon the field of Gettysburg or the Wilderness. Most heartily do we tender them our thanksgiving to-day. This monument we dedicate is a monument to their heroism and love of country, as well as to the patriotism of those who are no longer with us. It shall speak to us of the living defenders of our liberties as well as of the dead. It shall help us, I trust, to remember the debt of gratitude we owe to those who have fearlessly hazarded life and limb in the nation's defence, as well as to those whose lives have been actually paid as the price of our country's redemption.

A monument is usually the expression of regard and sorrow. And so it is with this. It is the expression in marble of our townsmen's grateful regard for those whose names the monument hands down to posterity, and of our sympathizing sorrow with the families and kindred whom their death has caused to mourn. The early loss of so many of our young men, who have shown by the heroism of their death that they were so fit to live, is surely an occasion for sorrow. And yet I cannot look upon that monument as an expression of grief alone, but also of pride and rejoicing. The darkness of our sorrow is but the shadow of a great joy. If it saddens us to remember that forty-six of our young men have been sacrificed in this war, it fills us with patriotic pride and pleasure to remember the nobleness of the cause to which their lives have been given.

In the history of ancient Rome, we are told that a vast chasm, opening in the very heart of the city, filled its inhabitants with anxiety and alarm. All efforts to fill it were vain. But on consulting the soothsayers (the historian tells us), they declared that if the Roman commonwealth was to be everlasting, the most valuable thing that Rome possessed must be sacrificed to this yawning chasm. On hearing this answer, the young hero, Marcus Curtius, deeming that Rome owned nothing more valuable than the lives of her young men, cheerfully offered himself for the sacrifice. Arraying himself in full armor, and mounting his war-horse, he leaped into the chasm and disappeared. Its horrid jaws at once closed over the victim, and Rome was again peaceful and prosperous. But the name of Marcus Curtius was not forgotten. For ages it was treasured and honored by the nation with exultant pride. His family instead of sorrowing over his loss triumphed and gloried in his sublime death.

The Roman fable has become an American fact. The demon of slavery has opened through the heart of our republic a yawning chasm, which threatened to devour not only our prosperity and peace but our very existence as a nation; and one of the most sublime spectacles the history of any people ever saw, was the zealous promptness with which, not one alone, but thousands upon thousands of our young men came forward, like Marcus Curtius, to offer themselves in sacrifice, if necessary, for the closing of the chasm and the riveting of our Union.

The work has been accomplished. The chasm has become the grave of Slavery itself, and our Union is more firmly compacted than ever before. And now, are we to look upon the death of those who have fallen in this sublime service with nothing but sorrow and mourning? Shall we not rather rejoice, as did the family of Curtius, with a patriotic joy, that our sons and brothers have died such a noble death in such a noble cause? And, if the Roman Senate erected over that closed abyss a triumphal column to give expression, not to their grief, but to their joy and pride that Rome had given birth to such a hero as Curtius, should not we, much more, look upon this monument we dedicate to-day as an embodiment of our pride and rejoicing that so many of the sons of Reading should have been willing to give life or limb for their country? It is, indeed, something of which to be proud,

— something over which we may, and should, rejoice with a patriot's joy. And in all the years that are before us, during which (as we may rationally hope) our regenerated nation is to stand before the world as this marble shaft stands on yonder hill, no longer, like Nebuchadnezzar's image, part of iron and part of clay, but homogeneous throughout, — pure, erect, symmetrical, and strong, based upon the eternal granite of justice and freedom, and crowned with the proud symbol of our nationality, spreading its guardian wings over the whole; in all these coming years it will be an occasion of grateful pride for our children, and our children's children, to point to this marble emblem of our nation's purity and power, as a monument to the patriotism of Reading in the dark days of our country's peril.

And while recording the patriotism of the past, may it perpetuate this same spirit for the future. May it inspire our young men with a new readiness for self-sacrifice and a new love for their country. May it aid them to see and to feel that it is a noble thing to suffer or to die in the cause of humanity. May it teach them — may it teach us all — that, precious as are life and home and friends, there are things far more precious still; and that no price is too great to pay for personal manhood and nobility, or for the triumph of national righteousness and constitutional freedom.

ODE BY MRS. P. H. HANAFORD.

Air — "Pleyel's Hymn."

To this sacred spot we come,
Half triumphant, half in gloom,
Thinking of the brave and blest
Gone to share a patriot's rest.

Now the marble shaft we rear, —
Hero-names recorded there,
Telling to all coming Time
Of their patriot deeds sublime.

And though far from us repose
Some that bravely met our foes,
Near or far, they all shall be
Honored by the pure and free.

Lord! may we life's conflict meet,
As they went, with willing feet;
Crowned as victors may we rise,
Meet our brave ones in the skies!

HYMN BY MISS ELIZA EVANS.

Tune — "Shining Shore."

Our fall'n heroes, glorious dead!
  In Freedom's cause enduring;
Through toil, privation, prisons, death,
  Our liberties securing.
For them we raise the sculptured pile,
  Their names we'll fondly cherish
With deep devotion in our hearts,
  When other names shall perish.

When in the nation's darkest hour,
  Rank Treason's host assailed,
Then Freedom's champions quick arose,
  And mightily prevailed.
Oppression from her seat was hurled,
  And Right became victorious;
And lasting days of peace shall crown
  The victory so glorious.

The loved have fall'n, — the true and brave
  The fearful numbers swelling:
Our mourning households, stricken, lone,
  The tale of woe are telling.
On battle plain, by treason slain,
  Their precious dust is sleeping;
God knows His own, and He, our trust,
  That hallowed dust is keeping.

Our Honored Dead! let history's page
  Record their deeds of glory,
That generations yet unborn
  May know, and read the story.
When with our Heroes we shall meet,
  Beside the peaceful river,
To God, our great Deliverer's praise,
  We'll strike our harps forever.

JAMES S. CAMPBELL,
SOLON A. PARKER, } *Trustees.*
JOSEPH L. PRATT,

O.

NAMES OF THE OWNERS OR OCCUPANTS

OF DWELLING-HOUSES IN THE FIRST PARISH (NOW WAKEFIELD) IN 1765, WITH THE NAMES OF THOSE WHO OCCUPIED THE SAME HOUSES, OR SITES, IN 1795, IN 1812, AND IN 1865, OR LATER.

1765.	1795.	1812.	1865, or later.
Rev. Wm. Hobby.	Rev. Caleb Prentiss.	Burrage Yale.	J. F. Hartshorne.
Samuel Poole.	Wid. Sam'l Poole.	Stephen Hale's Inn.	Taken down.
James Barrett.	Nathan Eaton.	Aaron Bryant.	Aaron Bryant.
Eben'r Nichols.	Thos. Rayner.	John Rayner.	Dr. J. G. Brown.
John Vinton.	—— Vinton.	Samuel Wiley.	Willis' Building.
Cornelius Wotton.	Cornelius Sweetser.	Cornelius Sweetser.	Quanapowitt House
		Joseph Bryant.	S. O. Richardson.
	Paul Sweetser.	Paul Sweetser.	Cyrus Wakefield.
Sam'l Felch.	Reuben Eaton.	Pomp Putamia.	Adam Hawkes.
Michael Sweetser.	—— Sweetser.	Paul Sweetser, Jr.	Asa N. Sweetser.
Isaac Smith.	Dr. John Hart.	Dr. John Hart.	Taken down.
Benja. Smith.	Ebenezer Smith.	Dr. Hart's old house.	Do.
Jona. Evans.	Jona. Evans.	Samuel Evans.	Do.
Daniel Gould.	—— Gould.	Tenement house.	Ezekiel Pitman.
Richard Upham.	Wid. Spear.	John Waitt.	P. H. Sweetser.
Wm. Green, Sen'r.	Aaron Green.	Aaron Green.	Chas. W. Green.
Wm. Green, Jr.	Aaron Green.	Aaron Green.	James Lord.
Thos. Green.	Daniel Green.	Chas. Green.	C. W. Green.
Capt. Dan'l Green.	—— Green.	Reuben Green.	Judge Nash.
Do. old house.	Daniel Green.	Nathan Green.	A. Drake, &c.
Lt. John Walton.	—— Walton.	Benj. Walton.	
James Smith.	H. Richardson.	Ezek'l Oliver.	Mr. Oliver.
John Smith.	T. Emerson.	T. Emerson.	Almshouse.
Amos Boardman.	Benj. Emerson.	Benj. and Peter Emerson	
Capt. Sam Bancroft.	Thos. Green.	Thos. and Jeremiah Green.	C. Wakefield. Tenement house.
Jona. Poole, Jr.	Jona. Poole.	Nath'l Wiley.	Leon'd Wiley.
Thos. Wiley.	James Wiley.	James Wiley.	Mrs. David Wiley.
Nath. Wiley.	Nath. Wiley.	Eli Wiley.	Irish family.
Ephr'm Weston.		Caleb Eaton.	Mrs. Spaulding.
Noah Eaton.	Lilley Eaton.	Jacob Eaton.	Tenement house.
Wm. Gould.	Wm. Gould.	John Gould.	Taken down.
	Jere'h Bryant.	Jere. Bryant.	A. Young.
Wm. Stimpson.	John Gould.	Lilley Eaton.	Eunice Eaton.
Thos. Burnap.	Jere'h Brown.	Jer'h Brown.	John and William Brown.
Thos. Emerson.	John Sweetser.	John Sweetser.	Dr. Cushman.
Joseph Underwood.	Do.	Do.	Dana Clayes.
Dr. Oliver Swain.	Oliver Swain.	Thos. Swain.	D. Batchelder.
Do.	—— Lewis.		A. Foster.
Thos. Parker.	Dea. T. Parker.	T. Parker.	Suel Winn.
Nath. Swain.	Jos. Burditt.	Wid. Burditt.	—— Wood.
Capt. John Swain and son.	Jacob Parker.	Issachar Stowell.	Issachar Stowell's old house.
Jeremiah Brown.	Benj. Peters.	Wid. Peters.	Ed. Upton.
Nath. Brown.	J. Brown.	John Brown, Jr.	H. Eaton.
John Walton.	O. Walton.	Oliver Walton, Jr.	—— Austin.
Jotham Walton.	Oliver Walton.	Oliver Walton.	Oliver Walton, Jr.
Jona. Brown.	—— Walton.	A. Hawkes.	D. P. Emerson.
Jona. Cowdry.	Oliver Pope.	Col. Jas. Hartshorn.	Col. J. Hartshorn.

James Emerson.	J. Emerson.	J. Emerson, Jr.	J. E. Emerson.
Eben'r Gould.	Dan'l Gould.	Charles Gould.	Clarissa Gould.
Capt. John Goodwin.	J. Goodwin.	Wid. J. Nichols.	J. Eustis.
Thos. Hay.	Amos Boardman.	Amos Boardman.	Mrs. Benj. Emerson.
Dr. Wm. Hay.	Dr. John Hay.	Dr. John Hay.	
Thos. Damon.	E. Eaton.	Benj. Swain.	Mrs. V. Holt.
Benj. Hartshorn.	James Hartshorn.	James and Jer'h Hartshorn.	Jos. Hartshorn.
Eben'r Damon.	Phineas Parker.	Suel Winn.	Mrs. Winn.
Widow Lambert.	Will'm Lambert.	David Smith	Tenement house.
Jeremiah Bryant.	J. Bryant.	Wid. J. Bryant.	Taken down.
James Bryant.	Dea. Francis Smith.	James Bouttell.	Do.
	Capt. Johnson.	Davis Foster.	Burnt.
Nath'l Cowdrey.	Nath'l Cowdrey.	Aaron Cowdrey.	H. L. Eaton.
Cap. John Goodwin.	James Nichols.	Wm. Beard & Co.	M. F. Leslie.
Joseph Gould.	J. Gould.	Wid. Newhall.	J. F. Emerson.
Joseph Emerson.	Joseph Emerson.	Eben'r Nelson.	Hon. Tho. Emerson.
John Batchelder.	T. Evans.	Thos. Evans.	Tenement house.
Munroe, formerly of Nichols.	—— Newhall.	Wm. Stimpson.	Mrs. F. B. Eaton.
John Batchelder.	J. Nutting.	Jos. Corditt.	Removed.
Gen. Benj. Brown.	B. Brown, Esq.	Thos. Clement.	Lucius Beebe.
Joseph Brown.	J. Smith.	Do. farm-house.	Taken down.
John Pratt.	Wid. Nichols, of Salem.	Tenement house.	L. Beebe.
Dea. B'wn Emerson.	Wid. Edes.	James Gould.	Dr. F. P. Hurd.
John Nichols.	David Smith.	Noah Smith.	Tenement.—C. W.
James Woodward.	T. Stimpson.	Penniman&Tileston.	W. Stimpson's heirs.
Wm. Eaton.	—— Hill.	Cornelius Sweetser.	
Ensign Hopkinson.	Dea. Hopkins.	Joseph Hopkins.	E. Sumner Hopkins.

P.

DEDICATION OF WAKEFIELD HALL.

The dedicatory exercises of the new Town House occurred on Wednesday, Feb. 22, 1871.

The day was pleasant, fulfilling in this respect the fondest anticipations, and the fact that it was the anniversary of Washington's birth made the selection all the more appropriate.

Though business in town was generally suspended, the stores closing at an early hour, our streets throughout the entire day never presented a more animated appearance. Visitors were present, not only from the towns adjoining, but from Lynn, Chelsea, Cambridge, Salem, Peabody, and other places even more distant.

The mansion of Mr. Wakefield was open during the day, and hospitalities were dispensed to all visitors.

Though the exercises did not commence until two o'clock, the people began to assemble at the building at half-past twelve ; and when the doors were opened, at half-past one, a vast audience had assembled, who eagerly made their way through the spacious entrance and up the wide stairways, and in less than fifteen minutes every available seat and standing position in the Hall was occupied, — the galleries being filled with the delighted, expectant faces of the children from the public schools. Every aisle, nook, and corner, together with the stairways, corridors, and anterooms, were thronged; and the number present could not have been less than two thousand.

In the centre of the rear gallery was stationed the Wakefield Brass Band.

At the appointed time the President of the day,— Hon. P. H. Sweetser, — Cyrus Wakefield, Esq., the town officers, and distinguished invited guests, made their appearance on the stage.

The exercises commenced by the playing of "Hail Columbia" by the Band.

Mr. Sweetser then said: —

FELLOW-CITIZENS: On this national holiday, this anniversary of the birthday of Washington, we have assembled to dedicate this edifice. The service seems to me eminently appropriate to the day; for I regard this splendid structure, with all its grand purposes, one of the legitimate fruits of the free, paternal government of our country, — a government under which laudable ambition and worthy enterprise are better stimulated and rewarded than in any other country on the face of the globe; a government, for which and all its attendant blessings, we are under greater obligation to Washington than to any other human being. It is proper on this occasion that we acknowledge the Infinite Giver of all our benefits.

Prayer was then offered by Rev. Charles R. Bliss, after which "Hail to Thee, Liberty," was finely sung by a select Choir.

The following Report of the Building Committee was then submitted by the Secretary, Daniel Allen, Esq.: —

FELLOW-CITIZENS: It will be well remembered that, during the year 1867, the erection of a Soldiers' Monument and the building of a new Town House were matters that were freely discussed among our citizens, and that during the year a Soldiers' Monument Association was organized, and a small amount of funds raised towards carrying out the purposes of the Association.

At a town-meeting held April 15, 1867, an article appeared in the warrant, to see what action the town would take in regard to erecting a Soldiers' Monument; and the subject was disposed of by choosing a Committee, consisting of Hon. Lilley Eaton, B. F. Bancroft, James M.

Sweetser, James F. Mansfield, P. H. Sweetser, James Oliver, Cyrus Wakefield, and Dr. S. O. Richardson, to take the whole matter into consideration, and report at the next town meeting.

At a town-meeting held Nov. 2, 1867, the above committee reported, that they had not been able to agree upon any definite plan in regard to a monument, and requested further time to consider the subject.

At a town-meeting held Jan. 20, 1868, the committee reported, instead of the erection of a Soldiers' Monument, that they had the pleasure to say to the town, that one of our patriotic and generous citizens had proposed to the town, through the committee, to donate to it a lot of land on the Noah Smith lot, on Main Street, of suitable size and surroundings for a Town House; also, in addition to the above donation, a sum not less than Thirty Thousand Dollars, — and an additional sum of Five Thousand more, if necessary — for the purpose of erecting a Town House, of sufficient capacity to furnish a suitable Hall for town-meetings and public lectures, a Soldiers' Memorial Hall, Room for the Town Library, Town Officers' Rooms, and Rooms for Military and Municipal purposes.

This committee also reported that another of our wealthy and liberal citizens proposed to donate the sum of One Thousand Dollars, provided the house was located on said Noah Smith lot, for the purpose of adorning and furnishing the new Town House.

The town then unanimously voted to accept both of the munificent donations, and with much enthusiasm passed a vote of thanks to the generous donors. At the suggestion of Mr. Wakefield, a Building Committee was chosen to carry out his proposition to the town, and the following persons were chosen that committee: Cyrus Wakefield, Dr. Solon O. Richardson, Hon. Lilley Eaton, Daniel Allen, P. H. Sweetser, Dr. J. D. Mansfield, and Thomas Emerson, Jr.

FEBRUARY 22. The committee met at the house of Dr. S. O. Richardson, and organized by the choice of P. H. Sweetser as Chairman and Daniel Allen as Secretary. Mr. Wakefield then gave the committee some general outlines of his plans and ideas of the building he contemplated erecting for the town, and proposed, at the next meeting of the committee, to present to them full and complete plans of the building. At the next meeting of the committee, full and complete plans *were* presented, of a building much more elaborate and expensive than the committee supposed was intended by the donor. After a very full examination and explanation of the plans, the committee unanimously voted to leave the whole subject of the erection of the building to the liberal donor.

The committee would further report: that thus far the expense of the building to the town is: Services of the Building Committee, by a vote of the town to serve without pay — Nothing. Paid by the town for land and building — Nothing. It will thus be seen that the position of the committee has been somewhat novel, but easy and pleasant. No funds to spend, no early or late suppers, no junketings; but, with our fellow-citizens, to quietly look on and witness the erection of this noble edifice, much more expensive than was proposed by the donor, fully satisfactory as well as gratifying to the committee, as we feel it must be to all our fellow-citizens.

All of which is respectfully submitted in behalf of the committee.

DANIEL ALLEN, *Secretary.*

WAKEFIELD, Feb. 22, 1871.

The reading of the report being concluded, Mr. Allen then read the deed, by which Mr. Wakefield conveyed the building to the town, as follows: —

Whereas, I, Cyrus Wakefield, of the Town of Wakefield, in the County of Middlesex and Commonwealth of Massachusetts, in consideration of my attachment to the place in which I have established and conducted the business by which I am enabled to make the gift hereinafter set forth, and in recognition of the honor conferred on me by my fellow-citizens, in giving my name to said Town, have recently erected upon the parcel of land herein described, a building designed for a Town House and for municipal uses; but also with the desire and intent that such portions thereof as are adapted thereto shall be from time to time devoted to use for patriotic, charitable, scientific, military, literary, æsthetic, educational, moral, and religious purposes, and for meetings, lectures, and addresses promotive thereof; and whereas I desire to present the said land and building as a free and unrestricted gift to said Town for its acceptance: —

Now, in consideration of one dollar to me paid, the receipt whereof is hereby acknowledged, I, the said Cyrus Wakefield, do hereby give, grant, and convey unto the said town of Wakefield, the parcel of land situated within said town, bounded and described as follows, viz.: —

Westerly by Main Street; southerly by Water Street; northerly by a new street fifty feet in width recently laid out by me; and easterly by a street sixty feet in width recently laid out by me; together with the Town Hall thereon erected by me, and all the rights, privileges, easements, and appurtenances thereto belonging. To have and to hold the same to the said town of Wakefield, to its use forever, for the uses and purposes above set forth.

In testimony whereof, I, the said Cyrus Wakefield, with Eliza A. Wakefield, my wife, in token of her release of all right of homestead and of dower in the above granted premises, have hereto set our hands and seals, this twenty-second day of February, A. D. eighteen hundred and seventy-one.

In presence of
THOMAS RUSSELL, to C. W.
GEO. H. WORTHLEY, to E. A. W.

CYRUS WAKEFIELD.
ELIZA A. WAKEFIELD.

MIDDLESEX SS., Feb. 22, 1871.

Then personally appeared the above named Cyrus Wakefield, and acknowledged the foregoing to be his free act and deed.
Before me,
LILLEY EATON, *Justice of the Peace.*

The reading of the deed was received with shouts of prolonged and enthusiastic applause.

The President then introduced Cyrus Wakefield, Esq., whose appearance was the signal for renewed cheering, waving of handkerchiefs, and demonstrative greetings such as are seldom witnessed. Mr. Wakefield delivered the following address, in a voice clear and distinct, every syllable of which was heard to the remotest corner of the hall: —

MR. PRESIDENT, LADIES AND GENTLEMEN:

The occasion which has called us together to-day is one of peculiar interest to me, as I doubt not it is to all of my fellow-townsmen here assembled, — marking, as it does, a fresh event in the growth and progress of this town, which has always sustained an enviable reputation for its enterprise in all that pertains to the industrial interests of a community, as well as for its maintenance of everything which affects the welfare of society in education, law, and religion.

Every thoughtful member of society, whatever may be his occupation, his religious creed, or bias in politics, knows that the happiness and welfare of a community are wholly dependent on the virtue and intelligence of its members. Every well-wisher to society, then, should do all in his power to encourage and sustain the various means adapted to secure to every man, woman, and child, intelligence, refinement, well being, usefulness, and virtue.

Early instruction at the fireside of home, and at the village school, deeply imbued my mind with the value of education, — a blessing which is imperishable. "It is," as has been well said, "a companion which no misfortune can depress, no clime destroy, no enemy alienate, no despotism enslave; at home a friend, abroad an introduction; in solitude a solace, in society an ornament." "Whence," said one of the most distinguished promoters of education in Massachusetts, "whence have come all those mechanical and scientific improvements and inventions which have enriched the world with so many comforts, and adorned it with so many beauties; which to-day give enjoyment and luxuries to a common family in a New England village, which neither Queen Elizabeth of England nor any of her proud court ever dreamed of, but a little more than two centuries ago? All history and experience affirm that they have come, and must come, from the people among whom education is most generous and unconfined. These are the results which you can no more have without common education, without imbuing the public mind with the elements of knowledge, than you can have corn without planting, or harvests without sunshine."

This truth is obvious to every one who has been a student of the history and growth of our civilized community. And for myself I can truly say, that though from early youth to the present time my life has been one of constant, daily activity in business pursuits, yet have I never lost sight of the fact that all the blessings of social life are given us on one condition, that of intelligence, viz. education — intellectual, moral, and religious. This truth, indelibly stamped upon my mind in early life, has been more and more deeply engraven there by the observation and reflection of maturer years. And to-day, more than ever before, do I love and respect that time-honored institution established by our fathers almost at the moment they set foot upon this, our New England soil. I mean the common school. We are all proud of our free public schools, — and justly so; for they make education co-extensive with the community. They place the children of the rich and the poor on a level, as regards the advantages of intellectual culture. It is education, and it ends in general intelligence, which makes labor reputable and the laborer respected; a result, which in this country gives the workingmen a place in society, not merely as laborers, — furnishing for others the comforts and luxuries of life, — but as MEN, claiming an equal share in all the domestic, civil, and religious privileges of freemen.

Out of universal education come talent, skill, and enterprise. All the improvements in mechanical and useful arts, whether in greater or smaller operations, come as directly from intelligence as the light from the sun. The pursuits and attainments which constitute, adorn, and elevate civilized life, wherever a sound education is given, grow up as naturally as an oak grows out of an acorn.

The various and almost infinite improvements in machinery, in implements of husbandry, and all those ingenious inventions which have enriched this part of the country, and helped to build up the prosperity of other communities, as well as our own, have come from minds which have had an early awakening by being put on scientific trains of thought in the common school.

The late Hon. Edward Everett, when Governor of this State, in a public address on education, exhorted the fathers and mothers of Massachusetts in these words: "Save," said he, "save, spare, scrape, stint, starve, do anything but steal, to educate your children." And I doubt not that every father and mother in this audience heartily responds to this sentiment of Massachusetts' great scholar and statesman. Yes,

"'T is education forms the common mind."

Domestic training and the public schools are the means of moulding the mind. They give the first impulse and direction to the thoughts and cast to the feelings of the young. They are the springs or fountain-heads of education. From them commences the flow of that stream of virtue and intelligence in youth, which, as we grow to maturity, widens and deeps by the influx of its many tributaries, until it becomes the majestic river, in its onward course to swell the great sea of universal knowledge.

When we leave the public school our education is, as it were, just begun. We have but come into possession of that rudimentary knowledge which awakens the mind to a desire for higher attainments, and gives it the power of progress. On leaving the school we enter upon the various occupations of life, its duties and responsibilities. But the mind hungers and thirsts for knowledge, and needs its natural aliment for daily sustenance and growth, as much as the body. The advantages of higher institutions of learning, of colleges and universities, are available to but few. To meet, therefore, this need and demand of the great body of the people, it is necessary that such means and institutions for mental advancement should be established in every community as will not interfere with the daily vocations of life, and such as can be made available at a small cost. Hence have arisen the evening school, the Sunday school, and the town library, accessible to all. We have also the cheap weekly and monthly periodicals, and that great educator, the daily newspaper, all of which are placed within the reach of every class of the community, and, thanks to our public schools, can be understood and appreciated by all, — the mechanic, the farmer, and the day-laborer, as well as the professional scholar. We have, also, for the advancement of education, discourses delivered, sermons preached, conventions held, and associations formed. And one of the most popular and important means for the promotion of general intelligence, for preserving from neglect or perversion the knowledge acquired in the public school, for enlarging its boundaries and strengthening its foundations, is the lyceum. Through its lectures, disquisitions, and discussions, the lyceum becomes a powerful educational force. Here, in a few hours and for a small price, we are presented with the results of years of hard study and research, as conducted by the ablest thinkers, investigators, and explorers in the vast realms of science, history, and philosophy ; and not less so with the practical fruits of personal application and inventive industry which are gleaned by the diligent hand of the artisan.

It is here we are instructed in many of the most important points, in all departments of useful and entertaining knowledge, whether within the range of science, strictly so called, or miscellaneous and useful information. The great leading truths of abstract science are here brought down to their direct and useful applications, in all the varied forms which the actual business of life or the interesting associations of thought prescribe for our guidance.

Discussion and investigation of such themes, it is needless to say, serve equally the purpose of advancing, in degree, the field of human knowledge, and of enlarging and enriching our sources of true and noble enjoyment.

To the observer of human progress throughout New England, the fact is familiar that the foundation of a village library is often found to be the first of a long succession of onward steps in the general diffusion of knowledge, whether popular or scientific. But for the full accomplishment of the purposes of the benevolent founders of such institutions, the addition to the village library of a permanent course of instructive lectures has always been found indispensable. And wherever, in the local history of our communities, the order just referred to has been inverted, and a course of popular lectures on the applications of science has taken the lead, the establishment of a library has always been sure to follow as a result. A judicious course of lectures naturally leads the general mind to an earnest desire for opportunities for acquiring more thorough and extensive knowledge on the subjects whose elements have been successfully presented.

In many of our New England villages, accordingly, the village library and the lyceum course of lectures have gone on, hand in hand, mutually strengthening and enlarging each other. Hence the New England village of to-day so often proves itself the worthy successor of that whose foundations were laid amid the uncertainties and deficiencies of earlier times. Nor can we advert to such facts without indulging in a glance at what the larger future so surely offers to those who shall succeed us in the cultivation and improvement of all social opportunities of general advancement in enlarging knowledge and its consequent advantages.

In these institutions, then, — the library and the lyceum, — which throw open their doors of invitation to the whole community, we have secured to us the definite and practical means of a wide and ample diffusion of knowledge and of intellectual enjoyment.

To secure and make permanent such results, therefore, every town or village needs a building of ample and inviting accommodations, for a library and lyceum hall ; and, my friends, it has been with special reference to this need that the building in which we are now assembled has been erected. And with the confident assurance of your efficient co-operation in advancing the common well-being, it is now thrown open to you, fellow-citizens, for the purposes already mentioned, and placed at your disposal, in whatever form you shall deem most appropriate for the accomplishment of the purposes to which it is devoted.

As a body of freemen, it is your social home for the enjoyment of every noble privilege which a gracious Providence has made the peculiar blessing of our common New England life, as members of the great national community on the grand footing of equal rights and privileges, the most exalted in their character and the most enduring in their stability with which humanity has yet been favored.

In compliance with the arrangements assigned for the occasion, I have little further part to perform than to propose your acceptance of this edifice, as proffered for the purposes already mentioned. May it long continue to benefit you and yours in all the relations of life, — civil, social, and individual! To all your families may it ever prove, on a larger scale, an efficient means to the wider diffusion of social and intellectual enjoyment, when the coming years of our great national future shall have rendered their accumulated additions to the general well-being of humanity!

My only remaining duty, in further compliance with the arrangements of the day, is to surrender to your trust and keeping, Mr. Chairman, as a representative of your fellow-citizens, in this transaction, the KEYS of this edifice, and, virtually, the control of its future arrangements.

I hereby, accordingly, give and make over to you, sir, personally, these keys, and with them the sole charge and disposal of these halls, in connection with the purposes for which they were erected.

Mr. Wakefield closed by formally presenting the title-deed and keys of the building to the Chairman of the Selectmen, Richard Britton, Esq., who replied as follows:—

SIR: It falls to my lot, in behalf of the Board of Selectmen, to accept, in the name of the town, your munificent gift. The offer made by you to the people of Wakefield, some months since, has received a fulfilment which has far exceeded their expectations. You now place at their disposal a public edifice, unsurpassed for the beauty of its architectural designs, the thoroughness of its workmanship, the convenience of its numerous apartments, and the elegance of this spacious and magnificent hall. The citizens of Wakefield appreciate the liberality which has so far exceeded your first generous proposals, and they honor the public spirit which has provided for the wants of the future in meeting those of the present. They reciprocate your well-known sentiments upon popular education, and the best means of perpetuating its advantages, after the school-room shall have been exchanged for the scenes of active life. The library, the lyceum, and the scientific lecture are but the common school carried into maturer years; and it is a matter of common congratulation that we now have a building so well adjusted to these and other uses. They think with you, also, that the affairs of municipal bodies can be conducted with economy and efficiency only when suitable and safe offices for public business are established under one roof, and within reach of various public records; and upon the attainment of these objects, so long deferred and so long needed, they congratulate each other. Recent events, too, have taught us all that the world has not yet passed beyond the need of military organizations, and that it is the part of true wisdom to keep in training a small force of drilled soldiers, competent to meet the nation's emergencies when they shall arise; and those same events have laid upon those who survived the terrific shock of war the most solemn obligations to keep fresh and green the memory of those who fell. These objects, too, which commend themselves equally to our patriotism and our grateful memories, have received abundant and faithful care within these walls. And believe me, sir, all classes of our people are deeply thankful to you for a gift so costly and noble in itself, and so well adapted to these already pressing and growing needs. Look into the faces of your neighbors and friends before you: do you not see their gratitude? Look at the faces of these children in the galleries, who for a generation to come will reap the fruits of your beneficence: do you not read their joy and their thanks?

Sir, we accept this noble structure as a sacred trust. May it long stand a monument of your forethought and generosity! For yourself, sir, may your prosperity continue; may your widening plans be fulfilled; may your life be spared till old age shall come, and then may you be gathered in peace and hope to that better land!

The following dedicatory hymn, by Hon. P. H. Sweetser, was then sung to the tune of *America*, by the choir and children of the public schools, under the direction of Solon Walton, Esq., the audience rising and joining in the same: —

>Thanks to our God belong!
>Praise Him with joyful song,
>   Extol his name!
>Within this temple's walls,
>Through its resounding halls,
>Where'er His mercy falls,
>   His love proclaim!

>May this be Learning's home,
>Where youth and age shall come
>   For precious lore;
>For light to shine abroad
>Along life's darksome road,
>Brighter than gift bestowed
>   Of shining ore.

>May those who congregate
>For counsel and debate,
>   Within these walls,
>Exclude all party hate:
>Loyal to home and state,
>To truth be consecrate,
>   As duty calls.

>A nobler gift we own
>Than other climes have known,
>   At princes' cost!
>God of our fathers' land,
>Long may this building stand,
>In purpose wise and grand,
>   Our pride and boast!

> Speed on the happy day
> When all shall choose the way
>   The wise have trod;
> And may this temple be,
> This offering rich and free,
> Honored and blest of Thee,
>   The mighty God!

Hon. Lilley Eaton then delivered the following address:—

MR. PRESIDENT, AND LADIES AND GENTLEMEN:

Rising to speak, for the first time, from this high position,— as I look around upon this multitude of earnest eyes and expectant countenances, this throng of the youth and beauty, the fashion and chivalry, the rank and file of our village and its environs, and find myself standing within these spacious and elaborately finished walls, beneath this lofty ceiling, which is bright and radiant with iridescent and artistic taste and lustre, and realize that I am in the presence of the learned, the honorable, the reverend, the venerable,— among statesmen, philosophers, and poets; and when I call to mind the interesting and eloquent speeches, and animating music, to which we have just been listening, and have respect, in anticipation, to the flowing verse and other exercises that are still to come, with hallowed memories of the sainted and majestic character of *him* whose honored birthday this is, mingling with other stirring suggestions,— although my breast swells with the excitement and inspiration of the occasion, and emotions too big for *my* utterance seem welling up within me; yet, in view of all the attendant circumstances, I find myself totally unable to command language with which to express my emotions, or suited to meet the just expectations of this audience. For here let me say, that I occupy this position, not from any supposed *peculiar* ability to discharge its duty, but by the favor of the Committee of Arrangements, who in this case, having more regard to *age* than to talent, have thought that, because I have been somewhat closely identified with the history and progress of the town for the last half-century, it was therefore proper that I should have a place in the programme of exercises on this interesting and crowning occasion; and in an unguarded moment I assented to the arrangement. I am consoled, however, with the reflection, that whatever I may lack has already been abundantly supplied by those who have preceded me, and will be more than made up by those who are to follow.

Mr. President, we have heard, in the report of the Building Committee, as read by their Secretary, a brief history of the enterprise which culminates in this day's celebration. From that report we learn that our illustrious fellow-citizen, who, some three years ago, proposed to erect, at his own expense, a building suitable for municipal, scientific, and other purposes, and would present the same, with a lot of land, to the town of Wakefield, has most honorably and overflowingly redeemed his promise, and more than met the most sanguine expectations of all.

We have now witnessed, with pleasing and graceful ceremonies, the conveyance of this splendid property to the town of Wakefield. This beautiful civic temple, with its eligible site and all its numerous, ample, and elegant conveniences, is now all our own. The cost and intrinsic value of the property considerably exceed what the whole real and personal estate of all the inhabitants of the town was appraised at by the town assessors within my own recollection; and it comes to the town the free gift of the munificent donor.

We have listened, with much interest and delight, to the eloquent words, the kindly wishes, and the valuable suggestions with which the donor has accompanied the delivery of the title-deed and keys of the premises to the possession and custody of the town authorities; we have highly enjoyed the pleasant and successful manner in which the ceremony of the reception thereof has been performed by the chairman of the Board of Selectmen. And we, the people, are now here to ratify the official acceptance, and to signify for ourselves our warmest gratitude for this rich and noble present; we are here to consecrate this building, with its appurtenances, to the important objects of its erection; and with invocations and petitions, with music and poetry, with sentiment and song, to express our joyful congratulations and thanksgiving, and to render to Heaven the tribute of our sincere and devout acknowledgments for the bestowal of that influence that induced our friend to make this princely donation.

We accept, with modest diffidence and pleasure, the very complimentary allusions of the donor to the character and enterprise of his adopted fellow-citizens; we concur most sincerely with him in his high appreciation of the value and importance, to the rising generation, of education, and an early training in the practical principles of science and art, and the higher principles of morality and virtue, in order to secure an intelligent, moral, skilful, successful, and happy community; and we fully agree with him in his opinion of the adaptedness of common schools, free libraries, and public, scientific, and moral lectures, to the promotion of such education and training. We rejoice, therefore, that our friend, who has heretofore contributed to the encouragement of our schools, has now given this further and signal proof of the sincerity of his convictions, by furnishing such ample arrangements for the public library, public lectures, and other municipal and social purposes, as that now we have accommodation for an indefinite increase of books, maps, pictures, and works of art, and lecture room sufficient for the tallest orators.

Mr. President, I shall not attempt to give a particular, technical description of this fine building and all its numerous accommodations; it is not necessary to do so; for you have seen it and it speaks for itself. But I will refer briefly to some of its more important subdivisions and conveniences, and the purposes to which we would consecrate them.

Behold this beautiful and capacious municipal, civic Hall, with its wide area, its extensive galleries, its comfortable and substantial settees, its broad and commanding forum, its adjacent corridors and anterooms, its lofty canopy, its elaborate and æsthetic finish, and its capacity for holding its thousands!

The purposes to which we trust this fine room will ever be devoted are municipal, scientific, patriotic, industrial, charitable, social, and moral. Here let the citizens assemble, exercise the right of franchise, transact their municipal business, discuss important local and public questions, and proclaim the principles of American liberty, independence, and union. Here let the people come to listen to the eloquent and gifted, who shall here pour forth, from time to time, the treasures of knowledge, of science, and of wisdom. Here may the muses delight to resort, and chant the melodious strains of music and poetry. Here may the true spirit of patriotism, of equity, and of philanthropy ever reign and excite. Here upon this stage may our rising youth, catching the inspiration of the place, be trained in those practices of public speaking and debate that shall enable them, in subsequent life, at home or elsewhere, to defend the right with eloquent ability, in whatever exigency may arise. And may this costly and excellent Hall, now clean and nice, never be desecrated by any low, rude, or immoral occupation, but be carefully preserved in its present purity and elegance.

Below and under this main hall, on either side of the Ionic Hall, with its capital-crowned pillars and tessellated pavement, are other rooms, designed for various important public and useful purposes. On the one side, in front, are rooms for town officers, large, light, and convenient, with fire-proof safety vaults to protect the municipal records and treasures. On the same side, in the rear, is a large room, convenient for many civic purposes, sometimes called the court-room, where, we trust, whenever it shall be used as such, the scales of justice in the hands of those whose sacred ermine shall be unsullied, will ever give that "just weight which is the delight of the Lord." On the other side of the Ionic Hall, in front, is the Library Room, of ample size, fitted up with much cost, convenience, and elegance, and with especial reference to providing for a large increase of books, the funds for which are already secured; where the "Beebe Town Library," so named from a munificent patron, is to be installed, and where the fountains of knowledge, bursting forth from ten thousand springs, shall ever flow with refreshing and reviving influences. On the same side, in the rear, is the Soldiers' Memorial Hall, to be decorated and made interesting with tablets of marble, inscriptions, busts, medallions, portraits, trophies, and other mementoes of the heroes, dead and living, who were connected with the Union army in the late War of the Rebellion. These decorations, as yet incomplete, are being furnished from the voluntary contributions of the loyal citizens, and are especially designed to render this hall a place where the names and the memory and the laurels of those young warriors of our town who died for their country and for freedom, shall be kept forever fresh and green; and where our children and children's children and their successors shall early learn to love patriotism and valor, and to hate cowardice and treason. Above this main hall are rooms for our military bulwark, where our guardsmen shall deposit their arms, and equipments and where our young men shall meet to stir up one another's brave minds in love of country and of liberty, learn the science of war, and be trained in those exercises that shall qualify and enable them to do in the future as they have repeatedly done in the past, viz. rally at a moment's notice, don their armor, and march to the defence of their country. These military rooms are to be fitted up and furnished in tasty and convenient style from funds generously given by the foster-father of the Richardson Light Guard, the "beloved physician" who has long been a sincere friend and liberal patron of that excellent and popular corps.

Above also, and adjoining the military rooms, is the social Banquet Hall, roomy and commodious, which we hope will ever be open to all the gatherings of friendship and philanthropy, to all innocent festive occasions, and all useful meetings for which it is adapted.

And so (without further detail) this whole edifice, with all its many suitable and beautiful appurtenances and belongings, including the latest and most approved modes of heating and warming, is now donated, conveyed, and consecrated, to be from henceforth for the free use of the inhabitants of Wakefield for all useful purposes. May we who are the fortunate recipients of this rich gift, and our successors, ever show our gratitude therefor, and our appreciation of its value, by a wise improvement of its facilities.

Mr. President, let us not forget that this building stands on historic, classic, and hallowed ground. Here, one of the early and learned Puritan divines, the second minister of this town, erected his family altar more than two centuries ago ; here he courted the muses, here studied, and went hence to preach philosophy and ethics to the early settlers, and here sought that power his youthful muse to inspire,

" That touched Isaiah's hallowed lips with fire."

Here, too, were the birthplace and home of some of the most eminent, honorable, and revered sons of our town. The venerable mansion that was recently removed to give place for this structure, which was the home of that eminent divine, and had sheltered many generations of his successors, still stands in near proximity. Long may it remain, a relic of the olden time and a memento of departed worth ! Let us rejoice that this ancient site is still to be historic and classic ; that in the shadow of that retreating old parsonage this lofty temple has arisen, — massive, towering, grand, capacious, convenient, beautiful ; sacred to social, scientific, and moral improvement and happiness.

Towards heaven it lifts its turret fair,
With golden dials beaming :
The nation's flag is waving there,
With starry banner streaming.

Mr. President, while we admire this fine house, in its skilful design and artistic execution, let us not omit to award due credit and commendation to the accomplished architect whose wisdom planned it, and to the ingenious mechanics whose cunning hands have fashioned this complete and elegant work ; like the laborers who built Bunker Hill Monument, may they, in the sentiment of the immortal Webster, look up and around here, and be proud of the results of their toil.

And what shall we say of *him*, the moving, living cause of the grand result that we this day celebrate ; of him whose generous impulses and wise regard for the people's welfare first originated the plan and objects of this important work ; of him whose inexhaustible generosity and apparently inexhaustible purse were fully equal to the utmost extent of the architectural pencil, in its demands for magnitude, proportion, convenience, artistic taste, and beauty; of him who now turns it all over a free gift to the town of his adoption, the ancient home of his ancestors; of him who is now the cynosure of all eyes, the exponent of munificence, the Leo of the occasion, — our godfather, our namesake, and our friend? Of him I am led to exclaim, O fortunate man! Fortunate in possessing that business skill and enterprise that have enabled him, in honest trade, to amass the means of his unbounded liberality. *Unbounded* liberality, we say, for we forget not that this rich gift is only one of many emanating from that abundant liberality on which might justly be inscribed the stately motto, *E pluribus unum*. Fortunate man, we repeat, in having been favored of heaven with a disposition to avail himself of the heavenly sentiment that "it is more blessed to give than to receive"! Fortunate in being moved to expend his means upon objects of high, generous, and permanent usefulness, thus securing the power to enjoy the sweetest kind of earthly felicity, viz. a consciousness of having made others wise, useful, and happy! This sweet felicity may he long live to realize! Long may he have the delightful satisfaction of witnessing, going forth from the recesses of this beautiful temple, the light of knowledge, of science, and of liberty, and the principles of good order, justice, and philanthropy. And after he shall have become fully rich in the merchandise of wisdom, and shall have fully served his generation here below, may he find an abundant entrance and welcome and home in the Celestial Temple, the house not made with hands, eternal in the heavens; and may the memory of his name and good deeds long live after him, and their influence bless posterity.

John S. Eaton, Esq., then pronounced the following poem, written by himself for the occasion: —

> He who performeth noble deeds,
>   Rears temples with his gold, —
> For him the future hath its meeds,
>   His fame the centuries hold!

> And he whose own unaided power
>   Makes shining treasure his,
> Then scatters it, — a golden shower, —
>   The grandest victor is!

APPENDIX.

Wearing to-day no regal crown,
    Unheralded by drums,
Yet laurelled with a high renown,
    Cyrus the conqueror comes.

For he, a youth, within the fold
    Of hills that shut him in,
Beheld, as on a map unroll'd,
    The trophies he might win.

Unfettered, from that mountain door
    His daring thought outwent;
In dreams he held — as now, *in store* —
    Wealth of the Orient.

Uprose the height he fain would tread,
    Bright flashing in the sun;
His tireless steps then upward sped,
    And the rich prize was won!

Now at his wish earth's agents yield;
    Steam and the winds his slaves,
Speeding his forces, myriad-wheeled,
    His products o'er the waves.

An army marches at his word,
    Guiltless of battle stains;
No sabre in their ranks, nor sword,
    Their only weapons, — *canes*.

Where'er this powerful army moves,
    Along these plains of ours,
Vave musical the leafy groves, —
    And in its footsteps, flowers.

Their leader's keen, sagacious glance
    Brings distant thousands near,
And in the van of their advance,
    Old landmarks disappear.

The levelled hill, with smoother sod,
    Discloses lovelier views;
The narrow lane and winding road
    Stretch straight, broad avenues.

The quaint old roofs of earlier days
    Scarce meet our vision more;
While statelier dwellings in their place
    Embellish slope and shore.

Thus, while the ancient relics fade,
    And vanish from our view,
Our town, in fresher robes arrayed,
    Prepares to greet the *new!*

March on, transforming army, march,
    With beauty crown each vale!
While we inscribe on laurelled arch, —
    "*Cyrus, the prince, all hail!*"

. . . . . .

It stands complete, — this promised gift, —
    Munificent and fair;
Skyward its pointed turrets lift,
    Cleaving the wintry air.

Complete each graceful arch and niche,
    Complete from base to tower;
While all its ample walls are rich
    With scroll and leaf and flower.

A gift so precious and so grand,
    So excellent and rare,
The rhythmic praise at our command
    Seems incomplete and bare.

We note in this exalted gift,
    One name outshines the rest,
As one tall pine may grandly lift
    Above a mountain crest,

High o'er the trees whose branches throw
    Their shadows at its feet, —
Yet *valued all*, the high, the low,
    The landscape to complete;

So in this glittering coronet
    We have a *central gem*,
While *lesser jewels*, proudly set,
    Complete our diadem.

Secure, these lofty walls shall hold
    Their wealth of classic lore;
Bright gems of thought in leaves of gold, —
    A rich, increasing store;

A fountain ever full and free,
    Alike for age and youth.
Perpetual may its blessings be,
    Drawn from the wells of truth!

APPENDIX.

Secure, these guarded vaults retain
  Their records, worn and brown;
The olden records which remain, —
  The archives of the town.

This ample and attractive room,
  With tasteful colors bright,
Shall bring to thousands, as they come,
  An *ever new* delight.

And from this platform, which *we* tread
  With diffidence and doubt,
Scholastic essays shall be read,
  And polished lines go out;

And Music, here, its notes shall lend,
  In melodies most sweet;
Science and Art, congenial, blend,
  To make its charms complete.

While, over all, in ordered line,
  Keeping sure watch and ward,
The burnished barrels, silent, shine, —
  The muskets of the "Guard."

And here the rich "Memorial Hall"
  Its precious names shall hold;
Its roll of honor, 'neath the pall;
  Its heroes, framed in gold.

Their fame shall fadeless marbles tell
  Through all the coming time,
Who 'neath the Starry Banner fell,
  And made their deaths sublime.

New lustre, then, shall gild their names,
  As the bright years increase,
Who died in battle's awful flames
  To give their children — *Peace*.

And here, on freedom's holy ground,
  Her green slopes bright with dew,
For earnest souls, it shall be found,
  Peace hath *her* triumphs, too.

Marches progressive, now begun,
  Will test the zeal of youth;
For he with tireless steps must run
  That holds the race with Truth!

The Future on the glorious heights
    Marshals her shining ones,
And to the fields of bloodless fights
    Summons her fearless sons.

Her white tents grace the shadowy hill;
    I see her camp-fires gleam;
I hear her bugles, echoing shrill
    From mountain-peak and stream;

I hear the mustering of the hosts,
    Her thousands fair and strong, —
To reach the high, commanding posts,
    For conflict with the Wrong.

Those legions, girt with strength from Heaven,
    And panoplied in light, —
To them, rich conquests shall be given,
    The victories of *Right!*

. . . .

While the procession of the years
    Its steady march shall keep,
In time with the revolving spheres,
    In their sublimer sweep, —

Here may this massive temple stand,
    Unmarred its walls and pave, —
Memorial, undecayed and grand,
    Of princely hands which gave;

Bearing its treasures rich and fair
    Unstained as in their prime,
With all its cherished emblems, there,
    Down to the latest time!

Greet it, earliest light of the dawn;
    Let it bathe in the golden day;
And radiant tints, from the sunset drawn,
    On its turrets linger and play!

"These moments entrancing," was next sung by the choir. The President, Hon. P. H. Sweetser, then made the following congratulatory address: —

It was said of Hannibal that all he needed to complete his martial virtue was, that when he had gained a victory he should know how to use it. I think, ladies and gentlemen, *we* shall not say of our distinguished fellow-citizen, to whom we are indebted for this splendid and commodious edifice, that, having gained treasures, he does not know how to use them.

It has been common for those who possess great wealth to hold on to it, as with a miser's grasp, until, in the providence of God, their palsied hands *must* let it go; and then, perchance, to leave it to contentious heirs, or bequeath it in some direction where the half of it never should be heard of more.

The pious Baxter put aside a sum of money with which he intended to endow a school. By some fatality the money was all lost. He blamed himself for the misfortune, and resolved never to defer another opportunity for doing good.

Our late distinguished fellow-countryman, Mr. Peabody, is widely known and honored for his more than princely benefactions. He seemed to appreciate the poet's sentiment, that charity is twice blessed, blessing him that gives and him that takes; he seemed to believe that money invested for the well-being of mankind returns a higher and surer interest than stocks and bonds; that while commerce brings gold, generosity makes it permanent *gain*.

Other wealthy individuals, prompted, I trust, by the precepts and example of Him who went about doing good, are performing noble deeds by contributing of their ample means to promote the welfare of their fellow-men.

I congratulate you, fellow-citizens, that *we* are the recipients of a costly bounty, and that we receive it from one of our own citizens, whose worthy ambition, and splendid enterprise, and public spirit, and liberal hand have won for him the treasures and the honors he enjoys.

We did not expect, when we heard that a Town Hall would be erected for us, such a temple as this. It is builded costlier and better than we knew. What the giver intended, I cannot say; but he has given us a surprise. Surprises are sometimes dangerous. Let us endeavor to bear this with becoming fortitude, and turn it to the best account.

You are aware that this is not the first token of Mr. Wakefield's regard for the interests of the town. The beautiful diploma, which, for several years, our High School graduates have received, and which those who hereafter graduate will receive, is an evidence of his desire to stimulate the young in the pursuit of knowledge, and of his appreciation of the value of education. His address, to which we have all listened with delight, clearly evinces that the education of the people is an object very precious in his sight.

Mr. Peabody, to whom I have alluded, on a public occasion expressed the following sentiment: "Education — a debt due from present to future generations." I know that this sentiment has the hearty approval of Mr. Wakefield; that it is, indeed, his sentiment. I know it is his desire that this town especially, whose educational reputation first attracted his attention and induced him to locate here, shall preserve and increase its educational privileges, and transmit them to its future generations.

And I rejoice that his liberality is not restricted by the limits of a town; his public spirit and his generous purse are known abroad; his generosity is becoming chronic. Who will remonstrate if it become contagious? If our ever-vigilant Chief Magistrate should learn that it was spreading into other towns in the Commonwealth, especially in the form in which it is presented to our delighted vision here to-day, I do not believe he would hasten to appoint Commissioners to stay its progress; but that, instead, he would exclaim, "All right! Let it spread!"

In the old Town Hall — the first that I remember; and that in which many of us cast our first ballots — there was but a single room, and a single key gave entrance to all its accommodations. A large bunch of keys is required to open the various halls and rooms of this commodious structure. It is a noble edifice, grand in purpose, admirable in design, costly and beautiful in build and finish; an honor to the town of Wakefield, and to the renowned old Commonwealth of Massachusetts.

For myself, as a citizen of the town, I thank the noble donor for his munificent benefaction. For the more than four thousand inhabitants of the town of Wakefield, I tender heartfelt, earnest thanks. And I am justified in saying that the people's gratitude to Mr. Wakefield will increase, as the privileges and blessings he has conferred upon them shall be accepted and enjoyed.

I cannot doubt that the citizens of the town will receive the gift with a desire, and with the purpose to regard the donor's wishes in relation to its use. And I know his aspirations will be satisfied, if the keys which unlock these material doors shall be the medium to unlock human hearts; to open to the light of truth and knowledge immaterial and imperishable minds.

The Secretary of the Building Committee, Mr. Allen, here read a letter from His Excellency Gov. Claflin, regretting his inability to share in the delights of the occasion.

Dr. George B. Loring, of Salem, was introduced to the audience, and spoke as follows: —

LADIES AND GENTLEMEN:

I have listened with great interest to the exercises of the afternoon, in which your own citizens have in graceful and appropriate phrase dedicated the gift which your generous townsman has made, and around which he has woven his own well-expressed views upon the value and importance of education to a free community.

But it is not alone the liberality of him who has presented this beautiful hall to the town which bears his name, that we are called upon to remember; for there is a significance in the gift itself which should not escape our notice. The earth is strewn with representative and significant structures, designed to mark the memorable events of history, or to perpetuate the memory of the great and good, or adapted to the civilization by which they are surrounded. The forms of heroes have been preserved with ideal beauty in marble and bronze; to the memory of saints has the grandeur of churches and cathedrals arisen; to gratify a depraved and savage taste, the splendors of the amphitheatre have been dedicated; to mark the lines of social distinction, gorgeous and resplendent halls have been devoted. To art and architecture do we owe the elaborate and interesting records which man has left behind him of his religious faith, his personal distinction, his social relations, and his civil institutions. All around us stand the monuments which he has erected to himself, to society, the church, and the state. Among these significant structures shall stand this building, which you now dedicate to the intellectual and civil service of this town. Here may the inquiring mind find opportunity to traverse the paths of knowledge, led by those who, in the form of public address, would instruct their fellow-men. Here may the municipal duties of this thriving and prosperous town be discharged in a manner worthy of intelligent freemen, clothed with the responsibilities of citizenship. Tell me, if you can, what nobler structure can arise than that which has for its foundation the cultivated mind and the broadest civil freedom of an American community. Nowhere but in our own land is a place to be found for such a public edifice, — a hall for popular lectures, and a citadel for the defence of the highest popular rights. You may well congratulate yourselves on the possession. You may well congratulate yourselves that prosperity has attended the path of one who knows so well how to use her gifts.

To the old and the young I would commend the example of your benefactor. Recognizing the privileges which are the inheritance of every American, he has done what he could to perpetuate them. An enterprising citizen, he would develop an enterprising town. I am sure he learned in his youth the value of public instruction and the advantages to be derived from courteous demeanor in public places. And we have before us a noble illustration of that mature wisdom and philanthropy which gave Wakefield a name, and opened these ample doors for the instruction and elevation of her people.

Judge Thomas Russell, collector of the port of Boston, who was introduced as "a citizen of no mean city," made the subjoined address: —

MY FRIENDS: I am glad to have the opportunity of joining with you as you dedicate this magnificent building to free government, to loyalty, and to enlarged education. The sunshine without is reflected on your faces; and how happily you have united the past, present, and future. We are all enjoying the present; Mr. Eaton has told us of the past; and when you announce the Governor of the Commonwealth, and then call upon Dr. Loring for a speech, you certainly borrow from the future.

But what shall I say? As I looked at your long order of exercises, all to be exhausted before dinner, I thought not of your poet, but of Gray's famous ode on "A Distant Prospect of Eton." Yet variety and fitness have made the exercises seem short; and I am still without a subject. I looked to the children in the galleries, and thought how soon this town would be ruled by these boys — and girls. (O wise forethought! which doubled the size of this hall, so that the men in a few years might bring their wives and sisters with them to town-meeting.) I was glad, not only to see the boys, but to hear them. Even their shrillest whistles reminded me of the young declaimer, who thus repeated a famous passage of Chatham: "The poor man's house is his castle; the wind may whistle round it; but the King of England cannot whistle in it." Long life to these young republicans, and may they never know rattan, except as a material for manufacture! And the sight of these boys and girls suggested education as a fit theme for the day; but Mr. Wakefield has already said all that can be said on that subject, and more than he has said he had done long ago. Before coming here I had glanced at a geographical gazette, and learned that the thriving town of Wakefield, in Yorkshire, was most famous for its grammar school, from which have gone some of the first scholars of England. It is a happy coincidence that the name has already been associated with devotion to learning. To-day we have one illustration more of the effect of education: the wealth, of which this generous gift is a fragment, sprung from a humble red school-house in New Hampshire.

I would have spoken of towns, and of the influence of town-meetings on American history; but that subject has already been made familiar to you. Only let me say this, Does any one think this hall more spacious than is needed? Then let treason raise its head once more, let rebellion again threaten the Union, and every inch of space shall be thronged by your loyal people. Nor would the living come alone. Every name on those marble tablets beneath would be represented. From hospital and prison and battle-field your departed heroes would rally once more for the endangered land and the insulted flag.

The building is a natural subject of remark, but it speaks for itself. From foundation stone, from Ionic pillar, from frescoed ceiling, come praises of that spirit which gains wealth, not for sullen hoarding, not for selfish pleasure, but for wise and beneficent liberality. I admired the report of your committee. Indeed, I always admire Farmer Allen. Years ago when I went as a boy to hear him lecture, I used to wonder whether he was not connected with the Daniel of whom we read; and I was inclined to believe it, because that Daniel's countenance, also, was "fairer and fatter" than the faces of his neighbors. No wonder that the lions would not eat him, we used to think, as we pictured them listening all night to his stories, and roaring, not with rage but with laughter.

You must all have been pleased with the financial part of the report, "Services and expenses of building committee — nothing." Your expenses down to zero; the generosity of your fellow-citizens up to fever heat. It is one benefit of such gifts as this, that they stimulate other givers. Mr. Wakefield was not without generous example at home, but his own example seems to have inspired him most, for beginning with a promise of thirty thousand dollars, he ends with this munificent donation. He wisely enjoys his gifts, instead of postponing his liberality till his estate ceases to be his own. The poet says: —

"Die, and endow a college — or a cat."

You [to Mr. Wakefield] know a trick worth two of that. Live, and long as you live enjoy the fruit of your beneficence to your neighbors.

The 22d of February is a good day for this dedication; and while we are all familiar with the patriotism of Washington in war, let us remember to-day that he showed his public spirit, also, by developing the resources of the country and by furnishing employment to the people. He did not disdain to be, with one exception, the richest man in America; he knew that wealth is honorable when it is gained by honest work and consecrated to noble uses; he knew that before a man of business can gain the means to support a poor family by charity, he has fed a score of families by the industry which is better than charity. Foremost in promoting internal improvements, always the friend of commerce, it is one of the glories of Washington that, after securing the independence of America, he sought so to foster the industrial arts that every citizen might achieve personal independence.

In this, as in other fields, President Grant follows in the footsteps of our great deliverer. He recommends measures for the revival of commerce; he urges them on an unwilling Congress; he repeats them even to deaf ears; he begs that legislation may restore to the sea that stainless flag under which he triumphed on the land. Honor to the statesmen who make the employment of people their care; and honor to-day, and always, to the merchant and the manufacturer who organize labor; who develop the wealth of nations; who "maintain the state of the world." The poorest of us should look upon their riches not with envy, but with respect and gratitude. A hundred homes must be supported in comfort before a great fortune can be accumulated by commerce.

It is a gratifying thought that one busy brain here in quiet Wakefield is employing and feeding men and women in all parts of the globe; that richly-freighted ships (eighteen last year) are now, in obedience to a single will, crossing the Atlantic and Indian Oceans; that these ships are bringing cargoes valued at millions of dollars, and destined to gain by labor millions more of value; that in the jungles of India, by the water-side of Singapore, in the perfumed forests of the Spice Islands, men are now gladly doing the work of our friend. You are resting to-day, but resting in comfort and in peace, because so many of you are sure of well-paid employment, provided by the industry of your fellow-citizen.

It was said of Washington, in words now familiar to all ears, "Heaven left him childless that a nation might call him father." Oh [to Mr. Wakefield], how large a family receive their daily bread from your hands! Long may you live to enjoy the gratitude of your neighbor; long may this good town thrive and grow; long may this building stand; and as long as it stands, it shall be a monument of business ability, of successful enterprise, and of wise liberality.

After another performance by the band, the benediction, by Rev. M. B. Chapman, concluded the afternoon exercises.

At six o'clock there was a grand banquet in the upper hall, to which about four hundred persons sat down, Mr. A. A. Currier, of this town, being the caterer. Daniel Allen, Esq., presided; Rev. Francis Smith, of Providence, invoked the Divine blessing. When all had partaken to their satisfaction, the President announced Thomas Winship, Esq., as toast-master. The applause which followed showed that the company considered the nomination "fit to be made." The toasts were as follows : —

The President of the United States. — He seems to be distinguished for great *deeds*, rather than great *speeches*. And yet the greatest speech made during the Rebellion — the key-note to his character — was that in which he said : "*I propose to fight it out on this line.*"

Response — "Hail Columbia," by the Band.

Francis Smith was an early settler of this town, whose residence was near where is now the Junction railroad station. He was authorized by the Colony Court, in 1650, to draw wine for *earthly* travellers, for which he received money and price. To-day, his lineal descendant and namesake of the eighth generation is authorized by a higher Court to offer to *heavenly* travellers wine and milk without money and without price.

Response by Rev. Francis Smith, of Providence, R. I.

The State of Massachusetts. — While she encourages education, together with the arts and sciences, she also delights to honor with the highest office in her gift one who is a well-known representative of an important branch of her manufacturing interests.

Response by Hon. Harrison Tweed, a native of this town, and now President of the Taunton Locomotive Works.

The Merchants of Boston. — While they are justly proud of their reputation for business sagacity and wealth, let them not despise the day of small things, — since one of their number, who in early life was known only *as the son of a Carpenter*, is now an enterprising and successful merchant.

Response by George O. Carpenter, Esq., of Boston, recently of this town.

The Clergy. — However much we may have enjoyed the "benefit of clergy" in the past, we associate unalloyed *Bliss* with the "benefit" which has been arranged for us on this occasion.

Response by Rev. C. R. Bliss.

Our Manufacturing Industries. — Since they profitably employ the *wealth* of our capitalists, the *brains* of our mechanics, and the *hands* of the great mass of the people, they should be regarded as the *chief* source of our material prosperity.

Response by Cyrus Wakefield, Esq.

Dr. S. O. Richardson. — His interest in the "Richardson Light Guard" and Wakefield band, and the *material aid* he has given to both, together with his liberal donation towards furnishing the rooms in this building, entitle him to the lasting gratitude of our soldiers, musicians, and citizens generally.

Response by the Band.

Public Schools. — May those who attempt to "teach the young idea how to *shoot*," always bear in mind that they will *miss the mark*, unless their *aims* are right.

Response by Hon. P. H. Sweetser.

The Farmers of New England. — The general intelligence which they exhibit affords us abundant evidence that their own heads, as well as their cabbage-heads, improve by cultivation; and we are well assured that one intelligent head will do the head-work of farms better than a hundred head of — block-heads.

Response by Dr. George B. Loring, of Salem.

The State Printer. — An indescribable *type* of character.

Response by Robert K. Potter, Esq., of Boston.

Though obliged to omit all reports of the responses, we cannot forbear noting the fact that Dr. Loring touched upon the woman's suffrage question; and as for "woman's rights," said he, "I go for them." Still he thought we did not duly consider the fact that in many respects the women held the men completely in their power. A man could not deed away a rod of land without the consent of his wife. For instance, he noticed that the deed by which the town came into possession of this edifice also contained the name of Eliza A. Wakefield. [Loud applause.] And here the eloquent speaker expatiated on the power as well as the rights of women; and when he closed, three thundering cheers were given for Mrs. Wakefield.

Remarks were also made by Prof. B. F. Tweed, of Charlestown, Rev. Francis Smith, of Providence, Henry D. Smith, Esq., of Worcester, and others. The mirth-producing tilt of words between Messrs. Allen, Potter, Tweed, and Smith, added zest and interest to the occasion, and could not well have been dispensed with.

Thus ended one of the most memorable days in the history of the town of Wakefield, the records of which occasion will be perpetuated to remote generations.

Q.

[From report in the "Wakefield Citizen."]

THE DEDICATION OF THE NEW HIGH SCHOOL HOUSE.

For practical interest in education, our town, whether under its old name of South Reading or its newer one of Wakefield, has always borne an honorable reputation. The old South Reading Academy, which for years was the compeer of many of the best seminaries of the land, and sent forth some of our ablest citizens from its halls, was a potent agent in creating that advanced sentiment which caused the establishment by the town of a High School, when possessed of only a degree of the population and property deemed essential in most towns for the formation of so advanced a grade.

The advance of the general standards of education, the upbuilding of the town, and the long insufficient accommodations of the old High School edifice, have for some years forced upon the attention of our citizens the daily increased demand for more adequate provision for prospective and even present needs. An article was introduced into the warrant for the town-meeting of April 3, 1871, by the Hon. P. H. Sweetser, a life-long friend to the educational interests of the town, and for many years the chairman of its School Board, under which action might be taken towards the establishment of a more commodious structure, better fitted in all ways for the purposes of a High School. The action upon the article provided for the appointment of a committee of five to consider the whole subject of the educational needs of the town, and report at a future meeting. This committee, consisting of five of our most esteemed citizens, Messrs. Cyrus Wakefield, Lucius Beebe, Oliver Perkins, Richard Britton, and George Packard, reported at the town-meeting, May 1, 1871, in favor of the immediate purchase of land and the erection of a suitable edifice for the accommodation of the High School. The report of the committee was adopted, and they, as the building committee, proceeded at once to the fulfilment of their duties, the result of which is the very elegant and ample structure situated at the corner of Common and Lafayette Streets, on the site formerly occupied by the old Prentiss house, long familiar to our older citizens, and which was removed after the purchase of the land for school uses.

The lot purchased has a front upon Common Street, overlooking the old Park, of one hundred and forty-six feet, and upon Lafayette Street of two hundred and four feet, and contains 28,154 square feet, affording ample room for the building, and leaving space for ornamentation of the surrounding lawns.

The building consists of a main and an L addition, the former thirty-five feet eight inches, by seventy-four feet six inches, the latter forty-eight feet by fifty-two feet eight inches, and is a blending, in several points, of the various styles of architecture, the porticoes and their ornamentation being beautiful specimens of the Ionic order, while there are delightful croppings out, here and there, of some of the other ancient divisions, with expressions of the modernized lines. The base is of rough granite two and a half feet in height, the steps of hammered stone, and the exterior finish is of wood in furrowed sheathing, the front façade on Common Street being relieved by the projection of a tower and portico, and by heavy based pilasters surmounted by Corinthian capitals in relief. The corbels and consoles are all fine specimens of carved work, and the pediments show a remarkably pleasing effect in the arrangement of their dentels. The south façade is relieved by a portico rather less pretentious than that on the front, and by similar pilasters. The L addition has along its southern face a piazza, the roof of which is supported by Ionic columns. The rear and northern façades present the same general features as the others. The front has a fine mullioned window over the portico, its general finish being a close approach to the Gothic, and very elaborate in design. The gutters and conductors are of copper, the belt about the roof is surmounted by a heavy balustrade, the roof itself being the Mansard pattern, slated with the best Welsh slate, and crowned with two ventilators of the Robinson pattern. The workmanship throughout is of the best description and reflects credit upon the artisans. The entrances to the building are four: the large main entrance in front, closed with double doors, their upper panels and the large windows over the doors furnishing a portion of light for the main hall; the southern entrance to the main building opening into a wing of the main hall, lighted in the same manner as the main hall; the entrance from the southern piazza to the L of the building; and another door upon the northern side of the L, intended rather as a special way of exit in case of fire than an ordinary avenue of ingress. Passing in at the main entrance from Common Street we enter the main hall, eighteen feet six inches, by twenty-two feet ten inches, from which doors open on either hand, and from the inner end of which the broad double staircase ascends to the second floor.

Taking the first door to the right, we find ourselves in the Chemical-Room of the High School, nineteen feet by twenty-six, the only apart ment occupied by them, except the cloak rooms, on the first floor. This room is elegantly finished, as is the whole of the interior of the building, in selected ash, the mouldings of which are very heavy, and the windows are fitted with inside ash shutters entirely excluding external light whenever experiments requiring darkness render it desirable. Too much cannot be said in praise of the wonderful beauty of the workmanship throughout the building, and as every part displays the same degree of excellence we notice it here as applicable to the whole. From this room a doorway gives exit through the janitor's room and one of the cloak rooms of the Grammar School in case of fire, to the escape door, on the north of the building, and the hall-way opening in the south adjoining the Chemical Room, and opening from the hall is the Janitor's Room, which communicates with the cloak-room of the Grammar School, and thence with the western part of the building, and the cellar, thereby giving the Janitor ready admission to all parts of the edifice. On the left of the main hall is the large and finely appointed cloak-room for the young ladies of the High School, communicating with the water-cabinets in the basement, and furnished with a marble-topped stationary wash-bowl and case, supplied with water from a great tank in the tower.

Still farther to the left opens the side wing of the main hall, communicating with the southern entrance to the main building from which opens the cloak-room for the young gentlemen of the High School, communicating with water-cabinets in the basement, and furnished like the ladies' room.

Ascending by one of the wings of the fine staircase, we find ourselves on the second floor of the building, the whole of which without reservation is devoted to the use of the teachers and scholars of our High School; and we certainly believe that nowhere are afforded finer accommodations or greater opportunities for the culture and the refinement that tasteful surroundings give. Occupying the whole front of the building on one side of the passage which separates them from the High School room proper, is a range of recitation rooms communicating with each other, and furnished with blackboards and with speaking tubes and bells, communicating with the Principal's room.

A door opens into the High School room at each end of the hall, and at the southerly end of the wall-way is a library room for the school, and at the opposite end a teachers' retiring room, furnished with water-cabinet, set bowl, etc., while the hall itself is supplied with the uniform marble bowl and case before described, at either end. The High School room itself, fifty-two feet by fifty-one feet six inches, is without doubt one of the finest in New England, well lighted and ventilated, and having all the new and approved conveniences of school furniture. A low, roomy platform for the teachers occupies the space between the two entrance doors, and convenient to the Principal's chair are speaking tubes and bell-pulls communicating with all the rooms under his charge. In brief, no want seems unprovided for, and under so favorable influences we cannot doubt that new aspirations and increased vigor for study will be given to the young ladies and gentlemen who are to occupy these advantages. Arrangements are made for lighting the entire building with gas, and the heating apparatus will be referred to in another connection. Returning to the hall, we pass up a wing of a second double staircase leading to the third story, and find ourselves in the space formed by the Mansard roof, the portion of which immediately above the High School room it is intended to devote to the purpose of an Exhibition Hall, though we doubt the utility of this, from its elevation, its inconvenient arrangement of iron rods which support the floor, from the facts that it cannot be heated by the furnace, and that the High School room is so much better for the purpose. The front part of the roof is occupied by large rooms suitable for various uses, and the tank room in the tower, where the water of the roof is collected and thence distributed to the various water-pipes of the building.

Returning to the outer air, we pass around the southerly façade of the main building and enter from the beautiful Ionic piazza the hall of the advanced Grammar School, for which arrangements of equal completeness and beauty with those of the High School have been provided. On the left of the hall as we enter is the first door opening into the school-room proper, and on the right, immediately opposite, is the teachers' retiring room, furnished like those on the second floor, with water-cabinets, marble bowl, and other conveniences, the hall being also provided with the uniform marble-topped bowl and case for the use of the scholars. The second door on the right enters the girls' cloak-room, communicating with water-cabinets in the basement, and the third door to the right enters the boys' coat-room, also communicating with water-cabinets below stairs. The fourth door on the right leads to the large recitation room, fourteen feet ten inches, by twenty-two feet, for the Grammar School, provided with all the facilities of the other recitation rooms in the building; and the fifth and last door upon the right of the hall opens into the small vestibule of the north door, valuable chiefly as a fire escape. The second door on the left of the hall and at its northerly end, directly opposite the entrance to the recitation room, enters the school-room proper of the Advanced Grammar School, thirty-five feet by forty-one feet six inches, and equal in all its appointments to the High School room immediately above. Descending to the basement by one of the four flights leading thereto, we find a spacious and well-arranged area for coal bunkers, fuel, and heating apparatus, and separated from this area by brick partitions, the water-cabinet arrangements for the several schools, also subdivided by brick walls. The materials throughout the building are of the best quality, and of the workmanship enough has already been said. The tower of the edifice beautifully surmounts the whole, and its platform affords a fine view of the surrounding scenery, and we presume will often attract the young star-gazers of our High School with their new telescope.

To this completed and elegant temple of learning there gathered a large and appreciative audience on Thursday afternoon (Oct. 10), to participate in the dedication of the structure to the purposes for which it was designed, and there has rarely occurred in our time a more richly enjoyable occasion of happy expression and retainable merit than was afforded in the exercises of the day and the event. John S. Eaton, Esq., by invitation of the School Board, filled most acceptably the position of Chairman of the day, and among those invited who favored the occasion with their presence were Prof. B. F. Tweed, of Charlestown, Gen. H. K. Oliver, of the Bureau of Statistics of Massachusetts, Rev. Dr. J. W. Chickering, Henry D. Smith, Esq., Edward Mansfield, Esq., long connected with the School Board, the Board of Selectmen, the School Committee, and representatives of the press.

The members of the High School occupied seats on the extreme left of the house, and every available foot of space was occupied by the refined and intellectual audience. The Wakefield Orchestra furnished acceptable music, their renderings being in fine taste.

The exercises commenced at two o'clock by invocation by Rev. W. F. Potter, of the Universalist Church, followed by music by the orchestra.

Richard Britton, Esq., acting for the Building Committee, then transferred the charge of the building to the Chairman of the Board of Selectmen, John S. Eaton, Esq., in the following brief but comprehensive address: —

MR. CHAIRMAN : On me unexpectedly devolves to-day, as the representative of the building committee of the town, charged with the construction of this edifice, the pleasant duty of consigning to your hands the care and custody thereof.

The foresight of our citizens which anticipated the demand for increased educational facilities, caused by our rapid growth as a town, and which has eventuated in the erection of this beautiful structure, found its earliest public expression in an article introduced into the warrant for the town-meeting of April 3, 1871, by a gentleman whose name has for years been honorably identified with the educational interests of this municipality, the then chairman of the School Board, now gone to his rest, the Hon. P. H. Sweetser. The action upon this article, which contemplated the possible conversion of the old town house to school purposes, resulted in the appointment of a committee of five, who should take into consideration the whole subject-matter of construction, and report at a future meeting. On this committee were appointed Messrs. Cyrus Wakefield, Lucius Beebe, Oliver Perkins, Richard Britton, and George Packard. The report of this committee, after a careful review of the needs of our entire school system, unanimously recommended the immediate purchase of land and the erection of a commodious edifice for High School purposes, and this report was adopted. The eligible lot on which this building now stands, containing 28,154 square feet, was purchased at a cost of nine thousand eight hundred and fifty-four dollars, and ground was broken for the new enterprise on the sixteenth day of September, 1871.

From the various plans submitted, that of John Stevens, Esq., one of our citizens, was selected as most nearly meeting the necessities of the case, and according to its provisions the building has been erected at an expense closely approximating forty-three thousand dollars. In addition to ample accommodation for a High School of large numbers, the building contains provision for an advanced Grammar School, an exhibition hall, and every advantage and convenience that the advanced state of culture in school architecture has suggested and found desirable.

It has been suggested that the considerable expense which the completion of this structure has occasioned the town, largely in advance of previous investments in this line, and even of the expectations of our citizens, is ill-considered and unwise; but far in advance of the consideration of cost is to be placed the expectation of return therefrom. The gold that glitters is not to be placed in the scale against the richer worth of the culture and education of mind and heart given by such surroundings as these. Who shall predict what achievements in all that is good and great shall here have their germs planted in the minds of some of the most humble of birth by the refinements that here alone shall greet the eye whose home is amid poverty and wretchedness ! To the liberality of heart and hand which makes such agencies of education as this possible, and which resides pre-eminently in our midst, is due the position of America to-day among the nations ; and the people of this community will doubtless long enjoy, not less the commendation of their own hearts, than the congratulations of all who shall visit us, upon the possession of so glorious a monument to one of our cardinal principles, — the education of the common people.

To the citizens for their liberality and their patience, to the faithful endeavors of the artisans, one and all, to those who have aided in manifold ways the labors of your committee, we desire to express our profound sense of gratitude ; and it is no small degree of satisfaction and relief that we feel in witnessing the completion of what must prove in such an undertaking, at best an arduous and trying task.

In discharge of the trust committed to the committee, and in their behalf, I have the honor to surrender to you the keeping of this edifice, and the emblems thereof.

Mr. Eaton, on receiving the keys, responded as follows : —

MR. CHAIRMAN, AND GENTLEMEN OF THE BUILDING COMMITTEE :

To my present official position am I indebted for the honor, as well as the pleasure, of receiving from your hands, on behalf of the town of Wakefield, this magnificent temple of science. Our citizens, never backward in furnishing such educational facilities as from time to time have seemed to be required, for the erection of this school edifice have poured wealth from their treasury in unusual measure ; and they have watched its construction with peculiar interest and pride, as under skilful hands it has grown into symmetry, with added cornice and column and capital, until it stood completed and commanding.

Appropriately reared upon a site alike historic and venerable, around which cluster cherished memories of ancient worthies and teachers, it reveals its ample and admirable proportions in finished beauty, an ornament and an honor to our town. Its eminent location, flanked by churches, in accordance with the true New England custom, would seem to render it secure from all *heretical* influences ; and we may readily adopt the familiar lines of Whittier : —

> " Nor heed the skeptic's puny hands,
> While near our school the church-spire stands ;
> Nor fear the bigot's blinded rule,
> While near our church-spire stands the school."

In the years that are yet future, may there go forth from this temple an army of scholars, thorough, earnest, brilliant, for such will ever find full scope for the finest culture in the broadest fields of humanity. May it prove indeed a treasure-house of knowledge, and may the wealth which shall be gathered from within its walls exceed the material wealth which constructed them a thousand fold!

In this place, and on this occasion, we cannot forget those familiar forms which are missing from this assembly, or the voices which are silent to-day. One amidst the snows of winter, and one amidst the freshness and fragrance of June, they both passed serenely on before us to a celestial atmosphere within a grander temple, and to the enjoyment of a knowledge perfect and perpetual.

> Them shall no sunshine from the fields of azure,
>   No light of home or hall,
> No summons sent from crowded marts of treasure,
>   Again to duty call.
>
> And all life's problems and equations,
>   So intricate before,
> Now solved, amid the infinite creations,
>   Are mysteries no more!

In closing, permit me to express to you, Mr. Chairman, and to the members of the committee whom you represent, on behalf of the citizens of Wakefield, their full appreciation of the fidelity which has marked the performance of the duties assigned you, and of the satisfactory result of your efforts. And now I shall be pleased to transfer the keys of this new school building to the chairman of the school committee, upon whom its immediate care will devolve, confident that under such guardianship it will ever remain uninjured and beautiful.

On receiving the keys from the chairman of the selectmen, Rev. Mr. Bliss, in the subjoined excellent address, delivered the keys to the principal of the High School.

It is with great pleasure that the school committee accept, for the purposes of education in Wakefield, this beautiful edifice. They congratulate the people of the town that a need that was beginning to be deeply felt has been supplied. Though they are not as a body to be credited with any active participation in the work of planning or rearing this building, having been wholly relieved of that responsibility by the labors of another committee appointed by the town for the purpose, they yet have watched the progress of the work, and believe that it has been carried forward with great skill and care. They hope that the building, so beautiful both without and within, will be found in its use to be fully adapted to all the purposes for which it has been reared.

The liberality shown by the town in the erection of this house has been very great, so great, indeed, as to have provoked the remark that it has been excessive; and there are, perhaps, some who would have preferred a less imposing and expensive structure. Far shall it be from me to defend extravagance, whether it be in school-houses or dwelling-houses or churches; and yet there seem to me to be good and sound reasons why a building devoted to the uses of education should be one of the most commanding and comely in the town. Taxes are indeed sometimes onerous; debts are generally curses, whoever have them to pay: nevertheless, good buildings are educators of no mean power; and when devoted not to purposes of folly, nor yet to purposes of gain, but to the noble end of educating the young, they can hardly be too good. Without discussing the question whether a few thousand dollars less might not have sufficed for this building, I yet count upon the agreement of all present when I say, that it is altogether fit and proper that the finest architecture which any town is able to display should be that devoted to the twin purposes of religion and education. Those things which we prize most, as the sources of our prosperity and our strongest safeguard, should receive the most emphatic expression. There is an incongruity in building for ourselves fine private dwellings and then erecting a cheap and uncomely church, — and were this the place, we would congratulate our Baptist brethren upon the elegant structure with which they have graced our street. They have taxed themselves heavily, but the cause is one worthy of being taxed for. It deserves an adequate expression of the regard in which Christian men hold it. The same is true of education; it is important enough to receive at the hands of any community the acknowledgment contained in handsome and costly structures. A house like this is an emphatic public declaration that good learning is held in very high esteem here, and many persons, children among the rest, will have higher ideas of the importance of education from the fact that old people have given this proof of their judgment concerning its legitimate requirements. Besides, there is an imperceptible, perhaps, but none the less powerful influence, constantly exerted by a tasteful public edifice. A great many valuable lessons are continually being derived from it. It is true it may be a source of self-flattery, as too many of our possessions unfortunately are; for it is seldom that we can look upon any excellent object, if it be our own, without spreading a little more widely the wings of our pride; but if used as it ought to be, it is a source of much instruction and of many incentives. An evil which is very perceptible in our busy lives is that we cannot stop for details, but content ourselves with general impressions, and I think are more apt to be vain in consequence. Many persons, in looking at a fine building, will be content with a single glance, and be unable to give any account of the architecture of it; or if they glance at it will speak in general and perhaps contemptuous terms of the gingerbread work about it, being quite unable to see the study and taste that were employed in producing the general effect which they feel and acknowledge. But there is a change in prospect in this respect; object teaching will do much to remedy this bad habit. When children shall be taught, not less from books, but more by external observation, and learn accurately to notice and describe everything about them, they will derive from nature and from paintings and from architecture many of the most valuable lessons, and lessons which we, who have been taught by the old methods, never learned. For that day this edifice will be an excellent teacher. It is the desire on the part of many of us that our High School should be developed into a school of greater influence and usefulness than it has hitherto been. It should, we think, have a larger number of scholars, a wider range of studies, and should reach a position of so much evident importance that parents will not be content to suffer their children to go into the shops and factories till they have enjoyed its full advantages. Hitherto it has labored under great difficulty in the narrowness of the quarters assigned to it, in the want of suitable recitation rooms, and in the lack of various facilities for the prosecution of school duties. That much excellent teaching and much hard study have been performed are facts which many before us can affirm by direct testimony; and all honor to the teachers who in remote and recent years have used to the full extent all possible facilities that the old building afforded. They have their reward in the consciousness of having done their duty, and in the gratitude of their pupils.

But we have come to a new era. The town has passed beyond its old boundaries. New streets, new stores, and new dwellings say very plainly to us that new responsibilities rest upon us, and a new career is opening before us. The schools already feel the impulse. Though three new ones have already been established within one year, yet some of the old ones are now overcrowded, and admonish us that still more ample accommodations will soon be required. From this greatly increased number of scholars in the lower schools, we shall certainly gather a larger number for the High School, and we shall doubtless find that it was wise to have anticipated our wants in providing beforehand these greatly enlarged accommodations. One reason for the early withdrawal of scholars from the High School has, perhaps, been the fact that the teaching force of the school has not been sufficiently great to perform the labor required by the course of study the committee thought it wise to lay down.

Two teachers have had neither the time nor strength to give to the pupils that thorough drill upon the studies of the course which was necessary to fix their interest in the school. Hence the scholars of less studious habits were willing to leave school, and too often, perhaps, their parents were willing to have them, and hence the school has suffered both in its usefulness and reputation. Therefore, no sooner was there a near prospect of transferring the High School to this building, than the committee decided to add another teacher to the force already employed upon this school. In other words, they took the younger and less proficient of the pupils, who, under the old arrangement, would have entered the High School, and made a separate school, and placed them under an experienced teacher for a year's thorough drill. It will be no small advantage to the scholars of the school to have three competent and faithful teachers where they had but two before. And with this additional teaching power, coupled with the attractiveness of this building, the committee believe this school can and will enter upon a new career of usefulness.

The natural sciences have been very faithfully and successfully taught in the school during the past year, but with the new facilities afforded by this building, a still larger degree of success may be obtained. The languages and mathematics have also been thoroughly studied, but with the opportunity for longer recitations, and with the more direct personal care of the teachers, these branches can and doubtless will be more fully acquired.

The new apparatus which the school has in part purchased, and for which the town has made an additional grant of money, will add to the facilities of the teachers for imparting, and the advantages of the scholars for acquiring knowledge, and the committee are confident that the school may become far more proficient and useful than ever it has been, and that an increased conviction of its value will obtain a place in the minds of the people of the town. And that a school in order to be useful must have the hearty sympathy of the people, is a fact of prime significance. A school cannot thrive upon money alone; it must have something else; it must rest upon the good will, and to some extent, upon the warm solicitude of the community. It must be pervaded with the feeling that not a few pairs of eyes are upon it, but hundreds of them; that not a few persons, and they perhaps officials, are anxious for its prosperity, but that all its patrons and all the town are so likewise.

Teachers need such support; for however conscientious in the discharge of their duties they are, and however deeply they may love their calling, yet if they tax their invention to find methods to interest their pupils, and work, in school and out, for their benefit, and then gain no recognition of their faithfulness from the parents of the children, who perhaps are too inattentive to their efforts even to know that they have been thus at work, they will be very likely to lose heart, and cease special effort. Indeed, it often seems to me that parents are too little acquainted with the peculiar difficulties of a teacher's profession, and do not estimate at its true worth the labor which a teacher expends upon their children. Greater familiarity with the working of all the schools, on the part of parents, would inevitably greatly increase their efficiency. It would make the judgments of parents more discriminating and more just, and would stimulate both teachers and pupils in the most effective and healthful manner. Pupils need this manifested sympathy of their parents. The want of this has been the secret influence that has paralyzed the efforts of many a teacher. It is too much to ask of teachers that they, unaided, shall put the fire of enthusiasm in study into the hearts of pupils. They can do it often, but had they the co-operation of parents, they could do it almost always. Let scholars know that every step of their progress is noted by the parents, and that there is an actual understanding between the teachers and their parents, and frequent consultation, and let them often see their parents in the school-room and witness their open pleasure in their advancement, and this advancement would be far more satisfactory than it sometimes is. And perhaps there is no school in town upon which such attentions would have more direct and palpable effect than upon the two that are to occupy this building. The pupils have arrived at a sensitive age; they are having more and more self-respect; they would be pained by paining their friends, and they would be pleased in pleasing them, as a few years ago they would not; and the effect which parents by their frequent presence in the school-room, and by their constant interest in the progress made might produce, would be very marked and powerful.

The School Committee, then, would take this occasion, so auspicious for these schools and for the interests of education among us, to urge upon the acceptance of parents the privilege and the duty of giving the decided help of their sympathy to these schools. They are a possession of which any town might be proud; and it is for us, with these additional facilities, to make them foundations of increased usefulness and power.

It but remains for me, in behalf of the School Committee, to pass the custody of this building into the hands of the efficient Principal of the High School. We are glad to do this, for we are confident that you, sir, and your trusted assistant, will spare no pains to preserve its finish and beauty, and use it well for the purposes which you labor to advance. We bid you use, use it carefully, of course, but use it, every part of it; let this room witness to the hard work and good conduct of this school. Let these other rooms, these halls, the apparatus you will have, also bear evidence to the good quality of your work; and you will be sustained not only by this Board and the people of the town, but by the higher authority and the more satisfactory approval of your own conscience.

Mr. M. J. Hill, the Master of the High School, on receiving the keys, ably and happily responded as follows: —

These keys, sir, mean for me a double responsibility. I refer not simply to the duty of caring for this beautiful building, the finest school edifice of wood in the State, if not in New England, but to that higher and more difficult duty of guiding those who shall henceforth study within these walls. Upon the first I enter with some measure of confidence. Surely this elaborate and graceful structure will wellnigh protect itself; so cheery, spacious, and elegant, it cannot fail to invite the kindest treatment from all those whose good fortune it shall be to use it.

I believe, too, in its educating power. We readily enough appreciate the influence of a truly noble man. He need not act; he need not even speak. His very presence is a power for good. His nobility beams forth from his countenance, it cheers with its warmth, it illumines with its splendor. True, the warmth is not always present, and the glory of the illumination may vanish like the tints of evening. But the memory of such a man will live. Should all our memories be as exalted as that, we would be stones did we not lead better, purer, and nobler lives.

There is a companion truth, whose force some realize more than others. I think those to whom we owe this structure fully comprehend it. It is this: Things may be powers for good as well as persons.

Things that are voiceless and soulless may educate. A beautiful statue, or painting, or model of architecture, works upon the mind, awakes emotions such as beauty only can kindle, makes it more susceptible to other beauties, and hence, with great power or little, but always with some, it promotes that rich culture essential to a well-rounded education. But more precious than the building and its surroundings, is the school itself, whose highest success will depend in large measure upon the manner in which the parents and the scholars shall perform their respective duties. I am impressed more and more with the magnitude and importance of my calling the longer I labor in it. Say what you will of the great questions of the day, political, social, and others, I know of none greater than the problems that concern the human mind. Surely if the best intellects fail to solve them, I may be pardoned if, in spite of attempted solutions, some of them to my mind continue mysteries as before.

It will be my aim, however, to merit the confidence you have reposed in me. In this aim I ask your sympathy, your *charity*, and your cordial co-operation. In behalf of the Wakefield High School, I thank the town for its munificence. With thanks equally hearty for this token of renewed trust, I accept these keys and the burden of duties they symbolize. And, scholars, as these keys are the means whereby I am enabled to unlock the various apartments of this temple of learning, so may the training and culture you can acquire in your early years (if so disposed) become, as it were, *keys* to Nature's vast store-houses of unlimited knowledge.

The principal address of the day, by Prof. B. F. Tweed, of Charlestown, was then delivered, and by his courtesy we are permitted to give it below.

Mr. Chairman: I confess it was with a feeling akin to pride that I received an invitation from the School Committee of my native town to take part in the exercises of this interesting occasion. And it is not without emotion that I now stand in this presence, surrounded by the scenes and associates of my childhood and youth, and looking into the faces of so many of my life-long friends. My thoughts naturally revert to the little brown school-house in which I took my first lessons in scholastic lore, and the faces of my early teachers rise before me, idealized as seen through the vista of lengthened years, and hallowed by the affection with which I ever regarded them. I don't know that my early teachers were especially handsome, using that term as young men usually employ it in speaking of young ladies ; from the fact that most of them were never married, I might presume it to be otherwise. But (begging pardon of the ladies present for any seeming want of gallantry) I must say that I don't see any such young ladies nowadays as appear to my mind's eye when I think of Miss Symonds, Miss Bancroft, Miss Newhall, and Miss Evans ; and here I may say, incidentally, to the young ladies teaching in Wakefield, that they have it in their power so to impress themselves on the plastic minds committed to their care, that in after years, when whatever of beauty they may now possess shall have faded, it will still exist as " pictures in memory, not changed, but translated."

Nor can I deny myself the privilege of referring to those who visited our schools at the stated examinations, and watched over their interests. Could I summon them in fact, as in fancy they appear before me, with the venerable form of him at their head who for so many years ministered at the altar in yonder church, and whose interest in our schools never flagged, it would afford me unmixed pleasure to express to them personally, and through them to the good old town, which, under whatever name, has always been liberal in support of schools, my heartfelt gratitude. Nor must I forget the public-spirited men, through whose influence and liberality the South Reading Academy was established, which furnished opportunities for a higher course than our public schools then provided. For the ability to occupy a responsible, and I hope useful position in life, I feel indebted more to these schools, and to the self-denial and wise foresight of parents who appreciated their value, than to any effort of my own ; and I am glad that you have given me an opportunity thus publicly to acknowledge my obligation. But, sir, not to dwell on what is, in some sense, personal to myself, though equally applicable to hundreds of others, I will pass to what I hope will be regarded as an appropriate theme for this occasion. It is this : The influence of our school system on New England character and on great public interests.

It has been said, and with some show of truth, that the only natural production of New England is ice, but that its manufactures include every conceivable thing, from wooden nutmegs to brains. Anything combining utility with cheapness, from an apple-parer to a sewing-machine, is known, the world over, as a Yankee notion, and I wonder that no biblical commentator has found a special reference to the universal Yankee in the text, " Man has sought out many inventions."

It is true that, by dint of industry, the scanty and sterile soil does yield some other products than ice, yet it is only by the most persistent tickling with a hoe that it is made to smile with a harvest. Or perhaps

I should rather say, using Yankee phraseology, it is only by swapping a full equivalent of labor and dressing that the farmer secures a scanty return. The resources of New England, therefore, and those to which she is indebted for her prosperity, are not in the soil, but in the strong arms and fertile brains of her people. Nay, even in the case of the one natural production, it was in the alembic of the Yankee cranium that ice was first converted to gold. What had remained insoluble for the purposes of pecuniary liquidation, from the beginning, yielded only to the alchemy of the Yankee brain. Notwithstanding the transparency of ice, it was only the keen sight of our Tudors, Gages, and Hittingers that could see *money* in it.

That climate, soil, and other physical conditions should have produced marked peculiarities of character might have been anticipated, though what they would be could hardly be foreseen. A weaker race than our fathers might have been discouraged, and yielding to what seemed a necessity, might have dragged out a miserable life of poverty. In them, however, it stimulated to industry and perseverance, and developed a fertility of resource in an inverse ratio to that of the soil.

Somebody has said that in certain parts of our country a whiskey-shop and lager-beer saloon only are necessary as the nucleus of a village. With our fathers it was a church and a school-house. Around these two institutions clustered the settlers, and the germ there planted has developed into our present liberal system of public education. From these spring material wealth, our social and political institutions, and the patriotism, public spirit, and intelligence requisite to preserve them, and to advance the interests of a progressive civilization.

Humboldt has said that "science and manipulative skill must be wedded together, that national wealth must be based on an enlightened employment of national products and forces." Our fathers may not have had this in view as the prime object in founding our school system, but the results of New England thrift have abundantly proved that educated labor *pays*, regarded even from a pecuniary point of view; that by utilitizing all our material, — the brains of the masses, — we increase indefinitely national wealth. And here we have a fine illustration of the fact that the highest and truest interests of society are best promoted by providing for the welfare of its individual members; that justice to all, even the weakest, is, like honesty, the best policy, not only of the individual, but of the state.

From time immemorial, and everywhere, the greatest waste had been that of humanity. The great mass of mankind had been little better than mechanical implements or tools directed by the intelligence and for the benefit of the few, — mere hewers of wood and drawers of water, — all the elements of a distinctive humanity, that which constitutes the image of God, undeveloped, lost to themselves and the world. The Reformation, making every man directly responsible to God, and carrying with it, as its correlative, the right of private judgment, tended to a system of education qualifying every man to exercise this right.

But the world is slow to admit the logical consequences of a proposition which disturbs time-honored institutions; and there were not wanting those who supposed that such a consummation would work a social revolution, threatening the very stability of the state. It was only after the lapse of many years, and in a new country, that the experiment was inaugurated and developed. It is, then, a problem first solved in New England and by our school system, that the education of the whole people is the most important element in the material prosperity of a nation. It has become an axiom in political economy. There is no one question now exciting so much interest among educationists, both in this country and in Europe, as the inquiry how to bring our school systems into more direct relations with the industry of the people; and though we may justly claim to have taken the lead in a general educational system, we are forced to admit that some of the nations of Europe have outstripped us in the practical character of the instruction imparted.

At the World's Fair in 1851, the palm of excellence in manufactures was, in nearly every department, awarded to England. Sixteen years later, when the nations again displayed the results of their skill and labor, England excelled only in ten of a hundred departments. This excited so much alarm among the manufacturing interests of England that Parliament appointed a committee of investigation, and the report of the committee is equally instructive to us as to England. It is this, " That the success of the Continent was owing to its admirable technical schools; that no nation can excel in manufactures unless it provides facilities for scientific education for all that converts the mere workman into the artisan." It was this report, and the fact that so many of the foremen in our manufacturing establishments were foreigners, that led immediately to legislation in behalf of industrial drawing, under which technical schools are springing up in all our cities and large towns.

It was seen that we were in danger of being crushed by the very wheel which we set in motion; that not only general intelligence, but technical knowledge and skill, add immensely to the material wealth of a nation. Such is the uniform testimony where "*brains* sit at the loom, and *intelligence* stands at the spinning-wheel." But mechanical drawing is only the beginning of a course of industrial training which is to extend to every department of skilled labor. The establishment of technical schools, whose advantages shall be accessible to every apprentice in any branch of human industry, is strongly recommended by our Governor in his message. Such schools, where they are in operation, as in France, Belgium, and Switzerland, have already, says Professor Waterman, one of our ablest statisticians, created a productive capital of many millions. What, then, may we expect of them in this country, where so many great interests are only waiting for development? But not to dwell too long on this part of my subject, I have said that our social and political institutions, and the public spirit and intelligence requisite to preserve them, rest securely only on a general system of education.

A distinguished English writer on history, in the early part of this century, attributed the lack of patriotism and of elevated sentiment, which he affirmed to exist among the people of his own country in the eighteenth century, to the fact that they had been engaged chiefly in the value of estates, the balance of trade, and profit and loss. And he goes on to say that the only way in which this elevated sentiment of patriotism can be preserved among men whose minds are occupied with their bargains and their markets, the article they are to produce and the price they are to receive, is by the education of all; by accustoming every man to interest himself in the concerns of his country, and thus giving him an idea of his social and political importance.

This was but theory with the philosophical Englishman. Has not the experience of the last few years in this country proved the practicability of preserving noble sentiments of patriotism, where peaceful industry and the pursuits of trade are the engrossing subjects of all classes; and was it not accomplished by the very means suggested by the writer mentioned? The quiet determination and patriotism sleeping in the breasts of the loyal millions, educated in our Northern schools and colleges, were roused by the first roar of the artillery of rebellion. Never was there a more striking proof in the history of the world that peaceful industry, accompanied by intellectual, moral, and religious culture, do not render men parsimonious and effeminate, but rather fit them to become the truest and most liberal supporters, and the best soldiers of freedom and right. For proof of this we have only to consult the army roll and the records of the Sanitary Commission.

Just as surely as the early discipline and habits of study acquired in our schools give the best assurance of success to a young man, so surely are they the presages of national welfare. There is something in our very nature, after we have once started on the road of progress, that beckons and impels us on. The cry of Oliver Twist for "more," which so horrified the astonished Mr. Bumble, is the cry of humanity; and the only alternative is more education, more opportunities for usefulness, or more anarchy, more blood. The atmosphere of the workshop, as suggested by the author just quoted, is too arid for constant breathing. Daily infusions from cultivated social life, from books and lectures, are necessary to health. Who shall say how much the immediate vicinity of Cambridge has done to extend, elevate, and purify public sentiment in Boston? Neither the annual nor triennial catalogue contains the names of all the students educated *by*, if not *in*, our colleges. And so also with our public schools: when the father returns to his family at evening, surrounded by his children conning their daily lessons, he finds himself in a different world; and he is a wise man if he can answer all the questions that are puzzling the brains of all the members of his household. The common school, therefore, is not only the educator of the children between five and fifteen, but of the whole community. It is the nature of all good institutions, as well as good men, that "virtue goes out of them."

The indirect influence of our colleges is yearly recognized by honorary degrees conferred on those who have attained excellence in some department of learning, outside the walls, but not without the aid of those institutions. It is no less a claim of influence, on the part of our higher institutions, than a compliment to the recipients of the degrees. To many a man, who never paid a tuition fee, or attended prayers in the college chapel, is old Harvard the alma mater, in a stricter sense than to hundreds whose sonship is chiefly evinced by a scrap of parchment. I know it is common to speak of men who have become distinguished, though they have not had the benefit of a college course, as self-made men; and this, in a limited sense, is just; but, I believe, as a class, they will be found to have as lively a sense of obligation to the great institutions that have furnished the best books in science and literature, as those more favored ones who have received instruction from the lips of tutors and professors. If other proof were wanting that our schools and colleges do in fact educate the community at large to higher views and a juster estimate of life, it might be found in the fact, that the same brains that convert ice into gold are not satisfied till the gold itself, purged of its baser dross, is transmuted into wisdom, virtue, and religion. There is scarce a college, an academy, an asylum for the blind, the insane, or the dumb, a hospital of any kind, or any beneficent institution, that is not a monument of the generosity of those who, by the discipline and knowledge obtained in our schools, have amassed wealth, without forgetting that the worth of the dollar consists in its exchangeable value for that which is more precious than rubies. Hence those immense sums invested in institutions whose dividends stand accredited to the *world*, and whose accounts are audited and approved in Heaven. What, then, is the distinguishing character of our boasted system of public institutions? Not the superior scholarship of the favored few, however desirable that might be; but that it has raised the general character of learning and intelligence to a higher plane than has been done elsewhere. Though we can boast, perhaps, of no peaks of the greatest altitude, yet our table-lands are more extensive, fertile, and productive than those of any other country.

Guizot, in his History of Civilization in Modern Europe, says, "that when we consider separately, any particular development of the human mind, in literature, in the arts, in any of the ways in which human intelligence may go forward, we shall generally find it inferior to the corresponding development in the civilization of antiquity; but as a set-off to this, when we regard it as a whole, European civilization appears infinitely more rich and diversified." May we not hope that the future historian of American civilization may be able to say that, though Europe may, perhaps, boast of individual instances in which literature, the arts, or sciences have been carried to a higher pitch of excellence than in our comparatively young Republic, that we have given to the world a civilization, which, regarded as a whole, is infinitely richer, deeper, and broader than that of the Old World. If not, it will be because we as individuals have not used the opportunities so richly furnished us by the far-sighted wisdom of our ancestors, and watched over and strengthened by the wise and good of later generations.

And now, sir, shall I trespass on your patience with a word more especially adapted to this occasion? This beautiful and spacious building, which you have set apart and dedicated to the purposes of education, is itself a witness of the essential truth of the views I have advanced. The contrast between this and the one-storied, unpainted building of my childhood, is a fitting exponent of the astonishing increase of material wealth in New England, and, may I not say, a proof that an appreciation of the value of common-school education has fully kept apace with it. I would not be misunderstood, in any degree, to detract from the inestimable value of our religious institutions. But I cannot help noticing that the little school-house, which formerly nestled humbly, as if for protection, under the shadow of the more pretentious church, with its heaven-pointing spire, now stands boldly by its side,—not indeed as its rival, but as its trusted ally. And as that is dedicated to the worship of God, which is the first and great commandment, so, also, by these exercises we now dedicate this to the service of humanity, which the Master has said is like unto it. Nor is there any respect of persons. It beckons to its embrace all your sons and daughters, and points your *sons* at least — I hope it soon will your daughters — to Harvard and Tufts, or to lucrative and honorable positions in industrial pursuits. In this institution, at least, the poorest have as much stock as the richest, and it is not unlikely that the largest dividends will be found accredited to their children. It is the common school which constitutes the Commonwealth; nor does its influence stop here. The *physical* geography of our country is well defined. Its mountain ranges rim a basin capable of feeding the world. Its great watercourses, with their thousand tributaries, are ample to waft its wealth of productions to our ports. Its *political* geography, thanks to the boys in blue, educated in our Northern schools, and led on by our great captains, has been preserved intact; and now the little brooklets of learning, springing from every hillside in New England, have converged and united, till they have become a mighty river, which, augmented by its magnificent tributaries of the North and West, has swept across the continent, bearing upon its ample bosom the rich treasures of civilization and learning to the far Pacific.

Music by the orchestra, followed by a remarkably amusing and enjoyable, but altogether unreportable address, abounding in reminiscences of school-days, and replete with fun, from Gen. H. K. Oliver, he in turn being followed by Rev. Dr. Chickering in a brief but entertaining address, congratulating and encouraging in tone.

The thanks of the town were at this juncture returned to Henry D. Smith, Esq., by John S. Eaton, Esq., for the very elegant copy of Worcester's Dictionary presented by him to the High School before the commencement of the exercises. Mr. Smith briefly, happily, and humorously responded, and with a bit of pleasant repartee from Prof. Tweed the addresses closed.

R.

COPY OF AGREEMENT

BETWEEN A COMMITTEE OF THE TOWN OF WAKEFIELD AND MILL OWNERS ON SAUGUS RIVER, AS TO THE WATER-LEVEL OF LAKE QUANNAPOWITT.

Whereas, a Committee chosen by the town of Wakefield, together with the mill owners upon the stream that runs out of Lake Quannapowitt, met at the outlet of the Lake, August 7, 1871, and, after examination, have failed to find any sign of a log that was placed in the outlet by direction of the town authorities, some twenty-seven years ago, to define low water-mark, and as there is no record of any bearings being taken at that time with permanent objects, its location cannot be ascertained.

Recognizing the importance of having a fixed water-mark, to regulate the flow of water, to retain it at a proper depth in the Lake, and to direct its flow to the best advantage of the mills on the stream, the following mutual arrangement in regard to the water-mark has been decided upon, with the assent of all the parties concerned.

First, That the stream shall continue to flow, during the present season, without further obstruction, until the water is on the increase.

Second, That the basis for the level of the water-mark shall be a foundation timber on the north side of the stream, forty-nine feet from the west edge of the road bridge.

Third, That the low water-mark shall be at twelve inches above the level of said timber, from the first day of April to the first day of August; and from the first day of August to the first day of April, the mill owners shall have the right to draw the water six inches lower than the said low water-mark.

Signed,

JAMES F. EMERSON,
JOHN G. ABORN,
SAM'L PARKER, JR.,
LUCIUS BEEBE,
LILLEY EATON,
C. W. EATON,
Town Committee.

PRANKER & CO.,
ANDREW A. SCOTT,
AMOS BINNEY,
(By S. G. LANE),
HOYT & WILEY,
Mill Owners.

S.

[CHAP. 335.]

AN ACT

TO SUPPLY THE TOWNS OF WAKEFIELD AND STONEHAM WITH WATER.

Be it enacted, etc, as follows:

SECTION 1. Cyrus Wakefield, Lucius Beebe, James F. Emerson, John Hill, H. H. Mawhinney, Onslow Gilmore, Francis H. Knight, their associates and successors, are hereby made a corporation under the name of the Quannapowitt Water Company, for furnishing the inhabitants of Wakefield and Stoneham with water; with all the powers and privileges, and subject to all the duties, restrictions, and liabilities set forth in all general laws which now are, or hereafter may be in force, so far as the same are applicable to this corporation.

SECT. 2. Said corporation, for the purpose aforesaid, may take, hold, and convey, into and through said towns, the waters of Lake Quannapowitt or Crystal Lake, or both, in the town of Wakefield, together with the tributary waters which flow to either in said towns; and may take and hold, by purchase or otherwise, such land, on and around the margin of such lake or lakes, or tributaries, not exceeding five rods in width, as may be necessary for the preservation and purity of said waters; and may also take and hold in like manner such lands as may be necessary for erecting and maintaining dams and reservoirs, and for laying and maintaining conduits, pipes, drains, and other works, for collecting, conducting, and distributing such waters through said towns of Wakefield and Stoneham. The said corporation shall, within sixty days from the time of taking any land as aforesaid, file in the Registry of Deeds for the County of Middlesex, a description of the land so taken, sufficiently accurate for identification, and state the purpose for which it is taken.

SECT. 3. Said corporation may build aqueducts, and maintain the same by any works suitable therefor; may erect and maintain dams; may make reservoirs and hydrants, and may distribute the water throughout said towns of Wakefield and Stoneham, by laying down pipes, and may establish the rent therefor.

Said corporation may also, for the purposes aforesaid, carry its pipes and drains over or under any water-course, street, railroad, highway or other way, in such manner as not to obstruct the same; and may enter upon and dig up any road, under the direction of the selectmen of the said towns respectively, in such manner as to cause the least hinderance to the travel thereon.

SECT. 4. Said corporation shall be liable to pay all damages that shall be sustained by any persons in their property by the taking of any land, water, or water rights, or by the constructing of any aqueducts, reservoirs, or other works for the purposes aforesaid. If any person who shall sustain damage as aforesaid cannot agree with said corporation upon the amount of said damages, he may have them assessed in the same manner as is provided by law, with respect to land taken for highways; and all damages for the taking of lands for the purposes aforesaid shall be paid for by said corporation before entering upon said lands.

SECT. 5. No application shall be made to the County Commissioners for the assessment of damages for the taking of any water rights until the water is actually withdrawn or diverted by said corporation. Any person whose water rights are thus taken or affected, may apply as aforesaid, at any time within three years from the time when the water is actually withdrawn or diverted.

SECT. 6. Said corporation may hold, for the purposes aforesaid, real estate to the amount of one hundred thousand dollars, and its whole capital stock shall not exceed three hundred and fifty thousand dollars, which shall be divided into shares of one hundred dollars each. And no liability shall be incurred by said corporation until at least thirty thousand dollars of its capital shall have been paid in in cash.

SECT. 7. Any person who shall maliciously divert the water, or any part thereof, of the sources which shall be taken by the corporation, pursuant to the provisions of this Act, or who shall maliciously corrupt the same or render it impure, or who shall maliciously destroy or injure any dam or reservoir, aqueduct, pipe, or hydrant, or other property held, owned, or used by said corporation for the purposes of this Act, shall pay three times the amount of actual damages to the said corporation, to be recovered in an action of tort; and every such person, on conviction of either of the malicious acts aforesaid, shall be punished by fine not exceeding one hundred dollars and imprisonment not exceeding six months.

SECT. 8. The towns of Wakefield and Stoneham, or either of them, in case the other declines to participate in said purchase, may at any time within three years from the time this Act takes effect, take or purchase the franchise of said corporation and all its corporate property, by paying therefor the amount expended for the construction, maintenance, and repairs of said water works, and all necessary incidental expenses, together with interest thereon at the rate of ten per centum per annum, less the amount derived therefrom, with interest thereon at the rate aforesaid, and may assume all its rights and privileges from the corporators aforenamed. And in case said towns cannot agree as to the portion of said amount to be paid by each, the Supreme Judicial Court or any justice thereof, upon application of either town so purchasing, shall appoint three commissioners to award the amount to be paid by each, which award shall be final.

SECT. 9. For the purpose of defraying the cost of such franchise, corporate property, lands, water, and water rights as are taken, purchased, or held for the purposes aforesaid, and for constructing works necessary and proper for the accomplishment of the purposes authorized by this Act, and paying all expenses incident thereto, each of said towns may issue, from time to time, scrip, notes, or certificates of debt: the town of Wakefield to an amount not exceeding two hundred thousand dollars; the town of Stoneham to an amount not exceeding one hundred and fifty thousand dollars. Such scrip issued by the town of Wakefield shall be denominated on its face Wakefield Water Fund Bonds; that issued by the town of Stoneham shall be denominated on its face Stoneham Water Fund Bonds. All such scrip shall bear interest at a rate not exceeding seven per centum per annum, payable semi-annually, and the principal shall be payable at periods of not more than twenty years from the issuing of said scrip, notes, or certificates respectively. And such town may sell the same, or any part thereof, from time to time, or pledge the same for money borrowed for the purposes aforesaid, on such terms and conditions as such towns shall deem proper. And each of said towns is further authorized to make appropriations, and assess from time to time, such amounts, not exceeding in any one year the sum of ten thousand dollars, towards paying the principal of the money so borrowed, except in the year when the same may become due, and also a sum sufficient to pay the interest thereon in the same manner as money is assessed and appropriated for other town purposes.

SECT. 10. When said towns, or either of them, shall assume or purchase the franchise, property, rights, and privileges of the corporation established by this Act, said town or towns shall hold and may exercise all the powers and authority conferred upon said corporation by this Act, and shall be subject to all the restrictions, duties, and liabilities herein imposed on said corporation, and may act by such commissioners, three in number, from each town, as the selectmen of each town shall from time to time appoint; and said town or towns shall be liable to pay all damages to which said corporation shall have become liable and shall not have paid.

In case both towns shall have united in assuming or purchasing the franchise and property of said corporation, the commissioners appointed by the selectmen as aforesaid shall constitute a joint Board of Water Commissioners, who shall have power to regulate and control the use of the water of said lake, and exercise all the powers and authority conferred by this Act; and said towns, in case they shall have united as aforesaid, shall be jointly liable to persons having claims under this Act; but the apportionment between the towns of any expenses incurred under this Act, and the determination of any other question which shall arise between said towns under this Act, shall be made by said joint Board; and in case said commissioners shall be equally divided upon any question, it shall be determined in the manner heretofore provided in the eighth section of this Act for apportioning the amount to be paid for the franchise and property of said corporation.

In case one of said towns shall alone assume or purchase said franchise and property under the provisions of this Act, its commissioners shall have the powers conferred by this section upon said joint Board.

SECT. 11. The rents received for the use of water within the limits of each town shall, when collected, be paid over to the treasurer of the town, and after the payment therefrom of the semi-annual interest upon said scrip, and after deducting all charges of distribution and repairs and other expenses incident to the same, shall be set apart, with all amounts appropriated from time to time by said town, for the payment of the principal sum of said scrip, as a sinking fund, which, with the accumulated interest upon the same, shall be devoted to the payment of said scrip of said town at maturity. Said sinking fund may be invested in the scrip authorized by this Act, at a price not exceeding its par value, or on such loans or in such securities as by law the funds of savings banks may be invested in, except that no portion of the same shall be loaned, directly or indirectly, to either of said towns, or upon mere personal security.

SECT. 12. The accounts of such sinking funds shall be kept apart from the other accounts of the town, and in each town shall at all times be open to the inspection of the water commissioners of said town. The treasurer of each town shall annually make a written report to the town, at its annual meeting, of the condition of the fund of the town, and the changes of investment during the then preceding year. The selectmen and water commissioners shall jointly, as often as once in each year, examine the accounts and securities of the fund, and shall report the result of their examination to the town, in connection with the report of the treasurer.

SECT. 13. It is hereby provided that if in the future the supply of water shall prove insufficient for more than one town, for domestic purposes, the town of Wakefield shall be first supplied.

SECT. 14. Nothing in this Act shall be construed to preclude the right of the town of Reading to take water from either or both of said lakes, whenever so authorized by the Legislature.

SECT. 15. This Act shall take effect upon its passage. [*Approved May* 4, 1872.]

THE END.

INDEX

ABBOT, 279
ABBOTT, 42 43 75 76 215 221 261
　271 279 287 288 291-293 314
　338 339 473 474 553 564 573
　600 633 650 652 693
ABORN, 3 82 152 220 221 279 328
　338 342 367 376 382 519 588
　593 595 600 601 604 633 651
　653 654 657 657 727 810
ADAMS, 165 179 180 208 266 279
　366 421 517 523 554 559 600
　601 602 633 651 654 657 693
ADDEN, 265 269 401 401 405 410
　426 523 550 533
ADDINGTON, 692 693
AELWELL, 35
AHAWAYET, 30
ALBEE, 253
ALBERT, 633
ALDEN, 297 351 355 660
ALDRICH, 194
ALEXANDER, 70 601
ALIENE, 496
ALLEN, 116 212 238 260 271 292
　313 326 362 364 452 530 542
　553 601 607 633 650 651 654
　656 706 725-727 729 761-763
　782 785 788 787

ALLIN, 49 55
ALMSHOUSE, 112
ALPAUGH, 601
ALSHOUSE, 166
AMES, 346 473 487
ANDERSON, 280 601 653
ANDRE, 720
ANDREW, 556 574
ANDREWS, 601
ANDROS, 35
ANGIER, 43 103
ANGLICE, 691
ANOUGH, 43
ANSORGE, 651
ANTRIM, 56
APPLETON, 91 107 116 147 165
　240 265 267-269 294 313 334
　398 480 514 515 523 531 537
　538 544 552 553 633 659 671
　678 752
ARCHER, 147
ARMINIUS, 200
ARMOUR, 654
ARNALL, 32
ARNOLD, 22 38 43 56 132 633 714
　718-720
ARRINGTON, 408 601 654
ASH, 84

ASHE, 601
ASHLEY, 215
ATKINS, 229
ATKINSON, 523-525 552
ATLINS, 241
ATWELL, 115 138 141 190 246 261 288 291-293 305 346 395 399 403 463 474 483 624 654 656 657 698 727 394
ATWOOD, 318 319 601
AUSTIN, 166 266 294 358 376 382 544 633 759
AVERY, 233 255 329 388
BABCOCK, 252 421 537 651
BACCHUS, 160 694
BACHELDER, 7 11 16 19 20 22 34 38 40 59 73 528
BACHELLER, 25 32 47 61 167 471 474
BACHELLOR, 712
BACON, 43 424
BADDGER, 207
BADGER, 52 68 243 249 260 261 266 287 288 323 337 346 370 373 375 376 388 410 411 414 417 474 527 694 736
BAILEY, 309 314 355 378 654 708 718
BAKER, 87 131 220 329 382 633 656
BALCH, 239
BALDWIN, 193 220 268 289 294 602 694
BALINK, 633
BALL, 251 269 528
BALLEY, 694
BALLOU, 210
BANCHOR, 564
BANCROFT, 7 22 23 32 34 35 39

BANCROFT (Continued)
40 43-45 52 58 61 64 68 80 97 99 102 104 107 108 113 118 120 122 126-128 132 138-141 143 145 147-154 156 164 166 168 170 172-174 176 179 180 182 183 185 205 216 220 221 225 226 236 247 251 259 266-268 274 276 282-287 290 294-299 302-307 309 313-318 330 346 365 367-369 384 395 399 405 406 446 447 461 471 472 475 479 480 513 520 521 524 528-531 534 542 545 546 548-551 560 568 570 602 633 651 652 654 683 693 697-699 701-706 708-710 713-715 731 734 752 759 761 803
BANKS, 597
BAOTS, 35
BARBER, 602 653
BARBERY, 221
BARDEN, 211
BARKER, 28 77 280 424 602 650 654 698
BARNARD, 56 137 278 279 344 346 358 370 579 602 661 672
BARNES, 633 652
BARRET, 169
BARRETT, 45 97 107 165 349 382 694 759
BARRON, 653
BARROWS, 216 219 220 265 267 480 514 553 554 566 752
BARRUS, 236 240 265-267 269 294 295 480 511 514 517 540 541 550 555 566 700
BARRY, 167
BARSTOW, 473

BARTLETT, 124 261 364 419 633 650 652
BARTLEY, 524 561
BARTON, 565 705
BASSE, 89
BASSET, 535 678
BASSETT, 266 267 688-690 241
BATCHELDER, 4 38 45 99 101 109 115 117 138-140 147 160 162 166 167 169 174 175 221 247 248 264 269 271 272 276 280-283 285-287 289-291 293 296 300-302 307 308 314 315 317 331 334 371 384 385 426 439 445 456 472 474 476 479 513 527 529 538 550 564 602 650 651 652 693 698 699 705 759 760
BATCHELLER, 103 145 170 205 355
BATES, 492 561
BATT, 153 376 697
BATTELLE, 634 652
BATTETTE, 633
BATTS, 431
BAULDWIN, 140
BAUMISTER, 602
BAXTER, 75 266 496 781
BAYRD, 369 404 654
BEACH, 654
BEAL, 252
BEALS, 728
BEARD, 36 118 119 161 163 170 173 298-300 304 306 310 311 318 403 404 511 525-528 694 700 760
BEATIE, 634
BECK, 119
BECKWITH, 280 587 602 609

BEEBE, 3 50 109 167 261 294 329 330 338 467 471 499 500 588 656 727 740 760 789 794 810 811
BEECHER, 238 239
BEERS, 82 307 527 532 693
BELCHER, 140
BELKNAP, 47 107 108 658
BELL, 524 634
BELLFLOWER, 11 14-16 19 20 47 60
BELLINGHAM, 10 18 31 51 692
BELLOWS, 246
BEMIS, 634
BENDER, 253
BENNET, 271 168
BENNETT, 45 47 160 213 218 698 699
BENT, 651 653
BENTLEY, 340 650
BERD, 188
BERMINGHAM, 651
BERRIER, 609
BERRY, 225 407 473 563 634
BESSEY, 634
BICKFORD, 299 308 309 602 651 698
BICKNELL, 654
BIGELOW, 168
BILL, 111
BILLINGHAM, 241
BILLINGS, 156
BINNEY, 810
BISHOP, 654
BIXBY, 280 603
BLACKINTON, 252
BLACKMAN, 693
BLACKSTOCK, 383
BLADDEN, 602

BLAIR, 345 715
BLAKE, 556
BLAKNEY, 602
BLANCHARD, 142 155 379 382 392 451 459 487 489 491-494 634 652 654
BLANDIN, 473
BLISS, 205 261 589 654 729 761 787 796
BLOCK, 473
BLODGETT, 155 156
BLOOD, 9 249
BLUNT, 529
BOARD, 530
BOARDMAN, 112 113 166 169 188 206 209 247 260 261 274 325 344 347 348 364-366 368 395-397 401 402 405 410 411 419 463 497 654 693 694 699 759 760
BODGE, 694 715
BOLLES, 252 372 421
BOND, 603 651
BOOTH, 88
BOOTHBY, 230
BORDEN, 634
BORMAN, 47
BOSWELL, 246 261 289 293 294 473 656
BOUTELLE, 705 760
BOUTWELL, 19 20 32 34 38 47 48 59 61 62 64-66 68 79 86 87 91 93 94 99 109 112 116 120 132 138 139 141 146 149 152 170 205 221 249 282 284 297 299 300 303 310 315 318 319 337 346 364 372 391 397-399 401 407 446 523 541 694 698-700
BOWDITCH, 543

BOWEN, 215 651
BOWSER, 241 523
BOYCE, 235 354 515 526 539 598 634 652
BOYD, 132
BOYNTON, 115 333
BRADFORD, 76 650
BRADLEY, 225
BRADY, 191
BRAGG, 61 230 250 694 699
BRALEY, 403
BRANT, 718
BRASTOW, 597
BRATTLE, 53 106
BRAYFORD, 137
BRAZELL, 603
BREED, 271 291 292 294 363 540 543 700
BREEDEN, 497
BRETT, 634
BREWSTER, 329
BREYMAN, 714
BRIANT, 139
BRIDGE, 121 700
BRIDGER, 233 603 634
BRIEN, 634 650
BRIERLY, 654
BRIGGS, 220 252 459 480 555
BRIGHAM, 253
BRIGHT, 100
BRITTON, 289 292 471 603 654 727 728 769 789 793 794
BROCK, 6 14 16-18 20 27 33 34 49 90 104 132 204 351 352 442 731
BRONSON, 215 271
BROOKS, 75 96 121 155 176 180 248 302 457 459 473 475 528 543 603 634 700 701 703 704 706 713 714 734 752 694

BROUNE, 57
BROWN, 3 10 22 51-53 55 57 63 66
    81 94 97 98 100 117 120 125 126
    132 133 138-141 144-146 150
    151 155 160 162 163 166-169
    171 173-176 179-186 188 199
    205 206 210 216 220 221 225
    243 247 250 255 258 266-268
    274 277 281 282 284 285 288-
    290 292-294 297 298 302 309
    327-330 332 334 335 345 349
    350 354 358 364-366 370 375
    378 381 382 386 392 401 410
    417 438 440-443 457 463 466
    472-474 476 497 511 523 528
    540 560 563 564 569 603 617
    634 653 654 694 696 697-699
    711 713 728 732 734 744 759
    760
BROWNE, 5 6 11 12 14-21 25 26 28
    29 32 33 34 37-40 44 49-52 58
    68 86 130 132-134 136 204 244
    248 274 282 283 688-690
BRUCE, 68 337 367 368 603 634
    651 653
BRYAM, 225
BRYAN, 604
BRYANT, 19 20 32 34 43 44 48 55
    56 68 81 84 94 112 114 115 125
    126 132 133 137 139-143 145
    148 149 151 152 163 165 167
    172 206 274 275 277 282 283
    290 296 303 310 319 326 327
    330 333 343 348-350 352 358
    364 368 370 376 377 384 394
    397 401 410 474 530 603 604
    658 694 697-699 759 760
BUCHAM, 344
BUCHANNAN, 560
BUCHOLIZER, 54
BUCK, 119 319 399 515 522 523
    634 635 652 654 698
BUCKE, 267
BUCKLEY, 68 88
BUCKLY, 51
BUCKNAM, 143
BUDINGHAM, 239
BULL, 417 457 458 736
BULLEN, 209 261 654
BUMBLE, 807
BUNKER, 635 652
BUNTIN, 490
BURBANK, 393 495 654
BURCHAM, 30 33
BURDETT, 500
BURDETTE, 598
BURDITT, 246 251 259 261 279 280
    332 345 379 386-389 407 410
    472 474 603 604 650 651 653
    654 694 759
BURGESS, 654
BURGOYNE, 183 545 705 706 712
    714 715 719
BURNAM, 160
BURNAP, 11 14 16 19 20 26 30 32
    34 38 51 56 57 64 68 73 85-87
    95 97 111-113 116 124 127 132
    136 138 139-142 144 148 149
    154 164 166 169 170 172 186
    213 216 249 274 281 282 299
    300 304 308 317 378 395 442
    471 475 694 699 700 759 23
BURNHAM, 274 275 326 328 350
    367 379 403 406 474 604 693
BURNS, 78
BURR, 526
BURRELL, 650
BURRILL, 59 75 95 267 287 300

BURRILL (Continued)
383 528 535 654 688
BURRINGTON, 222
BURSHAM, 100
BURT, 31 32 34 58 135-138 140 314 392
BUSHNELL, 220
BUTLER, 291 387 555 556 604 625 654 657
BUTTERFIELD, 653 654
BUTTERS, 58 635 694 699
BUTTERY, 15 19 58
BUTTRICK, 298
BUXTON, 74 169 266 316 604 650 694 698 700
CABOT, 628
CALDER, 564
CALDWELL, 604 651
CALIFF, 717
CALL, 147
CALLEY, 694
CALNON, 307 697
CALVIN, 200
CAMP, 694
CAMPBELL, 181 271 287 291 293 294 308 524 635 651 709 750-752 758
CANBY, 610
CANN, 40 133
CANNON, 558
CAPEN, 715
CARDELL, 654
CAREY, 298 604 635 654 715
CARLETON, 650
CARLEY, 515 524
CARNES, 157
CARNEY, 635
CARPENDER, 59
CARPENTER, 278 344 403 580 787

CARR, 650 652 654
CARROLL, 422
CARTER, 58 119 172 196 237 251 266 274 291 310 339 343 364 368 386 410 512 513 519 527 539 546 604 635 651 653 654 694 699 713
CARTWRIGHT, 259 604 653
CARVER, 85
CASE, 22 220 235 650
CASH, 654
CASSIDY, 604
CASTINE, 35
CATE, 220 269 278 294 389 511 554 635
CATO, 182
CAUGHLIN, 635
CENTRE, 377 400
CHADWELL, 7
CHADWICK, 58 93 137 492 654
CHAMBERLAIN, 127 137 218
CHAMBERLIAN, 497
CHAMBERLIN, 132
CHAMBERS, 401 605
CHANDLER, 14 45 58 91 132 305 383 398 406 605
CHAPMAN, 206 229 270 271 390 486 605 635 650 651 654
CHASE, 95 474
CHATHAM, 784
CHEEVER, 45 191
CHENEY, 300 518 527 605 654 657
CHEVEY, 238
CHEWTE, 546
CHICKERING, 793 809
CHILDS, 336
CHITTENDEN, 526
CHOATE, 551
CHURCHILL, 605 654 657

CHUTE, 216 247 310 516 531 545-547
CLAFLIN, 782
CLAFTER, 713
CLAPMAN, 786
CLAPP, 329 694
CLARK, 3 7 15 17 19-21 38 53 58 90 115 132 193 206 236 238-240 266 267 281 323 325 365 519 556 564 605 654
CLARKE, 8 10-12 21 32
CLAY, 221 395 401
CLAYES, 120 166 384 497 759
CLEAVES, 215 271 635 636
CLEMENT, 635 760
CLEMENTS, 329 654
CLEMONS, 605
CLERK, 605
CLEVELAND, 239
CLIFFORD, 394 493 539 605 651 656
CLUMMONS, 699
COATES, 408
COBB, 421 678 679
COBURN, 539 597 635
COCHRANE, 249
COFFIN, 35 259 272 635 656 671 752
COGGIN, 238 386 392 534 698
COGGINS, 119 221
COLBURN, 225 288 293 528 652
COLBY, 473 565 605 654
COLE, 58 208 266
COLEMAN, 606
COLLINS, 606 650
COLMAN, 106 469 523 699
COLSON, 20 33 38 58 63 137
CONANT, 68 124
CONEY, 280 544 606 635 650 652

CONNELL, 377 391
CONVERS, 70 694
CONVERSE, 31 41 267 277 544
CONVERSSE, 28
CONWAY, 606 635
COOK, 58 83 84 215 280 311 513 530 556 606 635 636 650 652 694 752
COOKSON, 227 268
COOLEY, 126
COOMBS, 294 606 654 694
COON, 606 654
COOPER, 230 259 606 653
COPELAND, 241 523 636
COPER, 7
COPLEY, 552 559
COPP, 654
CORCORAN, 651
CORDIS, 167 247 248 330-332 334 364
CORDITT, 760
COREY, 606
CORKINS, 556
CORRIE, 636
CORWIN, 106 131
CORY, 694
COTTON, 104
COULSON, 32
COVERLY, 715
COWDREY, 3 6-8 11 13 15-20 23 25 26 32 33 35 37 38 45 47 51 58-61 63 68 81 90 96 97 100 101 114 115 136 139 146 163 166 167 169 189 205 261 274 281 288 289 291 299 311 329 339 352 376 384 392 394 395 403 411 430 432 464 474 606 651 654 656 657 694 698 727 759 760

COWELL, 394
COWLES, 204
COX, 107 367 379 525 636 653 654
COYTMORE, 12
CRAIN, 388
CRANDALL, 10 11 517
CRANE, 255 650
CRASKIE, 607
CRAWLEY, 228
CREESEY, 539
CREESY, 530
CRISTY, 266
CROCKER, 119 386 391 399 656
CROOKE, 235
CROOKER, 405
CROSBY, 253 636
CROSS, 120 308 650
CROUCH, 299 319 636
CROW, 653
CROWE, 539 636
CROWELL, 539
CUMMINGS, 187 200 249 291 371 519
CUNNINGHAM, 227 261 473
CURMICK, 650
CURRIER, 607 654 749 786
CURTIS, 694 698 699
CURTIUS, 756
CURWIN, 32 60
CUSHING, 241 370
CUSHMAN, 166 384 759
CUTLER, 14 15 19 20 31 32 34 35 38 47 60 71 106 112 120 140 143 169 261 282 294 329 442 473 564 651 694
CUTLERS, 389
CUTTER, 651 654 657 694
DAGER, 654 656
DALAND, 259 654

DAME, 650
DAMING, 547
DAMON, 3 7 11 16 19 20 22 23 30-32 34 38 40 47 60-62 65 66 69 72-75 94 97 99 101 109 111 113 115 118 119 126 132 137 139 140 145 147 149 160 162-164 166 167 169 170 174 180 184 189 205 220 221 236 240 247 268 271 276 281 283-286 296 298 299 301-305 307 308 312 317-319 321 334 353 354 366 384 400 436 437 443 449 522 524 529 531 536 542 547 548 550 636 650-652 694 698-700 705 712 760
DANA, 249 294 636
DANE, 249 487 650
DANFORTH, 115 333 370 607 651 653 654 657
DARLING, 500 651
DARRACOTT, 651
DAVIES, 36
DAVIS, 3 7 10-12 16 19-21 43 47 48 62 65 88 90 102 126 139 206 207 220 250 252 259 269 281 291 310 346 377 404 407 418 421 473 475 479 513 521 523 527 539 549 550 607 636 637 650 651 653 654 657 694 699
DAVY, 215 228 271
DAWES, 559
DAY, 267 350 360 476 521 539 607 651 654
DEADMAN, 84 191 208 277 391 401 464 607 637 653 654 694
DEAN, 297 355 607 650 654
DEANE, 71 255
DEARBORN, 278 588 607 654 727

DEARHORN, 580
DEARINE, 607
DEBLOIS, 78
DEGEN, 278 279 588 597 608 653 654
DEJEAN, 529
DELAY, 637 652
DELVER, 65
DENNET, 654
DENNIS, 697
DENVER, 178
DERBY, 329 379 382
DEVEREAUX, 249
DEWBURST, 637
DEWEY, 514 540-542 557
DICKERMAN, 38 62
DICKEY, 608
DICKINS, 565
DICKSON, 608
DIKE, 403
DIMON, 249
DINSMOOR, 637
DINSMOORE, 267
DINSMORE, 527 528 550
DIX, 19 20 34 38 46 52 62 69 72 119 129 137 138 140 169 175 249 280 284 285 307 312 337 367 370 379 471 608 653 671 694 698 699
DIXE, 32
DIXTON, 650
DOAK, 715
DODDRIDGE, 496
DODGE, 63 133 146 248 653
DOE, 259 650 654
DOLAN, 608
DOLAND, 694
DOLE, 123 473 524 654
DOLLIVER, 288 597 656

DONNAVAN, 656
DONNELL, 651
DONOGHUE, 653
DORR, 637
DOSS, 162
DOTON, 372
DOUCETTE, 523
DOUGLAS, 694
DOUNTON, 73
DOW, 249 608 657
DOWNS, 201
DOYLE, 608
DRAKE, 279 366 608 654 759
DRAPER, 279 608 653 654 657
DRESSER, 68
DRINKWATER, 252 421
DRIVER, 214 269 271
DUBLIN, 528
DUDLEY, 104 307
DUFFIN, 608
DUNBAR, 241
DUNHARE, 546
DUNN, 126 193 235 580 582 608 609 654
DUNTON, 3 7 11 14 16 20-22 32 38 63 69 94 193 281
DURGIN, 557
DUSTIN, 3 7 11 13 14 16 18 19 21 32 37 38 58 63 119 439
DUTTON, 14 34 63 694
DYAR, 17
DYER, 609
EAGER, 609 654
EAMES, 220 221 267 287 292 294 306-308 363 378 395 529 540 652 654 655
EASTMAN, 212 271 637
EATON, 3 7 10 11 13 16 19-22 25 28 32-35 37 38 41 44 48 57

EATON (Continued)
63-70 74-76 80 94 95 97-101 103
107-110 119 122 126 132 135
137 139 140 143 145-155 160-
164 167-172 175-177 183 184
186 188 189 194 206-210 212
213 222 225 226 228 245 247
252 255 256 260 261 271 274
277-285 288-294 297 302-304
307 310 314 323 326 327 330
332 333 335 336 338-340 345
346 349-351 353 356 364 366-
372 375 377 381 383 387-389
391 393-395 398 403 404 410
411 420-423 426 427 432-436
445-447 452 463-465 467 471-
474 482 496 498 500 510 516
518 524 525 530 532 546 549
564 571 573 578 580 583 588
590 596 598 609 610 637 650-
657 665-667 694 696-700 705
706 709 725-727 729 741 759-
762 764 771 776 784 793 809
810
EBERDON, 694
EDES, 127 328 338 715 760
EDMANDS, 126 353 367 371 610 694 715
EDMOND, 550
EDMUNDS, 381
EDSON, 637
EDWARDS, 15 16 18 20 25 32 34 67 70 87 107 238 282 610 662
EITZHENRY, 132
ELD, 119
ELESLY, 312
ELLENWOOD, 694 699
ELLIOT, 527
ELLIOTT, 557 564 565
ELLIS, 96 610 637
ELLSLEY, 46 301
ELLSWORTH, 582 586
ELSELEY, 102 317
ELWELL, 637
EMERSON, 3 4 45 47 48 51 57 59
61 62 66 68 69 80 91 93 101 112
113 118 120 122 124 133 138
139 143 145-148 152 153 155
157 160 162 163 166-170 172
177 179 183-186 188 189 199
204 205 207 213 215 216 220
221 237 238 240 247-249 259-
261 266 269 271 274 276-278
283-286 288 289 291 292 294
295 297 299 300 302-306 314
316 319 327 328 331 335-341
343-346 349-351 356 360 365-
368 370 372 375 383-389 391
394 395 399-401 406 407 410
411 421 425 426 431 439 441
445 449 458 460 464 471 472
474 483 495-497 504 513 519
528 582 583 606 610 618 630
637 653-657 663-668 672 694
698-700 703 705 711-713 726-
728 759 760 762 810 811
EMERY, 356 526
EMMONS, 200 230 610
EMORY, 293
ENDICOTT, 69
ERSKINE, 377
ESTES, 610 653
EUSTIS, 80 99 149 152 166 280 288
397 398 426 458 593 611 653
653 655 760
EVANS, 69 70 79 84 114 119 120
143 162 166 169 210 225 226-
228 246 259 261 274 275 277

EVANS (Continued)
  288 291 317 334 335 338-340
  350 363 364 371 372 374 375
  377 410 412 415 420 439 470
  474 496 497 526 570 611 637
  651 652 654-656 694 699 753
  758-760 803
EVERETT, 70 106 249 250 701 766
EVES, 284
FABENS, 458 472
FAIRBANKS, 221 280 379 611 650
  655 656
FAIRBERN, 651
FAIRCHILD, 222
FAIRFIELD, 12 15 70 71 100
FARLEY, 23 305 694 698
FARMER, 83 305 319 694 700
FARMERY, 637
FARMING, 638
FARNHAM, 74
FARNSWORTH, 655
FARNUM, 338 651
FARRAR, 68 694
FARRELL, 653
FARRIER, 541 699
FARRINGTON, 688
FARWELL, 638 652
FAY, 611
FELCH, 8 11 13 15 19 20 32 34 37
  38 71 112 128 134 137 139 148
  149 160 166 281 282 305 356
  435 694 698 699 759
FELLOWS, 52
FELT, 140 142 694
FELTON, 383 611
FERSON, 41
FETCH, 125
FIELDS, 655
FIFIELD, 612 655 657

FILLEBROWN, 716
FISH, 33 71 137 139
FISK, 34 612 653
FISKE, 38 51 58 68 141 324 390 555
FITCH, 3 6-8 10 11 13 14 16 19 20
  25 32 34 36 38-40 45 56 62 63
  71 72 107 108 146 154 205 274
  281 282 290 341 430 431
FITTS, 8 13
FITZ, 564
FITZPATRICK, 228 638
FLAGG, 528 651
FLANDERS, 611
FLANNIGAN, 638
FLAXINGTON, 638
FLEIG, 638
FLETCHER, 280 371 383 396 522
  523 612 638 652
FLINT, 22 24 31-34 46 57 61 66 72-
  80 91 97 102 119 131 133 135
  136 140 144-146 148 169 170
  173-175 179 182 184 185 201
  213 247 249 250 267 270-272
  277 282 283 285-287 290 292-
  294 296 300 313 316 319 320
  348 354 371 372 398 404 426
  445 446 452 453 456 460 461
  470 471 500 527 638 650-652
  655 694 697-699 734 284
FLOWERS, 360
FLOYD, 386
FLYNN, 638
FOGG, 249 612 655
FOLGER, 73
FOLSOM, 340 597 631 656
FOLSON, 612
FONDE, 638
FOOTE, 274 318 519 557 566
FORBES, 612 657

FORD, 656
FORREST, 612
FORRESTER, 329
FORTISS, 652
FOSDICK, 715
FOSS, 299 560 638
FOSTER, 48 68 75 79 80 82 97 110 132 139 158 170 170 182-185 250 261 266 268 280 283 285 288 291-293 297-299 303 305 306 310 311 315 328 356 357 358 368 371 385 402 426 436 441 457 464 471 475 495 496 512-514 518 523-525 528 533 540 541 551 612 638 650 651 655 668 679 694 697-699 701 704 705 759 760
FOWLE, 118 612 651 694 698
FOWLER, 274 275 365 498
FOX, 55 105 106 183
FRANCIS, 80 306 638
FRANKLIN, 537 565
FREEMAN, 179 252 259 334 394 512 543 651 694
FREMONT, 477 584
FRENCH, 77 200 265 287 378 527 598 638 663
FRINK, 401
FROST, 75 235 308 513 517 522 526 540 638 652 750 751
FROTHINGHAM, 47 48 56 64 196 456 694
FRY, 253 650
FRYE, 157 158 249 284 564
FULLER, 115 227 228 250 268 472 566 652 653 692
FULLINGTON, 402
FULTON, 385
FULTZ, 306

GAFFIELD, 309
GAGE, 402 472 474 804
GALE, 91 104 652
GALLAGHER, 221
GAMBELL, 638
GAMMON, 655 656
GARDINER, 235
GARDNER, 72 155 160 194 326 355 377 391 392 421 426 517 656 698
GARFIELD, 530
GARLAND, 612
GARRISON, 516 517 740
GARY, 140
GASSETT, 305
GATES, 183 191 447 491 650 651 709 712 714
GAY, 254
GENDNEY, 691
GEORGE, 255 267 688
GEORGE-NO-NOSE, 687 689
GERRISH, 52 710
GERRITSON, 639
GERRY, 35 61 84 93 261 277 300-302 322 350 351 365 392 399 400 639 650 699
GIBSON, 66 108 149 346
GIHON, 612
GILBERT, 58
GILCHRIST, 651
GILL, 388
GILMAN, 79 246 612 651 653 655
GILMORE, 81
GLEASON, 223 287 511 512 517 524 525 530 542 564 694
GODDARD, 493
GODFREY, 613 655 657
GODSHECK, 330
GOING, 140

GOLD, 81 341
GOLDTHWAIT, 561 639
GOODALE, 121
GOODELL, 476 651
GOODHUE, 639
GOODRICH, 555
GOODWIN, 20 30 32 34 36 38 52 59
  80 81 85 94 95 102 103 115 126
  132 138 139 146 148 149 152
  160 162 163 166 167 169 170
  185 205 271 274 282 284 289
  290 297 349 397 398 404 474
  539 613 639 650 652 655 657
  694 697 699 712 760
GOOING, 137
GOOLD, 140
GOULD, 35 63 65 75 80-83 96 103
  113 121 140 143 154 162 163
  166 167 169 187 189 192 247
  261 274 275 286-289 291 303
  304 309 311 318 322 323 326-
  328 332 338 341 342 360 361
  372 374 376 379 380 381 383
  403 408 410 411 415 416 420
  430 463 473 474 523 525 529
  550 557 625 655 656 694 697-
  699 712 721 739 740 759 760
GOWING, 35 61 74 136 145 267 305
  316 445 480 652
GRANT, 599 650 786
GRAVES, 31 42 73 75 145 170 241
  247 271 286 290 557 694 697
  698
GRAY, 45 120 229 240 241 319 329
  338 515 525 558 784
GREBLR, 586
GREEN, 5-7 9 10 55 69 70 75 82-85
  102 106 113 116 121 124 126
  140 142 143 146 162 166 169

GREEN (Continued)
  173 179 191 199 204 217 230
  246 260 261 274 275 279 283-
  286 288 305 309 317 323 334
  336 338 353 355 358 363-366
  368-370 375-377 381-386 391
  400 410 411 438 439 442 463
  471 474 485 526 570 613 639
  650 652 653 657 694 698 699
  731 734 744 759
GREENE, 31 438 656 698
GREENLEAF, 694
GREENOUGH, 253
GREENWOOD, 523
GREGG, 272 370
GREGGS, 280 588 593 613
GRENVILLE, 118
GREY, 655
GRIFFIN, 143 148 393 655
GRIGGS, 639
GRISWOLD, 213
GROSVENOR, 135 252 269-271
  421 474 659 671
GROUARD, 312 527 528 545 704
GROVER, 57 85 639 652
GUILFORD, 213 228 271 295 752
GUIZOT, 808
GULLIVER, 239
GUNN, 558
HADLEY, 83
HAGGERTY, 614
HAIES, 34
HAINES, 60 324 399 416 417 736
HAIR, 13
HALE, 275 318 345 399 405 558 662
  759
HALL, 155 156 223 267 383 385 530
  614 639
HALSEY, 6

HAMBLIN, 259 614 655 657
HAMILTON, 473 614 653
HAMMOND, 255 293 358 651
HAMMONDS, 375
HANAFORD, 480 565 752 757
HANCOCK, 179 539 706
HANGLE, 614
HANGLIN, 655
HANLEY, 524
HANNAFORD, 473
HANNAH, 402
HANSON, 517
HARBORN, 639
HARCUM, 65
HARDING, 239 655
HARDY, 75 122 389 656
HARMERS, 614
HARNDEN, 20 31-33 85 118 129 133 136-138 213 267 282 295 317 370 461 518 521 523-525 527 528 539 541 551 552 564 598 614 616 652 653 657 696 732 733
HARRIMAN, 639
HARRINGTON, 117 280 558 614 653 655
HARRIS, 95 112 403 650 652
HARRNDEN, 132
HARSEY, 688
HART, 3 7 11 14 16 20 32 34-36 66 73-75 77 81 85 112 114 127 137 138 140 141 166 170 188 191 195 201 202 247 250 261 280 286 291 292 323 338 343 354-357 360 362 363 369 372 387 392 410-412 437 457 471 473 474 503 504 613 652 655 659 694 697 699 716 734 759
HARTS, 456

HARTSHORN, 3 7 8 14 20 22 25 34 59 60 65 91 94 96 115 117 132 136 139 145 146 149 152 160 162 163 166-170 175 186 206 220 221 246 247 260 261 268 269 275 276 281 284 287-289 294 295 299 300 306 307 314-317 326 343 344 345 366 368 392-394 398 399 401 403 406 439 472 478 479 483 487 514 567 613 614 639 653 664 694 697-700 727 752 759 760
HARTSHORNE, 8 32 35 36 38 46 47 51 55 62 64 79 85-87 100 119 259 289 655 697 698 759
HARTWELL, 280 613 639
HARVEY, 392 639
HASELTINE, 86 87
HASKELL, 614 655
HASSELTINE, 555
HASTINGS, 87 180 711
HATSON, 694 695
HAUGH, 6-9 12 14 16 17 23 27 33 49 87-90 92 98 111 123 204 351 354 442 731
HAUPT, 563
HAVEN, 167 168 172 182 187 200 215 216 312 705
HAWES, 318 558
HAWKES, 71 125 126 140 166 209 261 290 322 323 355 368 369 379 383 384 389 435 474 535 614 653 655 657 695 699 759
HAWKINS, 30 695
HAWTHORNE, 18 693
HAY, 83 90 91 106 126 139 140 152 163 166 168 169 187 189 190 198 247-250 276 277 284 299 339 349 365 393 394 397-399

HAY (Continued)
  404 407 416 473 474 694 695
  699 714 760
HAYDEN, 280 614 615
HAYE, 21
HAYES, 302
HAYNES, 372 650
HAYSEY, 32
HAYWARD, 280 552 615 639 752
HAYWOOD, 78 120 136 170 212
  222 271 518 699
HEALY, 328 384
HEATH, 214 226 251 261 271 348
  394 615 651 655 709
HEBARD, 317
HEBBETTS, 615
HEMENWAY, 122
HEMINWAY, 677
HEMPHILL, 119
HENCHMAN, 151 248
HENFIELD, 379
HENNESEY, 639
HENNIGAR, 233
HENRY, 19
HERBERT, 32 38 87 92 98 99 114
  128 129 130 133 248 282 289
  317 444
HERKIMER, 719
HERO, 397
HERRICK, 75 170 213 247 249 285
  299 300 358 399 471 474 695
  699
HERSEY, 97
HERVEY, 253
HESCEY, 6 92 282
HESCY, 107
HESELTON, 639
HETLER, 639
HETTLER, 651

HEWES, 42 215 221 472 655
HEWITT, 60
HIBBENS, 14
HICHBORN, 211
HIGGINS, 228
HILBORN, 615 651
HILBOURN, 655
HILER, 716
HILL, 12 181 228 249 258 261 267
  297 298 305 340 352 404 495
  500 571 655 656 695 697 700
  801 811 760
HILLIARD, 249
HILLS, 32 92
HINGHAM, 60
HINMAN, 650
HITCHCOCK, 711
HITCHENS, 699
HITCHINS, 408
HITTINGER, 804
HOBBIE, 512
HOBBY, 44 61 132 146 147 150-154
  156 157 165 204 345 443 447
  471 569 732 759
HODGKINS, 92 615
HODGMAN, 20 21 32 34 38 92 93
  139 141 147 152
HOLBROOK, 214 640 652
HOLDEN, 61 66 119 140 220 267
  293 403 518 522 533 540 694
  749 750 751 753
HOLLIS, 2 558 655
HOLMAN, 337 338
HOLMES, 10 11 346 615
HOLT, 13 45 75 136 166 170 186
  221 271 286 364 399 400 402
  640 650-653 655 695 698 699
  760
HOOD, 323 615 689

HOOPER, 4 7 11 15 20 26 31 34 38 63 93 117 137 282
HOPH, 9 10
HOPKINS, 102 149 167 188 200 206 259 285 299 404 405 406 410 449 571 640 652 655 695 699 760
HOPKINSON, 86 167 168 343 392 399 405 663 760
HORNE, 564
HORTEN, 598
HORTON, 291 640
HOSMER, 280 615
HOUSEMAN, 640 652
HOUSEMANN, 640
HOUSTON, 486
HOW, 45
HOWARD, 50 51 65 68 138 236 238 240 277 294 307 337 365 375 401 539 561 652 750
HOWARDS, 653
HOWE, 615 708
HOWES, 265 266 267 267 558 752
HOWLET, 693
HOWLETT, 18 230
HOYT, 266 280 537 615 640 655 810
HUBBARD, 79 259 392
HUCKINS, 207 421 423
HUCTHINSON, 652
HUDSON, 694 698 701
HULL, 204 230
HUMBOLDT, 804
HUMPHREY, 609
HUMPHREYS, 547
HUNNEWELL, 225 226 652
HUNT, 73 74 265 269 318 514 515 540 558 559 564 616 640 657 695

HUNTER, 650 651 652
HUNTINGTON, 559
HUPPER, 32
HURCOM, 138
HURCON, 170 175
HURCUM, 284
HURD, 51 68 167 328 332 385 395 495 615 652 655 656 760
HURLEY, 615
HUSSEY, 97
HUTCHENSON, 38
HUTCHINGS, 241
HUTCHINS, 267 558 695
HUTCHINSON, 31 32 34 72 73 93 95 136 138 213 261 267 283 293 314 350 388 401 472 496 498 655 692 695
HYDE, 564 640
ILSLEY, 551
INGALLS, 370
INGOLS, 178
IRESON, 315
JACKSON, 32 93 119 179 252 417 421 616 657 706 708 714 721
JACOBS, 252 421
JAMERSON, 404
JAMES, 110
JAMESON, 616 655
JAQUES, 52
JAQUITH, 309 546
JARVIS, 716
JEAGGLES, 139
JEFFERDS, 335
JEFFERSON, 421
JEFFERY, 153 213 640 697 752
JENKINS, 32 58 93 113 118 138 360 640 650 652 653 655 697 698 739
JENKINSON, 93

JENNINGS, 229 330 374 392
JENNISON, 616 652
JEWELL, 211
JEWETT, 123 210 560
JOHNSON, 9 28 45 68 80 82 164
    196 204 230 241 274 274 299
    369 377 385 402 403 432 457
    481 511 512 521 532 616 688
    695 699 751 760
JONES, 8 212 271 277 291 292 316
    358 616 640 641 650 653 655
JONSON, 128
JORDAN, 261 473 655
JOSSELYN, 18
JOY, 147 160 652
JRFFERY, 93
JUDD, 293 472 514 524 540 559 701
JUDSON, 216
KAIN, 401
KAKA, 616
KANE, 583
KEAWLEY, 650
KEBBE, 93 137
KEEFE, 641
KEEMER, 407 408
KEENE, 655
KEITH, 266
KELHAM, 564
KELLA, 716
KELLEY, 616 641 657
KELLY, 650
KELSEY, 652
KELSON, 93
KEMBLE, 713
KEMP, 186 268 558-560 694
KEN, 93 324
KENDALL, 4 7 11 15 19 20 30 34
    44 47 48 56 64 73 93 94 97 99
    101 103 128 205 253 281 302

KENDALL (Continued)
    310 407 431 432 443 550 653
    698 713
KENDRICK, 641
KENNEDY, 616 655
KENNEY, 404 616 695
KENNISON, 652
KENT, 180
KIDDER, 90 93 248 280 616 652
    655 695
KILLIAM, 250
KILLOM, 695
KILLORIN, 259
KIMBALL, 75 154 220 252 263 313
    335 371 421 475 565 641 656
    698
KINERSON, 85
KING, 457 650 688-690
KINGMAN, 235 259 266 269 277
    278 288 291 294 305 404 405
    497 511 516 517 527 528 531
    539 550 561 573 616 653 655
    656
KINGSTON, 403
KINNERSON, 616
KINSMAN, 397
KIRBY, 616 655 657
KIRK, 238
KITTREDGE, 659
KNIGHT, 66 84 115 140 143 214
    223 246 265 269 274 277 346 394
    395 514 540 542 560 561 617
    641 653 655 656 697 698 811
KNIGHTS, 279
KNOWLES, 252 340 364 419 421
    609 656
KNOWLTON, 94 112 362 652 717
KOSCIUSKO, 709
KUMMER, 641

KUNKSHAMOOSHAW, 687 688 689 690 691
LABADOR, 129
LABARON, 655
LACLAIR, 653
LACLAIRE, 641
LAFAYETTE, 704
LAIGHTON, 250
LAKIN, 94
LAMBERT, 97 162 167 261 284 396 401 402 464 472 474 695 699 760
LAMPSON, 44 45
LAMSON, 22 31 32 34 38 45 51 64 85 94 98 139 148 271 283 305 641 695
LANE, 41 249 259 617 655 656 657 810
LANG, 519 539 540 564 617 641
LANGWORTHY, 238
LANSING, 218
LARIFORD, 58
LARKIN, 383 716
LARNED, 178
LARRABEE, 383
LARRIBEE, 85
LATHROP, 158 218
LAUGHTON, 114
LAUKIN, 4 7 11 12 14 16 94 95 281
LAWRENCE, 116 140 205 249 403 617 655
LAWSON, 132
LEAMAN, 94 127
LEATHE, 45 266 277 287 291 294 296 297 311 314 320 426 522 535 641 711 752
LEATHERBEE, 371
LEATHERS, 617 655 657
LEAVITT, 655

LEE, 392 617 641 652
LEFFERTS, 492
LEFFINGWELL, 106 114 333
LEIGHTON, 93 258 655
LEMAN, 61 108 137 138 140 716
LEONARD, 252 337 421
LESLIE, 31 37 101 149 167 397 403 760
LEVERETT, 106 252
LEVISTON, 695
LEWIS, 35 46 47 71 73 94 130 138 140 145 169 170 212 248 271 277 298 299 319 320 385 395 396 514 617 641 655 691 695 697-699 759
LEWY, 35
LIDE, 50
LILLEY, 15 19 20 36 40 57 59 64 66 95 111 128 139 166 310 311 698
LILY, 589
LINCOLN, 254 511 560 565 642
LINES, 39
LIST, 394
LITTELL, 265 514
LITTLE, 650
LITTLEFIELD, 278 292 529 597 617 653
LIVINGSTON, 695
LOCKE, 58 118 278 279 371 378 575 588 597 618 652 655
LONDON, 695
LONG, 325 396 618
LORD, 280 365 558 618 655 759
LORING, 267 421 548 642 656 783 784 788
LOVEJOY, 45 109 119 267 527 642 698 752
LOW, 72
LOWE, 655

LOWELL, 395
LOYD, 642
LUCAS, 92 398 655
LUES, 175
LUFKIN, 364 618
LUND, 345 346
LUNN, 22
LUNT, 80
LYMAN, 653
LYND, 12
LYNDE, 39 103 112 243 248 397
LYON, 211 586
LYONS, 618 657
M'GEE, 280
MACDONALD, 642
MACK, 489
MACOMB, 417
MADDEN, 618 657
MADOCHAWANDO, 35
MAGEE, 618
MAGLATLIN, 253
MAGNER, 655
MALCOLM, 421
MALCOM, 252
MALLORY, 421
MALTBY, 277
MANATAHQUA, 30
MANLEY, 561
MANNING, 47 228 291 514 515 527 548
MANSFIELD, 92 127 169 209 210 233 234 255 259 261 279 288 291-295 327 348 371 379 382 386 393 398 404 470 473 495 496 500 573 576 578 584 588 589 597 618 619 651 652 655 656 726 727 762 793 289
MARBEL, 698
MARBLE, 84

MARCH, 43 261
MARRETT, 200
MARSH, 688
MARSHALL, 4 6-8 11 12 14 20 35 95 115 277 281 619 642 652 653 655 700
MARSTON, 213
MARTIN, 4 6-8 11 16 95 201 281 619 652 655
MARTINDALE, 563
MASON, 44 64 186 230 248 305 345 650 655 695 700
MASSEY, 642
MASURY, 642
MATHER, 105 131
MATTHEWS, 214 271 388
MAURIZO, 642
MAVERICK, 95 112 359 504
MAWHINNEY, 811
MAXIM, 655
MAY, 517
MAYO, 619 655 657
MAYSON, 655
MCALEAR, 642
MCALEER, 653
MCALLISOR, 642
MCALLISTER, 642 653 655 695
MCCABE, 619
MCCALL, 528
MCCARTY, 619 655
MCCLEARY, 619
MCCLELLAN, 622
MCCLURE, 237 238
MCCORKLE, 235
MCCURDY, 229 230
MCDONALD, 268 619
MCDOUGALL, 408
MCGANN, 642
MCGEE, 619

MCINTIER, 31 32 34 699
MCINTIRE, 19 96 110 120 136 137 169 170 221 241 267-269 317 377 517 530 642 650 651 653 695 697 698
MCKAY, 233 280 358 540 583 596 619 642 655 752
MCKENSIE, 619
MCKENZIE, 280
MCLAUHLIN, 620
MCLEOD, 121 352
MCMAHAN, 655
MCMASTERS, 655
MCMILLAN, 642
MCMILLIAN, 695
MCMUNUS, 650
MCPHERSON, 620
MCQUEENEY, 657
MCQUEENY, 620
MCQUILLAN, 620
MEAD, 113 230 249 529 533
MEANS, 115
MELANCTON, 54
MELBURN, 328 394 407
MELENDA, 299
MELENDY, 305 382 695 697
MELLEN, 194 198 201 642 652
MELLON, 36 133
MERIMAN, 347
MERRIAM, 72
MERRIAN, 655 701
MERRILL, 240 324 386 396 655
MERROW, 19 20 32 34 36-38 80 96 97 101 137 139 148 150 154 296 298 299 306 316 446 529 541 543
MESSENGER, 168 187
MESSER, 642
METCALF, 44
METCALFE, 44
MILIGAN, 653
MILLER, 97 207 208 376 527 620 653
MILTON, 290 659
MINGAY, 492
MINGO, 698
MINOT, 248 267 268 472 551 559
MITCHELL, 49 401 410 564
MONTOWAMPATE, 30
MOODY, 655
MOOR, 642
MOORE, 31 63 211 261 620 653
MORGAN, 697
MORPHY, 586
MORRILL, 15 92 97 111 165 200 279 359 620 653 655
MORRIS, 358 651
MORRISON, 206 259
MORSE, 116 210 213 269 655
MORTON, 105 228 269 478 523 620 650 652 653 655 657
MOSES, 279 620 653
MOULTON, 241 319 320 372 598 619 655
MUCKLAND, 620 653 655
MUDGE, 160
MUNJOY, 124
MUNROE, 167 255 312 348 385 393 421 642 650 653 760
MURPHY, 642
MURRAY, 303 620 706
MYERS, 642 653
MYRICK, 92 393 398
NANEPASHEMET, 30
NASH, 166 192 294 365 561 642 652 656 759
NASON, 241
NELSON, 76 161 193 201 206 226

NELSON (Continued)
266 307 316 335-338 382 472
474 565 642 664 760
NEWCOMB, 442
NEWELL, 32 210 338 362 371 377
NEWHALL, 55 57 84 97 102 243
302 311 356 357 365 372 385
386 395 398 407 423 520 620
621 652 653 656 691 695 712
760 803
NEWMAN, 43 286 426 513 621 653
655
NICHLAS, 441 442
NICHOLS, 13 20 22 31 32 34 37 38
45 52 61 64 65 68 73 81 91 92 94
97-100 107 115 118 121 126 127
131 132 137-141 143 146-152
154-157 160-163 165-167 169
171 175 186 188 205 220 245
247 259 260 267 269 271 274
280 282-284 286 287 290 292
296 299 300 303-308 310 311
313-318 322 329 333 334 340
350-352 354 370 377-380 385
388 391 394 397 398 402 404
406 412 415 416 418 419 432
464 472-474 476 477 523 528
530 542 550 560 621 643 650-
653 655 656 695 697-700 705
752 759 760
NICK, 300 695
NICKERSON, 77 655
NILES, 539 561 562 655
NOBLE, 643
NOCHOLS, 114
NOLAN, 643
NORCROSS, 206 259 293 350 351
362 463 473 656
NORISH, 137

NORRIS, 235 266 287 524 561 643
651
NORTON, 111
NORWELL, 562
NORWOOD, 301 650
NOTT, 210
NOYES, 113 119 698
NURSE, 64 86 100 110 111 137 145
283 695 699
NUTTING, 167 331 695 713 760
NYE, 258
O'LEARY, 655
O'NIEL, 655
O'REARDON, 621
OAKES, 84 365
OCONNELL, 643
ODELL, 404
ODIORNE, 344
OLIVER, 89 113 136 166 173 206
248 261 277 288 291-293 340
345 359 360 366-368 378 418
504 621 651 655 656 727 759
762 793 809
ORCUTT, 212 650
ORNE, 194 311 367
ORR, 84 366 716
OSBORN, 219 716
OSGOOD, 51 73 77 86 294 295
OTIS, 564
OWEN, 560
PACKARD, 292 655 789 794
PAGE, 716
PAINE, 238
PAIRPOYNT, 27
PALFREY, 14-16 70 100 112 281
360 437
PALMER, 557
PALMERSTON, 118
PARDEE, 366

PARKARD, 289
PARKER, 4 7 11 16 19 20 23 25-32
    34 36-38 44 45 47 48 50 51 53
    59 61 64 66 68 72 79 81 83 94-
    96 100-103 108 109 115-118 120
    121 128 130-133 135 137 139-
    141 143-150 152 155 156 160
    163 164 166-170 175 179 180
    187 205 206 214 215 220 221
    233 234 236 238-241 244 245
    247 249 266-269 271 274 276
    277 280-287 289-293 296-300
    302 304 306-317 338 349 351
    367 372 377 379 380 381 385
    387 388 391 392 397 398 400
    401 403-406 413 426 441 442
    446 449 458 471-473 475 476
    478 480 511 513 514 516 517
    519-523 525 527 529-532 534
    540-542 544 545 548-551 555
    564 568 598 621 643 644 653
    655 656 695 697-700 702-705
    710 751 752 758-760 810
PARMENTER, 271
PARROTT, 377
PARSONS, 55 280 456 621
PASCO, 622 657
PASSACONAWAY, 30
PATCH, 261 274 355 378 386 655
PATTEE, 259
PATTISON, 149
PAYSON, 383
PEABOBY, 236
PEABODY, 155 221 238 249 265
    266 294 306 477 479 513 516
    517 565 644 781
PEACOCK, 655
PEARSON, 4 7 8 11 14 27 34 40 44
    46 65 80 81 86 94 96 103 126

PEARSON (Continued)
    140 205 250 562 652 653 695
    699
PEASE, 371 527 562 620
PEASLEE, 652
PEASLEY, 644
PEIRCE, 212 271 277 302
PEIRPOINT, 28
PEIRPONT, 28
PELSUE, 698
PENDEXTER, 297
PENNEY, 267 644
PENNIMAN, 327 644 760
PEPPER, 93
PERKINS, 27 103 121 204 259 267
    268 290 317 383 511 515 516
    518 522 525 527 532 533 536
    540 552 564 644 653 655 740
    789 794
PERPOINT, 28
PERRY, 85 241 418 473 652 695
PERSON, 57 170 205 281 568 698
PERSONS, 132 456
PERVEAR, 377
PETAGUNSK, 30
PETERS, 378 379 381 759
PETERSON, 280 622 644
PETGOONAH, 30
PETTEE, 335
PHELPS, 31 32 34 73 103 135 136
    137 170 473 546 698 699
PHILBRICK, 265
PHILIP, 22 44 86 440 732
PHILIPS, 107
PHILLIPS, 13 35 208 209 259 261
    530 575 580 644 655
PHILPOT, 655
PHILPS, 169
PHINIS, 712

PHIPPS, 39 564 622 655 657
PICKETT, 217 218 269 452 457 542
PIERCE, 65 110 112 119 132 287
    291 305 335 338 341 418 511
    523 525 538 560 622 644 655
    657 698 716
PIERPONT, 27 35 38 39 41 43 91
    103 104 106 130 132 134 139
    204 248 351 352 358 398 443
    568 569 732
PIERSON, 132 140 179 298 314 714
PIGEON, 180
PIKE, 14 16 19 20 22 31 32 34 36 38
    60 106 132 318 392 695
PILLING, 622 654
PILLINGS, 655
PILLSBURY, 266
PINCHON, 9
PINION, 8
PINKHAM, 266 287 644 652
PITMAN, 166 268 655 759
PITT, 118
PLACE, 653
PLATTS, 650 653
PLUMMER, 46 655
POLAND, 404 461 473 583 622 695
POLLEY, 58
POLLY, 101 106 137
POND, 381
POOL, 45 83 311 319 542 543 570
    705 716
POOLE, 4-8 11 16-26 35 36 38 41 44
    45 47 48 64 66 67 69 91 92 97-
    99 106-109 122 126 132 138-141
    143 145 146 149 153 155 156
    162 164-166 169 170 187 247-
    250 261 274 275 281-283 285
    289 291 296 297 303 307 326
    333 345 346 349 367-369 374

POOLE (Continued)
    375 387 392 404 407 426 440
    442 471 474 475 498 520 568
    650 695 697-699 712 731 739
    759
POOR, 62
POORE, 46
POPE, 73 74 92 103 108 117 187
    351 368 372 374 392 398 403
    404 408 434 519 609 622 653
    655 659 759
POQUANNUM, 30
PORTER, 91 255 256 266 277 294
    298 299 305 398 518 583 644
    655
POTAMIA, 543 695
POTTER, 212 229 261 293 359 473
    688 788 793
POWERS, 650
PRA--, 215
PRANKER, 810
PRAT, 713
PRATES, 140
PRATT, 38 46 50 61 75 84 96 109
    112 118 119 121 122 132 138
    160 162 167 169 170 171 183
    188 191 220 225-227 236 245
    247 249 250 251 265-269 276
    280 283-287 289 291 293-295
    300 304 307 308 310 313-319 329
    345 357 364 372 385 386 388
    402 405 426 445 451 463 464
    471 472 475 477 480 511 513
    514 518 519 521 522 525-527
    529 531 532 534 540-542 545
    549-551 560 622 644 645 652
    653 655 695 698 699 701 705
    712 740 751 752 758 760 700
PRENTICE, 712

PRENTISS, 133 151 165 168 184 187 188 193 194 196-198 201 204 216 249 250 327 343 345 361 367 449 459 464 471 564 569 571 645 652 653 659 661-663 733 759 789
PRESCOTT, 65 93 220 236 266-268 287 290 293 294 302 303 447 460 472 479 499 514 518 524 540 544 549 550 560 585 706 717 718
PRESTON, 259 645
PRICE, 693
PRITCHARD, 397
PROCTOR, 223 291 514 540 542 562 598 650 752
PROVEN, 622
PUDNEY, 135 137
PURCHAS, 688
PURINGTON, 288
PUTAMIA, 355 418 759
PUTMAN, 271 696
PUTNAM, 72-74 76 103 135-137 141 142 147 154 169 173 184 212 213 247 248 284 286 290 383 447 471-473 474 523 526 645 699
PUTNEY, 655
PUTTEN, 645
PUYNAM, 285
QUAILAN, 650
QUANAPOWITT, 759
QUANNAPOWITT, 58
QUIGLEY, 645
QUINCY, 111 179 248
QUINT, 752
QUONOPOHIT, 687 688 689
QUONPOHIT, 690 691
RADDIN, 92 291 366 367 398 407

RADDIN (Continued) 656 695
RAHN, 280
RAHR, 622 645
RAINER, 698
RAINSFORD, 87
RAND, 50 60 193 349 655 716
RANDALL, 251 358 645 654
RANSOM, 279 622 655
RANTOUL, 421 473
RAPER, 146
RAYNER, 65 98 136 165 213 271 280 288 289 303 323 326 327 349 350 364 377 392 406 410 426 493 622 623 650 655 697 759
READ, 706
REAGAN, 655
REED, 156 179 261 309 324 366 399 454 478 522 559 623 645 655 698
REID, 217 223 269 516 517 522
REMICK, 523 525
RESTERICK, 623
RESTERRICK, 357 654
REYNOLDS, 500 623 651
RHOADES, 138
RHODES, 141
RICE, 32 37 38 57 109 110 135 137 139 650 659 671 695
RICH, 111 135 137
RICHARDS, 252 623 652
RICHARDSON, 31 32 35 68 75 103 108 110 118 119 121 145 165 170 205 221 225 236 240 248 250 252 260 265 266 268 277 278 287 293 294 297 298 302 313 314 316-318 327 348 352 374 375 378 387 395 408 421

RICHARDSON (Continued)
426 433 473 476 478 483 511-
514 518 519 523 524 527 529
532 535 540 551 564 574 578
579 587-589 592 593 597 601
602 608 623 645 652-655 657-
661 671-676 695 697-699 724
727 728 736 750 751 759 762
774 738
RIDGWAY, 115 695
RILEY, 655
RIMREY, 655
RING, 104 398 91
RIPLEY, 249 623 655 657
ROAFF, 695
ROBBINS, 22 31 34 110 127
ROBERTS, 22 34 65 79 100 110 139
298 303
ROBERTSON, 221
ROBINSON, 280 370 564 623 645
ROBY, 157 165 200 298
ROGERS, 110 129 248 249 387 402
564 645 652 652
ROLF, 171
ROLLINS, 375
RONDE, 645
ROOT, 271 293
ROOTE, 8
ROPES, 226
ROUNDY, 280 329 623
ROWE, 277 366 645
ROWELL, 652
ROWLAND, 623 657
ROYAL, 623
RUFFE, 32
RUGG, 374 383 386
RUGGLES, 267 269 312 514 524
525 527 539 564 645
RUMMERY, 623

RUSSELL, 65 76 110 137 140 146
169 285 306 318 402 655 679
695 698 699 764 784
RUTTER, 333
RYANT, 167
RYDER, 558 623 655 657
S, 200
SADLER, 17 18 31 110
SAFFORD, 223 267 524 525 530
560 652
SAGAMORE, 687
SALTONSTALL, 457
SAMUELS, 230
SANBORN, 101 115 167 189-191
200 216 221 237 310 312 354
450 454 456 472 473 478 513
520 521 545 546 646 704
SARGENT, 229 268 313 524 646
716
SAUNDERS, 308
SAVAGE, 32 33 36 38 51 87 88 90
105 111 123 137 274 327 490
493 655
SAWYER, 8 57 74 75 104 111 137
169 170 173 207 226 246 247
249 253 254 271 284 471-473
656 695 698 699
SCANLAN, 623
SCHAGER, 646
SCHOOLEY, 528
SCHUYLER, 718 719
SCHWEIZER, 515
SCOLLEY, 111
SCOLLY, 32
SCOTT, 324 402 586 810
SCULLY, 494
SEAGRAVES, 695
SEAVER, 623 624 655-657
SEVERNS, 624

SEWALL, 87 106
SHANNAHAN, 371
SHARP, 225
SHARPE, 656
SHATTUCK, 537
SHAW, 336
SHAYES, 188
SHEA, 624
SHEAFE, 259 624 656
SHELDON, 108 170 271 286 650 651 654 655 695 697-699
SHELTON, 110
SHEPARD, 55 279 289 624 716
SHERIDAN, 599
SHERMAN, 85 113 114 127 280 511 513 561-563 599 624 646 657
SHORT, 241
SHOVE, 53
SHUSTER, 646
SHUTE, 220
SIBLEY, 47 374
SIDELINKER, 651 653
SIMES, 309 646
SIMMES, 90
SIMMONS, 652 656
SIMMPSON, 650
SIMMS, 656
SIMONDS, 85
SIMONS, 656
SIMPSON, 400 624
SKILTON, 310 473
SKINNER, 346 369 377 382 391 401 463 624 651 654 656 727
SKIPPERWAY, 70
SKYES, 214 271
SLACK, 233-235 699
SLAVE, Cato 542 Cesar 542 Chester 542 Dinah 543 Fillis 542 Frank 88 89 90 Keemer 543 Mary 88

SLAVE (Continued) 89 90 Pegg 542 Prince 542 Sandy 542 Sesar 542
SLEEPER, 216
SLOCOMB, 259 277 358 370 377-379 381 388 463
SMALLEY, 238 624
SMART, 519
SMILEY, 311 474 624
SMILIE, 656
SMITH, 4 6-9 11 14 16-20 23 32 35 38 56 57 60-62 68-71 82 83 87 92 95-97 100 109 111-114 116 126 132 133 139 146 147 149 152 154 155 160 162 163 166 167 169 188 199 200 205 206 208 210 212 220 227 245 247 260 261 274-276 280-284 286 287 289 291 293 298 301 302 316 323 326-328 330 331 344 346 348 351-357 359 360 362 363 367 368 371 377 378 383 384 389 393 395-397 401 402 404 410 411 414 415 432 437 438 444 471 472 474 503 504 519 521 523 532 540 543 550 562 564 570 624 625 646 650 652 656 657 698-700 724 759 760 762 787 788 793 809 695
SMITHETT, 234
SMYTH, 12
SNELL, 625 654
SNOW, 255 258 561 652 695 729
SOMERS, 625
SOMES, 646
SOULE, 266 515
SOUTHWICK, 38 92 114 145 367 445
SPAULDING, 145 149 166 249 261

SPAULDING (Continued) 292 345 389 426 433 458 473 518 625 655 656 759 362
SPEAR, 268 331 364 417 655 759
SPINNEY, 221
SPOFFORD, 249
SPOKEFIELD, 313 522
SPOKESFIELD, 269 529 530
SPRAGUE, 12 51 126 154 370
SPURR, 83
SQUIER, 114
SROWELL, 647
STACEY, 394
STACK, 699
STACY, 121
STAFFORD, 654
STANLEY, 8
STARR, 194
STEARNS, 35 52 57 60 140 200 259 310 327 344 346 379 381 403 473 550 562 651 655 678 679 695
STEEL, 221
STEELE, 238 550
STEPHENS, 280 625
STETSON, 95 572 625
STEVENS, 251 259 382 388 646 655 732 794
STEWART, 487 651
STILES, 155 382
STILLMAN, 560
STIMPSON, 15 20 32-34 37 48 59 96 99 114 115 117 120 127 148 150 160 167-169 186 189 216 250 306 307 327-329 333 340 366 370 379 394 400 403 421 473 546 625 647 652 654 655 695 697-700 759 760
STIMSON, 36 381

STOCKER, 58 407 695
STOCKWELL, 564 718
STODDARD, 625 655 656
STONE, 76 77 82 83 155 196 198 200 212 218 250 271 355 369 375 449 454 456 471 523 548 625 647 652 695 699 716 718
STOODLEY, 267 527
STOODLY, 523
STORER, 146 165
STORRS, 217
STORY, 72
STOW, 139 205 226 329 379 473
STOWE, 239
STOWELL, 115 166 210 255 259 260 366 374 381 385 388 404 440 519 625 655 656 759
STRICKLAND, 221
STRONG, 417 655
STURGIS, 609
SU-GEORGE, 687-691
SUDERICK, 145
SULLIVAN, 210 259 340 371 625 647
SUNBURY, 625
SUTTON, 20 115
SWAIN, 24 42 47 57 58 69 83 84 86 87 95 103 111 116 117 121 124 131 138 139 145 148 150 153 158 160 162 163 166-170 187 201 206 213 246-249 260 271 274 282-284 288 290 317 324 330 344 349 356 369 370 372 380 381 384 385 391 399-401 410 415 426 456 471 473 474 569 625 652 655 657 698 712 731 752 759 760
SWAINE, 26 56 282
SWALLOW, 121 135 137

SWAN, 651
SWAYNE, 4 7 11 14 15 19 20 22-29 31-36 38 40 41 440 443
SWEET, 464
SWEETSER, 46 62 69 72 82 84 92 95 112 114 160 162 166 169 189-191 210 220 221 247 252 255 256 260 261 269 274 276 277 279 280 285 286 288 290-295 298 302 304 314 317 321 323 327 332 341 342 346 349 350-356 360 364 366 367 371-374 377-379 384-389 394 398 401 404 408 410 411 414 416 418 420 421 423 426 430 449 458 463 472 474 483 496 513 517 518 520 527 528 531 534 536 539-541 544 545 560 583 595 625 626 647 651-656 668-670 695 698 699 702 703 710 726 727 750 751 759 761 762 770 780 788 789 794
SWETT, 71 249
SWEYN, 569 688
SWEYNE, 569
SWIFT, 656
SYKES, 459 460
SYMES, 141
SYMMES, 111 248 652 716
SYMMS, 49 87 88-90 200
SYMONDS, 61 114 170 225-228 233 234 247 268 285 286 301 304 306 308 313 317 371 442 445 472 478 479 626 647 654 695 699 705 803
TABER, 652
TACKNEY, 626
TAINTER, 83
TALBOT, 626
TAPLEY, 127 371
TAPPAN, 54 55
TAPPIN, 249
TARBELL, 124 382 487 489
TARBOX, 8 656 695 699
TASKER, 295 382 656
TAY, 45
TAYLOR, 4 7 8 10-12 16 19 20 22 29 32 34 37 61 67 75 80 86 93 94 110 117 137 139 140 170 213 271 282 299 306 333 446 550 626 627 647 653 656 695 696 699
TEAL, 127
TEMPLE, 44 117 118 119 122 139 148 150 153 156 160 164 165 170 171 173-176 179 205 220 221 225 226 236-240 247 267-269 276 283-285 287 289 290 292 296-300 304 306 314 316 318 364 447 461 472 475 476 478 480 513 515-519 522 523 530 531 534 536 540 542 549 550 557 560 647 695 699 700
TEPREL, 115
TEPRELL, 333
TERRY, 647
THACHER, 564
THAYER, 310
THOMAS, 563 656
THOMPSON, 19 20 22 32 47 56 59 61 86 91 119 120 131 136 248 280 386 398 564 627 647 651 654 656 657 695 701
THOMSON, 706
THOYT, 695
THOYTS, 697
TIBBETTS, 233 280 306 308 588 593 627 652 654 656

TIBBITTS, 647
TILESTON, 327 651 760
TILTON, 408
TINKCOM, 699
TITUS, 752
TOBIN, 647
TODD, 161
TOLMAN, 239
TOMPSON, 53 233 700
TOMSON, 34
TON, 282
TONY, 119
TOOTHAKER, 261 305 473
TOPPAN, 656
TORREY, 517
TOTTEN, 28 529 539 647
TOTTINGHAM, 391 392 695
TOWER, 18 20 63 119 698
TOWLE, 241
TOWNLEY, 627 652
TOWNSEND, 35 47 61 69 80 83 111
    117 119 120 125 138-140 146
    171 227 255 279 285 306 318
    627 656 698 700
TRAIN, 76 226
TRASK, 656
TRAVIS, 651 656
TREE, 716
TREFETHEN, 654
TREVITT, 58
TROW, 307 486 523 656
TRULL, 344 368 378
TUCKER, 76 379 519 627 647 656
TUDOR, 804
TUFFS, 155 156 291 358
TUFTS, 367 624 628
TURNBULL, 259 627 628
TURNER, 12 216 402 523 530 561
    647

TUTTLE, 96 259 371 628 656
TWEED, 66 256 261 287 293 302
    311 354 355 357 358 474 495
    496 523 647 787 788 793 802
    809
TWISDEN, 656
TWISS, 280 628 656
TWIST, 807
TWOMBLY, 496
TWULL, 653
TYLER, 51 146 150 230 280 628
    653 654 657
TYLOR, 656
TYTHINGMEN, 39
UMPHRYES, 547
UNDERWOOD, 60 101 120 152 166
    184 248 250 384 385 759
UNRAH, 654
UPHAM, 37 84 120 140 142 143 146
    147 163 166 169 259 319 345
    364 371 463 573 628 656 759
UPTON, 3 31-34 39 50 57 65 68 73
    75 79 114 119 120 121 135 136
    138 145 158 166 170 173 179
    180 185 213 227 247-249 261
    271 276 283-287 290 293 294
    299 302 314 337 368 372 374
    377 381 387 446 471-473 475
    532 628 653 654 656 695 698
    699 759
USHER, 87 88 90
VARNEY, 656
VAUGHAM, 539
VAUGHN, 647
VAUX, 279 628
VERY, 60
VILES, 221
VINTON, 28 83 102 121 127 163
    165 169 184 189 291 333 351

VINTON (Continued)
352 364 370 384 394 695 698 759
VOSE, 204
WADE, 252 266 371
WADLIN, 628 648 657
WADSWORTH, 106 200
WAIT, 695
WAITE, 656
WAITT, 166 221 261 274 275 357 364-366 476 629 759
WAKEFIELD, 68 79 107-109 121-123 149 217 220 230 236-238 247 250 251 255 261 266-269 276 286 289 290 292-295 297 299 302 311 315 316 354 355 368 369 384 426 442 445 449 454 457-459 467 468 472 473 475 477 478 480 483 484 486 487 489 495 500 513 514 517 518 524 525 529 530 540 541 543 544 546 548 550 551 598 648 671 675 677 679-683 695 700 702 704 705 724 726-728 739 740 759-764 769 781 782 784-786 788 789 794 811
WALCOTT, 213 283
WALDO, 250
WALKER, 4-7 9 11 12 15 19 27 33 34 87 111 123 274 280 281 288 289 312 313 353 369 401 432 490 628 656 657 696 731
WALKUP, 48
WALLACE, 220 472
WALLIS, 96 478 759
WALLS, 651 653
WALSH, 648 651
WALTON, 57 69 84 113 114 117 123 124 140 153 160-163 166

WALTON (Continued)
169 173 174 181 199 201 233 234 249 259 261 274 284 285 288 289 292 294 307 314 334 335 345 352 355 364 366 372 374 376 377 379 380 382 383 397 398 410 449 463 464 474 504 571 573 628 629 654 656 695 697-699 727 734 759 770 192
WARD, 277
WARDWELL, 280 648
WAREY, 632
WARNE, 207 252 421
WARNER, 238 370
WARREN, 179 253 259 280 370 578 585 629 651 653 712
WASHBURN, 342 564
WASHINGTON, 179 182 538 548 559 560 630 648 675 703 707 709 718-720 761 786
WATERMAN, 806
WATSON, 315 695
WATTAQUUTINUSK, 30
WATTS, 191 199 651
WAY, 716
WAYNE, 407
WEARE, 249
WEARY, 648
WEBB, 113 130 147 248 249 252 421 700
WEBBER, 92
WEBSTER, 44 249 271 272
WEEDEN, 648
WEEKS, 648 706
WEETAMOO, 30
WELCH, 385 648 656 696
WELDON, 656
WELLINGTON, 319

WELLMAN, 35 125 140 654
WELLS, 419
WELLSTEAD, 147
WELMAN, 378
WENCHESTER, 697
WENDALL, 334
WENEPOWWEEKIN, 687 688
WENEPOYKIN, 30
WENTWORHT, 552
WENUCHUS, 30
WESSON, 143 145 146 148-150 162
    164 708
WEST, 398 518 651
WESTGATE, 230
WESTON, 14 15 17 20 23 32 34 38
    56-59 68 81 114 118 125 132
    137 139 146 148 152 166 171
    184 186 225 241 247 250 252
    266 267 268 276 280 282-286
    291 293 296 297 297 299 300
    304 305 308-310 316 318 319
    345 346 351 403 421 433 447
    460 471 475 511 513 518 520-
    525 528 532 533 535 536 543
    544 549 552 564 630 648 651-
    653 695-703 705 759
WETHERN, 563
WHEELER, 255 279 288 294 345
    373 377 394 400 526 563 588
    589 630 656 678 727
WHEELOCK, 288 376 597 656
WHIPPLE, 52 651
WHITAKER, 249
WHITBY, 200
WHITCOM, 712
WHITE, 13 46 66 84 109 114 167
    206 259 264 265 288 329 333
    334 335 338 339 426 439 648
    651 656

WHITEFIELD, 151
WHITEHEAD, 630
WHITEHOUSE, 651 653
WHITFORD, 630 652
WHITING, 218 219 314 695
WHITMAN, 648 653
WHITNEY, 186 656
WHITON, 277
WHITTEMORE, 193 211 400 489
    727
WHITTER, 30 795
WHITTERIDGE, 170
WHITTIER, 267
WHITTING, 217
WHITTINGHAM, 89 90
WHITTREDGE, 74 372 404 653 699
WHITTRIDGE, 270
WICKLIFFE, 512
WIDDEFIELD, 716
WIGGIN, 656
WIGGINS, 649
WIGGLESWORT, 248
WIGHT, 530 648
WIGHTMAN, 237 265 268 287 289
    293 524 536 750-752
WILCOX, 239 240 265 267 268 353
    752
WILDER, 632
WILELE, 28
WILEY, 4 7 20 21 27 28 32 34 38 61
    62 66 81 97 108 113 121 125-
    127 133 139 145 149 153 155
    160 162 165 166 169 188 201
    209 210 225 234 246 247 252
    255 259 261 274 275 277 278
    280 282 285 288 290 292-294
    303 304 316 326 327 330 340
    345 351-353 355 357-359 368-
    372 374 379 381 383 394 398

WILEY (Continued)
  399 402 410 420 421 423 426
  438 439 451 456 463 464 472
  474 518 560 579 580 630 631
  649 651 652 656 657 695 696
  698 699 712 727 728 759 810
WILIS, 211
WILKINS, 18 120 121 280 632 649
  656 657
WILKINSON, 692 693
WILLAN, 632
WILLARD, 9 309 353 671
WILLETT, 718
WILLEY, 324 385 386 563
WILLIAM, 358
WILLIAMS, 68 69 106 116 124 127
  131 140 143 147 160 308 310
  315 338 344 350 366 368 381
  392 410 631 649 653 656 657
  695 698 699 834
WILLIS, 259 261 293 351 473 524
  649
WILLMARCH, 261
WILMARTH, 209 210 649
WILSON, 121 250 371 517 649 695
WIN, 283
WINBORNE, 32 85 127
WINCHESTER, 698
WINEGAR, 630
WINN, 4 102 123 166 167 261 274
  276 288 300 343 365 387 394
  400 401 410 432 451 649 759
  760
WINNEPURKITT, 30
WINSHIP, 259 261 269 288 394 395
  495 630 654 656 695 727 787
WINSLOW, 554 678 679
WINTHROP, 82 586 630
WINTHROPE, 118
WINZER, 712
WITHERSPOON, 345 404
WITTER, 5 10
WOLCOTT, 253
WOLLEY, 699
WOLTON, 81
WOOD, 60 111 389 649 759
WOODBERRY, 268
WOODBRIDGE, 310
WOODBURY, 227
WOODFIN, 575 632 651
WOODIS, 632 651
WOODMAN, 113
WOODS, 656
WOODWARD, 32 34 38 44 57 73 74
  127 139 150 167 169 327 369
  376 377 388 483 632 656 696
  698 760
WOODWOOD, 370
WOOFINDALE, 632
WOOLLEY, 695
WORMALL, 566
WORMWOOD, 16 127
WORRALL, 233
WORTHLEY, 764
WOTTEN, 169
WOTTON, 165 352 759
WRIGHT, 61 95 138 222 223 269
  277 292 293 295 397 423 454
  472 515 521 563 564 632 649
  651 653 656 695 699
WRIN, 652
WYLEY, 11 16 19
WYMAN, 280 302 355 632
YALE, 214 251 252 325 327 346-
  348 396 410 411 421 423 474
  557 588 659 728 759 408

YOST, 719
YOUNG, 192 303 316 342 343 402
　479 528 649 696 700 759
YOURE, 649